BOOKS OF THE BRAVE

THE ARRIVAL OF THE SPANISH CONQUISTADORS

BOOKS OF THE BRAVE

BEING AN ACCOUNT OF BOOKS AND OF MEN IN THE

SPANISH CONQUEST AND SETTLEMENT OF

THE SIXTEENTH-CENTURY

NEW WORLD

Irving A. Leonard

1949

CAMBRIDGE · MASSACHUSETTS

HARVARD UNIVERSITY PRESS

PUBLICATION OF THIS VOLUME WAS AIDED BY A SUBSIDY FROM
THE AMERICAN COUNCIL OF LEARNED SOCIETIES

TO MY TEACHERS

Frederick B. Luquiens (1875-1940)
E. C. Hills (1867-1932)
Rudolph Schevill (1874-1946)
Herbert E. Bolton

LOS CONQUISTADORES

Como creyeron solos lo increíble,
sucedió: que los límites del sueño
traspasaron, y el mar y el imposible ♣
Y es todo elogio a su valor, pequeño.

Y el poema es su nombre. Todavía
decir Cortés, Pizarro o Alvarado,
contiene más grandeza y más poesía
de cuanta en este mundo se ha rimado.

Capitanes de ensueño y de quimera,
rompiendo para siempre el horizonte,
persiguieron al sol en su carrera ♣

Y el mar, alzado hasta los cielos, monte
es, entre ambas Españas,
solo digno cantor de sus hazañas.

—Manuel Machado

TO WHOM IT MAY CONCERN

THIS IS A BOOK ABOUT BOOKS, PARTICULARLY BOOKS OF
fiction. The chief characters of this story are not the heroes of the
Spanish conquest and settlement of the sixteenth-century New
World but, rather, the books which they and their descendants
knew and read, the entertaining writings which fired the imaginations of these pioneers, stimulated their unparalleled achievements,
amused their restless leisure, and consoled their bitter disillusionment. These printed products of creative spirits played a silent but
not wholly passive part in shaping the events of the first act in the
drama of Europeanizing the globe, and their participation is still
an unwritten chapter in the history of that great enterprise. In this
narrative the secular works of nonfiction and instruction figure as
minor characters, while the purely religious and theological literature, though dominant in that great age, is only briefly seen.
This account of the share of humane letters in an epochal adventure
of mankind, therefore, makes no profession of being a critical essay
on Spanish letters of the period, and much less does it presume to
be an intellectual history of early Hispanic America. It seeks only
to focus attention upon a neglected aspect of the early diffusion of
European culture in the newly discovered portions of the world,
and to demonstrate the existence of a relatively free circulation of
books in the former colonies of Spain, a fact hitherto obscured by
prejudices and misapprehension.

In the study of modern history an often subtle interaction between literature and events in human affairs, particularly since the
invention of the printing press, is not fully appreciated. Fictional
writings are not only the subjective records of human experience,
but sometimes the unconscious instigators of the actions of men by

conditioning their attitudes and responses. Often the works of imagination that were most influential in this respect at a given time and place are not the supreme creations of genius; they are frequently inferior manifestations of artistic expression which, because of special circumstances, sway the thoughts and emotions of their readers more profoundly. As a result, they sometimes alter the course of history or modify contemporary customs and manners. Few would claim *Uncle Tom's Cabin* to be a masterpiece of American letters, but few would deny it an influence all out of proportion to its esthetic merits in the thoughts and subsequent actions of the people of the United States of the middle nineteenth century. The effect of the wide reading of the rags-to-riches tales of Horatio Alger by the youth of a generation or two ago on the economic conceptions and individualistic philosophies of older, conservative businessmen of recent years might prove a fruitful inquiry. And who can tell to what extent the dime-novel fiction of the athletic superman, Frank Merriwell, helped to bring about a shift of juvenile interest from going west to kill Indians to the tremendous enthusiasm for sports during the last four or five decades? Such writings can hardly be termed literature, yet they had an appeal to a mass of readers of an impressionable age which, in some measure, conditioned their habits of thought and conduct. It is possible, then, that the Spanish Conquistador offers an early example of this interaction between the fictitious and the real. His matchless courage and driving force did not spring from brawn and endurance alone; his febrile fancy had much to do in spurring him relentlessly on to unprecedented exploits. Some of the visionary passion that animated him had its inspiration in the imagined utopias, adventures, and riches alluringly depicted in the song and story of his time. The texture of dreams became corporeal in the new medium of leaden type, and these men of the Spanish Renaissance were moved to work miracles greater than those performed in the pages of their books. In the first chapters of this account an attempt is made to appraise, to understand, and to explain these men and the fiction they emulated.

This book about books of the Conquistador and his descendants strives to serve a threefold purpose: first, to explore the possible influence of a popular form of contemporary literature on the mind, attitudes, and actions of these sixteenth-century Spaniards; second, to describe the mechanics of the associated book trade in the New World, including the related legislation and routines of shipping and conveying these wares to purchasers in the Western Hemisphere; and third, to indicate the universal diffusion of Spanish literary culture throughout the expanded Hispanic world of that great age. The first six chapters deal with the conqueror and the romances of chivalry that he knew, and the possible reaction of books on men is indicated particularly by the quest of the Amazons in America. Chapters VII to XII follow the fortunes of printed volumes through the House of Trade at Seville, on board the trans-Atlantic galleons, and into the ports of entry of the Spanish colonies. Chapters XIII to XIX are a series of case histories of individual shipments which symbolize the universal dissemination of books throughout the sixteenth-century colonial empire of Spain, including the outlying Philippines. This procedure was adopted because the surviving records in the archives of Spain and Spanish America are of such fragmentary nature that a statistical approach to the problem of book distribution is impossible. The total number of volumes which crossed the ocean in the sixteenth century can not be determined, though it clearly ran into the thousands annually, nor can the specific titles sent in the largest quantities be identified. The names which recur often on the surviving lists may be assumed to be among the most desired, and chapter IX suggests these seeming favorites, judging by a large number of ship manifests consulted in the Archive of the Indies at Seville.

The seven chapters of case histories are based on a selection of nine representative book lists, all but one from Spanish American repositories. They range from 1576 to 1613; book lists before the earlier date are extremely rare and the few discovered are short and of relatively slight interest. Of the nine, three are fairly long inventories for New Spain, dated 1576 and 1600; five are shorter ones for the viceroyalty of Peru, of 1583, 1606, and 1613; and one, still shorter but of considerable interest, is from the Philippines, dated 1583. Each chapter is based on one or more of these inventories and includes a historical sketch of the social and cultural life of the locality represented, together with an account of the special circumstances relating to the particular book order or shipment and an analysis of the lists of titles, with emphasis on belles-lettres. Because of its exceptional value in giving insight into Mexican intellectual life at the end of the sixteenth century, the list discussed in Chapter XVI is subjected to detailed commentary on all types of literature noted in it. Chapters XIII to XVI consider general belletristic and secular writings more broadly, while the following three chapters are concerned with specific masterpieces of the Spanish novel, namely, *Guzmán de Alfarache,* by Mateo Alemán, and *Don Quijote,* by Cervantes, whose arrival in the colonies marks the close of an epoch in popular literary preferences. As the novel enters an eclipse at the beginning of the seventeenth century, the introduction of Don Quixote into the New World is the climactic event with which the book closes.

The whole question of fictional and secular books in the former Spanish colonies has long been beclouded by prejudices engendered by the so-called "Black Legend" of the obscurantism allegedly practiced by Spain in America, and by the antipathies arising from the wars of independence in the early nineteenth century. It is not the purpose of the present work to transform the denigration of Spanish colonial policies into a "White Legend," but this account of the often denied circulation of books and ideas in viceregal Hispanic America, added to the investigations of others, may help to demonstrate that the true color of the "legend" was something like, perhaps, a light gray. The conviction, which some historical evidence seems to support, that Spanish authorities tried to seal off the colonies from European thought by excluding all books save those of approved orthodox religion still dominates the minds of many; it is almost a dogma which even scholars hesitate to question. Perhaps the first to shake the firm belief in the extremely limited circulation of nonreligious literature was the venerable Spanish investigator, Francisco Rodríguez Marín, who, in 1911, published two well-documented lectures in a little volume entitled *El 'Quijote' y Don Quijote en América.* By a somewhat cursory inspection of the ship manifests of the fleets sailing to America in 1605, which he found in the Archive of the Indies at Seville, he proved the exportation of several hundred copies of presumably the first edition of the famous novel. His discovery of these *registros* thus opened a rich vein for research. In 1914 an important collection of documents, *Libros y libreros en el siglo XVI,* published by Francisco Fernández del Castillo, revealed the possibilities of Mexican repositories for related material on the colonial book trade, besides throwing much light on the importation of printed literature.

In the winter of 1930-1931 it was my good fortune to be able to carry forward the researches of Sr. Rodríguez Marín in the *Contratación* records at Seville, which include the surviving registers of the annual fleets. I had photostatic copies made of many of these documents of the last decades of the sixteenth century and the first years of the seventeenth, and I took copious notes of many more. In 1932 and again in 1940 these archival investigations were continued in Mexico City; also in Lima, Peru, in 1937 and 1938, with briefer delvings into similar repositories of Chile, Argentina, and Colombia. These accumulating manuscript materials were first exploited in a short monograph, *Romances of chivalry in the Spanish Indies with some registros of shipments of books to the Spanish colonies* (Berkeley, 1933), which gave the fullest discussion then available of the circulation of light literature in those regions, and reproduced the first group of these curious book lists with a check list of titles. Subsequent utilization of other documents of this character occurred in a series of articles printed in scholarly journals, chiefly from 1940 to 1947. In considerably modified form some of the latter and parts of the monograph are incorporated in the present work.

In 1940 my good friend and fellow worker in the Archive of the Indies at Seville, the distinguished Argentine historian, José Torre Revello, published his monumental *El libro, la imprenta y el periodismo en América durante la dominación española,* a magnificently documented work with an appendix of ninety-seven book lists and related material, practically all from the great repository at Seville, where he labored for many years. Three chapters of this landmark of cultural history are devoted to the question of the circulation of books, and they have done much to shatter the legend of Spanish obscurantism in this respect so long maintained. More recently a compatriot, Father Guillermo Furlong, has brought out a similar work, *Bibliotecas argentinas durante la dominación hispánica,* which leans heavily on Sr. Torre Revello's monograph but adds a few book lists for study. This succession of important, documented studies has opened perceptible fissures in the hard rock of the traditional belief in Spanish intolerance towards humanistic literature in America, and the present work, with its further analysis, elaboration of details, and additional book lists mainly from Spanish American archives, seeks to advance this disruptive process.

I have a heavy debt of gratitude to acknowledge for help received from numerous institutions and individuals. Without their support and coöperation the long quest of materials, chiefly in foreign archives, on which my investigations are based, would have been impossible. In 1930 the American Council of Learned Societies of Washington, D. C. granted a generous fellowship which permitted me to spend a full year in Spain, with incidental excursions to France and England, for archival research. Subsequent aid from this source continued these efforts in Mexico in 1932. Research funds of the University of California assisted in the acquisition of photostatic copies of *registros* preserved at Seville. In 1936 the John Simon Guggenheim Memorial Foundation bestowed a fellowship enabling me to carry on my investigations in various countries of South America. The editors of the *Hispanic Review*, published by the University of Pennsylvania Press, and the *Hispanic American Historical Review*, published by the Duke University Press, have kindly given permission to reprint in modified and enlarged form several articles and book lists first published in those journals. The original forms of chapters XV, XVI, XVII, XVIII, and XIX appeared in vol. XV, No. 1 (January 1947), vol. IX, No. 1 (January 1941), vol. XI, No. 3 (July 1943), vol. VIII, No. 4 (October 1940), and vol. IX, No. 3 (July 1941), respectively, of the first-mentioned review, and chapters IV and XIV in vol. XXII, No. 1 (February 1942), and vol. XXIV, No. 4 (November 1944) of the second. All have undergone revision in this book, varying from slight changes in text to a complete rewriting with the insertion of many new data.

First claim to my gratitude among individuals is held by Guillermo Lohmann Villena, a distinguished young scholar of Peru who made my visits at the National Archive in Lima fruitful by helping me to locate colonial book lists in that repository and later by sending me copies and transcriptions of other inventories that he encountered. The distinguished Spanish paleographer, Dr. Agustín

Millares Carlo, rendered similar service in my work in Mexico City. In the difficult and sometimes trying task of identifying the abbreviated titles of works on the colonial lists I have called upon numerous friends and colleagues, including Professors R. K. Spaulding and C. E. Kany of the University of California, and especially Dr. Otis H. Green of the University of Pennsylvania. The entire analysis of the book list contained in chapter XVI is, with slight changes in wording, entirely the work of Dr. Green, who generously authorized its use in this book. It appeared originally in the *Hispanic Review* (vol. IX) in an article of the same title as the present chapter and under our joint names. For the benefit of their advice and for reading the drafts of some chapters I wish to thank Dr. Earl J. Hamilton of the University of Chicago, Dr. Federico Sánchez y Escribano of the University of Michigan, and Dr. Otis H. Green. The failure to heed their counsel in some respects will account for some of the book's imperfections.

IRVING A. LEONARD

Heathbrook
South Tamworth,
New Hampshire
September 1947

CONTENTS

ILLUSTRATIONS

THE SPANISH CONQUISTADOR I

The extraordinary actions and adventures of these men, while they rival the exploits recorded in chivalric romance, have the additional interest of verity. They leave us in admiration of the bold and heroic qualities inherent in the Spanish character which led that nation to so high a pitch of power and glory, and which are still discernible in the great mass of that gallant people by those who have an opportunity of judging them rightly.

Washington Irving[1]

The cause of the killing and destroying such an infinite number of souls by the Christians [i.e., Conquistadors] has been simply that their whole end was to acquire gold and riches in the shortest time so that they might rise to lofty positions out of all proportion to their wealth: in a word, the cause of such ills has been their insatiable ambition and covetousness. . . .

Bartolomé de las Casas[2]

OF THESE TWO QUOTATIONS INSPIRED BY THE DEEDS OF the Spanish conquerors in America, the second probably accords more closely with the impression held by the majority of that unnumbered throng who have been stirred by their prodigious feats. Indeed, its unflattering characterization of these sixteenth-century adventurers remains so firmly established and so pervasive as to partake of the nature of a hallowed tradition which blots out all other considerations. If a momentary skepticism should raise a fleeting doubt of the fairness of such a harsh judgment, this uncertainty is quickly dispelled by the knowledge that this cherished conviction traces its origin to a contemporary Spaniard of world renown, a Dominican clergyman, Bartolomé de las Casas. Thus the Spanish conquerors are condemned forever by the evidence of a star witness, a conspicuous countryman who had seen their works.

Why, therefore, examine the matter further? Why regard the Conquistador as anything better than a ruthless brigand? Yet there are good reasons, aside from the obvious special pleading of the great "Apostle of the Indians," to suggest the greater justice of the more dispassionate opinion expressed nearly three centuries later by the North American writer, Washington Irving, in the first quotation.

The Spanish Conquistador, like all other human elements before and after him, was the creature of his own age, molded and conditioned by the contemporary influences of his environment. If in retrospect he appears excessively primitive, fanatic, proud, cruel, and romantic, it is only because he reflected more conspicuously than did other Europeans of his age the dominant traits of his own time and of his Western European culture, and only in this light can he be rightly judged. If indeed he did sin more in these various respects than his neighbors on the Continent, it was mainly because his opportunities and temptations were so much greater than theirs.

But why, it may be asked, were the Hispanic peoples singled out to be the first instruments of history in the Europeanizing of the globe through the discovery, conquest, and colonizing of many of its unknown parts? Why did Spain particularly attain a momentary greatness that enabled her to achieve a historic destiny unequaled in human experience? These questions are always likely to provoke discussion, and the answers to them are not easy to find. Periods of greatness of a people or a nation frequently arise from the conjunction of the effect of environmental factors of their own milieu and of historic movements, the latter often set in motion by distant and weaker human aggregations reacting to peculiar local conditions. The peninsularity of the Hispanic peoples and the Commercial Revolution, with its development of trade routes and the international exchange of goods, were the coöperating factors which contributed greatly to the spectacular rise of Portugal and Spain and conferred upon these countries leading roles in ushering in the rise of modern imperialism, nationalism, and capitalism.

The capture of Constantinople in 1453 spelled the eventual doom of the Italian city-states which, in the later Middle Ages, had grown rich in the prosperous commerce with the Near East, and this historic event emphasized the pressing need of finding other pathways of trade. The course of the Commercial Revolution moved inexorably from the East to the West and hence could not fail to influence radically the destinies of the Hispanic peoples at the western extreme of the Mediterranean. This trend happened, also, to coincide with technical improvements in naval architecture, nautical instruments, and the like. The geographic proximity of the peninsula to the needed new routes, the great imagination, and the extraordinary energy and vitality of its peoples engendered by long residence on the edge of the Unknown and by centuries of successful warfare against the Moors were some of the environmental and inherent factors which prepared the Spaniards and the Portuguese for their mission in history. The Conquistador, endowed with tremendous courage, powerful imagination, and religious fanaticism, and flushed with triumph by his recent victory over the Mohammedan infidel, was the appointed agent to overrun a new world and initiate the westernization of the globe.

The first important step of this process, the spectacular conquest of America by the Spaniards particularly, has been explained alliteratively as the result of three basic drives, namely, "Gold, Glory, and Gospel." If this trinity of nouns sums up rather neatly the fundamental motivation of the sixteenth-century Conquistador in the New World, its brevity calls for some elucidation. Without analysis there is danger of an oversimplification which may lead to a less than adequate understanding of the singular achievements of the Spanish conquerors.

The quotation from Las Casas defines the basic drive of the Spaniards as the greedy pursuit of gold, and doubtless the quest of this precious metal is most widely associated today with the superhuman feats of the Conquistador. Inherent in this concept is the implication that the Spaniard, more than any other European, was animated by a lust for metallic wealth. Yet the inhabitants of the Spanish Peninsula are not today, and have never been, characteristically more acquisitive than their continental neighbors. On the contrary, the Spanish and the Portuguese are among the least materialistic peoples of western Europe. Why, then, the apparently fierce determination of Cortes and Pizarro to possess themselves of the mineral riches of the conquered Indian civilizations?

In the nascent Commercial Revolution, with its emphasis on the exchange of goods, the Hispanic peoples found themselves severely handicapped. Spain, particularly, was a relatively infertile land with few natural resources aside from its mines. Moreover, its human energies had for a long time been absorbed in intermittent warfare, to the detriment of manufacturing and agricultural activities, and Spain, therefore, produced relatively little that was useful for export trade. With the disadvantages of mountainous terrain, poor highways, and lack of navigable streams added to the clumsy and inadequate means of transportation of the time, the heavy ores and metal of the mines, among the richest of the national resources, could give the Peninsula no privileged place in the growing world commerce. Its people, consequently, were severely handicapped in the competition for the coveted spices and luxuries of the East. Inevitably the balance of trade was unfavorable for the Spaniards, and an equilibrium could be established most readily by the acquisition of precious metals whose value for exchange was out of all proportion to their weight and the space that they occupied in transportation. Since gold and silver were universally acceptable in facilitating commercial exchanges and credits, the economic disabilities under which they labored moved the Spaniards to feel keenly the need of possessing large quantities of these lubricants of trade. It is understandable, therefore, that the narrow mercantilistic philosophies in vogue at the beginning of the modern age should dominate the thinking of Spanish economists and that the Crown and the entrepreneur class should be intensely preoccupied with increasing the gold supply. The gradual realization that the newly discovered hemisphere was, in fact, a barrier to the trade routes to the Asiatic lands of spice and silk only strengthened the necessity of discovering and acquiring the precious metal, and it was natural that the colonies there should be valued mainly as a source of supply. The Conquistador, therefore, often sharing in the capitalistic ventures that many of their expeditions were, had a powerful reason for seeking so relentlessly the gold that was indispensable in the new economy. If he was too beguiled by a symbol of wealth and eventually paid dearly for his mistake in his own and his country's ruin, he was not unique in the history of mankind and there are indications in more modern times that others have not learned his lesson.

The second of the basic drives of the Conquistador, namely "Glory," is inextricably associated with the fierce pride and vanity

which marked the Spanish race during its period of political eminence in Europe and later, and these qualities have left an indelible
impress on its descendants on both sides of the Atlantic to the
present day. No one, perhaps, saw more clearly or inveighed more
bitterly against the false and worldly concepts of nobility, honor,
and valor which possessed the haughty Spaniard in the centuries of
his rise and decline than the great Spanish satirist, Francisco de
Quevedo (1580-1645), who, in searing terms, excoriated his countrymen's hypocritical practice of these virtues in one of his moral
satires, *The pigsties of Plato (Las zahurdas de Platón)*, published
early in the seventeenth century. This Spanish preoccupation with
the abstract quality of Glory, which was closely identified with
military distinction, probably crystallized during the more than
seven centuries of intermittent warfare against the Moors. The slow
but steady gains registered by successive generations against the
traditional enemy of a different race and creed engendered a glorification of the warrior even more pronounced than elsewhere in
Europe, particularly since the fighting man was a crusader against
a pagan faith. In these struggles individual combats were frequent,
and in them the successful contestant won fame and was quickly
enriched by the booty. Such rewards were far quicker and more
satisfying to personal pride than those of the slower and less spectacular ways of agriculture and the handicrafts, and inevitably there
emerged the false concept that soldiering was the highest calling and
that deeds of war were the duty and almost the sole honorable occupation of manhood. It was the apotheosis of the warrior brought to
a higher degree than elsewhere in contemporary Europe, which
learned to fear the tramp of Spanish soldiery during more than a
century. The prestige of Spanish arms and Spanish courage remained a source of pride to the nation long after its glory had
waned, and while other peoples of Europe shifted more and more
to a preoccupation with the profits of capitalistic trade, finance, and
industry, to the proud Spaniard these mundane occupations continued to be sordid pursuits unworthy of his talents and destiny.

The Spanish reconquest of the Peninsula from the Moorish invaders had associated the more methodical development of agriculture and the manual crafts of the latter with a debased paganism
and an infidel religion. To the Christian crusader these practical

activities and hard labor were suitable for the enemies of God and a befitting badge of servitude. In the form of *encomiendas*, he derived the benefits of the toil of the conquered as a legitimate reward for bringing them into the Christian fold; his position as a feudal lord was a mark of divine gratitude for his military prowess while the manual labor of his serfs was proper punishment for their allegiance to a false faith.

Toward the Jews, forced into the role of money changers and middlemen by the circumstances of their existence, the Spaniard felt a similar disdain. Again associating their occupational activities with penalties for adherence to a false faith and an equally hostile religion, he viewed with contempt the profitable careers which the growing capitalism of the modern age offered him through the development of these pursuits. Hence, with industry, agriculture, and finance bearing the marks of the foes of Christianity, and with God apparently favoring the forward sweep of Spanish arms, the one true path to Glory and material rewards was that of the soldier. This conviction became so deeply embedded in the Spanish character by the centuries of relentless warfare and steady triumph that it amounted to a dominant passion without which, perhaps, even the Conquistador would not have been equal to the formidable task of overrunning a vast continent of the New World and of enduring the tremendous hardships and sufferings of the Conquest.

The third of these basic drives of the Conquistador, symbolized by the word "Gospel," is the one which has brought as much obloquy as any upon the Spaniards. To reconcile the widely advertised plundering, massacres, rapine, and other crimes perpetrated by the early adventurers in the New World with the gentle Christian faith which they professed to bring to its natives is a difficult undertaking and posterity has seen in these acts only a cruel and wanton hypocrisy, forgetting that other Spaniards, with rare abnegation, consecrated their lives to the protection and education of the conquered. But again it is important, in judging the conduct of the Conquistador, to place oneself in the age in which he lived. In doing so it soon becomes evident that the sixteenth-century adventurers were in large measure merely reflecting the attitudes and inconsistencies general in the Western Europe of their time. If the Spanish Conquistador seems to have betrayed more discrepancies in his concepts of civilized behavior than other Europeans in the period of the Conquest, it is again because of his peculiar conditioning and because his temptations were so much greater than theirs.

For centuries the Spaniard had been in the front line of defense of European Christianity against a Mohammedanism which had flooded over his native soil. For other peoples of Europe the Crusades were a struggle against the infidel far from the homeland, but for the Christians of Spain their holy war was a hand-to-hand combat with the foe inside their own boundaries. From this close and continual conflict with the followers of Allah, who had invaded Europe by way of the Peninsula, came a hardening of the Spaniard's faith into a pitiless fanaticism, and from his ever-growing triumph over these pagan hosts came an unshakable conviction of his own righteousness and a concept of himself as the right hand of God. No other people had been similarly obliged to test its religious beliefs in the crucible of bloody struggle and ever-present danger, and it was probably inevitable, therefore, that the tough-fighting Iberian descendants, bearing the brunt of the infidel attack in their exposed position, should develop a more fanatic zeal for the faith which animated them than did their coreligionists beyond the Pyrenees. It was natural for them to view their final victory over the Moors in Southern Europe, after nearly eight centuries of warfare, as a sign of God's approval. The Spaniard could not but feel himself very precious in the eyes of the Lord, and this conception of his people as the chosen race of the Almighty could not fail to engender the pride and arrogance which came to characterize the ruling classes of Spain.

The profound individualism of the Spaniard, resulting in part from his relative geographic isolation and the long practice of warfare, manifested itself even in his relationship to his God. Religion was for the hard-fighting Spaniard a compact with the Supreme Being in which both were contracting parties. If he served God by expelling the infidel from the land or by converting him to Christianity by force, he felt himself clearly entitled to economic rewards for furthering God's work on earth. The prizes and booty that fell to the Spaniard in these efforts, whether in the form of lands, mines, estates or even of slaves, were thus considered tokens of appreciation bestowed by a grateful deity upon the victor. Hence, when the Conquistador brought what he conceived as the supreme boon of his faith to the natives of the New World, it did not seem unreasonable to him to extract as his legitimate reward for this service the maximum economic return from the bewildered native, even if the methods employed were dangerously like those of plundering and looting. The less pragmatic representatives of the Church accompanying the conquering expeditions usually possessed a much less primitive conception of the covenant with God and earnestly sought to control the excesses of the sixteenth-century adventurers against the Indians.

These abuses and the fanaticism of the Conquistador have created in the mind of posterity his enduring reputation for cruelty and brutality. The ruthlessness of Cortés and Pizarro is remembered more than the tremendous odds that they faced with a handful of followers far removed from their bases of supply, and the shrill protests of Las Casas in behalf of the conquered Indians have obscured the difficulties, which the Spanish leaders confronted, of establishing a new social and economic order. The wide publicity given to the barbarous acts of men facing desperate odds and to the lawless acquisitiveness of individuals who claimed the spoils of conquest helped to create among jealous contemporaries of Spain the so-called "black legend" of Spanish cruelty which has endured to modern times despite the findings of a generation of historians. Indeed, until recently "Conquistador" has seemed a name almost synonymous with ruthless savage and inhuman pervert, a sort of terroristic gangster of the sixteenth century. But again the tendency is to view his attitudes and acts outside of their historical setting and to forget that he reflected all too faithfully the spirit of the times in which he lived. The study of contemporary Europe reveals plainly the universal pattern of cruelty, intolerance, and inhumanity which characterized the social, religious, and economic life of the Continent. Humanitarianism was as yet a merely latent and undeveloped concept of human relations, and the disregard of the inherent rights of every individual was universal. For a conqueror to act with compassion toward the vanquished was still generally conceived as a sign of weakness.

That the Conquistador, dealing with an alien race and civilization, possessed no monopoly of brutality or cynicism as the representative of a conquering nation is made abundantly clear by the declarations of an Englishman of the same century engaged in a similar mission. Sir Humphrey Gilbert, in subjugating Ireland to the British Crown, had little compunction in putting men, women, and children to the sword in that island, and in a report on these activities he clearly revealed his frank acceptance of the current philosophy of his age and excused his atrocities by declaring that he was "constantly of this opinion that no conquered nation will ever yield willingly their obedience for love but rather for fear." So faithful was he in the practice of this conviction that, after his work was done in Ireland, one of his own countrymen, Sir Henry Sidney, commented that ". . . the name of an Englishman is more terrible now to them [the Irish] than the sight of a hundred was before."[3] Perhaps nowhere did the Spanish Conquistador receive so harrowing a tribute to his savagery as the one thus applied to the contemporary English conquerors.

Nearly a century later, when the Conquistador had passed from the scene and the inherent cruelty of the Spaniard was an article of faith among Europeans, certain Englishmen were treating the Indians of Virginia and even their own men with a barbarity reminiscent of the Spanish conquerors' fame. It is reported that Indians bringing food to the English colony were treated as spies. "Some of them S[r] Tho: Gates cawsed to be apprehended and executed for a terrour to the reste, to cawse them to desist from their subtell practyses."[4] And in the same region another Englishman was following merciless procedures.

> S[r] Tho: Dale haveinge allmoste finished the foarte, and settled a plantacyon in that p'te dyv[rs] of his men being idell, and not willinge to take paynes, did runne away unto the Indyans; many of them being taken againe, S[r] Thomas in a moste severe manner cawsed to be executed, some he appointed to be hanged, some burned, some to be broken on wheels, others to be staked, and some to be shott to deathe, all theis extreme and crewell tortures he used, and inflicted upon them, to terrefy the reste for attempteinge the lyke, and some w[ch] robbed the store, he cawsed them to be bowned faste unto trees, and so starved them to deathe.[5]

And more recently the eminent historian of the British Isles, A. J.

Toynbee, in his profound *Study of history*, has declared: "Habits of 'frightfulness,' acquired by the English in their prolonged aggression against the remnants of the Celtic Fringe in the highlands of Scotland and the bogs of Ireland, were carried across the Atlantic and practiced at the expense of the North American Indians."[6]

Perversity and man's inhumanity to man were not, then, traits unique to the Conquistador, and his aberrations were common enough among his fellow Christians in the times in which he lived. Yet because his Spain was then politically dominant and feared by other nations of Europe who envied the spoils of conquest, the Spaniard became the symbol of the collective cruelty of the European peoples engaged in the westernization of the world.[7] But the Conquistador, as the first to discover and exploit the riches of the New World, was no more than the expression of those drives which animated his generation, and a fairer appraisal of his character and significance comes from the pen of a famous English contemporary, Sir Walter Raleigh, who wrote in his *History of the world*:

> Here I cannot forbear to commend the patient virtue of the Spaniards. We seldom or never find any nation hath endured so many misadventures and miseries as the Spaniards have done in their Indian discoveries. Yet persisting in their enterprises, with invincible constancy, they have annexed to their kingdom so many goodly provinces, as bury the remembrance of all dangers past. Tempests and shipwracks, famine, overthrows, mutinies, heat and cold, pestilence, and all manner of diseases, both old and new, together with extream poverty, and want of all things needful, have been the enemies, wherewith every one of their most noble discoveries, at one time or other, hath encountered. Many years have passed over some of their heads in the search of not so many leagues: Yea, more than one or two have spent their labor, their wealth, and their lives, in search of a golden kingdom, without getting further notice of it than what they had at their first setting forth. All which notwithstanding, the third, fourth and fifth undertakers have not been disheartened. Surely, they are worthily rewarded with those treasures and paradises, which they enjoy, and well deserve to hold them quietly, if they hinder not the like virtue in others, which (perhaps) will not be found.[8]

If the Conquistador may be said to have possessed any one quality or trait in greater degree than his European contemporaries, it was what some writers have called "romanticism" or what, perhaps, might more accurately be termed "imagination." His emotional responses to stimuli of every sort were quick and warm, moving him to heroic action and intense enthusiasm. This characteristic has long been a distinguishing feature of Hispanic peoples and has tended to set them apart from the rest of the Continent. In the age of geographic discoveries this was strikingly true, and ever since it has manifested itself impressively in the art, literature, folklore, music, and in the innumerable myths, legends, and ballads which were the patrimony of every Spaniard. The relative isolation of Spanish life from that of the rest of Europe, the ever-present proximity of the unknown in the dark waters of the Atlantic, and the mingling of European and Arabic cultures, all tended to foster a sense of mystery and fantasy. This introspective preoccupation with the extraordinary was stimulated enormously, not only by the belief, current in the Middle Ages, in the truth of alchemy and astrology, or the existence of the elixirs of life and fountains of youth, but also by the tales of returning sailors and of such travelers from remote lands as Marco Polo, Sir John Mandeville, and Caballero Tafur. They brought rumors of mysterious islands with strange forms of life, hydras, gorgons, Amazons, mermaids, of weird Calibans and singing Ariels. The Spanish listeners, perhaps reacting to the stark realism of their immediate surroundings, escaped into flights of fantasy and, as their imaginations became incandescent, they flamed into a passion for adventure, for discovery. What they heard aroused an unquenchable curiosity and fired their will to see these wonders with their own eyes.

Before 1500 most of these fabulous legends came to Spanish ears through the oral narratives of storytellers or the chivalric ballads of troubadors and passed from mouth to mouth. But if these verbal accounts excited the credulity of the hearers, much more exhilarating and convincing was the visual evidence that they had after that date when the new invention of the printing press brought clear corroboration to their eyes in the magical form of type. Wisdom and truth had theretofore been imprisoned in written books down through the ages, the special domain of priests and wizards, but now the printed books offered their pages freely to all. What

appeared on them did not admit of doubt, and there were found
full confirmation and elaboration of the tales that the readers had
heard. Even the learned were often influenced by the apparently
incontrovertible nature that a statement seemed to take on when it
appeared in print. It has been repeatedly asserted that Christopher
Columbus was stirred to dreams by reading a tragedy of Seneca entitled *Medea,* in which occurs the following passage:

> There will come a time in the long years of the world
> when the ocean sea will loosen the shackles that bind things
> together and a great part of the earth will be opened up and
> a new sailor such as one who was Jason's guide, whose name
> was Thyphis, shall discover a new world, and then shall
> Thule be no longer the last of lands.[9]

And later Antonio Pigafetta, the chronicler of Magellan's voyage
around the globe, confessed that he was moved to emulation by
what he had read in books when he declared, "While I was in Spain
in 1509, certain people whom I met and several books which I read
revealed to me the marvels of the ocean sea and then and there I re-
solved to see such marvels with my own eyes."[10]

And so it was with the Spanish Conquistador who embarked on
the many expeditions to the new-found world. After 1500 particularly his imagination was kindled to an almost mystical exaltation of
adventure and romance by the many books which began to pour
from the presses. These volumes brought to his fevered mind seemingly authentic accounts of fantastic places, riches, monsters, and
enchantment, and he burned to discover and possess for himself
the realities that they described. To the Conquest itself, as a result,
was imparted a spirit of romance and chivalry which gave these
expeditions, as Irving has aptly remarked, "a character wholly distinct from similar enterprises undertaken by other nations."[11] It is
of importance, then, to consider briefly these early works of literature which exerted such a powerful effect upon the Conquistador
and which thus indirectly influenced the course of history.

THE ROMANCES II
OF CHIVALRY

HE TURN OF THE FIFTEENTH CENTURY HERALDED THE true beginning of the democratization of reading with the rise of the so-called "romances of chivalry," which were the first popular literature to demonstrate the commercial possibilities of the recently invented printing press. Taking its strongest hold in Spain soon after the discovery of America, this literary fashion spread like a contagion into the neighboring countries of Europe and, presently, crossed the ocean to the New World. Everywhere the appeal of this fiction proved overpowering and the literate elements of all social classes succumbed to it. And long before this enthusiasm subsided completely these fantastic tales had left their imprint on contemporary customs and manners, had fired the imaginations of adventurers in Europe and America, and had inspired the greatest masterpiece in Spanish literature.

These novels were usually long accounts of the impossible exploits of knightly heroes in strange and enchanted lands inhabited by monsters and extraordinary creatures, and they presented a highly imaginative, idealized concept of life in which strength, virtue, and passion were all of a transcendent and unnatural character. These prolix narratives were, indeed, the melodrama of their age, and readers, unrestrained by any knowledge of what are today the most elementary scientific facts, accepted avidly and uncritically the wildest extravagances that the authors generously offered them. As the public clamored for more of these romances, it identified itself completely with the world of these fictional knights. Like the motion pictures of a later day, these romantic novels exerted a profound influence on contemporary conduct, morality and thought patterns, and they furthered the acceptance of artificial standards of value and false attitudes toward reality. These books provided a pleasant escape from the harsh monotony of an essentially primitive existence, and they brought a touch of color to the drab lives of their readers. The latter, despite the denunciations of moralists against these "lying histories," continued to find in them authentic portrayals of life from which they derived not only patterns of behavior as well as ideas of a larger reality but incitement to greater endeavors.

The popularity of these romances in the sixteenth century was, in reality, a more democratic revival in the Spanish Peninsula of a medieval passion for the literature of chivalry. The folk ballads, which belonged to the whole people and still retained the affection of the less cultivated at the time of the Conquest, contained some of the same fanciful and idealistic elements, but rivaling them in appeal among the more aristocratic classes were the newer forms of chronicles purporting to give historical accounts of the past. As the Moorish frontier, where the conflicts of Christian and infidel supplied so many themes for artistic expression, was pushed farther south, leaving a greater degree of security and leisure in the northern provinces, these prose chronicles took on more and more a picturesque flavor. In time they were dominated by a spirit of poetic invention and chivalry which blended fact and fiction indistinguishably.[1] Hence the chivalric romances were but a step further and they reappeared with something of the aura of authenticity enveloping the contemporary chronicle. The multiplying agency of the printing press could not fail to make this revival far more widespread and influential, for the circulation of these romantic tales was no longer limited by the manuscript form to the wealthy aristocracy.

The vastly increased diffusion of secular knowledge and entertainment through the printing of books in the vernacular was a phenomenon of the sixteenth century as remarkable in its way as radio broadcasting in the early twentieth century, for the impact of this innovation on the daily lives and thoughts of an enormously expanded sector of the population was nearly as revolutionary. Reading was abruptly transformed from the special privilege of a small elite able to possess handwritten copies to the democratic opportunity of all classes, and a more widespread literacy was stimulated. The effect was not unlike that of radio communication later in widening the appreciation of music and in democratizing the enjoyment of that great art. But inevitably, when a mechanical agency suddenly gives access to an art medium to a large and unprepared audience, the common denominators of taste operate at a lower level and the vulgarization of a creative expression tends to debase traditional esthetic canons. The romances of chivalry, as the earliest genuinely popular literature made available by the printing press, illustrate this law. The literary merit of *Amadis of Gaul*, the first truly successful novel to circulate in print, was never equaled in the long procession of sequels and imitations that it inspired, and these continuations degenerated to such extremes of absurdity that, more than any other factor, they ultimately destroyed their own vogue.

With the origin and earlier manifestations of the chivalrous novel it is not necessary to be concerned here. Chronologically the first real work of this character in Spain was the *Historia del caballero de Dios que avrá por nombre Cifar*, a somewhat didactic novel with a mixture of realism and fantasy which marks it as a transitional composition and a link between obscure medieval beginnings and the later novelistic forms in Spanish literature. But the *Caballero Cifar* apparently did not appear in print until 1512 and hence was not widely known until more authentic romances of chivalry had already established the fashion. The earliest printed work of this sort seems to have been *Tirant lo Blanch*, published in the Catalan language at Valencia in 1490. This was a narrative of considerable artistic value with realistic elements and a relative lack of the magical incident that characterized the more typical tales of chivalry. The Castilian version did not appear until 1511 and its success was comparatively modest. Indeed, no documentary evidence of the transfer of copies, either of *Tirant lo Blanch* or of the *Caballero Cifar*, to the New World, soon to be an important market for Spanish books, has thus far been found in the records of the sixteenth century, and it is safe to assume that both works were far overshadowed by the phenomenally popular *Amadis of Gaul*, the first known edition of which was printed in 1508. In the last decade of the fifteenth century a number of French romances of the so-called Celtic and Carlovingian cycles were translated into Spanish and published, but it is doubtful whether they did more than prepare the way for the most famous knight of all, Amadis of Gaul, whose narrative may well have had an earlier edition during the same period.[2]

The complicated question of the obscure origin, antecedents, and authorship of this landmark of Spanish literature need not be discussed here, since the concern is primarily with the effect produced on many readers by the printed version of this work and its rivals. Suffice it to say that France, Portugal and Spain each claim the legend as originating in its own national literature. References to Amadis are noted in the Hispanic Peninsula as early as the fourteenth century and increasingly throughout the fifteenth. The first known printing, that of 1508 at Zaragoza already mentioned, was entitled *Cuatro libros de Amadís de Gaula*, with the author's name indicated as Garci-Rodríguez de Montalvo, though given in later editions as Garci-Ordoñez de Montalvo. Information concerning this writer is practically limited to the fact that he was a regidor of Medina del Campo and the belief that he wrote the preface of his historic work between 1492 and 1504.

The four books into which the novel is divided recount the origin, adventures and undying love of Amadis and Oriana, the daughter of Lisuarte, King of Great Britain. Amadis is born of the secret union of Perion, King of Gaul, and the Princess Elisena, who conceals his birth by placing the baby in an ark which floats out to sea. The infant is rescued by a Scottish knight, who rears the foundling in the court of the King of Scotland. There, in the course of time, young Amadis meets the charming princess Oriana to whom, at the mature age of twelve, he surrenders his heart, and, to quote the text, ". . . this love lasted as long as they lasted, for as well as he loved her did she also love him." The obscure origin of Amadis, however, made his suit presumptuous and left him no recourse but to sally forth as a knight errant and win by his own prowess the right to Oriana's hand. Then follows an involved narrative of the varied adventures of Amadis and his companions, including personal and collective combats, rescues, monsters, enchanted islands, and other extraordinary experiences. Through all these travels and encounters Amadis remains steadfastly faithful to his lady love and, quite properly, his remarkable constancy is rewarded by fame and by marriage to his beloved Oriana.[3]

This romantic tale has been characterized as "the first idealistic modern novel, the epic of faithfulness in love, the code of honor and courtesy which schooled many generations."[4] And, indeed, the medieval ideal of chivalry, cast in elevated prose, with emphasis on the theatrical aspects of knight errantry and its elaborate formalities, together with marvelous adventures in mysterious lands and among strange creatures, and all centered in an attractive hero and a beautiful heroine with whom the reader of either sex could identify himself, made this story of irresistible appeal. These fascinating features, including the novelty of human love depicted as permanent adoration, could not fail to assure the narrative the flattery of wide imitation. Other knightly heroes soon sought to emulate the deeds of Amadis, including an imposing number of his lineal descendants, but the *Four books of Amadis of Gaul* remained throughout the sixteenth century the favorite of innumerable readers, the manual of good taste, the model of valor and nobility, and the oracle of elegant conversation. To what extent its influence lingers in the ceremonial courtesy and courtly manners still practiced by the cultured elements of Hispanic society on both sides of the Atlantic is an interesting subject for speculation. Of more immediate interest is the certainty that the vista of exotic lands, strange peoples, and hidden wealth offered by the novel to contemporary conquistadors could not fail to lure them on to fantastic adventures abroad in the suddenly expanded world in which they lived.

The author, Montalvo, appears to have anticipated in some measure the resounding success of *Amadis of Gaul* and to have calculated shrewdly on the commercial advantages to be derived from the literary vein that he was tapping. Toward the end of the preface of his first work, in which he claims to have "corrected" the first three books of the novel and emended the fourth, he announces a forthcoming *Fifth book* to be known as *Sergas de Esplandián*. This continuation would recite the exploits of Amadis' illustrious son. Two years later, in 1510, the volume appeared and, although greatly inferior, it met with comparable success, attaining at least ten editions and probably more during the course of the sixteenth century. As will later appear, the inclusion in this sequel of the recently reinvigorated myth of the warlike Amazons may have caused the *Sergas de Esplandián* to have a more direct influence on the Conquistador than its superior predecessor.

The enthusiastic reception accorded the narratives of the legendary Amadis and of his son encouraged similar accounts of successive descendants until a lengthy genealogy of knightly heroes had evolved.[5] These continuations and the imitations of them by different writers poured forth, reaching a crest about the middle of the sixteenth century which slowly receded during the second half of the period. From 1508 to 1550 more than fifty different and bulky romances of chivalry appeared, but in the next forty years only nine new works of this character are known. In the last decade or so only three more were added, but practically all of the earlier favorites were reprinted again and again, even after *Don Quixote de la Mancha* appeared in 1605, and their fascination remained for many readers long after the vogue had passed. *Policisne de Boecia*, published in 1602, is usually regarded as the last of the long procession. Meanwhile, the sons, grandsons and great grandsons of Amadis and Esplandián carried on the family traditions, repeating the exploits of their forefathers in successive books, each with separate titles. *Florisando* came forth the same year as the *Sergas de Esplandián, Lisuarte de Grecia* in 1514, *Amadís de Grecia* in 1530, *Don Florisel de Niquea* in 1532, etc., until there were twelve books in the Amadis cycle.[6] These were collectively grouped as the "chronicles of Amadis," and the use of this designation was common when referring generically to the whole series, as was done in the prohibitory legislation by which authorities strove vainly to stamp out what they regarded as a pernicious reading habit.

Scarcely were the original heroes of the Amadis saga launched on their glamorous careers when a rival dynasty offered competition. This was the so-called Palmerín cycle,[7] the first novel being *Palmerín de Oliva*, who entered the lists in 1511. The son of this hero, Primaleón, like Esplandián, follows in the paternal footsteps and, from generation unto generation, invincible sires are exceeded in achievements by more invincible sons whose exploits and adventures grow progressively more fantastic and absurd. Still other rivals appear on the scene to captivate unsophisticated readers and these tales, like the themes of modern cinematographic drama, frequently incorporate palpable imitations of the characters, adventures, and plot of the original creation which scored a commercial success.

During the first half century of the truly epic feats by flesh-and-blood heroes, the Spanish conquistadors, the so-called Greco-Asiatic cycle of novels, which includes the Amadis series, appears to have enjoyed the widest appeal and exerted the strongest influence on the imaginations of Peninsular readers. Aside from the tedious repetition of the same combats and adventures, there were certain common features in these highly seasoned tales which seemed to give a convincing air of reality to the mythical knights that moved through their pages. Some of these characteristics were: the basing of the narrative on the alleged discovery of an ancient manuscript and its translation, thus giving the impression that the account was derived from an historical document; the obscure but noble birth of the hero who vindicates his lofty lineage by his extraordinary valor and daring exploits; the achievement of fame and fortune by individual effort, thus confirming the individualistic Spaniard's faith in his own sufficiency; the assured eventual triumph of the hero as an "Emperor of Constantinople" or monarch of some other exotic kingdom or enchanted island; and, finally, the fanciful geography of these romances with their vaguely located regions, wealthy cities, and magical isles. The apparent historicity of these tales, together with the enormous expansion of the physical horizons brought about by the recent discoveries in Africa and the New World, gave a plausibility to the wildest notions with which writers might season their stories. The vast possibilities that the earthly globe thus seemed to offer stirred the fevered imagination of readers to a high pitch of excitement and moved the more adventurous to seek out the mysterious wonders and the untold treasure with which the unknown lands were endowed so authoritatively. Exploring expeditions being fitted out for operations in the New World did not find the task of recruiting their members too difficult, for in that bright morning of the modern age nothing was impossible.

These tremendously popular works of fiction, then, stimulated the emotions and won the passionate devotion of all literate classes of Spain, from the great Emperor Charles V himself to the lowliest clerk in his service. Even the general addiction of twentieth-century

English-speaking readers to detective novels is hardly comparable, for the reading public of the early sixteenth century, much more credulous and uncritical than that of later generations, surrendered itself to these knightly tales with an abandon now seldom experienced by mankind except in childhood. The pages of this chivalric fiction were thumbed with an enthusiasm amounting to a passion, and their fascination spurred the illiterate to master quickly the art of reading. In the royal palace and in the humblest hut these novels were read, often aloud, so that a completely unlettered audience could enjoy vicariously the seemingly real and historical experiences of noble heroes. The aristocracy of every shade and degree, including its womenkind, and even the clergy, devoted much of their ample leisure to this diverting pastime.

This universal devotion to the popular fiction is clearly reflected in the contemporary protests of moralists and the prohibitory legislation of the mid sixteenth century and later against the "lying histories" which consumed so much time of youths and maidens, particularly, and inspired them to ape so slavishly the manners, habits, and speech of imaginary heroes and heroines. Indeed, the allegedly depraved younger generation, and some of its elders, seemed to prefer the dubious ethics and doubtful codes of chivalry to the sterner doctrines taught by the Church. Mothers who left their daughters at home locked in their rooms for safety from the dangers besetting their virtue were only exposing these damsels to corruption and imperiling their eternal salvation, for it too frequently happened that the young ladies occupied themselves during this incarceration with reading secreted copies of chivalric novels. And often as not the mother herself read them, openly or clandestinely.

Even before the appearance of the published version of *Amadis of Gaul*, a partiality for similar light reading existed in the highest social spheres. Pious Queen Isabella was known to have in her castle at Segovia a scroll copy of a chivalric tale *Historia de Lanzarote*,[8] which was probably the *Demanda del Sancto Grial con los maravillosos fechos de Lanzarote y de Galaz*, first printed in 1515 after her death. But it was her illustrious grandson, Charles V, who really fell under the sway of this literature. His imperial enthusiasm for the knightly *Belianis de Grecia*, it is said,[9] induced its author to write a sequel, and a similar work in French was translated into Castilian verse at the Emperor's command. And when this titular head of the Holy Roman Empire abdicated the throne of Spain, he took into retirement with him one or more of these chivalric narratives.[10] Nor was he unique among European monarchs in this fondness for romantic fiction, though his responsibility may have been large for the fondness of his royal prisoner, Francis I of France, for these books, whom he seems to have introduced to them. A later French king, Louis XIV, and William the Silent were also among the royalty who succumbed to their charm.[11]

The favor of princes encouraged the diffusion of chivalric literature among their subjects and stimulated the translation of these Spanish novels into various languages of Europe, thus making them accessible to the literate classes everywhere. The statesmen and diplomats of politically dominant Spain sought relaxation from the heavy strain of their responsibilities by reading such fiction much as their counterparts in a later age find momentary release in detective mysteries. One of the most distinguished diplomats of sixteenth-century Spain, Don Diego Hurtado de Mendoza, while traveling to Rome as ambassador, took copies of *Amadis of Gaul* and the *Celestina* as his only books on the journey.[12] The informant complains that this dignitary seemed to derive more inspiration from these contrasting works of entertainment than he did from the Epistles of St. Paul. The catalogue of Ferdinand Columbus, the titled son of the discoverer of America, shows that he had many early editions of these romances in the rich library that he assembled.[13] A prominent humanist, Juan de Valdés, well known in courtly circles, who also went to Italy, confessed in his famous *Diálogo de la lengua* that he had spent ten of the best years of his life in palaces and courts where he did not employ himself "in any exercise more virtuous than in reading these falsehoods," which gained such power over him that when he picked up a more respectable work he was never able to finish reading it. He had firsthand knowledge of most of the romances of chivalry of his time and, in his judgment, *Amadis of Gaul*, *Palmerín* and *Primaleón* were the best written.[14]

People of distinction with a passion for the current literary fashion were by no means confined to the secular elements of society. Although the clergy railed at the widespread reading of the

novels of chivalry, many of their own number, including some renowned for their piety and mysticism, were addicted, at least
briefly, to this worldly vice, as a few ruefully admitted later. Ignatius
Loyola, founder of the Jesuit Order, was accustomed to peruse such
"vayne Treatises" and asked for them to relieve the tedium of con-
valescence from a broken leg suffered at the siege of Pamplona in
1521.[15] Under the influence of some traumatic experience it seems
likely that this great saint's early enthusiasm for the lofty codes and
romantic idealism of the knights of chivalry was transferred to the
vastly profounder idealism of the Founder of Christianity, thus
spiritualizing the chivalric ideal. Indeed, one literary critic asserts
that Loyola's militant Jesuits were a kind of knight-errantry *a lo
divino*.[16]

Another great religious leader of the Counter Reformation who
succumbed to the fascination of Amadis and his tribe was no less
a figure than that profoundly mystical and eminently practical lady,
Santa Teresa de Jesús (1515-1582) of Avila. In the second chapter
of a sort of autobiography she states that she caught the contagion
of such fiction from her otherwise virtuous mother. "I began to
fall into the habit of reading them [romances of chivalry]," she
reports, ". . . and it seemed to me that it was not wrong to spend
many hours of the day and night in such vain exercise, though concealed from my father. I became so utterly absorbed in this that if
I did not have a new book [to read], I did not feel that I could be
happy. . . ."[17] This early contact with the literature of chivalry
undoubtedly had a psychological influence on her own mystical
writings, particularly in the militant symbolism of spiritual struggle
present in her most important work, *El castillo interior o moradas*.
Both courtly love and divine love were exalted by the same heroic
conception of moral obligation and, as a French student of the
Saint of Avila wrote, "La devise d'Amadis des Gaules et celle de
Thérèse pourrait être egalement 'aimer pour agir.'"[18] Indeed, it is
fair to assume that the exaltation induced in youthful, impressionable
minds by the idealism and fearlessness of these fictional heroes was
subconsciously transfused by some subtle process into the superhuman energy of those tremendous poets of action—the conquistadors—and of those incomparable poets of the spirit—the mystics.

Santa Teresa's sixteenth-century biographer, Francisco de Ribera, sought to exonerate her from this girlhood peccadillo by asserting that it was the Devil who induced her to read such literature. He adds that she spent much time in this way and ". . . her wit was so excellent and . . . she imbibed their language and style so well that, within a few months, she and her brother, Rodrigo de Cepeda, composed a novel of chivalry full of adventure and imagination, and it was such that a good deal might be said of it. . . ."[19] This youthful creative excursion of Santa Teresa, which was probably known to all the younger members of the family, may have had some repercussion many years later when one of her brothers, known as Agustín de Ahumada, who was in the New World seeking his fortune, wrote to the viceroy of Peru. In this letter, dated in Quito on October 25, 1582, he informed the king's representative in Lima that he was negotiating with the Royal Audiencia for aid in organizing an expedition of ". . . up to a hundred men to go in search of a certain province that some residents of this district came upon which they found was the most populous and richest in gold ever seen; from what they tell of it and the description that they give, one can believe that it must be without any doubt at all the El Dorado, in the pursuit of which thousands of leaders and men have been lost." Like all other such fantasy-inspired will-o'-the-wisps, it was so near at hand that ". . . in a week of journeying one is there!"[20]

If venerated saints of the sixteenth-century Church acknowledged strong though temporary attachment to these highly imaginative tales, it is certain that lesser members of the clergy were also addicted to them and probably more permanently. To cite one instance, Melchor Cano, a noted theologian of the time, reported that he knew a priest who was not only familiar with the deeds of Amadis and other knightly heroes, but believed that they were true because he had seen them in print![21] With varying degrees of credence, then, these romantic stories were read and accepted by the religious and lay alike, and the writers and poets of both groups were consciously or subconsciously influenced by this popular literature in their own artistic expression. Even in far-off Cuzco, the ancient seat of the Inca civilization in the lofty Sierra of Peru where the Conquistador had introduced this fiction, a youthful mestizo, offspring of a Spanish conqueror and an Incan princess, was steeping himself in chivalric narratives; this was Garcilaso de la Vega—el Inca, as he was called—who was to write the first truly American work, the *Royal Commentaries of the Incas*. Long afterwards he shamefacedly admitted this early fondness which, he claimed, was changed to aversion by reading the thundering denunciation of these entertaining books in the preface of Pedro Mexía's learned *Historia Imperial*.[22]

Doubtless a long list of such confessions by other more or less distinguished contemporaries who were enamored of the novels of chivalry could be compiled, but it is sufficiently clear that few able to read, whatever their class, occupation or social standing, lacked intimate acquaintance, at least in their youth and often late in life, with the highly colored exploits of Amadis, Esplandián, Palmerín, and other mighty heroes of fiction and were subtly influenced by their reading. If among the intellectuals this effect was largely limited to their own literary expression, the habits and manners of the majority of the less well endowed were modified, and many of the ordinary people, from whom the ranks of the conquistadors were recruited, were incited to adventurous action in distant lands, lured by the wonders and the wealth which the chivalric romances revealed to them so glamorously. Led by such intrepid captains as Cortés, Pizarro and Jiménez de Quesada, they performed flesh-and-blood prodigies of valor which, in boldness and daring, dwarfed those of the imaginary world of Amadis and his followers.

THE CONQUISTADOR AND III
THE "LYING HISTORIES"

SOME INDICATIONS HAVE BEEN GIVEN OF THE REMARK-
able grip of the chivalric romances on the popular mind of the first
half of the sixteenth century. The influence of this literature on the
thought and actions of readers is unmistakable, though it does not
lend itself to exact measurement. As the energetic and adventurous
element of Spanish society, the Conquistador could hardly escape
the incitement of these fictional narratives, whether he was literate
or not, though again the precise effect of such tales upon him is
not demonstrable by documentary evidence. In the next chapter
an effort will be made to trace a direct connection between inspiration from that source and a specific quest of the conquerors in the
New World, but the proof is not wholly conclusive. There can be
little doubt, however, that the young men of Renaissance Spain,
impatiently awaiting summonses to serve in their Emperor's armies
or eagerly volunteering for the expeditions to the New World, felt
themselves stimulated to heroic action by these exhilerating romances which glorified the warrior as the prototype of their culture.
It is reported that the extraordinary feats of one of Charles V's
celebrated captains, Don Fernando de Avalos, Marqués de Pescara,
were attributed to the noble ardor and desire for glory awakened
in his heart by the habitual reading of chivalric novels in his youthful
years.[1]

In a Portuguese work of the early seventeenth century there is
an amusing anecdote which bears witness to a similar influence exerted by these books upon a simple soldier in the ranks. Since it is
particularly apt and brief, it is worth quoting in full. It reads as
follows:

While a Portuguese commander had an enemy city under
siege during the fighting in India, a number of his soldiers
who camped together as comrades carried in their outfit a
novel of chivalry with which they passed the time. One of
these men who knew this literature less than the others regarded everything that he heard read as true (for there are
guileless people who think that there can be no lies in print).
His companions, playing on his gullibility, kept telling him
that such was really the case. When the time came for an
attack this good fellow, stirred by what he had heard read
and eager to emulate the heroes of the book, burned with a
desire to demonstrate his valor and to perform a deed of
knighthood which would be remembered. And so he leaped
wildly into the fray and began to strike right and left with
his sword among the enemy so furiously that only by great
effort and much peril his comrades and numerous other
soldiers together were able to save his life by picking him
up covered with glory and not a few wounds. When his
friends scolded him for his rashness, he answered: 'Aw, leave
me alone! I didn't do the half of what any of the knights did
in the book that you fellows read to me every night.' And
from that time on he was exceedingly valorous.[2]

Other such individuals, especially in Spain, animated less by
honor than by curiosity, were convinced that by participation in
overseas ventures they would see and experience in reality the
wonders, the riches and the adventures so seductively depicted in
the pages of the popular books. Giants, wizards, dwarfs, enchanted
isles, Amazons, fountains of youth, mystical Seven Cities, El Dorados
surely existed somewhere, in some part of the vast regions and
strange lands providentially revealed to the chosen people of
Castile!

Some explanation has already been offered of the undeniable
hold of the chivalric fiction on all elements of Spanish society, but
to comprehend more fully the hypnotizing effect of these romances
on the mentality and achievements of the Conquistador further
elaboration is desirable. It is convenient, perhaps, to limit this additional consideration to three basic factors: the historical events occurring in Spain and Western Europe which coincided with the
rise of this literature; the new invention of the printing press; and
the hazy distinction generally between fact and fiction.

Life was an exhilerating experience in the Spanish Peninsula at the close of the fifteenth century and during the decades following, for it seemed to hold more promise of great things for mankind than, perhaps, ever before or since in human history. The recently achieved union of Castile and Aragon had brought nearer the sense of nationality that was slowly evolving during the prolonged struggle with the Moors, and at the fall of Granada in 1492 Spain emerged as one of the first modern nations of Europe. This event coincided with the realization that—as the discoveries of Columbus made clear—the habitable world was a vaster space than theretofore conceived, and it thus marked a definite break with the Middle Ages or, at least, the point of fusion of the medieval and the Renaissance spirit. This sudden expansion of horizons, both physical and intellectual, to unbelievable limits, coupled with a sense of destiny as the instrument of God for the tremendous task of Christianizing the globe, released a prodigious amount of national energy and was a powerful stimulant to the imagination. The resulting meteoric rise of Spain as a political force was aided by the affiliation of the Peninsula with the Holy Roman Empire and particularly by the spectacular achievements of its soldiers in Europe and its conquistadors in America. So extraordinary were the feats of these men of arms that the recital of their deeds by prosaic chroniclers sounded like the current novels of adventure. Fact was outdistancing fiction and, however far fantasy might transport an individual, it might not be much in advance of the realities which the new lands beyond the seas would reveal to mankind. To be young in the Hispanic Peninsula during this period of human experience was to have faith in the impossible. An enormously enlarged world teemed with possibilities of adventure and romance in which one's wildest dreams and fondest hopes of fame and fortune could be fulfilled. Life had a zest and an irresistible allure in the bright Renaissance light which was rapidly dissipating the medieval gloom.

It was inevitable that there should be a mutual interaction between the contemporary historical events and creative literature, the imaginary influencing the real and the real the imaginary, thereby engendering a certain confusion in the minds of all. Vasco da Gama, Columbus, and the other navigators and explorers had unconsciously brought to the regions they discovered the mythical lore of the Middle Ages in which they were steeped, and hence these argonauts returned with reports of mysterious islands glimpsed, of Amazons inhabiting them, and of positive indications of the near proximity of the Earthly Paradise. And the new maps of a distending globe bore conventional cartographic ornamentation on the fringes, depicting curious anomalies; the broad, vacant expanses of sea and land now enlarged on them were specked with figures of strangely shaped beasts and men presumably existing in these unexplored areas. Were they not suggested in part by the fabulous creatures so vividly described in the current romances of chivalry, much as the latter had, perhaps, borrowed some of their notions from similar images adorning earlier charts? Did not the queer geography thus indicated with its out-of-the-way territories confirm the existence of exotic lands visited by the knights-errant in their wondrous adventures? The inaccurate and exaggerated reports of returning discoverers could, it seemed, be reconciled with or adapted to the stirring descriptions presented in the popular narratives. The exaltation of a people flushed with triumph and imbued with a faith in a unique destiny fostered a credulous receptivity to the fictitious accounts both of returning explorers and of novelists, and there was no strong desire to distinguish one from the other.

In these days of overabundant books, periodicals, newspapers, and pamphlets lavishly supplying literature for every taste, fashion, and mood, it requires an extraordinary effort of the imagination to appreciate fully the mystical awe which the written and printed word once inspired universally. The scroll and the book were the repositories and magical transmitters of occult learning, of the dark secrets of nature, and of miraculous power accessible only to that elite capable of deciphering their hieroglyphics. A ponderous black tome was an indispensable adjunct of the wizard's paraphernalia, a symbol of his supernatural wisdom and, in the folkloric myths of the Middle Ages, the accepted method of depriving these necromancers of their dominion of the black arts was to steal from them the book which was the source of their diabolic powers. The mixture of superstition and sacredness associated with the written scroll or manuscript did not vanish until long after the invention of movable type and the multiplication of printed works. During the centuries following, the residual veneration for these repositories of knowledge was an important factor in the slowness with which authoritarian learning or scholasticism yielded to experimentalism as a method of approximating truth.

The introduction of the printing press in Spain about 1473 had slight immediate effect on popularizing reading or in reducing the traditional reverence for the written word. If theretofore the scroll or volume—a rare and costly object, the product of laborious effort and exquisite workmanship of monkish scribes and illuminators— was the exclusive possession of royalty, the higher clergy, a few of the nobility, and a small number of scholars, the finely wrought incunables of the Peninsular presses, largely religious in character, did not greatly extend the circulation of books beyond the range of the earlier manuscripts. Moreover, Latin was the standard medium of most of these works and hence, in content and form, a book printed by movable type remained essentially an aristocratic privilege, virtually inaccessible to the overwhelming majority whose superstitious respect for the written word continued unaltered. With the printing in the vernacular of one of the first novels of chivalry, *Tirant lo Blanch*, in 1490, however, and the appearance of the dictionaries and grammars of Nebrija, along with the translation of certain French tales in the same decade, the process of democratizing the printed page in Spain got under way. The publication of *Amadis of Gaul* in 1508, or possibly at an earlier date, accelerated this trend and, while weakening the purely didactic function which a book was thought to serve solely, it revealed, more clearly than any of its predecessors, the commercial potentialities of the printing press. For the first time a wide public awoke to the realization that a book could also be a *means of entertainment*.

But this newer concept of the printed medium did not at once shake the traditional faith in books as an unimpeachable source of wisdom and a record of historical fact. Writing in this new form lost little of its mystical import, and this miracle of the talking page was too impressive at first to allow any skepticism to enter the thoughts of simple novitiates in the art of reading. The learned, perceiving the dangers involved, might view askance the flood of imaginative literature pouring forth from the clumsy presses, but the unschooled novice, who far outnumbered him, had no desire to question but, rather, preferred to believe uncritically all that the pages of type set so persuasively before his eyes. In the various strata of Spanish society there were probably innumerable counterparts of Melchor Cano's sixteenth-century country priest, previously mentioned, who was firmly convinced that nothing was false which had once gotten into print, ". . . for," he explained, "our rulers would not commit so great a crime as not merely to allow falsehoods to be spread abroad, but to bolster them up by privilege as well,"[3] meaning, of course, the granting of the official license to publish. He was, therefore, persuaded that Amadis and Clarian had, in reality, performed all the deeds accredited to them. It can hardly be doubted that many a youthful Conquistador, with even less formal education, had a similar naive faith in the accounts of knight-errantry and believed that he could emulate their fantastic adventures even in the very same places described in the *historias*.

Through the agency of the printing press the tales of magic, mystery and wonder, hitherto heard in groups and by oral tradition, now had a visual representation available at any time. Formerly enjoyment of literature was largely limited to occasions when traveling troubadors, wandering minstrels, or possibly less itinerant storytellers on the domestic hearth sang or recited songs and ballads to gatherings, large or small, and in these recitations facts and fables, indiscriminately confused, came to the individual, through his ears. This lore he received passively, storing it, perhaps, in the archives of his memory for repetition to other groups. Thus, besides being purely oral, the transmission of these legends and stories was associated with groups, either at home, on the village square, or in the church courtyard. Now, however, with the printed book in his hands, the vicarious experience which reading permitted him often became both active and solitary—active in that he created his own images from the cold type, and solitary in that he might enjoy the narrative in the privacy of his own chamber, his imagination working untrammeled by the presence of others, his identification with the hero of the tale complete. With the aura of authority and mystery still strongly investing the printed page and lending validity to the mental images it conjured up, the spell cast by the reading of the adventures of the knights-errant was hypnotic. As already asserted, the influence of these narratives on thought patterns and resulting conduct was immense. Minds conditioned by the accepted miracles of their religious faith, by the poetic and mythical lore of the Middle Ages, and by the chronicles of fabulous deeds performed by ancestors against the Moorish invaders, easily absorbed the effusions of creative writers with a credulity and conviction that seem impossible to the modern mentality.[4]

In considerable degree this uncritical acceptance of the romances of chivalry was prepared by the long series of Spanish chronicles, rich in variety, picturesqueness and poetry, which had flourished for two centuries. From bare recitals of fact they became in time accounts ornamented with unrealistic details and the injection of increasing doses of invented elements without, however, losing any of their prestige as authentic records. This evolution culminated in the *Chronicle of Don Roderick with the destruction of Spain* which appeared in 1511, almost coinciding with the publication of *Amadis of Gaul* and the *Sergas de Esplandián*. This work, which purports to relate the betrayal of Spain by Roderick to the invading Moors, is essentially a historical novel with purely imaginary figures mingling with those of Roderick himself, Count Julian, La Cava, and Orpas, the false Archbishop of Seville. These personages carry on invented dialogues, and impossible tournaments are described with kings moving about like knights-errant and ladies wandering around in distress. It was a revision of what passed for history in the old chronicles, incorporating details, incidents and characteristics of the now current romantic fiction but, since it dealt with a familiar historical episode, the ordinary reader did not question its veracity. Thus the complete acceptance of the parallel romance of chivalry itself was facilitated.[5]

In the popular mind, therefore, there existed an incongruous commingling of fact, fable, and wishful thinking which writers of chivalrous tales were quick to exploit. These purveyors of reading entertainment did not disdain the use of certain devices likely to beguile simple-minded readers only too ready to be convinced of the reality of what they read and all too eager to launch upon irrational adventures, as Don Quixote was to do later. Outwardly, many of these volumes resembled in appearance soberer works of erudition, particularly those of historical character. Indeed, many of the novels included the word "history" or "chronicle" in their titles as, for example, the *Chronicle of Don Florisel of Nicæa*. Since these terms connoted truthful records of the past, their use was inevitably misleading, and moralists therefore constantly branded these fictional works as "lying histories". But the so-called historical writings themselves, as already noted, frequently included accounts of miracles and supernatural phenomena, and hence the hazy distinction between fact and fiction in the ordinary reader's mind is not surprising.

Authors of the new literary genre did not limit their pretentions to authority by merely borrowing the standard terms associated with recorded history. A common practice was to profess the role of mere translator or emendator of a manuscript written in Arabic, Greek, or some obscure language of the Near East or Asia. This was a bluff which the uncritical reader was slow to penetrate, and which gave even the most absurd narratives an acceptable plausibility to the general public. Cervantes burlesqued this common feature of the chivalric literature by asserting in the second part of his *Don Quixote* that he was indebted to an Arabian historian, Cid Hamet Benengeli, for this continuation. Such attribution was usually set forth in the preface of a novel with other details, sometimes to the effect that the author or someone that he knew had happened upon the manuscript while traveling in a remote corner of the world. Often its discovery was alleged to be a chance one in some odd place of concealment, and the original text was supposed to be in a strange language which the author, by dint of much application and long effort, had at last deciphered and now placed before his reader. This device was used in the earliest novels of this type, including the *Caballero Cifar* and *Tirant lo Blanch*. The deceptive *Chronicle of Don Roderick with the destruction of Spain* professes to have been written by a certain Eliastras, one of its personages who is killed just before the end of the narrative, which was supposedly finished by Carestes, a knight of Alphonso the Catholic. It will be recalled that Montalvo stated in his foreword to *Amadis of Gaul* that he had merely "corrected" the first three books of the novel and translated and emended the fourth. At the same time he reported that his editorial work had extended to a manuscript concerning the offspring of Amadis entitled "*Sergas de Esplandián*, his son, which till now no man remembers to have seen but which, by good fortune, was discovered in a stone tomb beneath the floor by a hermitage near Constantinople and was brought by a Hungarian merchant to these parts of Spain in writing and on parchment so ancient that only with difficulty could it be read by those who know the languages."[6] Elsewhere he reports that the book was "written in Greek by the hand of the great master Elisabad," a physician mentioned in the third book of *Amadís of Gaul*, "who had seen much that he related and was quite attached to the father of Esplandián, whose *Sergas* later were translated into many languages."

Following the example of Montalvo, the writers of the sequels and imitations of his novels sought to give similar authority to their narratives by alleging an ancient and foreign source of the tales. The *Caballero de la Cruz o Lepolemo* (1521) was presumed to be a translation from the Arabic of a Moor "Xarton," *Amadís de Grecia* (1530) had allegedly passed from Greek through Latin to Spanish, and *Belianis de Grecia* (1547) was supposedly the handiwork in Greek of the wizard Friston. Gerónimo Fernández, the true author of this romance, states at the conclusion that he would like to relate further happenings, "but the wizard Friston, passing from Greece to Nubia, swore that he had lost the history and so he returned to look for it."[7] Thus an opening was left for a continuation if the writer thought there was a demand for it. If, in the course of time, such statements were accepted by readers with the recommended grain of salt, their faith in the essential veracity of the tales themselves lingered on. In such matters the public, on the whole, preferred to be fooled and was reluctant to abandon the cherished illusion that it might be reading a true narrative.

To the uncritical generation of the first decades of the sixteenth century these fascinating novels of chivalry constituted a mirror in which the reader saw himself in the valorous and triumphant role of the hero with whose fortunes he identified himself completely, and the customs so alluringly depicted in these exciting pages offered the models imitated in the Renaissance society of which he was a part. Individual courage valiantly contending with overwhelming odds, the stoic acceptance of hardships and the wounds of battle, the exalted sense of honor and personal dignity, the courtly manners and the chivalrous concept of love, all reflected the highest ideals of the Spanish character forged by a long and successful contest with the alien and infidel invader of the Peninsula. In these narratives, as in the contemporary historical events, the glorification of the warrior reached its supreme and glittering height. To the individualistic Spaniard the prodigious feats of these fictional heroes performed singlehandedly had a special appeal. The spectacle of the valorous knight, like the *torero* in the bullring, calmly facing the greatest mystery and terror of all—Death—filled the youth of Spain, swayed by a religious fanaticism, with a reckless determination to emulate such mighty deeds, which were invariably crowned with success and glory. In his suddenly expanded world of opportunity the individual soldier, and particularly the Conquistador, however humble and lowly his origin, might aspire to the highest rewards of wealth, to the loftiest seats of power. Like Esplandian and other legendary heroes, might he not also become an Emperor of Constantinople or at least, as Sancho Panza was promised long after, governor of some enchanted isle? With this ambition for power and position ran, of course, individual cupidity, the lust for material wealth in the convenient and negotiable form of gold and precious stones. Chapter 90 of the *Sergas de Esplandián*, published well in advance of Cortés' conquest of the Aztec empire, tells of the hero boldly removing with his own hands the lion standing guard at the portal of a tomb containing the enchanted treasure.

> And in this fashion it befell him in the tomb, of which he alone raised the outermost glass door; the inner one, colored sky blue, was guarded by a lock of pure emerald in which was inserted a key of diamond stone. The hinges were of very precious rubies. And when he had opened the tomb he saw within an idol of solid gold, all inlaid with enormous precious stones and a huge mother-of-pearl. And it bore a crown so marvellously wrought that it was regarded as a wonder by one who saw it later. On it were letters of burning rubies which read: 'Jupiter, the greatest of the gods'.

The Spanish Conquistador, boldly penetrating a vast new continent, his imagination fevered by such descriptions of hidden wealth recently read in camp and discussed on the march with his companions-in-arms, avidly seized upon any rumor of buried Aztec or Incan treasure wrung from a bewildered native. Shamelessly he violated the sanctity of pagan temples and tombs, and plundered these monuments of aboriginal civilizations in a frenzied quest of easy wealth which, the "lying histories" assured him, abounded in these remote corners and exotic lands of the globe. It was thus that he was incited, in no small measure, to accomplish superhuman feats of endurance and to commit acts of barbarism as he pushed along unknown trails and across unheard-of realms. The ruthless confiscation of the treasures of Montezuma, of Atahualpa, and of other victims of Spanish greed owed not a little to the imaginative quill of the storytelling regidor of Medina del Campo and to other practitioners of his craft.

AMAZONS, BOOKS
AND CONQUERORS—MEXICO IV

MANY WERE THE MYTHS WHICH HAUNTED THE MINDS
of the Spanish conquerors and their contemporaries as they ad-
ventured in the New World so recently revealed by the epochal
voyages of Columbus, but the one which perhaps most persistently
possessed these heroes was the legend of the warlike Amazon
women.[1] Wherever expeditions moved among the myriad islands
or in the vast reaches of the mainland the quest of these legendary
viragoes was pursued. The instructions issued to the Spanish leaders
and the contractual agreements between the conquistadors and
their financial backers—for the conquest of the New World was
largely a private enterprise, capitalistic in character[2]—frequently
included clauses requiring a search for these mythical women.
Again and again the chronicles and documents of the period contain references to the alleged existence or actual discovery of such
female tribes, and similar reports continued well into the eighteenth
century. Beginning with Columbus' account of his voyages and in
the writings of Peter Martyr, the first of the historians of the New
World, and of his successors, Oviedo and Herrera, as well as in
those of firsthand chroniclers such as Pigafetta of Magellan's voyage, and particularly Carvajal, who recorded the famous Odyssey
of Orellana through the heart of South America, the widely advertised legend appears conspicuously. Many other explorers and
adventurers of the sixteenth century and later, including Sir Walter
Raleigh,[3] have left testimony of their varying shades of conviction
concerning the existence of the Amazons.

The myth of a tribe of warlike women goes back to ancient
times when the Greeks reported them in Asia Minor, giving this

strange tribe the name of Amazons, apparently because of their alleged practice of removing one breast to permit the freer use of the bow and arrow, their chief weapon. The story persisted throughout the Middle Ages, gaining force as such travelers as Marco Polo, Sir John Mandeville, and Pedro Tafur, publicized their journeyings into remote parts. These female warriors were also reputed to be found in Africa, their island home lying in a marsh not far from the boundaries of the inhabited world, and also on the west coast near Sierra Leone.[4] But in all accounts the location of the Amazons is exceedingly vague. The older writers placed them anywhere between Finland and India, with Asia Minor, however, continuing to receive the most votes. It was probably inevitable that the discovery of an unsuspected continent in the western seas should open to the credulous new and likely possibilities of locating at last these elusive females. It was Columbus himself who first aroused such hopes by asserting that a number of these Amazons hid in caves on some islands of the Caribbean to which strong winds prevented his approach. And he was certain that still others of this race could be reached on the continental mainland by passing through cannibal country. Subsequent Spanish expeditions always seemed somehow to just miss discovering the realms of these strange tribes. Orellana, to be sure, was convinced that he had not only encountered some of these women but actually experienced their combative prowess, and for the mighty river of South America, which he was the first European to navigate, descending from the Andes to its mouth, the name of the Amazons in time replaced his own.[5]

Although the legend was of long standing, as already indicated, its strong revival in the early sixteenth century, and the universal belief in its validity among the Spanish conquerors roaming the New World, suggest that some recent and particularly vivid reminder had brought the subject sharply to mind. The fantastic rumors, including those concerning the Amazons, which flooded Spain and Europe soon after the fateful voyages of Columbus, found some confirmation in the apparently sober and trustworthy *Decades* of Peter Martyr, which appeared in 1516. Still further currency to the belief in the warlike women was afforded by a Spanish translation, first published in 1521, of Sir John Mandeville's *Travels;*

this was the very year in which Cortés was achieving his spectacular conquest of the Aztec capital. Two years later there came from
the press the official account of the circumnavigation of the globe
by Magellan's expedition, written by its chronicler and eyewitness,
Pigafetta, who stated in the course of his narrative that, after touch-
ing Java,

> our oldest pilot told us that there is an island called Acoloro
> which lies below Java Major where there are not persons
> but women, and that the latter become mothers by the wind.
> When they give birth, if the offspring is male, they kill it,
> but if it is female, they rear it. If men go to that island, they
> kill them if they are able to do so.[6]

But it is doubtful whether these historical works alone can account for the almost passionate conviction of early sixteenth-century conquistadors in the reality and the proximity of the Amazon
women. Such respectable books were hardly read by the ordinary
soldier if, indeed, he knew of them at all; the more literate of these
adventurers were likely to be addicted to other forms of reading
from which they derived no less fantastic notions. The more popular literature was, of course, the so-called romances of chivalry, and
to them it is logical to turn as a possible source of inspiration for
the renewed interest in the classical myth.[7] This quest quickly
brings one to the sequel to *Amadis of Gaul*, written by Garci-
Rodríguez de Montalvo and entitled *Sergas de Esplandián*.

In this prolix account of the adventures of the handsome son
of the great Amadis is intercalated the episode of Calafia, Queen
of the Amazons, who resided with her followers on a craggy island
significantly named "California." In the course of the first 122
chapters the narrative of Esplandián's exploits is carried forward to
the time when the King of Persia, named Armato in the novel, invites all the pagan princes to unite with him to capture Constantinople from the Christian allies of its Emperor. The response is
highly gratifying to the Persian monarch, for a mighty horde is
assembled to pit its strength against the outnumbered Christians
rallying about the Emperor. Conspicuous among the latter are
Amadis and Esplandián. Strangest of the heathen cohorts of the
Persian Armato is the tribe of Amazon women under Queen Calafia
who came with their man-eating griffins from the "islands of Cali-

THE SPANISH CONQUISTADORS AND AMERICAN TREASURE

THE AMAZONS

fornia" to fight for the Turks. Chapters 157 to 178 are devoted largely to the intervention of the Amazons in the ensuing struggle, particularly the personal encounters of the female leaders with the Christian knights, who fare badly at the hands of the so-called gentler sex. This success emboldens "Calafia, mistress of the great island of California, celebrated for its great abundance of gold and jewels" to challenge both Amadis and Esplandián to personal combat. As might be expected, the Amazon queen is overwhelmingly vanquished by Amadis' skill and Esplandián's beauty, and falls captive to these Christian heroes. Though enamored of Esplandián she philosophically acquiesces to his marriage to another and accepts Christianity, marrying a husband generously bestowed upon her by the ever-considerate Esplandián. Thus the hateful Turk is deprived of a formidable ally and Constantinople is saved for Christendom.

The fact that the main story of Esplandián is resumed after this incident and, save for the brief reference at the end, Queen Calafia and the Amazons do not reappear, has a certain significance. It suggests that Montalvo, the author, may have deviated from the original plan of the book and decided to capitalize on a recently renewed interest in an ancient legend. While he was engaged in writing this tale it is possible that there reached his ears an echo of Columbus' report of Amazon-like women on some islands past which he had cruised and of their alleged proximity to the Earthly Paradise. The revival of this scarcely dormant legend in the guise of an item of news possibly offered the storyteller, alert to the latest sensation, a theme for an exciting episode which he embroidered elaborately in his sequel to *Amadis of Gaul*. Later, his readers doubtless believed that they had found confirmation of a long-standing belief when they read the following passage in chapter 157 of the *Sergas de Esplandián*.

> Now I wish you to learn of one of the strangest matters that has ever been found in writing or in the memory of mankind. . . . Know ye that on the right hand of the Indies there is an island called California, very close to the Earthly Paradise, and inhabited by black women without a single man among them, for they live almost in the manner of Amazons. They are robust in body with stout, passionate hearts and great strength. The island itself is the most rugged with craggy rocks in the world. Their weapons are all of

gold as well as the trappings of the wild beasts which they
ride after taming, for there is no other metal on the whole
island. They dwelled in well-formed caves.

The novelist continues with further details on the manner of living
and fighting of Queen Calafia's warriors.

Some details offered in this quoted passage are worthy of note.
For the first time the shifting locale of these battling viragoes is
identified with the new-found lands of the Indies, though the hazy
geography of the novel places Calafia's islands within reach of
Constantinople and Asia Minor by sea. When Montalvo was writing the belief was probably still held that Columbus had actually
found a new route to the Asiatic mainland, the existence of the
intervening continents being still unsuspected. That Queen Calafia's
subjects "dwelled in well-formed caves" and that their island home
was "on the right hand of the Indies and close to the Earthly
Paradise" are further indications that the novelist may have derived
inspiration from the great Discoverer's reports of his voyages. From
the meager details of the latter Montalvo perhaps fashioned his
heavily embroidered episode, changing the name of the Amazons'
island abode from the ugly Matinino of Columbus' journal to the
more glamorous and euphonious "California".[8] As the existence of
a new hemisphere, to which the designation Indies adhered, dawned
upon the readers of Montalvo's popular work, the fugitive Amazons
now seemed tracked to their lair. Moreover, the positive assurance
that "their weapons are all of gold . . . for there is no other metal
on the whole island" made it certain that the physical discovery of
their insular realm would bring to the lucky finder a fabulous fortune. Thus the imagination of Montalvo elaborated the "facts" that
Columbus had reported and for the Conquistador the New World,
Amazons, and wealth became inseparable.

As already noted, the phenomenal popularity of the first romances promptly produced a formidable crop of sequels, carrying
the account through successive descendants of Amadis and Esplandián. The *Seventh book* of this series bore the title *Lisuarte de
Grecia* and is here mentioned because Queen Calafia again emerges
from her California isle and wanders through its pages, forming
further coalitions in the vicinity of Constantinople, though now
always on the side of the Christian knights. Thus, any readers who

may have missed acquaintance with the Amazon queen in the *Sergas de Esplandián* had an opportunity to meet her and receive assurance of the existence of her tribe.

At this juncture it is well to recall the dates of the various editions of these novels which revived the old legend in such a fascinating manner, in order to appraise the possible influence of these tales on the Spanish conquerors in the New World. Present bibliographic knowledge is insufficient to establish definitely the year of the princeps of the earlier romances of the Amadis cycle. For *Amadis of Gaul* the 1508 edition is usually cited as the first, though it is likely that there were earlier ones. Similar uncertainty surrounds the *Sergas de Esplandián* to which the year 1510 is ascribed as the date of the first edition.[9] This was printed by the Crombergers at Seville, a significant fact since it was from this river port that most of the conquerors embarked for their adventures in the Spanish Indies. It is apparent, therefore, that Montalvo's novel with its episode of the Amazons was available long enough before the spectacular conquests on the mainland for the Spanish soldiery to have read or heard of it. It is likely that various other editions appeared soon after 1510, though no data on them have yet come to light; however, there are clear indications of at least four new editions of the *Sergas* that were published during a spectacular five-year period of the Conquest: one in Toledo in May, 1521, one in Salamanca in 1525, one in Burgos in 1526 and another in Seville the same year.[10] This was a fairly rapid succession of reprintings for its time—and probably there were others unrecorded—but more important is the fact that this five-year period coincides with that in which Cortés was conquering and overrunning the broad realms of Mexico; in all directions his lieutenants, as well as he himself, were heading expeditions with instructions to locate the Amazons and other oddities, along with gold and silver mines. And it was during this period that Cortés was reporting to his emperor, Charles V, in his famous letter-reports, rumors of the existence in New Spain of tribes of warlike women.

The *Lisuarte de Grecia*, which again reminds readers of Queen Calafia and California, was evidently less popular than the earlier *Sergas* or, at least, fewer editions of it are known. The princeps appeared in 1514—also in ample time to influence the minds of the

Conquistador—and others probably followed, though only that of 1525, likewise printed by the Crombergers at Seville, is definitely recorded. While the references to the Amazons in numerous documents of this time, and particularly the bestowing of the name "California" on the peninsula to the west of the mainland of New Spain, point to the probable influence of these and other romances of chivalry, more detailed evidence is necessary before accepting this conclusion.

Most critics dealing with the chivalric novels have commented on the tremendous hold of these fictional works on sixteenth-century readers, though few have attempted any detailed analysis of this literary phenomenon. Occasionally one manifests a belief in some connection between these books and the deeds of the conquerors. One authority, for example, states that "the books of chivalry had their part in suggesting the heroic delirium of the Conquest" and elsewhere asserts that "it is well known that at that time the ballads of chivalry and novels of knight-errantry were on the lips and in the hands of the conquerors".[11] Benedetto Croce avers from abundant documentation that *Amadis of Gaul* and similar novels were favorite reading of the Spanish soldiers fighting in the Italian Peninsula,[12] which fact leaves little doubt that their companions-in-arms in contemporary America were also familiar with the same literature. As if to support this statement one of the foremost commentators of Cervantes' writings inserted an interesting footnote to the effect that twelve of Cortés' lieutenants banded together like the "Twelve Peers" of chivalry, solemnly pledging themselves with the vows of knights-errant "to defend the Holy Catholic Faith, to right wrongs, and to aid Spaniards and friendly natives"![13]

But much more direct evidence of the reading of the romances of chivalry by the conquistadors is supplied by that prince of chroniclers, a soldier in the conquering ranks of Cortés' army— Bernal Díaz del Castillo. In his famous *True history of the conquest of New Spain*, which is a firsthand account of the Spanish campaigns though written many years after the events, and which, in some passages, itself reads like a novel of chivalry, the soldier-author records the profound impression that the first glimpse of the

Aztec capital in the beautiful valley of Mexico produced on the approaching Spanish troops.

> When we saw so many cities and villages built in the waters [of the lake] and other large towns on dry land, and that straight, level causeway leading into Mexico City, we were amazed and we said that it was like the enchanted things related in the book of Amadis because of the huge towers, temples, and buildings rising from the water and all of masonry. And some of the soldiers even asked whether the things we saw were not a dream. It is not to be wondered that I write it down in this manner, for there is so much to think of that I do not know how to describe it, seeing as we did things never heard of or witnessed before.[14]

The mixed use of the first personal pronouns in this passage is of particular note. Where the plural *we* is employed it clearly indicates that Bernal Díaz, in alluding to the comparison of the scene before the Spaniards with descriptions found in *Amadis of Gaul* and its successors, did not express himself in terms of his own reading alone, but was conveying an impression shared by his companions who were also familiar with these novels. As they pushed inland on their spectacular conquest these bold adventurers doubtless talked of Amadis and Esplandián, and as they marched along they reminded one another of incidents and scenes described in the romances read or listened to. And thus they eagerly projected from their own minds into the exotic landscape about them the images evoked by their acquaintance with this literature of fantasy. And elsewhere the soldier-chronicler refers to a character in *Amadis of Gaul*, Agrajes, a name which became in Spanish slang the synonym for a braggart. These allusions to this romance of chivalry were plainly no literary affectation on the part of Bernal Díaz, whose entire narrative is characterized by its forthright and unvarnished style. Rather, they are the spontaneous and almost involuntary exclamations of one who is suddenly reminded of what he and his comrades had so often talked about. Either before embarking for the New World or after their arrival, he and many of his companions-in-arms had undoubtedly read more than one of the chivalric novels then available, and it is altogether likely that copies

of these fantastic tales, probably much the worse for wear, lay
about the soldiers' camps and served to divert the more literate in
the lulls between campaigns. In the famous chapter of *Don Quixote*
in which the luckless Sancho Panza is tossed in a blanket by the
roustabouts at an inn, Cervantes offers a realistic picture of the
reading of romances of chivalry in the sixteenth century by those
of a social status similar to that of many of Cortés' soldiers. In the
mouth of the innkeeper the great novelist puts the following passage
testifying to the universal enjoyment of this form of fiction.

> I cannot understand how that can be for, in truth, to my
> mind there is no better reading in the world, and I have
> here two or three of them [novels of chivalry] with other
> writings that are the very life, not only of myself but of
> plenty more; for when it is harvest time the reapers flock
> here on holidays, and there is always one among them who
> can read and who takes up one of these books; and we
> gather around him, thirty or more of us, and continue listen-
> ing to him with a delight that makes our grey hairs grow
> young again. At least I can say for myself that when I hear
> of what furious and terrible blows the knights deliver, I am
> seized with the longing to do the same, and I would like to
> be hearing about them night and day.[15]

It requires little effort of the imagination to translate this picture
from its rural, peasant setting to the camp of the doughty warriors
of Cortés and Pizarro where "there was always some one of them
who knew how to read." Surrounded by his comrades, "thirty or
more," and by the flickering campfire or in daylight, this literate
soldier read aloud the adventures of Amadís, Esplandián, and other
ideal heroes. If the innkeeper heard with special delight of the
"furious and terrible blows the knights deliver," the conquerors
doubtless found their enthusiasm stirred even more by the glowing
descriptions of the wealth of the fabled cities and mythical races
inhabiting strange lands. The marvelous exploits and fantastic accounts of persons and places thus brought to the eyes and ears of the
conquerors now encamped in the midst of an unknown continent
could not fail to stimulate their already fevered imaginations and
easily prepared their minds to accept avidly the wildest rumors of
riches which were forever luring them on. Absurd notions thus

generated were eagerly projected into the dim, remote regions lying ahead in this mysterious, new-found world, and anything was possible, even probable.

The conquerors readily found confirmation of their fiction-nurtured dreams through the poorly interpreted languages of the Indians who vaguely understood the questions put to them. These frequently fearful and bewildered aborigines, usually only too eager to be rid of the strange white invaders and not wishing to displease them, customarily answered all inquiries in the affirmative. And some were shrewd enough to perceive that they could easily satisfy their interrogators by agreeing that, whatever the latter sought, whether gold, treasure, fabled cities, or Amazons, it could be had by going only a "little beyond." To the excited Spaniards all information that accorded with their preconceived notions and desires was reliable; thus, with imaginations inflamed by books of chivalry, and convinced by the apparent corroboration of the natives that the enchanted places described in their favorite fiction really existed in this newly found world, the hardened campaigners could whip up the flagging vigor of physical bodies and goad themselves on to deeds more stupendous than those of the gallant knights who offered them such fascinating models. To the quills of sedentary novelists in far off Spain, Portugal, and France the extraordinary epic of the conquests of Mexico, Peru, and other regions of the New World indeed owes no small part of its realization! But to return to the quest of Queen Calafia and her California Amazons.

Columbus' early references to Amazon-like natives in the Caribbean islands, later reiterated by Peter Martyr in his *Decades*, seems, on the whole, to have excited slight interest in the Spanish settlers on Hispaniola, preoccupied in extracting gold and labor from reluctant Indians. Presently, however, curiosity began to develop regarding the shadowy mainland to the west and maritime expeditions skirted those shores. It was about this time that the *Sergas de Esplandián* and *Lisuarte de Grecia*, with their episodes of Queen Calafia, began to establish a hold on their readers, reinvigorating the age-old myth of the Amazons. The Governor of Cuba, Diego Velásquez, looking for further conquests, turned his eyes westward, and organized several exploratory expeditions equipped at his own expense. The first of these reconnoitered Yucatan in 1517 and brought back reports of a large town and considerable wealth. The following year and under the same auspices Grijalva coasted the shoreline from Yucatan to Pánuco, picking up a modest amount of treasure. Juan Díaz, a clergyman, has left a report of this expedition which includes a detail of immediate interest. Writing in May 1518, he states that "they turned back to the Island of Yucatan on the north side. We went along the coast where we found a beautiful tower on a point said to be inhabited by women who live without men. It is believed that they are a race of Amazons. Other towers were seen, seemingly in towns, but the Captain did not allow us to go ashore".[16]

The enterprising Governor of Cuba, moved by the long delay of Grijalva in returning and by his own impatience to learn the secret of the mainland, entered into an agreement with Hernando Cortés which was to result in the conquest of that vast region, though with little material advantage to Velásquez. Under date of October 23, 1518, Cortés received detailed orders for the important aims of the undertaking. Of particular interest is the twenty-sixth item which, after cautioning Cortés to exercise great care in taking formal possession of all islands discovered and in gathering all possible information regarding the land and its people, directed him,

> because it is said that there are people with large, broad ears and others with faces like dogs [to find out about them], and also where and in what direction are the Amazons, who are nearby according to the Indians whom you are taking with you.[17]

Here it is apparent that, only a few years after the first publication of the *Sergas de Esplandián* and *Lisuarte de Grecia*, Cortés and his financial backer, the Governor of Cuba, were definitely counting on the possibility of discovering, among other curiosities, a realm similar to that of the California isle of Queen Calafia. That the Indians accompanying the expedition are cited as authority for this expectation need not be taken too seriously, for it is probable that the idea was merely a projection from the minds of Velásquez and Cortés resulting from recent reading or listening which they unconsciously imposed upon the half-comprehending and overawed Indians, who then returned it to the true authors. It could hardly be expected that two hard-headed businessmen such as the Governor and the future conqueror would acknowledge the real origin of their belief—quite possibly a popular work of fiction—in a legal contract, if, indeed, they were aware of its source. That Cortés himself at least had firsthand acquaintance with some of the chivalric literature is evident in an anecdote related by Bernal Díaz del Castillo. When the great Conqueror was looking for the first time from his ship toward the shore near San Juan de Ulúa, one of his associates remarked to him pointedly,

"I say that you are looking on rich lands. May you know how to govern them well!"

To which Cortés calmly replied,

"Let God give us the good fortune that He gave the Paladin Roldán and, with your Excellency and the other gentlemen for leaders, I shall know well how to manage it!"[18]

This *idée fixe* of the existence of a race of warlike women somewhere in the New World remained with Cortés and other conquerors all through their campaigns and explorations. Occasionally, even in the legal documents of the period, there are unmistakable indications of this fact. In a decree of June 1530, signed by the Queen of Spain, granting a coat of arms to the conquistador Gerónimo López, it was stated that, among the services for which he was thus rewarded, he "had taken part in the *entrada* and conquest made in the South Sea [Pacific] and in the north in search of the Amazons."[19] Of more importance as evidence in this respect are the famous dispatches of Cortés to Charles V reporting his activities in Mexico. The earlier *cartas relaciones* deal mainly with a recital of the stirring events associated with the capure of the Aztec capital. The stern necessities of war against a powerful and numerous foe, and the quick maneuvers to frustrate the efforts of rival Spaniards bent on supplanting him, preoccupied Cortés too greatly for a methodical investigation of the secrets of the vast realm that he was subduing, and it is not until his *Fourth letter*, dated October 15, 1524, that exploration tends to replace the swift campaigns of conquest and more detailed descriptions of Mexican civilization are offered. Now, with subordinates heading expeditions in many directions to consolidate and extend his territorial gains, the old fables and legends claim greater attention. Perhaps by this time copies of the translation of Mandeville's *Travels* and of Pigafetta's report of the globe-girdling voyage begun by Magellan had reached the conqueror of Mexico, and these accounts seemed to offer their corroborative testimony to the reality of a California race of Amazons described in the novels of Montalvo and others familiar to him. At any rate, it is clear in the *Fourth letter* that Cortés was dispatching expeditions with instructions not only to search for the rumored treasure in the interior of New Spain, but to solve the mysteries of its hinterland. While the diligent quest of gold and precious stones thought to exist there in abundance continued unceasingly, the search for clues leading to the discovery of the fabulous kingdoms lying always a little beyond each horizon grew more intense. Chief among the latter objectives were the Amazon women, and again and again the proximity of their realm was reported. One of Cortés' ablest lieutenants, Cristóbal de Olid, with twenty-five horse and about eighty foot soldiers, had penetrated the rugged region of Zacatula and Colima near the west coast of Mexico, and they returned with a comparatively rich booty of pearls and an exciting report to the effect that only ten days' journey beyond where they had stopped was an island rich in treasure and inhabited by women only occasionally visited by men and who disposed of the resulting male offspring with distressing dispatch. This and other reports moved the Conqueror of Mexico to comment in his *Fourth letter* to the Emperor:

> In his [Olid's] description of these provinces there was news of a very good port on that coast, which greatly pleased me since there are so few; he likewise brought me an account of the chiefs of the province of Ceguatan who affirm that there is an island inhabited only by women without any men, and that at given times men from the mainland visit them; if they conceive, they keep the female children to which they give birth, but the males they throw away. This island is ten days' journey from the province, and many went thither and saw it, and they told me also that it is very rich in pearls and gold. I shall strive to ascertain the truth and when I am able to do so, I shall make a full account to your Majesty.[20]

Elsewhere in the same *Letter* Cortés reports that his lieutenant had seized "a woman whom all in those parts obeyed and everything quieted down because she sent to all the chiefs and commanded them to observe whatever was ordered in your Majesty's name, as she intended to do. . . ."

Now, indeed, the Spanish explorers were pushing closer to the "right hand of the Indies" where Montalvo had located the California island home of Queen Calafia's Amazons and, geographically, they were approaching the peninsula, long mistaken for an island, and destined to bear the name which the *Sergas de Esplandián* had advertised so attractively. So much importance did Cortés attach to the news brought by Olid that he not only passed it on to Charles V, but set about organizing another expedition which should push the exploration of the region beyond Colima to where the Amazon realm apparently lay. This momentous mission he entrusted to one of his kinsmen, Francisco Cortés, to whom he issued very detailed and specific instructions in writing. With twenty or twenty-five horsemen and fifty or sixty foot soldiers, mostly bowmen and musketeers and two pieces of artillery, he should find out the truth of the reports received "because," so ran the Conqueror's command,

> I am informed that along the coast adjacent to the towns of Colima there are numerous well-populated provinces where it is believed that there is much treasure; also, that in those parts there is a district inhabited by women without men. It is said that, in the matter of reproduction, these women follow the practices of the Amazons described in the *"istorias antiguas."* To ascertain the truth of this and the rest related to that coast will be a great service to God, our Lord and their Majesties.[31]

Particularly significant in this passage is the clear indication of the Conqueror's interest in the Amazons and the fact that his knowledge of them was derived from his reading. It will be remembered that he was a man of considerable education, having been a student in the University of Salamanca for two years. Despite his preference for action he had found time then and later for reading some of the *"istorias antiguas"* to which he refers in his instructions. The expression used was broad enough in his time to include the novels of chivalry as well as the allegedly more his-

torical chronicles. As has been observed, the romances frequently
contained the words *historia* or *crónica* in their titles and the loose-
ness with which these terms were applied to both fictional and
factual accounts produced confusion in the minds of general readers as to the nature of what they were reading; consequently, the
more interesting they found a book, the more inclined they were
to believe in its veracity. The sense of time as well as geography was
exceedingly vague in the tales of chivalry and usually the action was
placed "sometime after the passion of our Lord," hence sufficiently
remote for these self-styled chronicles to be thought of as *"istorias
antiguas"*. Since, as we know, the recognized histories contained
scarcely less of the marvelous than the acknowledged romances,
both were readily confused by the uncritical reader. Hence in this
reference in Cortés' instructions one may find confirmation of the
assumption that the Conqueror of Mexico, like most of his literate
contemporaries, was acquainted with the popular literature of the
day; and in his allusion to the Amazons and their habits, which both
Montalvo, the novelist, and Cortés' own lieutenants reported as
existing in this vicinity, it is fair to surmise that he, too, had dipped
into the pages of the *Sergas de Esplandián*, one of the more fascinating *"istorias antiguas"*.

Like most other attempts to track down the elusive Amazons,
Francisco Cortés' odyssey hardly measured up to the hopes of his
illustrious kinsman. One incident of this expedition, however, suggests that he had encountered a situation with some points of similarity to that of Queen Calafia. Beyond Jalisco he had found an
attractive district governed by a native woman during the minority
of her son. The female chieftain hastened to invite the white warriors to her realm, welcoming them with ceremonial acts which
included the erection of an arch bedecked with flowers and a hunting exhibition by her followers, who bestowed their game upon
the visitors. The Spaniards were then permitted to witness some of
the religious rites of the tribe at a pyramidal temple. After this
function they were comfortably lodged in the queen's palace where
their accommodating host thoughtfully provided women for the
entertainment of the soldiers. Apparently, this feminine company
did not enjoy the degree of pulchritude desired by the Spaniards
and Francisco Cortés reported that he had sent these females away

after due inspection and ordered his men to conduct themselves properly.[22]

What further interest Hernando Cortés may have taken in the solution of the vexing Amazon problem is not clear, though it is likely that he did not abandon his quest at once. Soon after dispatching his *Fourth letter* he set off on the ill-advised march to Honduras, absenting himself from Mexico City for two years during which his affairs there suffered severely from the machinations of his enemies. One of his most bitter foes was a certain Nuño de Guzmán, a partisan of Governor Velásquez with whom Cortés had been on bad terms since the founding of Vera Cruz in 1519. Guzmán had received jurisdiction over a broad strip of land called Pánuco, northeast of Mexico City and extending indefinitely inland. Overlapping and conflicting territorial claims soon brought friction between adherents of the two leaders, particularly during Cortés' long absence in Central America. Guzmán, too, had heard much concerning gold, jewels and rumors of Amazon tribes existing somewhere to the west, and he set out to penetrate the mystery. Cruel and unscrupulous by nature, he cut a swath of terror and barbarism as he swept through Michoacán and northwestward toward "the right hand of the Indies." From Omitlán, in the west, he dispatched a letter, dated July 8, 1530, reporting:

> The next day I made a procession with a Te Deum. Thence I crossed the great river of the Trinitie, and the River was full of Crocodiles, and there are many venemous Scorpions. Here was erected a Church and two Crosses. Azatlán is three days journey hence, where they prepared to give me battell. From thence ten days further I shall go to finde the Amazons, which some say dwell in the Sea, and some in an arme of the Sea, and that they are rich and accounted of the people for Goddesses, and whiter than other women. They use Bowes, Arrows and Targets; have many and great Towns; at certain times they admit males to accompany them, which bring up the males, and these the female issue.[23]

Nuño de Guzmán had also tried to track down the Amazons in the vicinity of Ceguatan reported by Cristóbal Olid and mentioned by Cortés in his *Fourth letter* to the Emperor. Concerning this effort he declared that he had sent out two mounted detachments, who came upon eight native villages of varying sizes along the Ceguatan river, inhabited by

> some warriors and a good many women quite different from those seen to date in both their garb and the manner in which they were treated. There were a few men, some well be-decked in war gear with large plumes, bows, arrows and clubs. These warriors stated that they were from neighboring villages and had come to protect the *señoras Amazonas*. . . . Later it was learned through the interpreters that these women said that they had come by sea and formerly lived in such a manner that they did not have husbands nor did they permit men among them. Rather, at certain times the men from the neighboring districts could come to them. Then the women who were pregnant and gave birth to males buried the latter alive, but raised the females. However, for some time now they did not kill the male offspring but reared them until they were ten years old or so when they were given to their fathers. We couldn't learn much about these secret matters because the interpreters that we had weren't very expert.[24]

From all the foregoing it is plain that a belief in the existence of Amazon women on islands somewhere along the northern mainland of the Indies was firmly implanted in the minds of the conquerors and explorers from their first tentative skirting of the Yucatan shore through the dramatic conquest and overrunning of the mainland. The preoccupation of these men of action with this legend and their repeated efforts to locate the warlike women can hardly be attributed to a mere intellectual curiosity regarding a strange human species. There was, perhaps, the unconscious drive of men who had left their womenkind behind to seek their own psychological counterparts, but a more impelling incentive for these tough adventurers was undoubtedly the rich treasure, particularly gold, with which the female warriors were inseparably associated.

But what made the Conquistador so certain that the Amazons could be found in the Indies? And what convinced him that their gold would amply reward him for his efforts to hunt them down? The answers to these questions are suggested by the words of Montalvo's novel: "Know ye that on the right hand of the

Indies . . ." and ". . . their weapons are all of gold and there is no other metal on the whole island." The great "South Sea" or the Pacific ocean, extending far beyond the west coast of the mainland, doubtless surrounded these mysterious isles, and the nearby peninsula, looking like an island and projecting like a finger into its blue expanse, came, somehow, to bear the romantic name of California which Montalvo used for the habitat of Queen Calafia and her colorful henchwomen. To be sure, no documentary evidence thus far unearthed has established definitely the connection between this novel of chivalry and the naming of Lower California, but by 1542, when the *Sergas de Esplandián* and *Lisuarte de Grecia* were still enjoying popularity, Juan Rodríguez Cabrillo made a historic voyage along that part of the Pacific coast of North America. In the log of this voyage he used the name "California" in referring to a portion of the coast skirted, thus indicating that the appellation was already a fixed one.[25]

Whether applied in derision or in earnest, the island realm of Montalvo's Queen Calafia seems surely to have bequeathed its name to an elongated strip of land, long mistaken for an island, lying approximately "on the right hand of the Indies"—proof positive that some conqueror or explorer who had glimpsed it was familiar with those exciting chapters of the chivalric tale, *Sergas de Esplandián.*

AMAZONS, BOOKS AND V
CONQUERORS—SOUTH AMERICA

T HE SPANISH CONQUEST OF THE AZTEC EMPIRE AND ITS neighboring territories was largely accomplished in the 1520's. If the booty of these campaigns and the treasure uncovered did not measure up fully to the febrile expectations of the conquistadors, it did not fail to excite the covetousness of other adventurers and stimulate the quest of an *otro México* which they could not but believe existed somewhere in the vast continents of the Indies. With the official approval of the Crown, which was slowly realizing the enormous extent of its new possessions and the importance of exploiting them, expeditions organized by promoters and led by enterprising spirits boldly pushed into the mysterious interior of the Americas in pursuit of quick wealth and fleeting will-o'-the-wisps.[1] In an astonishingly short time these explorations had brought into view the geographic configuration of much of the New World. That the prevailing faith in the marvelous, inspired by a medieval heritage and sustained by contemporary literature, had stimulated these extraordinary journeys, there can be little doubt. Disregarding the famous odysseys of Cabeza de Vaca, De Soto, Ayllón, and others in North America which followed hard upon Cortés spectacular feat—and their accounts betray the influence of contemporary myths—it is of interest to turn attention to similar, though possibly less familiar, epics of conquest and exploration in the southern continent. In large measure these efforts got under way in the 1530's, a decade and more after the fall of the Aztec capital.

There is nothing to indicate that the fantastic notions so prevalent in the earlier years of the century had suffered any appreciable loss of vigor by the time the Spaniards addressed themselves seriously to the almost superhuman task of subjugating the continent of South America. Indeed, as New Spain and its hinterland failed to disclose the location of the enchanted cities, the fountains of youth, the Amazons, and the many other wonders so plainly expected, there was a disposition to shift their locale to the still more mysterious and forbidding Tierra Firme to the south in which the unshaken faith of eager adventurers would be vindicated. And so, in the course of time, the search for the Earthly Paradise, the El Dorado, the City of the Caesars, and the Amazons was pressed with feverish zeal. In all this activity the still popular romances of chivalry undoubtedly played a part by constantly renewing the hopes and expectations of credulous adventurers often disappointed by the failure of the new lands to reveal the marvels with which their imaginations endowed them. The romantic youths who eagerly joined expeditions sent to all parts of South America were no less familiar with the literature of the day than were the followers of Cortés and his lieutenants in Middle and North America; and, even as the prodigious exploits of the conquerors were enacted, new editions, sequels and imitations of the favorite fiction steadily multiplied. When a member of Pedro de Mendoza's ill-fated attempt to plant a colony in the River Plate region in 1536 bitterly protested a death sentence imposed upon him by his superiors for insubordination, he declared that "some day things will be as God wills and the Twelve Peers will rule!"[2] This despairing allusion was quite possibly inspired by some acquaintance with the *Historia de Carlo Magno y de los doce Pares,* a romance of chivalry of the Carlovingian cycle which had appeared in print a few years before in 1525. And even earlier when the somewhat fanatic "Apostle of the Indians," Father Las Casas, sought to enlist settlers for an idealistic community on the northern coast of South America by dubbing them "Knights of the Golden Spur,"[3] he doubtless did so with the sure knowledge of the strong appeal such a designation offered to a generation under the sway of chivalric fiction.

In the 1530's and 1540's, when the major efforts to overrun the southern continent were in their most spectacular stage, the legend of the Amazon women had lost none of its pristine lure. The moralists and the learned might scoff at such nonsense, as they certainly did, but the common run of mankind, literate and otherwise, from which the soldiers and their leaders were largely drawn, obstinately persisted in its beliefs and continued to seek confirmation of them. Even at home in Spain the myth of a female race of warriors easily claimed adherents, as is evident in an incident reported in 1533 at Valladolid, then the capital of the Peninsula. In June of that year Don Martín de Salinas, a diplomatic official, wrote a letter from that locality to a Secretary of Charles V who was traveling in another part of his realm. Among other material is the following interesting comment:

> And so that you may have something to laugh about I'll inform you concerning an item of news which turned up here and was deemed authentic and reliable among educated and other people of repute. . . . I can hardly exaggerate how much credence has been given the report that seventy large ships had come into the harbors of Santander and Laredo, bringing ten thousand Amazon women who had come to mate with Spaniards because of the reputation for valor and virility of our men. The arrangement was that any Amazon who became pregnant would give fifteen ducats to the man concerned for his work, and she would remain to give birth. If the offspring were males, the Amazons would leave them here; if female, they would carry them away. This report caused the rates of the local "ladies of pleasure" to drop because of such a large and wealthy competition, and because their men customers are so well remunerated for their trouble. And rest assured that this news has been considered so well founded here that nothing else has been or is talked about. These things are noted down as worthy of report in view of the general gullibility of the people.[4]

Surely familiarity with the episode of Queen Calafia and her female minions, so engagingly presented by Montalvo in his *Sergas de Esplandián*, and later echoed in *Lisuarte de Grecia*, accounts in some measure for the "general gullibility of the people" with respect to such a grotesque rumor in the very Court of Spain. Little wonder that the authorities there and elsewhere feared the influence of such fiction on a guileless public and were already taking steps to banish such pernicious literature both in the Peninsula and in the Indies! And if the population in the more sophisticated centers, living in close contact with the spiritual and intellectual currents of the Renaissance, were so receptive to fantastic reports of this sort, how much less surprising it is that the rude and hardy Conquistador, battling his way into the interior of the dark and mysterious continents, was prepared to come upon the reality of the wonders projected from his own mind! Added to the newer editions of the novels so attractively reinvigorating the ancient myths, particularly of the Amazons, were the fresh printings of Mandeville's *Travels* in 1531 and 1540 which included references to the warlike women. Renewed opportunity of acquaintance with Queen Calafia and her fabled island was available in the 1539 printing of *Lisuarte de Grecia*, and the sales of *Sergas de Esplandián* still caused bookdealers to rub their hands in satisfaction. All these volumes were appearing in time to arouse strange thoughts in the minds of the recruits embarking on the exploratory expeditions to South America, and soon further reports of Amazon tribes filtered back from all parts of that continent. Some of these will be recalled in more or less chronological order.

In a report of the campaigns of conquest and exploration taking place in the lofty interior of present-day Colombia from 1536 to 1539 the authors pause to remark that

> While in camp here in this valley of Bogotá we got news of a tribe of women who live by themselves without men among them, for which reason we called them Amazons. They become pregnant by certain slaves which they buy and if they bear males, they send them to their fathers; if females, they rear them. It is said that these women only use the slaves for becoming pregnant, after which they send them away and so, from time to time, they summon them and dismiss them. In view of such a novelty in country like this, the lieutenant sent his brother with some mounted men and others on foot to see if what the Indians told us was true. He could not reach these women because of the mountain ranges in the way, though he came within three or four days' journey, getting more and more news that they existed and that they were very rich in gold.[5]

And later in this *relación* the same rumor crops up in another part of New Granada, as the land was named, in which "very strange news was learned of the region where we are concerning the aforementioned Amazons who possess innumerable gold."[6] Thus, in the locality in which the legend of El Dorado seemed traced to its source, the even more widely diffused myth of the warlike viragoes does not fail to appear.

Most famous of all the Spanish journeys in the southern mainland was that of Francisco Orellana through the Amazon basin. There is no need to recount in detail here the famous descent of the mighty river of this name to its mouth by a lieutenant of Pizarro and sixty odd companions in 1542, except to point out those incidents which relate to the alleged discovery of the Amazons. Starting from Guayaquil in present-day Ecuador in February 1541, Orellana overtook Gonzalo Pizarro's expedition which was striking eastward toward the great interior basin of the continent in search of El Dorado and the Land of the Cinnamon. Some ten months of futile wandering had reduced this adventurous band to virtual starvation. Orellana then volunteered to sail downstream with his threescore men on a rude brigantine constructed by the Spaniards and bring back food believed obtainable in that region, thus relieving the famished remnants of the main force. Among Orellana's companions was a Dominican friar, Gaspar de Carvajal, who was fated to lose an eye on this epic descent of the Amazon river to the Atlantic. More important, however, is the fact that he became the chronicler of this extraordinary feat of human endurance.[7]

The needed food did not materialize within the expected time or region and Orellana and his men were swept farther and farther downstream, leaving the luckless Gonzalo Pizarro and his followers far behind. It was on December 26, 1541 that the unprecedented navigation of the Amazon river began from its westernmost reaches and it ended at the broad mouth exactly eight months later. In his journal, Father Carvajal recites simply and graphically the mishaps and adventures that befell the small band during this period, and from this record are drawn some of the references to the alleged Amazons which Orellana later boasted of seeing.

Hardly two weeks after the start the Spanish leader learned from some Indians that Amazons of great wealth existed farther down the river. Always these curious phenomena were a few days beyond! Here, as in so many other parts of the New World, the wily natives, half comprehending the questions of the Spaniards and only wishing to be rid of their importunate guests, answered affirmatively if vaguely the queries of the white men. In this instance, it was a chieftain named Aparia who vouchsafed such encouraging news to Orellana, and thus moved him to hasten preparations for the construction of a larger brigantine, later completed farther downstream among more hospitable aborigines.

Late in May 1542, the Spaniards again received assurances of the existence of a realm of Amazons in the region. Much impressed by a carving on a tree trunk in the public square of a native village, the Spanish explorer questioned an Indian whom he seized and soon learned what was probably in his own mind. The replies elicited were to the effect that this local tribe was subject to Amazons of the interior to whom tribute was rendered in the form of parrot and macaw feathers. But it was on June 24 that the expedition had one of its more memorable experiences—the occasion when the chronicler, unfortunately, lost an eye. Some distance above the conjunction with the Tapajoz river, the Spaniards found a number of villages clustered together on a bend in the stream. The natives proved arrogant and warlike, and in the ensuing melee Orellana's men barely escaped defeat.

> I want it to be known why these Indians defended themselves in this manner. [wrote Father Carvajal]. It must be explained that they are subjects and tributaries to the Amazons, and our coming being known to them, they went to the Amazons to ask help. There came as many as ten or twelve of the latter, for we ourselves saw these women who were fighting in front of all the Indian men as female captains. These latter fought so courageously that the Indian men did not dare to turn their backs. . . . These women are white and tall, and they have long and braided hair wound about their heads; they are very robust and go about naked, their privy parts covered. With bows and arrows in hand they do as much fighting as ten Indian men. Indeed, there was one woman among them who shot an arrow a span deep into one of the brigantines, and others less deep, so that our boats looked like porcupines.[8]

From an Indian prisoner the Spaniards extracted further details, though again, with neither side understanding the language of the other, the information derived was probably what Orellana's men unconsciously supplied. They learned that the local chieftain was subject to a tribe of women living in as many as seventy villages only seven days' journey inland. Governed by a queen named Coñori, they lived without men in the traditional Amazon fashion except occasionally, and they possessed great wealth in gold and silver. Indeed, "all the mistresses of rank and distinction had only gold and silver eating utensiles," which seems but a distant echo of Montalvo's haunting words. In connection with this latest confirmation of their preconceptions Carvajal naively adds:

> and all that this Indian told us and more besides was told us six leagues from Quito because, regarding these women, there were a great many reports. . . .[9]

Thus he clearly confesses that Orellana's companions were mentally prepared to interpret every rumor and indication in the light of their own notions. How much Queen Coñori and her domain owed to the scarcely more imaginary Queen Calafia and her California realm invented by Montalvo must, of course, remain a matter for speculation, but the details of her wealth and, if Columbus' conjectures were right that the Terrestrial Paradise lay in the north of South America, her relative proximity to this Eden offered points of coincidence with the vague geographic data supplied by the author of the *Sergas de Esplandián*. Surely this novel played its part in the Amazon tale with which Orellana later regaled his listeners in Spain.

But even as this lieutenant of Gonzalo Pizarro was recounting his experiences with these strange women in the heart of the Amazon basin, elsewhere and further south other bands of Spaniards believed that they were finding corroboration. The first permanent European settlement in the southern continent was Asunción, capital of modern Paraguay, and from this base the Spanish search for sudden wealth was directed westward whence came rumors of the riches of Peru and of greater wonders. With the hope of running down some of these alluring reports to their source, Hernando de Ribera, with fifty-two men under his command, departed in a brigantine from the "Puerto de los Reyes" on December 20, 1543. The expedition sailed along a series of rivers until it came to the land of the Xaray Indians, who were considered a fairly intelligent tribe. From there forty of the Spaniards struck inland in a westerly direction and presently came upon the villages of the "Urteses" and "Aburuñes," natives who were accustomed to wear feathers like those of the inhabitants of Peru. Extended talks with these outlying Indian tribes elicited the information that the Spaniards always seemed so successful in acquiring. Perhaps once again the image of Queen Calafia and her Amazons projected itself upon the screen of the white explorers' minds, for the proximity of a realm of warlike women was excitedly announced. Again there seems a vague paraphrase of Montalvo in the Ribera report:

> These Indians, in perfect accord and without discrepancies in details, told him [Ribera] that ten days' journey westnorthwest from there some women lived in very large settlements, who possessed a great deal of metal, both "white" and "yellow", and the furnishings and service of their houses were all of this metal; as their leader they had a woman of the same tribe which is warlike and mates with Indians. Before reaching the land of this tribe of women there is another settlement of Indians (very small people) with whom the women fight and wage war. At a certain season of the year the latter have carnal union with these neighboring males. If the women who become pregnant give birth to daughters, they keep them with them; the male offspring they keep until weaned and then send them to their fathers.[10]

And the account adds that, far on the other side of these settlements of female tribes, there is a large lake called the "House of the Sun," a possible reference to Lake Titicaca where, according to the Inca legend, the founder of their royal dynasty first appeared. Ribera's report offers numerous other details which are not here of immediate interest. Though he does not use the term "Amazon" in his description of the alleged domain of warrior women, the statement concerning the abundance of precious metal in their possession and the use of gold in their personal utensils has a familiar ring. And though Ribera was informed, as were Cortés some twenty years before and many other explorers later, that the Amazon-like people were but "ten days' journey away," yet, somehow, they contrived to remain elusive and inaccessible.

Among the companions of Ribera in his explorations was a German by the name of Ulrich Schmidt[11] who, about a quarter of century after the event, published an account in his native language of his journeys on the tributaries of the River Plate. In the intervening years, it is possible that he refreshed his knowledge of the classics while, at the same time, his memory of his adventures grew somewhat hazy. Regarding the incidental quest of the Amazons on this occasion, his version varies somewhat from that given by the Spanish leader, and it would appear that in the details he was influenced more by an acquaintance with Scythian mythology than with the fictional writings of Montalvo. After stating that the chief of the Xarays gave a silver crown and a bar of gold to Ribera which he claimed that he had gained as spoils of war with the Amazons, the German chronicler continues:

> And when he [the chief] came to speak of the Amazons and gave us to understand of their great riches, we were very glad to learn of it, and our commander presently asked the chieftain if we could reach them by water, and how far it was to these Amazons. The Indian replied that we could not reach them by water but would have to go by land and travel during two whole months. Thereupon we decided to go to these Amazons. . . . These women, the Amazons, have only one breast, and the men come to their wives only three or four times in the year; and if the woman, being with child by her husband, bring forth a male, she sends it away to his father. But if it be a girl, she keepeth it with her, and seareth the right breast in order that it may grow no more. The reason for this is that they may be more fit to handle their weapons and bows, for they are warlike women, making continual war against their enemies.[12]

It is to be noticed that these viragoes, though they live on the conventional island, do *not* have either gold or silver. It would be well worth finding them, however, because "they are reported to have great riches on the mainland where their men live."

About the same time that Ribera and Schmidt were conducting their arduous investigations in the heart of the continent and gleaning information concerning the elusive female fighters, similar rumors were cropping up on the other side of the towering Andes and in the southern part of Chile where the Araucanian Indians were sturdily resisting the invading Spaniards. In 1543 a young secretary of the Royal Council in Spain, Agustín Zárate by name, was making extensive travels on the west coast and preparing a lengthy chronicle of the conquest of Peru. To the south of Chile, he reported, some fifty leagues beyond where the Spaniards communicated with the Indians, there existed, so the natives claimed, between two rivers

> a large province inhabited entirely by women who permitted men among themselves only at a time suitable for procreation. And if they bear male offspring, they send them to the father, and if they are daughters, they rear them. These women are subjects to Leuchengorma [a powerful Indian chief]; their queen is called Gaboimilla, which in their language means "heaven of gold" because, so it is said, they raise a great quantity of gold; and they make very rich goods, from all of which they pay tribute to Leuchengorma.[13]

But again, while positive indications of the truth of this information were secured, it was never quite possible for the Spaniards to reach the actual location of the strange women and discover the reality. And so it was in every case down through the century and later, with countless expeditions seemingly arriving within hailing distance but never quite contriving to push through to their objective.

It would be repetitious to list the many other recurrences of the Amazon legend in the voluminous literature of sixteenth-century travel and exploration in the wide reaches of South America and the New World. Not only the Spaniards continued to press this quest, but adventurers of other nationalities such as Ulrich Schmidt, as already noted, and also Sir Walter Raleigh, who was convinced that he had been within a short distance of an Amazon tribe on the Orinoco river in Guiana.[14] Doubtless these reports and rumors were as numerous as the eager queries put to the bewildered and uncomprehending Indians by gullible Europeans. Usually, of course, the communities of warlike women were associated with islands, but in the boundless continents through which the Conquistador traveled in his eager search, the locality of these strange realms necessarily became mediterranean rather than insular, as they were described in the books. But this circumstance did not alter the essential isolation and insularity of the abode of the female tribes, nor did it by any means eliminate the indispensable concomitant of great wealth, particularly gold. That this last association was inseparable and implicit in the minds of the Spaniards may well be attributed, in part at least, to the "best sellers" of the time, particularly the *Sergas de Esplandián*. There is little doubt that they were the fruitful source of so many of the fantastic notions possessing the Conquistador and that they were responsible in no small measure for the abiding spell which the ancient legend of the Amazon women cast over that flesh-and-blood knight of adventure, the Spanish Conqueror.

C IRCUMSTANTIAL EVIDENCE OF THE INFLUENCE OF current fiction on the actions of the Conquistador is so considerable that it prompts the question, why is so little direct testimony available? Why cannot more concrete proof in the form of allusions to fictional works be found in contemporary records? The only clear mention of one of these novels by any of the adventurers overrunning the New World is the passage quoted from Bernal Díaz del Castillo's *True history*, which was written long after the events it recounts. His awed comparison of the distant Aztec capital, glimpsed for the first time, with the cities described in *Amadis of Gaul* is the only positive reference to these imaginative works which has thus far come to light from the discovered reports of actual participants in the Conquest, though his use of the pronoun "we," as has been pointed out, is the best indication that his comrades shared his familiarity with the romances of chivalry. There is no doubt that the Spanish fighters everywhere had heard of them. Later in the century a celebrated commander and diplomat, Don Bernardino de Mendoza, whose *Commentaries* on the struggles in the Netherlands from 1567 to 1577 became a classic,[1] gives evidence of the continued fondness in the ranks for light literature. In his dedication of the volume to the Prince, he declared that he had written his *Commentaries* so that the Spanish soldiers "may put aside their fiction books, from the reading of which they derive no more profit than from listening to the water flowing by in a brook or river." The meagerness of more direct and corroborative testimony to this enjoyment of imaginative literature during the conquest period is disconcerting,[2] but this paucity of proof becomes understandable when some of its causes are analyzed. A few considerations of this character deserve attention.

In the first place, it is essential to recall that many of the followers of Cortés, Pizarro, Jiménez de Quesada, Valdivia, and other leaders were illiterate, or nearly so, and hence unable to leave written evidence of their possible attachment to the romances with which they were acquainted through hearing them read aloud or through the literary discussions of their companions-in-arms. And few indeed of those able to read and write were sufficiently articulate, or found themselves under any compulsion, to put on paper a subjective account of their extraordinary experiences. Of the uncounted number of adventurers participating in the great epic of the Conquest, only a minute fraction has left in writing any account of his part in it. There are a few personal chronicles, such as Cabeza de Vaca's report of his incredible peregrinations,[3] and a similar record of the unbelievable hardships of Pedro Serrano marooned on a barren island;[4] more numerous in the archives are the *relaciones de servicios*, or service reports rendered the Crown, usually composed for the purpose of obtaining due recognition and recompense in the form of pensions and other distinctions from remote royal authorities. These documents were ordinarily bare, soldierly accounts setting forth their writer's deeds, often with the matter-of-fact simplicity and stark realism of men whose instinctive medium of expression was action. In these unpretentious chronicles and in the documentary claims on royal bounty, there is little evidence or recognition of any subconscious motives impelling the authors to undergo the hardships that they endured with stoic courage.

But this diffidence or inability to acknowledge subjective influences, together with a tendency to dwell upon the purely external aspects of their exploits, may not have resulted from a total failure to analyze their own motives or to weigh the more imponderable factors affecting their conduct. As extroverts, the conquerors and explorers may well have been unaware of any connection between their excited imaginations and their acts, but the absence of any mention or hint of possible inspiration from current fiction in their written accounts could also be explained by the uncompromising hostility of authorities, both ecclesiastic and secular, toward the literature which the New World adventurers clearly read with passionate enthusiasm. Even before most of them had embarked upon their prodigious exploits in the new-found lands, the clamor of protest against the pernicious romances of chivalry was gathering volume. The profound effects of this vogue of reading on the credulous public were early perceived by the moralists and the intellectuals who, from pulpits and in moral tracts, vigorously denounced these "lying histories" and sought to have them banished by law. In the latter half of the century, the campaign waged by prelates and humanists against these fiction books assumed the proportions of a crusade, which fact is reflected, perhaps, in the sharply reduced number of new novels of chivalry published during that period. But these later denunciations were largely variations of the earlier diatribes aimed at the fictional works enjoyed by the generation of the conquistadors.

It is impossible to state exactly when these attacks began, but it appears that opposition to this popular literature soon developed as successive editions of the first parts of Amadis and the Palmerín series issued from the various presses of Spain, obviously supplanting the more respectable writings of the period. In general, the complaints against these imaginary tales arose from the fear of their influence on the manners and morals of impressionable maidens who, from the first, were extremely partial to them, but concern was also expressed for the welfare of the male youth of the land, likewise much given to such reading. But the moralists railed against this literature of chivalry not merely because readers showed what now seems an understandable preference for it as opposed to the too exemplary lives of saints, devotional works, and the more respectable chronicles, but because of the hypnotic effect which the descriptions of great wealth, gold, silver, precious stones, exotic lands, and fantastic creatures exerted on readers of the novels. Inevitably the suggestion of material riches was more attractive than the promised rewards of abstract virtue, and the clergy and the intellectuals fought a losing battle.

Possibly the most eminent opponent of the current literary fad was Juan Luis Vives, a friend of Erasmus and one of the foremost humanists of the Spanish Renaissance.[5] While profoundly preoccupied by the theological disputes precipitated by the Lutheran

Reformation, he also devoted much time to the preparation of moral guides for the laity. One of these treatises, which remained standard for many decades, was the *Instruction of the Christian woman*, first published in 1524. The fifth chapter sets forth the kinds of reading material which should and should not be placed in the hands of young ladies or, for that matter, of Christians. To this author it was far preferable not only to fail to learn how to read but, actually, to lose one's sight and hearing than to succumb to the poison of love stories and tales of combats. Every day fresh books were streaming from the presses of Spain to corrupt the minds and morals of mankind, yet no one was doing anything about it! Songs were sung and poems recited publicly of such demoralizing character, wailed the philosopher, that no right-minded person could listen to them without blushing. Indeed, questionable lyrics were the only kind that one heard these days! And he went on:

> All this should be remedied by laws and decrees if the rulers of the land wish to keep the public conscience sound. And the same things should be done to these other foolish books in Spain such as *Amadis, Florisando, Tirante, Tristón de Leonis, Celestina,* that go-between and source of depravity; those in France such as *Lancelot of the lake, Paris y Viana, Ponto y Sidonia, Pedro Provenzal y Magalona,* and *Melusina;* and those in Flanders such as *Flores y Blancaflor, Leonela y Cañamor, Curias y Floreta,* and *Píramo y Tisbe,* ... all of which books were written by idle and irresponsible individuals devoid of culture and full of vices and filth. And I wonder how there can be anything attractive in these books for anyone. ... When they set themselves to relate something about pleasure, what enjoyment can there be where they all prevaricate so deliberately, so impudently, and in such a silly fashion? One hero alone kills twenty men, another thirty, and another, riddled with six hundred wounds and left for dead, promptly recovers, God willing, and returns to the fray against two giants and kills them, thereupon sallying forth weighed down with so much gold, silver, precious stones, silks, and other things that a Genoese carrack could hardly carry them away. What idiocy it is to take pleasure in these stupidities![6]

The same writer's *Introductio ad sapientiam*, which also appeared in 1524, again inveighs against the reading of the same bad literature, but it was the translator of this work into Spanish, whose version was published in 1546, Francisco Cervantes Salazar, who amplified the condemnation of the original by dwelling specifically on the romances of chivalry. He deplored the thoughts that such works put into the minds of chaste maidens and adds: "Young men are just the same, for with their natural desires inflamed by evil reading, their one thought now is to dishonor young women and to shame matrons. All of which is the result of reading these books, and would to God that, for the good of their souls, those who have it in their power would prohibit them!"[7]

Vives reverts to the subject briefly in his *De officio mariti*, printed in 1529, alleging that "these books do hurt both man and woman, for they make them wily, and crafty; they kindle and stir up covetousness, inflame anger and all beastly and filthy desire." And many of the same sentiments recur in his *De disciplinis*, dated in 1531. As a leading philosopher and moralist of the Renaissance his opinions were certain to carry weight, but it may be doubted that his or others' denunciations greatly discouraged the reading of the fiction he attacked. However, they did, perhaps, serve to restrain the guilty from openly acknowledging their secret vice.

In 1529, the Bishop of Guadix, a famous preacher and spiritual advisor of the Emperor Charles V, Antonio de Guevara by name, published a book destined to be one of the most widely read of the sixteenth century. Disregarding his royal master's partiality for such literature, he took it upon himself to voice his pious protest against the prevailing reading fashion in the prologue of his *Libro áureo de Marco Aurelio*, which is the subtitle more commonly used than the original designation of his work, *Libro llamado relox de príncipes*.

> It is a pity to see the days and nights which many folk consume in reading silly books, that is, Amadis, Primaleon, Duarte, Lucendo, Calixto. Because of their doctrine I shall dare to state that they do not *spend* their time but waste their time because they do not learn in them how to avoid evil through the lure the books offer to greater vice.[8]

This worthy prelate again speaks his mind anent his liege lord's favorite reading, though he doubtless felt that royalty was exempt from the risks incurred by its subjects in entertaining themselves by such dubious means. In his *Aviso de privados y doctrina de cortesanos*, which appeared in 1539, he exclaims:

> Oh, how neglectful of what we write and recommend here is the State, for we see that men are only concerned with reading books which it is an offense to name, such as *Amadis of Gaul*, *Tristán de Leonis*, *Primaleón*, *Cárcel de amor*, and *Celestina*. All these and many others besides should be forbidden by law from being either printed or sold, for the lessons which they teach incite sensual natures to sin and weaken the desire to live rightly.[9]

It should be added that the good bishop's aversion to popular literature, particularly the romances of chivalry, did not deter him from employing some of their techniques in order to enhance the interest of his own brain children and give them the cloak of historicity to which they were not entitled. Indeed, this counsellor of the Emperor perpetrated a literary hoax, discovered in his own time, which caused him considerable embarrassment. Recognizing the advantage of giving an air of authenticity to his tale, as the authors of chivalrous novels were prone to do, by alleging the discovery of a manuscript which he pretended to translate, Guevara used this device in preparing his widely influential work entitled *Reloj de príncipes* which thus acquired the standing of a truly historical account. This bluff was exposed by a young ecclesiastic and, after vehement denials backed by the prestige of his eminent office, the bishop was finally obliged to acknowledge the falsity of his allegation.[10] This incident serves to illustrate the credulous naïveté of the sixteenth-century reading public as a whole, upon which even the most sanctimonious writers were tempted to play.

A less famous but more honest contemporary, Pedro Mexía, author of a renowned historical work, *Historia imperial y cesárea*, published in 1547, spoke with strong feeling against the chivalric romances. In his chapter on Constantine the Great, he bids for

> that attention which some give to the deceitful tales of Amadis, the Lisuartes and Clarians, and other monsters which rightly should be banished from Spain as contagious and harmful to the State, since they cause both the authors and readers to waste their time.

And he continues that, like Melchor Cano's parish priest and some of the conquistadors, many even believe them

> because they are men who think that things really happened just as they read and hear them when they are mostly profane and evil matters. It is a very grave and detrimental abuse for, among its objectionable effects, are the great ignominy and offense suffered by chronicles and true histories through permitting such infamous works to circulate equally with them.[11]

Mexía's concern, as expressed in these words, offers clear evidence of the prevailing confusion in the minds of readers between the allegedly historical chronicles of kings and saints and those relating the deeds of the knights and squires of Amadis' guild.

The following year Diego Gracián, the translator of Plutarch and Xenophon, heartily echoed the sentiments of the author of the *Historia imperial* regarding the discredit which worthy writings experienced as a result of the public's inability to discriminate between fact and fiction, thanks to its addiction to the novels of chivalry. Gracián bemoaned the fact that this devotion to purely imaginary heroes deprived the virtuous princes and illustrious captains of history of the appreciation to which they were justly entitled, and his tirade ends with unintentional humor.

> After all, [these romances] all strike the same notes and falsehoods exactly like the frogs of Plato's lakes which the poet Aristophanes, in his play, represents as singing and repeating only the same chorus "coax, coax, bebebex, bebebex, bebebex"; and this exercise in reading and writing these books is unworthy and unbecoming to grave and sober individuals.[12]

As already stated, denunciations of the offensive fiction increased in vigor and volume as the century progressed, but it would be tedious and repetitious to continue to quote the utterances of indignant churchmen, philosophers, and moralists, whose attacks were unceasing. These efforts to suppress light literature even extended to an endeavor to fight fire with fire by composing imitations of the popular models which strove to cloth saints and secular heroes with the glamour of fictional knights. These and other creative works designed to woo the public from its demoralizing obsession proved as ineffective as the oral tirades in banishing the original novels, and some of these pious parodies met a fate which did not befall the chivalric romances—proscription by the Inquisition. Ridicule, derision, satire, and angry condemnation were continually hurled by reformers at the popular fiction, and the evil effects of its reading were harped upon unceasingly. The *Suma de filosofía* by Alonso de Fuente, appearing in 1547, included a strong recommendation that such works be utterly prohibited and describes an individual rendered insane by reading so many fantastic tales, thus possibly supplying Cervantes with a suggestion for his masterpiece. It may be said that this inspired layman, the author of *Don Quixote*, succeeded where the churchmen and philosophers failed, perhaps because his genius substituted humor and compassion for moral righteousness and intolerance.

The inherent defects of these romantic tales and the absurdities to which their authors descended probably contributed more to the eventual eclipse of this literary vogue than all the rantings of moralists or the burlesquing of Cervantes. The evidence is fairly clear that, as the age of spectacular conquest in the New World ended toward the middle of the sixteenth century, there was a visible decline in the popularity of the purely fantastic romances. Whether this cooling of ardor was the result of a dawning disillusionment with the failure of the Indies to reveal the wonders which the books described, or was the cumulative effect of all factors operating against the permanent success of this type of fiction, it is impossible to say. A shift to the cloying and even more soporific pastoral novels is discernible about the middle of the century, though the earlier knightly favorites, Amadis, Primaleon and some of their progeny retained a prominent place in the reading fare of both sides of the Atlantic.

From the protests quoted concerning the chivalric novels, it is clear that the opposition of learned elements of contemporary Spanish society stemmed primarily from the deleterious effects which they professed to observe on the manners and morals, particularly of the younger generation which steeped itself exclusively in this type of literature. Scarcely less strong were the objections raised by the apparent undermining and destruction of the authority of the more respected and allegedly sounder works of history and devotion. Occasionally, there is a protesting reference to the tendency of the romances of chivalry to excite the cupidity and avarice of readers by glowing descriptions of wealth and treasure associated with the exploits of the imaginary heroes. There is, however, little to suggest that the purpose of these self-righteous critics was, primarily, to restrain the imitative zeal of the Conquistador in the New World or dissuade him directly from pursuing the will-o'-the-wisps which haunted his imagination as a result of his acquaintance with these books. But this vehement disapproval, voiced by such high authorities, could not fail to induce many sinners to be discreet about public confessions of their reading preferences and to abstain completely from written admissions of a surreptitious habit. The Conquistador, returning to the homeland or penning communications to royal officials, was thus disinclined to make any references to the books with which he was most familiar if, by any chance, he was aware of any stimulation derived from them. As the exploring expeditions fanned out in the newly found continents the resulting discoveries seldom harmonized with the rumors that launched the conquerors so eagerly on their adventures, and the progressive disillusionment slowly overtaking the Spaniards robbed the attractive myths and legends of their earlier validity. The prosaic reality fell far short of the dreams which had stirred their souls and now pride prevented the crestfallen adventurers from acknowledging the source of many of their fancies, the discredited and condemned chronicles of Amadis, Esplandian and Palmerin. Thus, with official disapproval of these chivalric tales rapidly mounting, with the extremes of absurdity to which their writers were descending, and with the growing realization of the falsity of the accounts that these novels offered, it is readily understandable why the conquistadors and others failed to make direct allusions of any sort to these fictional works in their *relaciones* and chronicles. As already indicated, only the forthright and honest soldier, Bernal Díaz del Castillo, writing in his old age and suddenly moved by his recollection of the wonder that seized him and his companions as they gazed for the first time upon the Aztec city in the middle of a lake, supplies the indisputable evidence that he and his contemporaries were intimately acquainted with the romances which attained an unprecedented popularity and influence in his time. This ingenuous reference of the soldier-chronicler gives substance to the more shadowy testimony so abundantly available, however, and leaves little doubt that such fantastic literature did, indeed, play its part in the "delirium" of the Spanish Conquest, despite the shrill protests of the aggrieved moralists.

LIGHT LITERATURE AND THE LAW VII

THE HELPLESSNESS OF DESPOTIC AUTHORITY TO OVERride the popular will of an individualistic people, particularly where their amusements are concerned, is clearly demonstrated by the vain efforts of the clergy, the moralists, and even of the monarchs of sixteenth-century Spain to destroy the passionate devotion of the reading public to the lighter forms of fiction. The novels of chivalry were especially invulnerable to such interference because they were too full of the sure-fire ingredients which make for the popular success of literature at any time or place, that is, generous portions of action, adventure, love thrills, virile heroes, gallant deeds, lovely ladies, vigorous tone, optimism, loyalty, and other virtues. Repressive measures were thus doomed to essential failure so long as writers retained their skill in serving up these basic elements in acceptable combinations; the ultimate neglect of authors to do so was, in fact, the most important cause for the eventual extinction of these highly romantic tales in popular favor. Meanwhile, despite the increasing pressure of intellectuals on the lawmakers to prohibit the reading and publication of the chivalric romances, no truly effective legislation resulted and the distribution and sale of all kinds of light fiction continued virtually unrestricted, both in Spain and in its overseas domains.

The strenuous efforts of the Counter Reformation to stem the rising tide of heterodoxy inspired by the Lutheran revolt did not fail to include stern measures against certain products of the printing press. Earlier decrees of condemnation were incorporated in an *Index of prohibited books* drawn up in 1559 by the Inquisitor Valdés at Valladolid, and this compilation became the cornerstone of all subsequent indices. Another inquisitor, Gaspar de Quiroga, revised and elaborated this list in 1583, dividing it into two parts, one of works prohibited in their entirety, and the other of those requiring expurgation. The Holy Office thus acquired a powerful throttle on freedom of thought, but in practice it was less oppressive than at first appears, for its restrictive activities were almost wholly limited to theological and religious literature. Considering the vehement denunciations of the romances of chivalry by ecclesiastical writers, some of which were reproduced in the last chapter, and the strange lack of reverence and the questionable taste that many of these novels betrayed, the tolerance of the Inquisition toward these books was truly extraordinary. It is curious, indeed, that not a single work of the profane variety was ever placed on the *Index*, while the *Celestial chivalry*, a religious romance written with the express purpose of destroying the popularity of the secular tales by imitating their form, found a place on the proscribed list.[1] And throughout the sixteenth century the Holy Office, though charged with the responsibility of preserving the purity of the faith and of public morals in the Spanish realms, continued to ignore the raucous clamor of the righteous against the preferred fiction of the laymen, a fact belying the traditional infamy which posterity associates with this institution.

Though the efforts of reformers proved unavailing in curbing or eliminating the universal enjoyment of chivalric literature through the organization of an allegedly all-powerful Church, this fact did not deter them from seeking the same objectives through the authority of the secular State. Among the many petitions presented to the Cortes or parliament convening at Valladolid in 1555 was one, numbered 107, which demanded the complete suppression of all light fiction. "Notorious is the harm done and being done to youths, maidens and other people in these realms," this document declares, "by the reading of such false and foolish books as *Amadís* and all others imitating its character and form which have come after it, and of couplets, love farces, and other nonsense."[2] Young people are employing their leisure in such idle diversions, so runs this protest, and they become so obsessed by the love affairs recounted and so entranced by the personal combats described that they are moved to cast aside all restraints in their desire to imitate such fascinating deeds. To quote the text, "often a mother leaves her daughter shut up in the house thinking that she is left in seclusion, but the daughter is really reading books like these and hence it would be far better for the mother to take the daughter along with her." And the petition dwells on the evil effects on the souls of the young people who become so captivated by these tales, by the customs that they portray, and by the language employed, that they lose all interest in books of sound doctrine and Christian dogma. To remedy this deplorable situation and to protect the unheeding from the fearful menace to their own salvation, the petitioners urge the strictest prohibition of the publication and reading of all such literature and the gathering up and burning of all existing books of this sort; henceforth, no light fiction of any kind should be published without a previous careful inspection and the approval of the Royal Council of Justice. Thus a great service would be rendered to God by putting a stop to such reading and by compelling the public to devote itself to more edifying works.

Perhaps Charles V, who abdicated that year, was too eager to retire to the peace of the Monastery of Yuste to give heed to this earnest entreaty of puritanical reformers; or perhaps he counted on devoting some of his new leisure to further perusal of the tales which had given him much entertainment in the past. Whatever his reaction to the proposal, he appears to have made no reply to it, but three years later Princess Juana, in the name of Philip II, then absent in Flanders, stated that a decree had been issued endeavoring to give effect to the substance of the petition presented to the Cortes. But this belated action had little visible result, judging by the continued sales of the favorite fiction and by the uninterrupted denunciations of moralists and the clergy throughout the remainder of the century. Unperturbed by these fulminations of preachers or by the disapproval of secular authorities, readers persisted in indulging their appetite for light literature, their tastes gradually shifting only as other literary fads made stronger claims upon their affections.

However unsuccessful were the efforts to ban such writings in Spain, it was long an article of faith that the Peninsular authorities were able to erect a nearly impenetrable barrier against the circulation of fictional works in their New World colonies. Only as contraband, so ran the traditional belief, did a few books of this character manage to evade the vigilance of despotic officials and enter those benighted regions. This legend inspired bitter recrimination of the mother country by Spanish American critics and historians of the nineteenth century and even by those of today. In some instances, where there is acknowledgment of a grudging acceptance of the accumulating evidence refuting this alleged obscurantism, the assertion is made that, while the Peninsular authorities may have displayed commendable liberality in permitting the exportation of fiction, this tolerance was largely nullified by the restrictions imposed on these books as soon as they reached the other side of the Atlantic. As one writer puts it:

> At the same time, it is evident in the archives of America that the freedom in shipping books on the consignee's account was not continued when these works reached their destination. Often the very contrabandist who succeeded in shipping them from the Peninsula would make the denunciation of them—I speak upon the basis of testimony of proceedings in the General Archive of the Nation [Mexico City]—and occasionally in the very fleet in which the cargo was transported there were papers ordering their seizure upon arrival. When these persecutions were put into effect, few books escaped, for the authorities wished to make patent their zeal and, in the majority of the cases, they were not only empowered to burn prohibited books, but also suspected ones. These facts explain the lack of works of light literature in the old libraries of America, notwithstanding the fact that they had gone out of Spain to the Indies.[3]

How unreliable this deduction is appears from surviving documents in both Spain and Spanish America, which demonstrate conclusively that large quantities of books of all sorts continually reached the colonies and circulated there during the whole colonial period. One can hardly suppose that commercially minded booksellers of Seville and elsewhere would persist, year after year, in sending hundreds and thousands of volumes, including even those officially banned, if the fate upon arrival of the majority or even a small part of them was confiscation or destruction by viceregal officials. These dealers—who could hardly be called contrabandists —were primarily interested, like businessmen everywhere, in profits accruing from a lucrative trade. Surely arbitrary methods beyond the sea would soon be reflected in diminished shipments of fictional works at least. During the sixteenth and seventeenth centuries, however, the available evidence shows no appreciable decline in the number of consignments of fiction. Popular tastes varied within the limits of imaginative literature, but the actual number of books increased.

But many Spanish American commentators have been unwilling to concede that any works of entertainment were even allowed in the former colonies, basing their contentions on extant prohibitory decrees of the Crown issued in the early sixteenth century.

> The Americans [of Spanish America] could not read poetry or novels or any work intended for amusement or diversion. According to the express wording of the law, which was not repealed, the colonists could not enjoy Don Quixote, or the plays of Calderón or Lope de Vega,

wrote a Chilean historian of the nineteenth century,[4] while an even more distinguished countryman avers:

> By command of the kings of Spain the colonists of America were forbidden under the severest penalties from reading what were called books of fiction, poetry, novels, plays, etc. It was not possible to read Cervantes, Vega, Quevedo, Moreto.[5]

A well-known Argentine scholar of a generation ago declared that

> such books of fiction, however, constituted a great part of the literature of the mother country at the time of this royal command, by which it is evident that such a prohibition was equivalent to depriving us Americans of all reading, assuming that all were not able or wished to read religious and juridical works.[6]

One of the bitterest utterances of all comes from a Colombian literary historian.

> No books except of a certain kind ever came to the colonies which were so jealously guarded; they wanted to make us a race of hermits and they made us a race of revolutionists.[7]

Even as late as 1940, when much evidence had accumulated dis-
proving this outworn theory, an estimable Mexican historian left
unchanged in the revision of his earlier edition a statement which
reads in part:

> Life, mute and monotonous, offered no incentive to lit-
> erary activity. Being isolated from every foreign influence,
> the colony, even more than Spain, was ignorant of the in-
> tellectual innovation which the world was undergoing. Cen-
> sorship prevented printed books from entering that were not
> subject to rigorous inspection: wherefore it is understand-
> able why so few entered.[8]

If accepted at face value these acrid comments of later writers
lead one to some curious conclusions. It is already clear that the
Conquistador read fiction books before and during the period of
his epic adventures in the New World, yet it would appear that
both he and his descendants were entirely cut off from this pleasure
on settling down in the overseas realms. That such hardy fighters
and rugged individualists would meekly obey the royal will in a
personal matter as small as their private reading while openly flouting imperial authority in economic and social questions such as
those raised by the so-called "New Laws of the Indies for the
Good Treatment and Preservation of the Indians" of 1542, is a
theory hardly tenable. Even if the decrees had truly sought to
prevent the Spaniards from enjoying their favorite books, the merchants and traders following close on the heels of the Conquistador
would have found means, legal or otherwise, to supply the demand.
But, since the conviction that Peninsular authorities did actually
exclude such literature from the colonies is still so firmly established in many quarters, it is worth while to examine the prohibitory
legislation producing this cherished belief. On close scrutiny these
laws reveal that the real intention of the repeated decrees has been
misunderstood and their purpose misinterpreted. To make these
facts clear the texts of a few, taken in chronological order, will be
quoted at length.

If the seventeenth-century historian, Fernando Montesinos, is
correct in his *Anales del Perú,* among the regulations which King
Ferdinand imposed in 1506 "for the good government of the Indies"
was one that ordered "that there should not be permitted the sale

of books dealing with profane, frivolous and immoral matters so that the Indians may not take to reading them."⁹ Isabella's spouse was obviously referring to the fiction books of the period, but be it noted at once that the prohibition was linked with the welfare of the Indians. Nothing is said of its application to their white over-lords.

The most famous of these royal decrees and the one so often quoted with damning effect by historians is the instruction of the Queen, acting as sovereign in the absence of her imperial lord, to the House of Trade at Seville, and dated April 4, 1531. It reads:

> I have been informed that many books of fiction in the vernacular which are unrelated to religion such as Amadis and others of this sort go to the Indies; since this is bad practice for the Indians and something with which it is not well for them to be concerned or read, I command you, therefore, from this time henceforth neither to permit nor allow any person at all to take any books of fiction and of secular matters there, but only those relating to the Christian religion and morality upon which the above-mentioned Indians and other inhabitants of the Indies may practice the art of reading, and with which they may busy themselves; no other kind is to be allowed. Done at Ocaña, April 4, 1531. I, the Queen.¹⁰

The wording of this royal order, which had the force of a law, is precise and the expectation of complete obedience to it is implicit. Yet in the instructions which the Queen issued to the first viceroy of Mexico, Antonio de Mendoza, under date of July 14, 1536, there is clear evidence that only five years later her earlier banning of "Amadis and others of this sort" was so ineffective as to require repetition. The underlying purpose of this prohibition becomes more apparent in the document handed Mendoza, which contains the following injunction:

> A few days ago the Emperor and King, my lord, ordained that no books of secular and fictional subjects in the vernacular should be carried to those parts [Indies] so that the Indians able to read may not take to them and thus neglect works of sound and healthful doctrine and, by reading such fiction, learn evil customs and vices from them. Also, because they [the Indians] do not know that these frivolous

books were written about what did not happen, and being
people still not firmly rooted in the faith, they may confuse
these tales with writings of genuine authenticity and authority such as the Holy Scriptures and the works of saints.
As we believe that there has not been due care in the enforcement of this matter, we strongly charge and command
you to arrange that from now on no books at all of this sort
shall be sold or brought in again, in order that these abuses
may stop. You will thus endeavor to see that Spaniards do
not have these books in their houses and that they do not
permit the Indians to read them, as we are informed that
some of the natives of that country are already beginning to
be adept in Latin. And you are to order the preceptors who
instruct them to read books of Christian and moral doctrine
always, for there are works among these in which they can
progress quite well in the Latin language.[11]

Obedience to these repeated commands of the Queen was apparently indifferent for, seven years later, still another order of the
same tenor was issued to the House of Trade's administration, this
time signed by the Prince, later Philip II, under date of September
13, 1543. Though in content it resembles the two documents
already quoted, its text is also reproduced in translation for purposes of comparison.

Know ye that much harm results from taking to the
Indies books in the vernacular of profane and imaginative
character such as those about Amadis and others of this type
of lying histories, because the Indians able to read turn to
them, forsaking works of sound and proper doctrine; from
these false tales they learn evil practices and vices. Moreover,
since they do not know that those frivolous books were
written about what did not happen, it is possible that the
authenticity and authority of our Holy Scriptures and the
writings of learned saints may suffer because, since they [the
Indians] are not firmly grounded in the faith, they may regard all books of equal truth and authority. To do away with
these and other objections I command you not to permit or
allow any book of this sort to go to our Indies. You will take
all necessary precautions so that, neither as contraband nor
in any other way, shall these books be taken, since this is for
the service of God our Lord. Done in the city of Valladolid,
September 13, 1543. I, the Prince.[12]

Later in the month instructions of the same character, with slight changes in phraseology, were forwarded to the Audiencia of Lima, to that of Santo Domingo, and presumably to all of these judicial and legislative bodies in the New World.[13]

Such were the decrees that remained in the law codes to inspire later severe indictments of Spanish rule in the former colonies. Historians have too often failed to realize the danger inherent in basing history on existing legislation, overlooking the tendency of many laws, particularly unpopular ones, to become dead letters in a brief time or to be honored in the breach. The need to repeat these commands at short intervals is in itself an indication that the prohibition of fictional books in the overseas realms was largely ineffective from the outset. But more serious, perhaps, is the misinterpretation of the intent of royal authorities in promulgating these laws. Even a cursory reading of the successive decrees and instructions produces a clear impression that the primary concern of the royal signers was not to prevent the Spaniards and Creoles in the New World from reading light literature but, rather, to keep such books out of the hands of the Indian charges of the Crown who were receiving the blessings of a Christian education. The fear that these natives, like many of the readers in Spain itself, might confuse fact with fiction and be unable to discriminate between works thought to be edifying and those which were not, undoubtedly suggested the advisability of banning the exportation of such profane writings. No doubt the royal household was anxious to discourage the Spaniards as well from indulging a dubious reading taste, and it hoped that the ban would prove effective among all elements of colonial society, but fundamentally the rulers were motivated more by consideration for what they deemed the moral welfare of the Indians than by a perverse desire to keep their overseas subjects hermetically sealed from European thought or creative expression, as was claimed by later critics. In the decree of April 4, 1531—apparently the only one known to many commentators—it is plain that the Queen was genuinely disturbed by the danger inherent in the false and misleading fiction books to the success of the Spanish efforts to elevate the aboriginal inhabitants through proper indoctrination to an equal status with other subjects of the Crown. A complete proscription seemed the surest method of removing such hazards and hence it was commanded that no such literature be transported to the Indies so that the "Indians and other inhabitants" should not have access to it. The "other inhabitants" mentioned might well include the Spaniards and Creoles themselves, of course, but it is possible that the term applied more directly to a new and increasing element of the population—the half-caste offspring of Spaniards and Indian women for whom schools were also being founded.

The Queen's primary concern is even more clearly expressed in the Mendoza instructions drawn up five years later in which she expatiates on the danger of confusion in the minds of the Indians and charges the viceroy to see to it that the Spaniards do not have fictional works lying about their homes where these natives may lay their hands on them. And again, in 1543, when the House of Trade is once more exhorted, this time by the Prince, to stem the flow of light literature to the Indies, the danger that the natives will succumb to the lure of fiction is reiterated. It is significant that in this instance nothing is said about the "other inhabitants" formerly included, and this omission serves to emphasize the limited application of this prohibitory legislation.

The frequent repetition of these commands in the space of a few years plainly indicates that these interdictions were ineffective in preventing the continued exporting of imaginative literature from Spain to her new colonies. There is direct confirmation of this fact in the phrase of the Mendoza instructions, "we believe that there has not been due care in the enforcement of this matter," i.e., stopping the shipment of disapproved books. It is likely that the officials of the House of Trade, to whom repeated decrees were directed, had discreetly disregarded the subsequent dispatching of fictional works by Peninsular merchants, especially by the influential guild of Seville, since the latter derived a profitable return from the popular literature sold to a growing clientele in the Indies. The necessity of instructing the House of Trade repeatedly, and the significant omission of any reference to the Spaniards and other segments of colonial society except the Indians, suggests that some connivance of this sort existed between booksellers and royal officials at Seville. The imperial household perhaps found it expedient, therefore, to word its commands so that they amounted to a tacit limitation of the restriction to the native elements of the overseas realms in the process of Christianization. The marketability of the popular novels among the white masters in the New World was much too great for the puritanical will of the Crown to prevail, and the economic need of the central government was far too pressing to provoke the hostility of the commercial guilds that were rapidly developing a profitable colonial trade.

In this question of the prohibitory legislation affecting the shipment of light reading to the Spanish Indies, there is an incidental interest, perhaps, in the fact that none of the related decrees or instructions was signed by the Emperor himself; all appear to have been issued during his absence, either by the Queen or by the Prince, later Philip II. One may speculate whether Charles V's private enjoyment of the scorned books made him indulgent with respect to this pastime, or whether more weighty affairs of state rendered him indifferent to its alleged dangers. Matters pertaining to the welfare of the souls of new converts probably assumed greater importance in the eyes of the virtuous and pious Queen, and certainly in those of his humorless and fanatic son and heir, Philip. It would appear that these two members of the imperial household, overconscious of their obligations for the moral and spiritual health of their subjects, took advantages of the numerous absences from Spain of their more tolerant lord and master to attempt remedial measures. The fact that these prohibitory injunctions did not come directly from the acknowledged ruler of the land but, rather, from members of his family temporarily exercising his sovereign authority, may possibly have played a part in the laxity of the enforcement which this legislation received from the outset. Whatever the truth, these successive orders were largely ignored and shipments of books of all kinds continued to pass through the House of Trade into the holds of vessels and ultimately into the hands of the retired Conquistador and his multiplying descendants. These overseas subjects, therefore, could, from the earliest period, enjoy the exploits of Amadis and his innumerable progeny, together with other and greater products of the creative genius of Spain.

That the idealistic Spaniards did embark on the ambitious undertaking to educate their Indian charges in the early sixteenth century by attempting to teach them both Spanish and Latin is abundantly clear in the records of the time. The high purpose of the Crown is patent in the magnificent efforts of the early Church to mitigate the cruelty of the Conquest and to perform its holy task of civilizing the aboriginal inhabitants of the Indies. Famous are the unselfish efforts and the devoted lives of such great missionaries as Father Pedro de Gante, a relative of Charles V, and Vasco de Quiroga, an Oidor of the Audiencia, who dedicated their lives to founding schools and training Indians in the arts and crafts of civilized society, including reading, writing, and singing. Much evidence is available testifying to the aptness and quickness of the natives in acquiring knowledge and new skills from their enthusiastic teachers. Juan de Torquemada, a contemporary historian, reported that each of the monasteries had a school beside its church where, in addition to music, the sons of the native chieftains were taught to read and write after they had mastered Christian doctrine,[14] while Motolinia, a humble but gifted friar working among the Indians, wrote: "In a very short time they [the Indians] learn to read both our Spanish vernacular and Latin, whether printed or written by hand." And they began to teach each other in their own languages, thus performing what seemed an inexplicable marvel to them, that is, making paper talk and convey thoughts to an absent friend.[15] Elsewhere the same author declared: "All know how to read, even those only just beginning to be taught."[16]

These statements were confirmed by the Viceroy, Antonio de Mendoza, to whom the Queen had issued instructions for the conduct of his new office, including the enforcement of the ban on light fiction. From Mexico City on December 10, 1537, this high official wrote Charles V urging his monarch to assist in the establishment of a *colegio* for the natives who were studying in the monasteries. "There are abilities in these Indians and they have a capacity to master literature, judging by what the instructor who teaches them told me. . . . I have chatted with these Indians several times when I have visited their schools, and it seems to me that they are quite advanced for the short time since they began to study."[17] Indeed, the obvious precocity and volubility of the aboriginal neophytes in using the new media of expression even aroused the misgivings of one of the Viceroy's advisors, Jerónimo López. This individual addressed a letter to the Emperor, dated October 20, 1541, in which he stated that the Indians had not only learned to read and write, play instruments and to become musicians, but they were learning Latin grammar so well that "there were lads, and more and more every day, who are talking as elegant Latin as Tullius." Their progress was so astonishing that they were even excelling their own teachers in the monasteries; advanced schools had been founded where these bright natives could read all kinds of books and immerse themselves in all forms of higher learning. Charles V's correspondent felt that there was actually grave danger in permitting the Indians to acquire such advanced knowledge, which included study of the Bible and sacred writings. In fact, a clergyman of his acquaintance had gone to one of these *colegios* to say Mass and was horrified by the freedom and facility with which some two hundred students of the conquered race asked questions and discussed recondite matters concerning the Faith of the conquerors. This situation was so dangerous, in the writer's view, that the only remedy was to put a stop to all that had been done so far, otherwise "this land will become a cave of Sibyls and all its inhabitants spirits who read theology."[18] One may ponder on the possible relationship between this communication and others like it testifying to the omnivorous reading habits of the Indian wards of the Crown and the subsequent royal decrees to the House of Trade and the various Audiencias in the colonies instructing those agencies to prevent the circulation of light literature which might be confused with alleged fact.

But the imperial government appeared to be undeterred in its good intentions with respect to the education of its charges in the New World, for a decree of the Queen, dated July 7, 1550 and directed to the Viceroy of Peru "and the President of the Audiencia," specifically enjoins the continued instruction of the Indians in Castilian.[19] And in the effort to carry out the high resolve to educate the descendants of the Incas, whose conquest was achieved a decade or more after that of the Aztecs of Mexico, the Crown pressed for the prohibition of profane literature in the newer viceroyalty of Peru. It appears that the great administrator, the Viceroy Francisco de Toledo, brought with him to Lima in 1569, as Mendoza had done years before in Mexico, instructions to prevent the diffusion of light literature in Spanish South America. Among the measures which this vigorous executive reported that he had taken upon his arrival in Peru was one requiring all book-dealers and private individuals to bring before the Royal Audiencia all *libros profanos* in their possession because such literature was forbidden to enter the realm. Significant is the statement included in this report that [this royal order] "had not been observed or executed up to now."[20]

At no time did the royal commands seriously affect the expor-tation from Spain of the proscribed literature, and a similarly lax enforcement of the laws was the rule among the receiving officials in the colonial ports. Occasionally, some conscientious clergyman in the overseas realms waxed indignant concerning the noxious effect of such reading on the morals of his flock and sought to implement the existing prohibitory legislation with edicts of his own. These efforts, however, were sporadic and, it may be judged, largely in-effective. Typical of these attempts was that of Bishop Fernando de Trejo y Sanabria of Tucumán in Argentina who assembled a diocesan synod in 1597 to consider means of "bringing about the salvation of all the faithful, especially the Indians, of our bishopric." Among the resolutions adopted was one concerning the "libros vanos," which reads in part:

> One of the matters most harmful to the Christian com-monwealth is the reading of immoral books and novels of chivalry which serves no good end but, rather, stirs up im-moral and lascivious desires and false and foolish fables in readers' minds; these foolish fancies impress chiefly young people to the great detriment of their souls which are cor-rupted by these books, for they are inflamed by them and begin to learn and try out what they did not know about or had not heard from other sources. For this reason we order every person of our bishopric, men and women of every status and class, under penalty of total excommunication, to bring to us and to send to our office within four days of the publication of this resolution, every book entitled *Diana*, by whatever author, every novel of chivalry and all immoral and vulgar poems.[21]

All such books were to be burned, for it was outrageous that, with so many worth-while and true works in existence, the reading of such stupid and lewd ones should be allowed. "And likewise, we command," the resolution continued, "that all merchants who have dealt in books of this sort shall cease to sell them in this bishopric" under heavy monetary penalties.

Stern as this resolution is, evidence is lacking that it was more than temporarily effective, and it is doubtful whether any of the condemned books were actually burned. The later synods of 1606 and 1607 make no further mention of books, and it is likely that this attempt to change reading habits met with no more success than had others. The incident serves, on the whole, to indicate clearly how wide was the diffusion of light literature in the six-teenth-century Spanish colonies of the New World.

As this period of expansion wore on, however, the Crown in-sisted less and less on the expensive process of educating the Indians in the languages of Spanish learning. It was too vast a task to in-struct so large a sedentary population of natives as that found in the richer parts of the Indies, to say nothing of the more nomadic tribes living on the periphery and in the remote interior. Rather than attempt to teach all the natives the speech of their overlords, it was simpler for the clergy to master the dialects of their flocks, converting and guiding them through the intricacies of the Faith with the aid of manuals, catechisms, and vocabularies. While in-struction in Castilian and Latin continued to be given to selected natives and mestizos throughout the century, and to some extent throughout the period of Spanish rule, the first educational at-tempts on a large scale were abandoned. The monarchy had neither the resources nor the disposition to realize the ideal of the first great teachers in the Indies, for the ominous threat of the Lutheran revolt and the dream of reducing all Europe to the Catholic fold under the aegis of Spain consumed all the available strength of the Penin-sula and soon left it exhausted. The feat of governing an empire so far flung in the New World became increasingly impossible for the harassed home government, and its economic and political pol-icies soon took precedence over the civilizing mission of Spain in America. The zeal of the first missionaries quickly yielded to rela-tive indifference, and the Indians became still greater victims of the exploiters in their midst, both ecclesiastic and secular. As the num-ber of literate natives ceased to increase and probably declined, the need to keep obnoxious books from falling into their hands diminished. There came to be little danger that the fictional works of the sixteenth century and later would confuse the Indians or wean them from the sounder books of doctrine, and thus the basic concern of paternalistic rulers, which had inspired the prohibitory decrees, largely disappeared. This situation, together with the Spaniard's individualistic determination to enjoy his romances of chivalry and similar reading anyway—a determination which profit-minded merchants did much to stimulate—explains why legislation banning "*libros profanos*," which remained in the law codes and was never repealed, had so little effect in stemming the flow of entertaining literature to the colonies throughout the entire period of Spanish dominion.

BOOKS FOLLOW THE CONQUEROR VIII

BOOKS OF THE BRAVE

THE AMAZING RAPIDITY WITH WHICH THE SPANISH conquistadors and explorers overran much of two enormous continents, overpowering vast populations of sedentary Indians, subjugating others less civilized, and adding great domains to Spain and to geographic knowledge, will always remain one of the supreme epics of human courage, energy, and endurance. The thrill which still emerges from the moving accounts of these astounding feats, retold by Prescott and others, tends to leave the impression, however, that the Conquest was solely a spectacular orgy of destruction or, perhaps, an exciting military success, daringly accomplished by almost lawless bands of audacious adventurers. Resounding and glamorous as were these first achievements in the Europeanizing of the globe, they actually pale into insignificance beside the constructive processes of settlement and colonization which the Spaniards at once set into motion. Even as Cortés was mapping out further campaigns of expansion a Spanish municipality was rising out of the ruins of the Aztec capital with all the characteristic institutions, laws, and practices of Spain itself firmly implanted. From the Antilles and the mother country a stream of missionaries, officials, merchants, artisans, and simple adventurers poured into this reorganized city and realm, all bent on reproducing quickly in the new locale the blessings of European civilization, which included, of course, material rewards and distinctions. Civil life took shape and form at once and, while the impatient search for treasures and sudden riches continued feverishly, the more sober and less speculative forms of economic exploitation began to operate. Mining, stock raising, agricultural pursuits, and the industrial crafts, in many of which the vanquished natives proved apt apprentices, were soon producing greater material returns for the capital and energy invested than did the restless expeditions pushing boldly into the dim mystery of the hinterlands.

But even before these more settled occupations yielded returns, merchants, peddlers, and traders, who had followed closely on the heels of the conquerors and even accompanied them, were busily bartering their wares and functioning as middlemen. Then as later "trade followed the flag," and the new lands subdued by the Conquistador opened up immensely profitable opportunities for the sale of Spanish goods and the exchange of native commodities. A large market for the manufactures of the Peninsula developed immediately, and its exploitation precipitated a scramble for monopolistic control in accordance with the mercantilistic theories of the time. Perhaps the most eloquent proof of the swiftness with which Spanish civilization and commerce took root in the New World is the fact that, from the earliest date, the importation of goods from the Peninsula included printed books of varied nature.[1] From 1501, and doubtless before, the clergy brought with them supplies of missals, breviaries, Bibles and other devotional literature, grammars and dictionaries; lighter forms of reading must have been brought by laymen almost as soon. The evident familiarity of Bernal Díaz and other soldiers of Cortés with the novels of chivalry point to the strong likelihood that similar fiction of entertainment was available from the first in the Antilles, particularly in Santo Domingo and Cuba, whence came many of the expeditions to the mainland. The multitude of planters living in comparative idleness on these islands, thanks to the Indian and Negro labor, had ample opportunities to peruse the fascinating pages of the romances supplied by energetic merchants in their midst, and doubtless these imaginary descriptions of exotic lands whetted the desire of these restless Spaniards to penetrate the secret of the shadowy mainland about which more and more rumors came to their ears.

It has already been suggested that, among the luggage of the historic company which embarked with Cortés from Cuba and probably that of most of the other expeditions of conquest and exploration on Tierra Firme, there were a few such books to fire the imagination and ease the boredom between campaigns. Evi-

dence of a positive character is not entirely lacking, for it is recorded that the leader of the ill-fated undertaking of 1536 in the
River Plate region, Pedro de Mendoza, had a small number of volumes in his personal baggage. These were works of Vergil, Petrarch
and, interestingly enough, writings of that witty humanist, Erasmus
of Rotterdam.[2] And almost at the same time the first Viceroy of
Mexico, Antonio de Mendoza, included among the effects brought
for his comfort in the new post a box of two hundred books[3] which,
incidentally, were exempted by special dispensation of the Queen
from the usual imposts on such goods. This was the same Regent,
it will be recalled, who exhorted this viceregal representative to
enforce her earlier decree banning the books of Amadis and the
like from the Indies. Unfortunately, the record of the new administrator's small library does not specify the titles or nature of
this reading material. Considering contemporary tastes in such
matters, it is reasonable to suppose that at least a few "libros de
entretenimiento" were among these volumes to distract their owner
from the oppressive cares and heavy responsibilities of administration. And perhaps the highly imaginative tales of the time, presumably represented in this book collection, had a part in conditioning his mind to a too ready acceptance of reports of the fabulous "Seven Cities of Cíbola" brought back from the land of the
Pueblo Indians to the north by the overcredulous Friar Marcos de
Niza. This incident, it will be recalled, gave rise to the vain quest
by Vásquez de Coronado whose expedition, organized with the
blessings of Viceroy Mendoza, started with the pageantlike trappings of medieval splendor on a two-year, futile search for the
emerald-studded cities. The story of this historic episode, which
resulted in the discovery of the Grand Canyon of the Colorado and
other wonders of the American Southwest, exceeds the narratives
of the novels of chivalry themselves in sheer adventure and color.[4]

As elsewhere the conquerors and others fortunate enough to
win *encomiendas* on the mainland or pension grants from the Crown
as rewards for their services were thus able to retire to their estates, where Indians and other dependents attended to their needs.
This lordly leisure permitted the more literate to enjoy the sequels
to the popular novels which had enlivened their long marches and
the tedious interludes of their hazardous campaigns. But already this

nucleus of a reading public was greatly augmented by the throng of officials and fortune hunters swarming over the viceroyalty, thus creating a rapidly widening market for books of fiction as well as volumes of more utilitarian character. Merchants were not slow to supply these demands by including printed works among their varied wares. There is direct evidence of the presence of one book-seller attracted by the possibilities of Mexico in the first decade of the Conquest. A contemporary notation, found on the title page of a surviving copy of a German treatise entitled *Erklerung des neuen Instruments der Sunnen* by Sebastian Münster and printed at Op-penheim in 1528, states that a certain Johannes Schick, a bookdealer, emigrated that year to a "far-distant island called Yucatan," lured by the fame of its riches. Apparently, he returned to Europe two years later somewhat disillusioned but possibly perceiving more assured if less spectacular gain in the furtherance of his own trade.[5] Others, however, whose names are unknown to fame, re-mained in the New World or journeyed back and forth on the cumbrous galleons like commercial travelers, extracting a larger measure of prosperity from their efforts. But more patent evidence of an early and lucrative traffic in books between Spain and its Indies comes to light in the story of the famous printers of Seville, the Cromberger family, who were instrumental in introducing the first printing press into the western hemisphere.

No city of Spain benefited more from the sixteenth-century discovery and exploitation of the trans-Atlantic continents than the colorful Andalusian capital, Seville, situated well up from the mouth of the Guadalquivir river. As the only authorized port for the transoceanic commerce, it was a bottleneck through which passed all the trade and migration to and from the Spanish colonies. Its population grew rapidly soon after Columbus' discoveries as artisans, craftsmen, workers, and adventurers crowded into the nar-row quarters of the city.[6] Its wharves were thick with the forest of masts of ships preparing for the voyages across the western seas, while waiting sailors and members of the innumerable expeditions bound for the New World loitered about the streets for months and even for a year or more. The merchants of the port grew opulent and powerful, exerting a determining influence on the commercial policies of the Crown, and the House of Trade, founded to direct this colonial trade, spawned a proliferating bureaucracy. From various parts of the Habsburg empire in Europe came foreigners to profit from the prosperity of Seville, often supplying the technological skills indispensable for the development of new crafts and industries. Not least important of the latter were the printing and manufacture of books, of which large quantities went to the rapidly expanding market overseas. In the seventeenth century, it is reported, unscrupulous printers of Seville reaped an enormous harvest from the colonial trade by shipping abroad great quantities of unauthorized editions, particularly of the three-act plays then phenomenally popular, and of printings of mediocre works falsely attributed to well-known writers. But during the age of the conquistadors the influx of bookmakers into the Andalusian capital brought the typographic arts to an unprecedented perfection. Probably the most famous of these craftsmen was the House of Cromberger, already mentioned, which, for many years, enjoyed exclusive rights as suppliers of books to the vast region which Cortés had conquered for the imperial Crown, a special concession in New Spain allowing a profit margin of 100 percent.

The head of this family, Jacob Cromberger, of German origin, was an expert printer and a shrewd businessman who came to Seville in 1500, where he set up a press; later he established others at Lisbon and Evora. The moment of his arrival at the Andalusian river port was opportune and perhaps deliberate, for it coincided with the rapid growth of the locality as the Spanish terminal of the new trans-Atlantic trade. Of even greater importance, he timed the founding of his printing house with the rising vogue of fiction which gave the book business its first great impetus as a commercial enterprise in Spain. These fortunate circumstances, together with the exclusive control of the expanding colonial trade, made Seville the foremost publishing center of the Peninsula during much of the sixteenth century. Titles of 751 different works printed there in that period are recorded, but this figure does not represent the total. The fast-selling novels of chivalry constitute a significant percentage of this output, though estimates of the number of volumes produced are, at best, approximate. For Spain at large one investigator finds that, during the century of conquest, 316 editions of chivalric romances were printed, of which 109, or roughly a

third, came from the presses of Seville. Forty-five of these, or
nearly one-half, bore the imprint of the Crombergers. Other centers
of Spain brought out fewer editions collectively than this firm did
individually, Toledo being the nearest with 32, Burgos next with
29, and Alcalá de Henares with 23.[7] The first known printing of
the *Sergas de Esplandián*, the novel which put strange notions into
the heads of many adventurers, came from the Cromberger press in
1510, and a large number of its sequels and rivals betray the handiwork of the same publishers. Into their *talleres* on the banks of the
Guadalquivir, where manufacturing and selling were comple-
mentary activities, undoubtedly wandered many of the soldiers who
loitered about the streets of Seville awaiting sailing orders, and
there they purchased copies of the highly seasoned fiction which
inflamed their imaginations and distorted their conceptions of the
lands they were to penetrate.

By some means this enterprising German firm contrived to win
from the Emperor a monopoly of the book trade with Mexico,
which privilege it enjoyed from 1525 on, though no similar concession was apparently granted for South America. In 1527 the
son, Juan Cromberger, broke away from partnership with his
father and set up a separate establishment.[8] On the death of the
elder Cromberger two years later, an inventory of his possessions
was made. This document, dated June 7, 1529, includes an extensive list of books in stock from which a few representative items
are extracted to throw light on the kinds of works apparently enjoying a good turnover. They are: 398 "Amadises," valued at 44,-
376 *maravedís;* 80 more "Amadises" (probably a different title), at
12,000 *maravedís;* 320 "Don Clarián," at 34,676; 1,501 "Rey Canamor," at 21,014; 162 "séptimos de Amadís" [*Lisuarte de Grecia*], at
9,234 *maravedís;* 405 "Oliveros," at 6,885; 209 "Cancionero general,"
at 22,347; 95 "Cavallero de la Cruz," at 6,650; and 50,500 "pliegos
de coplas," at only 1,500 *maravedís.*[9] Since Jacob Cromberger had
exclusive right of sale in Mexico, there is little doubt that many of
these books were destined for the colonial market and that many
copies of these and other titles had preceded them to that part of
the world.

The son, Juan Cromberger, who, about 1539, contracted with
Juan Pablos, a native of Lombardy, to set up the first printing press

in Mexico City, obtained from the Viceroy and the Archbishop of
New Spain the exclusive privilege of sending "the *cartillas* and
other printed material and books of all kinds" for sale there at a
net profit of 100 percent. At his death in 1540 his widow and
children begged Charles V to grant a twenty-year extension of this
monopoly. The Emperor compromised by reducing the limit to
ten years, possibly because of complaints by rival bookdealers in
Seville, who viewed with envy the favored position of the Crombergers in the prosperous overseas trade. These would-be competi-
tors laid a petition before the City Council of Seville on July 11,
1542, requesting that the special rights of the Crombergers be
abolished and pledging that, if these trade opportunities were opened
to them, they would fill orders at no more than 25-percent profit;
furthermore, they would set up printing presses in Mexico and
would charge the relatively low rate of four *maravedís* per page.[10]
This effort to share in the colonial book trade was unsuccessful,
apparently, but it clearly indicates that the traffic in a luxury item
was sufficiently lucrative to excite rival businessmen, and that the
volume of trade was great enough to interest these commercial elements in operating at a considerably reduced margin of profit.

The inventory of the stock left by the son at his death in 1540
is more impressive than the one made of his father's possessions
eleven years before. Not only does it offer a greater variety of
fictional titles, but it also records larger quantities of individual
works. With the exclusive right of sale in New Spain still held by
this firm and soon renewed, it is probable that a considerable proportion of this stock was destined for that market. Hence this list
may serve as an indication of the reading preferences of the conquerors and their associates in the colonies toward the middle of
the sixteenth century; its signficance is enhanced when it is considered in conjunction with the contemporary efforts of the Crown
to ban the exportation and reading of "Amadis and similar lying
histories" in the Indies. Once more it appears that the passionate
desire of readers overseas for light literature, and the commercial
advantage for profit-minded merchants accruing therefrom, co-
operated from the very outset to nullify almost completely the
prohibitory legislation. And this inventory serves to explain, perhaps, the apparent need of the regents to repeat unheeded com-

mands, and thus leaves the impression that the colonial reading public was at no time actually deprived of its preferred reading fare. According to this lengthy document,[11] the following titles were among the leading favorites, if one may judge by the numbers in stock:

No. of copies	Titles
446	Amadis de Gaula
1017	Espejo de caballerías
156	Palmerines
10	Septimos de Amadis [*Lisuarte de Grecia*]
171	Oncenos de Amadis [*Crónica de Florisel de Niquea*]
228	Trapisondas [*de Don Reynaldos*]
167	Caballero de la Cruz
696	Rey Canamor
550	Oliveros [*Caballeros Oliveros de Castilla . . .*]
325	Celestina [*Tragicomedia de Calisto y Melibea*]
823	Doncella Teodor
409	Tablantes [*Crónica de . . . Caballeros Tablante . . .*]
730	Alexos
377	Cid Ruy Díaz
370	Siete Sabios [*de Roma; o Grecia*]
281	Conde Fernán González
557	Robertos [*el diablo*]
194	Flores y Blancaflor
372	Magalones [*Libro de la linda Magalona . .*]
800	Troyanas [*Crónica Troyana*]

These figures for the various titles represent for their time a respectable number of books to be kept on order, particularly as there were many other works in smaller quantities, and they suggest a fairly constant demand from the trade and, perhaps, a rapid turn-over. They also point to the probability that book shipments to the colonies during the two decades following the fall of the Aztec capital ran into thousands of volumes, which fact readily explains the jealousy of rival dealers in Seville. With profits of 100 percent guaranteed and probably exceeded, the proceeds of this export monopoly were doubtless considerable enough to move the influential Cromberger family to bring pressure unostentatiously upon the officials of the House of Trade to honor in the breach the reiterated injunctions of the Emperor's household against the cir-

culation of light literature in the Spanish Indies. Where the monetary returns were so substantial it could hardly be a matter of
serious concern to the merchants involved that the "Indians and
other inhabitants" might mistake the chronicles of Amadis and his
progeny for the historical accounts of flesh and blood heroes, or
that these new and untutored subjects of the Crown overseas might
confuse the imaginary exploits of the fabulous knights with the
miracles of the Church saints. Thus books of fact and fiction flowed
with equal freedom into the New World colonies from an early
date, and clearly the monarchs were justified in their suspicions, as
expressed in subsequent prohibitory decrees, that their "command
was not being observed with the care required." 60523

The imposing array of books in the warehouse or on the shelves
of the Cromberger establishment admittedly does not furnish *prima
facie* evidence of a flourishing colonial trade, for it is possible that
these wares were distributed in the rich market of Seville itself and
elsewhere in Spain. There were, however, printers and booksellers
in many other cities of the Peninsula who served their local clientele
and also competed in other centers. It is clear that later they also
shipped their wares overseas, thus becoming rivals of the *sevillano*
merchants. In 1542 there were at least twelve of the latter in the
same business besides the Crombergers, judging by the number of
names signed to the document sent to the City Council of Seville
in an effort to break the monopoly held by the German house, and
there were possibly more.

With so large a number of bookdealers catering to the local
trade in the Andalusian capital and with the Cromberger family
enjoying the unique concession as suppliers to Mexico, it is virtually
certain that many of the fictional works listed on the inventories of
1529 and 1540 were destined for this export market and represented
the current stock awaiting shipment. More direct and incontrovertible evidence in the form of bills of lading or similar documents
is, unfortunately, lacking, owing to the fact that almost none of the
shipping records of the early sixteenth century survive. The few
registers extant rarely indicate more than the presence of a case or
fardo of books, nature unspecified, mingled with other freight.
Invoices of a later date are less laconic but are only relatively more
numerous and detailed. Despite the frequent repetition of prohibi-

tory decrees earlier, the desirability of listing titles of works dispatched was not felt, apparently, until the middle of the century. On September 5, 1550 the "Emperor Don Carlos y los Reyes de Bohemia" issued an order which, in abbreviated form, reads:

> We command our President and judicial officers of the House of Trade at Seville that, when any of the permitted books are to be taken to the Indies, they shall have each one specified on the register, stating its nature, and such books shall not be registered in lots.[12]

This instruction meant, then, that each shipping manifest should be accompanied by a list of the titles of the printed works in the consignment it covered. The historian has reason to be grateful for the fact that this imperial command received greater compliance than was accorded the prohibitory decrees, but the beneficial effect on this measure is not immediately noted in the surviving records. It is not until 1583, a third of a century later, that *registros* or manifests of the annual fleets to the New World are found with these useful addenda, and from that date on they are preserved in a fragmentary state only. For the period up to that year only one small bundle of papers relating to earlier book shipments has been found in the Archive of the Indies at Seville, the present repository of the remaining records of the long-extinct House of Trade. This solitary *legajo* contains a few registers of ships sailing to America from 1523 to 1526 inclusive, and some for the single years 1545 and 1557.[13] Even those of the latter date rarely give any indications of the nature or the title of the literature transported in the cases of books occasionally announced. The only exceptions occur in a couple of the 1545 manifests, from which it is possible to identify a small number of volumes. In that year a certain Fernando Pérez Jurada consigned four boxes of freight aboard the ship *San Juan* to "Joan de Escarraón" at Nombre de Dios on the Isthmus of Panama, and the *registro* records that these cases included two copies of Antonio de Guevara's currently popular historical novel, *Libro áureo de Marco Aurelio*, which first appeared in 1529. This writer was, apparently, a favorite, for the shipping document also declares "Los Quatro libros de don Antonio de Guevara," which possibly referred to his other works such as the *Menosprecio de*

Corte, Epístolas familiares, Monte Calvario and *Oratorio de religiosos*. And there were, besides, two copies of his *Década de la vida de los diez Césares*. Another item listed was "un libro de Mexia a los Emperadores," presumably Pero Mexía's *Historia imperial y cesárea*, a résumé of the lives of the Roman Caesars and the Emperors of Germany down to Maximilian I of Austria. This work was first published in 1544, only a year before the date of the invoice, which interesting fact offers early proof that the booksellers of Seville sent copies of the most recent publications of the Peninsula to their customers in the Spanish Indies. The time lag in the diffusion of printed works and hence ideas from Spain to the New World was much shorter than is generally acknowledged. Other random lists of these earlier years permit identification of an occasional work. In 1530, among various religious books, there was a copy of the chivalric *Los siete sabios de Roma*, printed that year at Burgos, and in 1557 some treatises on music were included.[14]

Though the extant shipping documents before 1583 are too few and contain too little detail to give more than the most meager data, they are sufficient, nevertheless, to validate the assumption that the flow of light literature was under way during the first and more spectacular decades of the Conquest. They give convincing indications of what is perfectly clear after 1583—that *libros de entretenimiento* were carried to the Spanish Indies on nearly every ship that departed from Seville. That many of them arrived safely and circulated freely in America is confirmed by existing testimony, though as yet it is as scanty for the earlier years of the Conquest as that of the shipping manifests preserved in the Peninsula. The archives of Mexico and Peru grudgingly yield a few crumbs of evidence which may in time increase in volume and weight as researches are continued.

Most useful of these early documents are legal instruments, such as receipts of book shipments, bills of sale, wills and testaments, inventories of local colonial libraries or private collections, etc., found in the surviving records of professional scribes charged with these notarial duties. The Spaniards displayed a commendable zeal in formalizing all legal actions and transactions of their nationals wherever or in whatever circumstances they might be, a fact which often makes Spanish and Spanish American repositories today, however disorganized, rich treasuries of historical information. The scribes accompanied every expedition, whether its purpose was conquest, exploration, or settlement, and they were frequently the "ghost writers" of the colorful reports which the sometimes illiterate commanders rendered to the Crown through its Council of the Indies. In the new townships and municipalities, which were quickly organized in the conquered territories, these indispensable officials aided greatly in establishing the orderly processes of civil life, and from the accumulations of their notarial records much information, both trivial and important, on social, economic and cultural aspects of colonial life can be extracted. Like the commonplace shipping manifests of the House of Trade at Seville, these formal and prosaic documents are fragmentary and scattered in the early period and relatively few are valuable for specific data until the sixteenth century is well advanced.

Further search for these barely exploited materials may bring to light more facts concerning the presence of books in the newly conquered regions, but the earliest record of this character at hand comes from the National Archive at Lima, Peru. This is a bare notation relative to the shipment of seventy-nine books of a certain Alonso Cabezas of that viceregal capital, made November 1, 1549 on the ship *La Magdalena* to a "Pero Hortiz" at Nombre de Dios.[15] Most of the volumes listed are brevaries, missals, and other religious works, but at the very end of the list appear the highly fictional *Chronicle of King Don Roderick* and, significantly in view of the recent prohibitory legislation, nine "novels of chivalry," titles unspecified, unfortunately. These last items are of special interest since they indicate that light literature had reached the viceroyalty of Peru in or before the year 1549—a bare fifteen years after the founding of Lima by Pizarro. Despite the royal proscription of fiction books allegedly in force at this time, and despite the chaotic conditions of civil strife still prevailing in the "City of the Kings," as the Peruvian capital was called, copies of the popular literature of the times were already present there to beguile the local *aficionados*.

Scattering, fragmentary, and unsatisfactory as is the available evidence of the diffusion of books in the New World during the dynamic decades of the Conquest, little doubt remains that, wherever the Conquistador turned his adventurous steps, the romances of chivalry he enjoyed so passionately accompanied him or followed closely upon his heels, offering incentives to further heroic action, vicarious adventure in the intervals between his own prodigious experiences, and a consoling balm to his frustrated aspirations.

FAVORITE FICTION IX

IN THE LAST CHAPTER SOME OF THE MORE POPULAR FIC-
tion carried in stock by the Crombergers at Seville was indicated.
The titles listed represented in most cases the highest totals of
copies on hand and, presumably, were the ones in most demand
among the clientele of these publishers. The belief that many of
the works figuring in these inventories were intended for the consumption of the Conquistador and his associates finds support in the
fact that a comparison of these lists with manifests covering book
shipments to the Indies at a later date reveals considerable similarity. This observation tends to strengthen the presumption that
the Crombergers kept fairly large stocks ready to meet a demand
abroad which, with their protected monopoly, only they could
supply. Since there is a certain coincidence of titles on these lists
of the Seville printers and those of shipping documents later in
the century, some commentary is desirable on these particular
books and others which colonial readers appeared to prefer. In
this discussion, however, it is necessary, as already pointed out, to
move forward into the very last decades of the sixteenth century
to make comparative evaluations, owing to the unfortunate gap in
surviving records. This procedure is less misleading as a reflection
of the tastes of the conquerors and the generation following if due
consideration is given to the fact that, while new works appeared
throughout the century, reprintings of earlier favorites were frequent and numerous, and both, presumably, went overseas without
interruption in the undocumented interim. Thus testimony is offered of the sustained popularity of the older writings that beguiled
readers on both sides of the Atlantic during the long reigns of
Charles V and Philip II. A sampling of the incomplete registers of

ships leaving Seville and of some of the contemporary receipts and book lists discovered in Spanish American archives will permit specific mention of many types of literature enjoyed by the Conquistador and his heirs. These records are far too fragmentary and imperfect for statistical purposes and only observations of a general character can be derived from them.

It will surprise no one that theological, moral, and religious writings usually outnumber all other works on a given list, for theology and its cognates were the privileged science and learning of the time. Since the Conquest of the Spanish Indies was, in fact, the last Crusade, the Church's role in the drama was great and it soon directed the intellectual as well as the spiritual life of the new communities. Under the increased pressure of the Counter Reformation this influence was preponderant in the colonies and, with a settled order rapidly established in conquered territories, the multiplying clergy constituted an important section of the book-buying public. Roughly speaking, works of ecclesiastical character represented 70 to 85 percent of most colonial lists; the remaining 15 to 30 percent were divided about equally between secular nonfiction (history, geography, treatises on veterinary science, medicine, precious stones, architecture, music, manuals of instruction for lawyers, scribes and other public officials, almanacs, grammars, dictionaries, etc.) and purely creative writings. This small percentage would seem to reduce fiction books to a negligible total, but the actual number, nevertheless, was considerable, owing to the surprisingly large consignments of books to the Indies. The reading public of the various colonies, especially Mexico and Peru, was obviously much larger than has generally been supposed, and the preponderance of theological works imported is less significant when the fact is realized that the more creative and utilitarian writings undoubtedly passed from hand to hand far more freely than the large folio tomes in Latin which often gathered dust by disuse through decades and centuries on the shelves of monastery and convent libraries.[1] The extreme rarity today of early editions of novels, poems, and plays in surviving colonial collections of books suggests that the lighter forms of literature enjoyed a much wider currency among the conquerors and their descendants than the theological tracts. It is altogether likely that the more eagerly

sought *"libros profanos,"* for which many of the clergy also had a
fondness, were quickly thumbed out of existence. The ponderous
and more respected works, appealing to a small elite, were less read
and thus more easily resisted the ravages of time.

In this story of the Spanish Conquerors' books the concern is
chiefly for those forms of creative expression which entertained
these heroes and their immediate successors during their leisure,
and solaced their separation from the motherland, the cultural sun
that warmed their universe. What, then, were the specific fictional
works that these literate expatriates devoured with probably
greater eagerness than their stay-at-home relatives in Spain, thanks
to the immense distance, and their nostalgic yearning and reverence
for all things Spanish? These books were as varied as the literary
productions of the creative spirits of the Peninsula in its most
fecund period, and only those works of most frequent recurrence
on the contemporary book lists and imported in the largest quantities will be noted. A more exhaustive account would degenerate
into a mere catalogue of sixteenth-century Spanish literature. In
later chapters selected shipments will be studied more carefully
for their variety.

Throughout the period of conquest and exploration the novel
in its multiple manifestations, the picaresque, the pastoral and, of
course, the adventurous and sentimental romances of chivalry, enjoyed immense popularity. On the shipping manifests the last-
mentioned group normally constituted the largest single class of
fiction until the appearance of *Don Quixote* in 1605. This classification, however, is broadly interpreted to include not merely the
so-called *novelas de caballerías,* but also the more amorous tales
of varying length which partake of the characteristics of the true
novel of chivalry, some indeed with possibly a very tenuous relation to the genre. The enthusiasm of the sixteenth-century reading public was by no means limited to the chivalric novel strictly
defined, but extended to all narratives of fanciful and exotic adventure. However broad the term, it is safe to say that nearly every
species was represented in the continuous book shipments to the
Indies, though one notable exception, perhaps, should be made. The
many registers examined offer no indications of *Tirant lo Blanch,*

generally regarded as the earliest printed novel of chivalry indigenous to Spanish soil.

Topping the list of these chivalric romances, of course, are the units of the Amadis and Palmerin cycles. The imperfect data available point to conclusions which are possibly misleading and they lend themselves to some curious deductions. *Amadis of Gaul*, the founder of the dynasty, though widely read even late in the century, met with less favor toward the end than did his great-great-grandson, *Don Florisel de Niquea*. The probable reason for this development will appear presently. Further sampling of the lists suggests that Amadis senior was compelled to share honors fairly evenly with his son Esplandián, whose influence on the quest for Amazons was noted, and with his great-grandson, Amadis of Greece. The grandson, Lisuarte of Greece, did not please so much as his grandsire. Similarly, the founder of the rival Palmerin family, Palmerín of Oliva, had to bow to the achievements of his adventurous descendants. The fortunes of his son Primaleon, related in the novel of the same name, must have been followed by a wide audience in the Indies, for this title appears more frequently in the records than any others of the series. Indeed, in the last decades of the century, it is noted almost twice as often as *Amadis of Gaul*, though the total number of copies seems much less than those of the *Crónica de don Florisel de Niquea*.

Among the many imitations of the heroes of the two leading dynasties the one contained in the *Espejo de príncipes y caballeros* (Mirror of princes and knights) by Diego Ortúñez de Calahorra was apparently an outstanding favorite. It was published first in 1562 and a succession of second, third, and fourth parts made their appearance between then and 1589. Another contender was *El caballero del Febo* (The knight of Phoebus) by Esteban Corbera, printed in Barcelona and said to be patterned closely on the model of the *Espejo de príncipes y caballeros*. Both are characterized as the most prolix, absurd, and wearisome of the romances of chivalry. The *Caballero del Febo* is branded as a "vast encyclopedia of stupidity which came to consist of five parts and more than two thousand pages in two columns folio."[2] Both titles rank high on the ship registers, though usually in small quantities on individual orders, which fact indicates, perhaps, a fairly steady demand.

Another novel of relatively less frequent occurrence and one that was more charitably regarded by critics is *Lepolemo o el caballero de la Cruz* (Lepolemo or the knight of the Cross), which ran through ten editions from 1521 to 1600. The many other romances of this class need not be enumerated as their sporadic appearance on the lists suggests that they were held in somewhat less esteem by the Conquistador's descendants. A passing mention of *Don Cristalián de España*, written by a woman, Doña Beatriz Bernal, and first published in 1545, is of interest as indicating that Santa Teresa was not the only woman to conceive a novel of chivalry despite the efforts of contemporary moralists to shield that sex particularly from this form of pollution.

But shipments of chivalric fiction to the Indies were by no means restricted to that of Spanish origin. Romances translated or adapted from French and other sources poured into the colonies continuously. Many were comparatively short, some scarcely more than short stories or brief novelettes, but this brevity had special advantages in the overseas market. For Peninsular printers costs of manufacture, freight and other charges per unit were relatively reduced and the financial returns proportionately greater; for the colonists, paying two or more times as much per copy as the reader in Spain, the shorter books permitted a wider variety of items for their money. The Cromberger press at Seville produced many editions of this sort of light fiction, indicating that these monopolists were alert to such opportunities for enhanced profit.

The so-called Carlovingian cycle of romantic tales of this character was chiefly represented by the *Cuento del Emperador Carlos Maynes e de la Emperatriz Sevilla* (Story of the Emperor Charles Maines and the Empress Sevilla), regularly sent in moderate numbers of twenty or thirty copies to an order, often more. Of the Arthurian cycle the most common is the short *Crónica de los muy notables Caballeros Tablante de Ricamonte y de Jofre* (Chronicle of the very remarkable Knights Tablante of Ricamonte and of Jofre), whose author was a thousand times blessed by Cervantes in *Don Quixote*.[3]

More numerous are the short tales of varied origin grouped under the heading of the Greco-Oriental cycle, among which belong the following three, listed in the order of their apparent popularity among sixteenth-century colonial readers: *Flores y Blancaflor*, *Libro del esforzado cavallero Conde de Partinuples* (Book of the hardy knight Count of Partinuples), and *Pierres de Provenza y la linda Magalona* (Pierres of Provence and the beautiful Magalona). The first is a sentimental tale of two lovers, one the son of a Saracen king and the other the daughter of a Christian slave, a theme utilized in *Aucassin et Nicolette*.[4] If one is permitted to draw any conclusions from the frequent appearance of this title on the extant records, one may deduce that Victorian sentiment was acceptable to the heirs of the doughty conquerors in America long before it was Victorian in Europe.

The second tale, usually listed as merely "Partinuples," was translated from a French novel. It appears conspicuously on the shipping manifests, and is represented by larger numbers than most of the novels of the Amadis and Palmerin series. Published at Alacalá de Henares in 1513 and, therefore, an early favorite, it is characterized as "one of the best narratives of its kind, one of the most rationally composed, and one of the most ingenious in details although, perhaps, not one of the most refined."[5]

The third of this popular trio, its title usually shortened to "Magalona" in the shipping records, is a comparatively short romantic tale with some resemblance to the first. It was written in Provençal or Latin by Bernardo de Treviez and had enjoyed high favor with Petrarch, who is said to have spent some time in his youth correcting and polishing its style. This work is one of the best of its kind and the conspicuous note of piety in it would have claimed the indulgence of the Inquisition if that institution had been inclined to be severe with such literature, though certain touches of sensuality in it appear to have aroused the indignation of the great Spanish philosopher and moralist, Juan Luis Vives, whose strong disapproval of the romances of chivalry has been noticed.

An even less objectionable tale was entitled *La historia de los nobles cavalleros Oliveros de Castilla y Artus d'Algarbe* (The history of the noble knights Oliver of Castile and Artus of Algarbe). The moral and religious tendency of this novelette, exalting virtue and repentance, probably moved the officials of the Holy Office to regard it benignly. This work was often shipped in single orders of

twenty, thirty, and sixty copies. Of the miscellany of romances of
French origin *La espantosa y maravillosa vida de Roberto el Diablo*
(The terrible and marvelous life of Robert the Devil) should be
mentioned. Another story of repentance toward which the Inquisition could well afford to be indulgent, it is rarely missing on
shipping documents in Seville or in orders for books drawn up in
the New World, and usually it appears in substantial numbers of
copies.

The vogue of the romance of chivalry was a vortex into which
fantastic and sentimental legends and stories of every kind and
origin were caught up and whirled about in an effort of enterprising printers to exploit the popular appetite for the adventurous
and the exotic. The inspiration of purely Spanish themes, added to
those of French extraction, was not enough. The literature of
Italy, Greece, Rome, and even the Orient were laid under heavy
contribution to supply the inexhaustible demand. Only those works
most frequently represented on the ship registers need be mentioned.

The *Espejo de caballerías* (Mirror of knighthood)—not to be
confused with the *Espejo de caballeros* (Mirror of knights)—was,
in the first of its three parts at least, a translation in prose of Boiardo's
Orlando innamorato.[6] This classic, together with the *Orlando
furioso*, which appears on many lists, enjoyed wide favor in the
colonies. Italian prose writings, sometimes in the original language,
were common enough on the list, including Boccaccio, the *Arcadia*
of Sannazaro, and the *Asolani* of Bembo, besides *Cortegiano* of
Baldassare Castiglione.

Another compilation from various Italian poems was called *El
libro . . . del noble y esforzado caballero Reinaldos de Montalbán*
(The book of the noble and hardy knight Reinaldos of Montalban).
Still another title often noted was the "Trapisondas de Don Rey-
naldos," which may refer to *La Trapisonda que es tercero libro de
Don Reinaldos* (The Trapisonda, which is the third book of Don
Reinaldos). Scarcely more than a short story but exceedingly popular was the *Historia del muy valiente y esforzado cavallero Clamades
hijo de Marcaditis, Rey de Castilla, y Clarmonda* (History of the
very bold and hardy knight Clamades, son of Marcaditas, King of
Castile, and Clarmonda), a tale apparently of Oriental origin which

entered Spain by way of France. Large quantities of this pamphlet went abroad in most of the sixteenth-century fleets to the Indies. Another work of unmistakable Oriental derivation was the *Doncella Teodor*, consisting of only sixteen sheets, usually dispatched in lots of a hundred copies and more. This was a version of a tale from the *Arabian Nights*, and the only one incorporated into popular Castilian literature directly from Arabic.[7] And with similar frequency in similar quantities the short *Historia del Rey Canamor del Infante Turian su hijo* (History of the King Canamor and of the Infante Turian his son) reached colonial readers.

At least two stories from the ancients were available to fiction lovers on both sides of the Atlantic in the century of the Conquest. One was the *Historia de los amores de Clareo y Florisea* (History of the love of Clareo and Florisea), written by Alonso Nuñez de Reinoso and first printed at Venice in 1552. Professing to write with a higher moral purpose than the authors of novels of chivalry, Nuñez de Reinoso succumbs to many of the exaggerations of the current reading favorites. But this book is of interest as having influenced Cervantes in his *Persiles y Segismunda*, which enjoyed considerable popularity in the Indies in the seventeenth century.

The second of the tales deriving from the ancients and often found in the registers after 1587 was *Teagenes y Clariquea*, sometimes called the *Historia Ethiopica* (Ethiopian History), by the Greek novelist Heliodorus. An edition of this work appeared in the year mentioned, the latest of a series of translations and one that continued to find acceptance late in the eighteenth century.

Of particular interest in this discussion of the conquerors' books is a sentimental work, reprinted many times, called *Selva de aventuras* (Forest of adventures). Divided into seven books, this tale contains nearly all the ingredients necessary to appeal to the most varied interests of readers. A fair maiden known as Arbolea politely spurns the offer of marriage by Luzman, a friend since infancy, and declares her intention of entering a convent. The disconsolate young man then wanders about Italy where numerous people insist on telling him more or less sad stories of their lives. Thus varied character types and pastoral episodes, interspersed with bits of lyric verse, enliven the narrative. Turning his steps homeward at last, Luzman has the customary ill fortune of falling into the hands of Moorish pirates. In due time he is ransomed, and reaches Seville just as Arbolea is taking the veil. Unshaken in her determination despite the convincing proof of love and fidelity given by Luzman, she urges him to seek another as his wife and to settle down. The hero nobly announces that he will follow a course similar to Arbolea's and spend the rest of his days in meditation at a hermitage not far from her convent. This ultrasentimental conclusion helped to give the novel an immense popularity among the more effete descendants of the conquerors and afforded an antecedent to *El peregrino en su patria* (The pilgrim in his native land) by the great Spanish dramatist Lope de Vega. Curiously enough this tender love story fell under the displeasure of the Inquisition and was placed upon the *Index expurgatorius,* a surprising fact since "everything in it breathes of seriousness and propriety and it is inexplicable that the Holy Office, which was so indulgent or indifferent to this type of literature, should make the rare exception of putting *Luzman and Arbolea* on the *Index of prohibited books.*"[8] Such an act seems strange, indeed, for the *Selva de aventuras* appears constantly on the registers throughout the sixteenth century and in such large quantities as to place it among the consistent "best sellers" in the Indies.

The widespread demand for chivalric literature was so insatiable that every resource of the imagination was strained to satisfy it. The adventures and loves of valiant knights were even composed in verse form for the voracious public, but they failed to arouse as much enthusiasm as the prose narratives and appear only occasionally on the registers. One of the earliest of these metrical narratives was *El caballero determinado* (The determined knight). This work was a particular favorite of the Emperor Charles V, for it was essentially an allegory of the life of his father, who was known as "Philip the Handsome." The author of this fiction, Oliver de La Marche, had been a servant of the Emperor's grandmother, María de Borgoña, and had written the tale for her entertainment or consolation. Charles V subsequently commissioned Hernando de Acuña to translate it into *antiguas coplas castellanas.* Both the French and the Spanish versions the abdicated emperor took with him into retirement at Yuste and his son and successor later kept them in his possession until his own death.[9] This composition met with considerable success, being reprinted seven times during the sixteenth century, a fact possibly attributable to the royal interest manifested in this chivalric novel. Other versified romances appearing with some frequency on the records of colonial shipments are *Celidón de Iberia*, by Gonzalo Gómez de Luque, published in 1583; *Florando de Castilla*, by Gerónimo Huesta, 1588; and *Caballero de la clara estrella* (The knight of the bright star), a poem in *octavas reales* by Andrés de Losa.

As already noticed, the Inquisition passed over all the romances of chivalry and sentimental tales in silence, the only exception being the comparatively innocuous *Selva de aventuras*. It is entirely true that these authorities were remarkably tolerant of popular taste in literature despite the clamor of moralists and reformers, and they seldom made use of the ready means of proscription. This fact should temper the harsh criticism of this institution since it indicates that, in the sixteenth century, at least, and during the full flood of the Counter Reformation, the sway of the Holy Office was less completely despotic than is commonly believed. With respect to books of fiction secular authorities had shown themselves less indulgent in the repeated decrees banning the literature of entertainment in the Indies, though they were animated primarily by concern for the welfare of the Indians rather than by a desire to suppress these books entirely. The Inquisition, of course, was not utterly indifferent and possibly some of the secular opposition was of ecclesiastical inspiration. Angry denunciations of the romances of chivalry by representatives of the Church were common in the pulpits and in print, but outwardly, at least, the Holy Office wisely chose to take no action. Exception to this policy is indicated toward the end of the century when, perhaps to fight fire with fire, it sanctioned the publication of romances *a lo divino* which exalted Christian virtues and were free of the cruder blemishes, though often stooping to the ridiculous. A few of these rather insipid antidotes found their way into the colonies in much smaller quantities than their more profane brethren, but it seems likely that these mild efforts to combat the plague were ineffective—the strength of the epidemic of chivalric romances was already spent. It suffices to mention only two of these pious tales found in the shipping records, *El caballero del sol* (Knight of the sun) by Pedro Hernández de

Villaumbrales, printed in 1552, and *Caballero Asisio* (Knight Assisi) by Friar Gabriel Mata, dated 1587. The latter was a prolix poem about St. Francis in the garb of a knight of chivalry and some of the saints of his Order.

The sentimental character of much of the fiction mentioned suggests that the conqueror and his descendants did not limit themselves to vicarious adventures of a warlike nature; on the contrary, they appeared to like the latter best when well diluted with tender sentiment and lofty idealism. In time this yearning for refinement and elegance in their leisure reading came to predominate. Even before the tumult of the conquest subsided this trend was visible, and the romances of chivalry that had falsified the glory of martial combat were yielding to another form of narrative which falsified even more completely the peace of bucolic existence. This newer literary fashion brought forth the so-called pastoral novel, which rivaled, if it did not equal or exceed, the earlier popularity of the chivalric fiction. The recounting in a mixture of prose and lyric verse of the idyls of rustic shepherds and lassies in idealized rural settings would seem an extreme of escape literature. Indeed, these saccharine tales appear even more soporific than the tediousness of repetitious knight-errantry, yet their acceptance was unmistakable, both in Spain and in the viceroyalties of the New World. If the *Arcadias, Dianas,* and *Galateas* individually did not total as high on the registers as the *Amadises, Belianis,* and *Trapisondas,* they were often on lists from which the chivalric novels were entirely lacking.

The highly artificial genre of the pastoral tale could trace its origin back to antiquity. The frequent appearance of Vergil's *Georgics* in sixteenth-century book lists is doubtless explained in part by the current vogue, while the occasional presence of Boccaccio's *Ameto* (1341) indicates more recent inspiration. Practically coinciding with the first known edition of *Amadis of Gaul* was the lachrymose *Arcadia,* by the Italian Jacopo Sannazaro, whose twelve doleful eclogues captivated colonial readers for a century and encouraged numerous imitations. Its cloying sentimentality and idealized landscapes contaminated contemporary novels of chivalry. *Don Florisel de Niquea,* by Feliciano Silva, which appeared in 1532, has its hero, in the first two parts, doffing his armor and assuming the garb of a shepherd in order to follow the shepherdess Sylvia, the object of his affections. The second book of the fourth part, which came from the press in 1551, includes an eclogue containing a dialogue between two shepherds, Archileo and Laris, and the poetical contests described therein anticipate one of the important features of Jorge Montemayor's later *Diana*. These pastoral episodes intercalated in a novel of chivalry doubtless account for the pronounced popularity that *Don Florisel de Niquea* appeared to enjoy among colonial readers in the second half of the sixteenth century. Even as late as 1601, in a register covering the largest single shipment of books noted in the surviving records, no other novel of chivalry approaches the total of 130 copies of *Don Florisel* included. The only other work with a comparable number in this particular consignment is Lope de Vega's pastoral novel, *Arcadia*.

But the work which definitely established the success of this ultra-unrealistic genre was the *Siete libros de la Diana* (Seven books of the Diana) by the Portuguese-born Jorge de Montemayor. First appearing about 1559, its acceptance in Spain and in the Indies was only less than that of *Amadis of Gaul*. It was reprinted seventeen times during the sixteenth century and at least eight more editions appeared in the next hundred years. Its fame is attested by the continuations it inspired, by the parodies it evoked, and by the translations into various languages it underwent, which spread its renown over Europe. Almost plotless, it recounts the fruitless wooing of the shepherdess Diana by the rustic Sereno (apparently Montemayor himself). The fantastic elements, such as enchantments, magic springs, and spells, and the insertion of extraneous episodes, so familiar in the novels of chivalry, partly explain the easy transfer from one literary vogue to another. But despite the undoubted refinement of language and the charm of its lyric passages, both prose and verse, the enthusiasm of sixteenth-century readers, particularly the heirs of the hardy Conquistador, for the pastoral theme remains a puzzling enigma. The shipping registers and other contemporary lists, however, attest unmistakably to its popularity, for they are sprinkled not only with Montemayor's masterpiece but with sequels by other writers such as Alonso Pérez (1564), and the more inspired *Diana enamorada* of

Gaspar Gil Polo (1564). Two of the giants of Spain's Golden Age of letters, Cervantes and Lope de Vega, exploited the profitable literary fad by writing similar works, the first his *Galatea* in 1585, and the second his *Arcadia* in 1598. Both these titles promptly made their regular appearance in substantial numbers in book shipments to the Indies.

Noted with particular frequency also is the well-written *Pastor de Fílida* (Shepherd of Filida) by Luis Gálvez de Montalvo (1582), a *nouvelle à clef*, reprinted five times in a few years, which rivaled Cervantes' *Galatea* in popularity. Proof that these sentimental tales strongly influenced the daily lives and thinking of their readers, much as the romances of chivalry had done, is evident in the denunciations of moralists who urged that the pastoral novels be banned as well. Montemayor's *Diana* played its part in the mental derangement of Don Quixote, for it will be recalled that the niece of this worthy knight urged that this particular book be burned along with the others in the library "because it's not too much to expect that, when my uncle has been cured of the disease of knighthood, he will take a notion, on reading books such as these, to become a shepherd and wander through the woods and meadows singing and piping and, what would be worse, become a poet which, they say, is a contagious and incurable affliction."[10]

If the popular taste of the sixteenth century ran rather strongly to fantastic adventure and soporific sentimentality, there was always a minority of readers who enjoyed a more protein fare of realism. To this discerning group the dialogued novel *Tragicomedia de Calixto y Melibea*, commonly called *La Celestina* and ranked as second only to *Don Quixote* as a work of art in Spanish literature, was a favorite modestly represented on many book lists. The fusion of idealism in the ill-fated passion of the aristocratic lovers, Calixto and Melibea, and the realism of the underworld of the wily go-between, Celestina, who could "provoke hard rocks to sensuality if she has a mind to it," constituted a masterpiece which insured steady if not large sales for over two centuries after its first publication in 1499. Despite the distinction of incurring the wrath of the moralists which the *Celestina* shared with the romances of chivalry, it had at least twenty-two editions in the sixteenth century and inspired numerous continuations. Invariably indicated as merely "Celestina" on the book lists of the period, it is seldom clear whether this designation refers to the original work or to some of its sequels also shipped for colonial consumption.

Even more completely realistic was the first and most famous of the picaresque novels *La vida de Lazarillo de Tormes* (The life of Lazarillo of Tormes), like the *Celestina* of obscure authorship. This satire, which appeared in 1553, is in the form of an auto-biography in colloquial and racy style and describes, among other aspects of contemporary society, the licentious life of some of the clergy, which fact subjected it to expurgation by the Inquisition. Thanks to this editing it again circulated freely in a somewhat subdued form under the title of *Lazarillo castigado* (Lazarillo chastened), often bound with a play entitled *Propalladia* by Torres Naharro. Possibly the severe pruning of the first novel of this sort accounts for the fact that, save for some inferior continuations, the picaresque theme remained largely unexploited until the very end of the sixteenth century when, amidst much moralizing, the enter-taining adventures of another earthy picaroon are recounted in the pages of Mateo Alemán's famous *Guzmán de Alfarache* (1599).

Colonial readers displayed a mild partiality for what they be-lieved was history. The hazy line between fact and fancy, which invested the "lying histories" of Amadis and his kind with so much authority, probably accounts for the fairly steady demand, particu-larly during the last decades, for works purporting to be factual accounts. The more popular titles on contemporary book lists were often little more than historical novels. Most of them borrowed the well-worn technique of the romances of chivalry by alleging trans-lation or adaptation from authentic accounts. Various early chron-icles in printed form recur in modest numbers, of which the most common is, perhaps, the previously noted *Chronicle of King Don Roderick, with the destruction of Spain*, by Pedro del Corral. Its acceptability is easily explained by the fact that it is merely a different sort of tale of knight-errantry presenting the legend of Roderick and the betrayal of Spain to the Moorish invaders, replete with descriptions of tourneys, jousts, individual combats, sumptuous gardens, and so on. Roderick becomes a reasonable and attractive

facsimile of Amadis of Gaul and both are fixed as historical personages in the imaginations of readers. This alleged chronicle was
actually the earliest historical novel on a national theme and was
reprinted again and again throughout the sixteenth century. Indeed,
its influence was felt long afterward in *The vision of Don Roderick*
by Walter Scott, in *Roderick the last of the Goths* by Robert
Southey, and in *Legends of the conquest of Spain* by Washington
Irving. The *Crónica Troyana* (Trojan chronicle), relating the fall
of Troy and a title used for several distinct accounts of the same
event, is another pseudohistorical work with chivalric trappings
that was read with pleasure by the heirs of the New World conquerors.

As already noted, the various writings of Bishop Antonio de
Guevara, particularly his celebrated *Libro áureo de Marco Aurelio*
(Golden book of Marcus Aurelius), are seldom missing from sixteenth-century book lists, thus tending to confirm the statement
that this work was as widely read as *Amadis of Gaul* and the
Celestina. A sort of epistolary novel allegedly based on letters of
the Roman Emperor, the maxims, admonitions, pedagogic precepts,
and pompous platitudes expressed in rhetorical style would appear
tedious fare for expatriated readers, yet they were seemingly devoted to it. The work was astoundingly popular, being translated
into the leading languages of Europe, including Latin, and it inspired a flattering crop of imitations, both in Spain and abroad. Its
universal acceptance encouraged other moral tracts by the good
bishop, and his *Menosprecio de corte* (Contempt of court life),
Aviso de privados (Counsel for favorites) and *Epístolas familiares*
(Familiar epistles) dot the shipping lists of the century.

Of historical origin is the charming tale of two Moorish lovers
protected by a magnanimous Spanish *alcaide* (warden), known as
the *Historia de Abencerraje y la hermosa Jarifa*. This sentimental
novelette rarely appears by title on the lists but is often present,
intercalated in or appended to other works such as the *Inventario*
(1565) of Antonio de Villegas.

Toward the end of the century a constantly recurring favorite
was the famous *Guerras civiles de Granada* (Civil wars of Granada)
by Gines Pérez de Hita, of which there were at least twenty editions published between 1595 and 1631. It was a fictional account

of the bloody feuds of the Zegríes and Abencerrajes during the last days of Moorish rule, allegedly based on an Arabic manuscript but obviously inspired by popular ballads growing out of the long warfare with the Moslems. Its episodes of adventure, love, personal combats of Christians and Mohammedans, and so on, made its appeal irresistible to readers long conditioned by the literature of chivalry. Indeed, its picturesque style makes the *Guerras civiles de Granada* one of the most readable products of Spanish letters of the period, and Washington Irving was not averse to imitating it in his *Chronicle of the conquest of Granada*. In the partly autobiographic novel *El periquillo sarniento* (The itching parrot) (1816) by the Mexican pamphleteer, Fernández de Lizardi, which mirrors the social life of the closing years of the colonial regime, this historical narrative of Gines Pérez de Hita, apparently, was still read with enthusiasm by the youth of the land, for the schoolmaster of the picaresque hero warns his pupils against reading such *boberas* as that sixteenth-century work.

The novel in prose had its counterparts in verse, for the century of conquest was the flourishing period of the epic or heroic poem, often inspired by the stirring models of Ariosto and Tasso. This glorious epoch of high adventure in the Old and New Worlds alike did not fail to offer themes for long metrical compositions reflecting the zestful spirit of the time. The most striking is the *La Araucana* of Alonso de Ercilla, which describes the struggle of the Spaniards and the Araucanian Indians in Chile. This lengthy poem played its part in introducing into Europe the concept of the "noble savage", later to find artistic expression in Continental literature. *La Araucana* is generally regarded as the greatest heroic verse in the Spanish language and its early recognition and popularity are confirmed by the continued presence of this title and its succeeding parts on contemporary book lists. Almost as frequently observed is a similar classic on the tremendous feat of Vasco da Gama, the *Luisiades* by the Portuguese poet, Camoens. Other narratives in verse commonly appearing are the *Austriada* (1584) of Juan Rufo, recounting in graphic fashion the successful suppression of Moorish rebellion by John of Austria, a contemporary event appealing greatly to the patriotism of Spaniards on both sides of the

Atlantic; the *Monserrate* (1588) by Cristóbal de Virués, relating the legend of the hermit Garín and the founding of the famous monastery overlooking the city of Barcelona; and the *Navas de Tolosa* (1594), a very dull poem concerning the epochal victory of Alfonso VIII over the Moors in the thirteenth century.

Other forms of poetry were also a part of the literary diet of the conquerors and their descendants. The romances or ballads dear to the heart of the Spanish people had, like the novels of chivalry, played their part in the conquest of the New World and the universal familiarity with and love of the traditional assonanted verse passed on to successive generations in the Indies. *Romanceros*, or collections of ballads, are found on practically every book list, often as the sole representatives of lighter literature in inventories of arid tomes owned by or consigned to some learned ecclesiastic. The poetic writings of Boscán, Garcilaso de la Vega, Juan de Mena, and Juan de la Cueva, along with translations of Italian epic and lyric poets, particularly Ariosto, Boiardo, Petrarch, and Sannazaro, also found a welcome in the far-off Indies.

Dialogued verse was still a potential rather than an actual indulgence toward the end of the century of conquest. The theater had already begun to win a preferred place among the popular amusements of the masses, but the reading of plays was, on the whole, slight until Lope de Vega's comedies appeared in print shortly after the turn of the seventeenth century. Before the great age of the Spanish theater, items such as the tragedies of Seneca and the dramatic writings of Aristophanes are occasionally noted. Now and then *comedias* by Lope de Rueda, the manager of a strolling company of players, whom Cervantes greatly admired, are found on the sixteenth-century lists, but more often the awkward and inartistic works of the Andalusian poet and playwright Juan de la Cueva, who spent a few years in Mexico, were offered to colonial readers. This inept dramatist's happy idea of utilizing national themes sung in popular ballads insured him a reading audience to which the artistic merits of his plays scarcely entitled him.

This lengthy but incomplete catalogue of the light literature of the Spanish New World settlers of the sixteenth century should not end without mention of a few works of miscellaneous character revealing the varied tastes of these readers. The weird and macabre had an appeal that prefigured a similar enthusiasm for the pulpwood fiction of the twentieth century, to judge by the frequency with which the *Historias prodigiosas* (Prodigious stories) is encountered. This was an excellent translation from the French of Pierre Bouaisteau, apparently by another enterprising bookseller of Seville, Andrea Pescioni by name, and it proved to be a remarkably profitable commercial venture. Apparitions, ghosts, nocturnal visions, malignant spirits, souls in torment, abnormal beings, and other perverse creatures of a fevered imagination flitted eerily through the pages of this swollen compilation of dark tales which must have sent chills up and down colonial spines. Scarcely less thrilling were the chapters on earthquakes, volcanic eruptions, floods, the spawning of monsters, and other dread aberrations of Nature, all solemnly recorded as actual facts. Full of the mythical lore harking back to the Middle Ages, this work also represented an early response to a taste for the fiction of pseudo science which Jules Verne, H. G. Wells, and others of a later age were to exploit so advantageously.

This French compilation, like many other writings of the time in Europe, owed much to Spanish sources, one of which was a similar assemblage of twisted fact and fancy with a long-standing popularity in Spain, its Indies, and in Europe generally. This earlier work was the *Silva de varia lección* (Forest [or collection] of various stories) by Pero Mexía, Charles V's chronicler, which first saw the light in 1540 and had some twenty-six editions in Spanish as well as many translations. Less preoccupied with the strange and abnormal than the *Historias prodigiosas*, it was an aggregation of curiosities of history, archaeology, and alleged science, anecdotal in character but bearing a stamp of authenticity. Written in a cultivated style and with obvious moral purpose, its apparent high authority as the handiwork of an imperial chronicler and its own inherent interest claimed for this work a renown not easily comprehended today. If the romances of chivalry had played their part in the delirium of the Conquest, compilations such as the *Silva de varia lección* and the *Historias prodigiosas* explain, perhaps, the persistence of superstitions and strange notions of later explorers and settlers concerning the mysteries of the physical world just beyond their horizon.

Booksellers found miscellanies particularly susceptible of sustained sales both in Spain and in the Indies, and the more enterprising of the guild devised numerous works of this character for their trade. One of the most successful or, perhaps, the most famous was Juan de Timoneda, a Valencian printer about whom little is known. In 1563, or possibly before, he brought together a collection of brief tales, little more than anecdotes extracted from various sources, which he called *El sobremesa o alivio de caminantes* (Relaxation for travelers). In the main the contents were mere synopses of stories by Boccaccio, Poggio, Bandello, Guevara, and others, succinctly and attractively phrased. The work appeared in two parts, the first containing ninety-three and the second seventy-two stories in digest form. While Timoneda's other compilations were acceptable and brought considerable sales, the most popular, judging by recurrence on colonial lists, is the well-known *Patrañuelo*, or Fabulous tales, consisting of a group of twenty-two short stories, fables or *patrañas*, the first collection in Spanish of novelettes imitating Italian models and written in easy, natural prose.

Timoneda's commercial success appears to have played its part in the formation of an important sixteenth-century collection of stories and anecdotes called *Floresta española de apotegmas y sentencias*, by Melchor de Santa Cruz, first published in 1574 and quickly popular in the Indies. It is largely a compilation of apothegms and sayings, folkloric in character, arranged in twelve parts and associated with categories of persons such as bishops, knights, soldiers, merchants, musicians, and students, and incidents such as duels, games, love affairs, thefts, and hold-ups, a rich mine that later storytellers and playwrights drew upon heavily.

But to continue this description of the light reading of the conquerors and their heirs in the Spanish Indies would be to undertake a long and tedious recapitulation of sixteenth-century Spanish literature. Many other works unmentioned doubtless deserve equal space and it is possible that some were more widely read. About this the surviving fragmentary records and the imperfect data they preserve permit no certainty. But whether or not proper priority and emphasis have been bestowed in this catalogue of the entertaining literature enjoyed in the contemporary New World, the main fact is abundantly clear that, during the century before the Pilgrims landed in New England, the luxury of light reading was well rooted in the broad realms to the south which the courage and daring of Spanish conquerors and Christian missionaries had won for the King of Spain, and that the descendants of these bold adventurers were privileged to enjoy the pleasures of the printed page which their English counterparts were not to know fully until generations later.

THE HOUSE OF TRADE AND X
THE CONQUERORS' BOOKS

T HE SAMPLING OF THE SIXTEENTH-CENTURY RECORDS
reveals a remarkable quantity and diversity of fiction books dispatched annually from Seville to the far-off Spanish Indies and it
gives a basis for the conjecture that a higher proportion of literacy
existed among the adventurers pouring into the new lands than has
hitherto been conceded. It is barely possible, indeed, that the percentage of these migrants to the New World who could read was
greater than that of the less active and less enterprising elements of
the population who remained in the Peninsula. Whatever the truth,
merchants of the Andalusian capital profited greatly from a surprisingly large volume of export business in books which passed
through their hands. The fact that light literature, such as that
reported in the last chapter, and secular nonfiction constituted a
relatively small part of the book trade with the colonies, strengthens
the impression that the traffic in these commodities, of which ecclesiastical works are the major portion, was very considerable.
Obviously, the expanding colonial communities required many
other manufactured articles from the motherland and the cases of
books occupied but little of the cargo space of the clumsy galleons,
yet the many consignments of printed works listed on the registers
indicate that the total commerce with the Indies must have filled
these diminutive vessels to capacity. To control this voluminous
trans-Atlantic trade the Crown found it necessary to set up a
special agency only a few years after Columbus' momentous discovery. This institution was the *Casa de Contratación* or House of
Trade or, as some prefer to call it, the India House, definitely established at Seville in 1503.[1]

In the light of conditions existing in the Spanish Peninsula at the beginning of the sixteenth century it was probably inevitable that the southern city on the Guadalquivir river should become the seat of an organization for regulating commercial activities with the New World possessions. There were, to be sure, sound reasons why the Andalusian capital should *not* have been designated as the sole terminal port of the colonial trade and why other cities with equally good or better claims to the same distinction, such as Cádiz, Málaga and Barcelona, should have been selected. These latter coastal centers had more accessible harbors and better facilities for ocean-going vessels, on the whole, than Seville, and some had other geographic advantages which that city sorely lacked. Seville was, in fact, an inland municipality located some twenty leagues up the Guadalquivir river; its approach from the sea necessitated a difficult and dangerous crossing of the bar of San Lucar de Barrameda at its mouth and a risky ascent of the narrow and tortuous stream to the city wharves—a feat hard at any time even for galleons of light burden, and progressively more hazardous as the channel silted up and as vessels became of deeper draught. Even in the first half of the sixteenth century, when the Conquistador was embarking at that port on his New World adventures, returning ships were obliged to discharge part of their cargoes some eight leagues below the city before tying up at its docks.[2] And all too frequently departing fleets tarried for weeks at the river mouth awaiting a favorable conjunction of wind, tide, and clear sky to permit a safe passing of the sandy bar. During this tedious maneuvering ships often became entangled, broke their cables, lost their anchors, and drifted on to the rocks. But despite these severe handicaps Seville retained a nearly complete trade monopoly until 1717 when its long-standing rival, Cádiz, became the terminus of the transoceanic commerce and the House of Trade transferred many of its activities to that Atlantic port.

That Seville thus retained its privileged place for more than two centuries is explained largely by certain historical, political, and economic factors such as often in the affairs of men outweigh for a time more logical considerations. Since its recapture from the Moors by Ferdinand the Saint in the thirteenth century, the city on the Guadalquivir had been a flourishing commercial center appended to politically ascendent Castile, which granted it special favors, and the resulting prosperity attracted many foreign merchants and industries to this community. More recently its importance was increased by the crowning triumph of Isabel and Ferdinand in driving the Moslems from Granada. Seville thus became the most populous and opulent city of Isabel's domain by the coincidence of this victory with the sudden acquisition of vast territories beyond the ocean sea; now the geographic inconvenience of the Andalusian city offered definite advantages to the monarch of landlocked Castile. The inland situation of the river port had a double merit, for thus it was relatively nearer the interior provinces where the Queen held court, and it was more secure from piratical attack by sea. Circumstances conspired, therefore, to give the merchants of the city on the banks of the Guadalquivir a trade monopoly and a privileged position in the affairs of the nation which they jealously guarded for generations.

Prior to the establishment of the House of Trade maritime expeditions had departed from various ports. The first voyage of Columbus, it will be recalled, started from the little town of Palos near the mouth of the Río Tinto and directly west of Seville; his second and larger expedition was prepared at Cádiz, which continued as the chief port of embarkation for nearly a decade thereafter. By this time, however, the multiplying activities of conquest, exploration, and trade called for an organization to facilitate preparation, equipment, and control of these new enterprises. If there was any hesitancy in deciding upon the proper location for this agency, the powerful commercial elements of Seville doubtless practiced an early sixteenth-century form of lobbying at the royal Court by which they convinced the Crown's advisers with little difficulty that such an institution belonged nowhere but in their fair city. By a decree of February 14, 1503, signed at Alcalá de Henares, the House of Trade was duly set up at the river port.

This governmental bureau of commerce was installed in the royal Alcazar, or Palace, near the magnificent cathedral and close by the towering Giralda, which still dominates the sky line of Seville, and on this site, with other buildings added as activities increased, the House of Trade remained in whole or in part until its final extinction late in the eighteenth century. The functions of this

SEVILLE AT THE END OF THE SIXTEENTH CENTURY

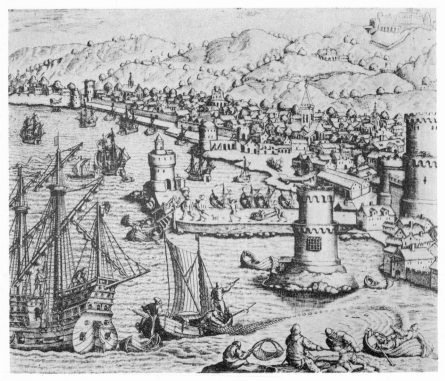

THE SIXTEENTH-CENTURY SEVILLE WHARF FRONT

agency were both administrative and scientific, and as its operations grew more complex—it supervised the trade with the Canary
Islands and with Spanish posts in North Africa as well as with the
distant possessions in America—the modest initial staff evolved into
a ponderous bureaucracy. Besides having to carry out the extremely
detailed operations of fitting out maritime expeditions, issuing licenses, registering cargoes, determining quantities of products for
the colonies, collecting export and import duties, inspecting outgoing and returning ships, taking care of the royal fifth of precious
metals, preventing contraband, receiving goods of deceased persons
and seeking their legal heirs, and so on, the House of Trade was a
legislative and judicial body. Its duties in these latter categories
multiplied enormously as claims, disputes, and perplexing differences
arose in the expanding commerce and as efficiency declined in the
enveloping bureaucratic red tape.

The remarkable scientific activities of this institution soon transformed it into a vast repository of geographic, cartographic, and
hydrographic information. Pilots and shipowners were compelled
to keep daily logs of their voyages, giving detailed descriptions of
places visited, tides, currents, winds encountered, bearings, and
other nautical observations. The House of Trade was also a school
of navigation, giving training, both theoretical and practical, to
pilots and mariners. The research and technical instruction thus
carried on made it the first and most important school of navigation
in modern Europe.

As originally organized this bureau of commerce had three main
divisions, each with its department head and staff. These were:
(1) a treasurer, charged with the care of the gold, silver, and
precious stones brought by returning ships, with setting apart the
royal fifth, and with collecting excise duties; (2) a comptroller,
responsible for the registers of persons and commodities to or from
the Indies; and (3) a factor or business manager, whose duties included outfitting and provisioning fleets for the round trip, pur-
chasing supplies and armaments, and taking charge of all merchandise except the precious metals handled by the treasurer. In
due course, expanding activities required the installation of other
officers, such as the Pilot Chief (the first of whom was Amerigo
Vespucci) to train pilots and sailors in nautical sciences; the Post-

master General, to direct the regular and special postal services, prescribing routes and similar details; and the Cosmographer, a sort of research official who devoted himself primarily to theoretical navigation and the collection of maps, charts, and other maritime records.

Thus the House of Trade at Seville was an important arm of the royal government for the control of the colonial trade of the Peninsula. Across its wharves and through its warehouses passed the coveted treasure of the Indies and the varied manufactures of Spain and Europe. Among the latter goods destined for the lands won by the blood, sweat, and valor of the Conquistador were many books, from the large folios to the small chapbooks, bound in leather, vellum or paper, all silent but eloquent partners in the great task of spreading western civilization and Spanish culture to the ends of the earth. In this world-wide diffusion of the creative spirit of Europe, of which Hispanic letters were the spearhead, it is of interest to study the mechanics of distribution beginning with the procedures at Seville preliminary to transportation overseas.

From the little printing shops of Castile and Aragon as well as those of Seville itself came pack trains of patient, plodding burros laden with boxes of books. They were headed for the port of embarkation of the annual fleets to the Spanish Indies; some of the small packing cases they carried were filled with assorted volumes ordered by colonial merchants, while others held a good part of an entire edition of a single work just off the press and now hurriedly forwarded to the Andalusian city before sailing time so that a whole year might not elapse before these literary novelties reached an overseas public willing to pay high prices for them. Along the sometimes dusty, sometimes miry highways, fording the sometimes shallow, sometimes flooded creeks and arroyos, and through the narrow, cobbled streets of villages trudged these diminutive beasts of burden until at last they came to a weary halt at the warehouses along the river front of the inland port. This scene was a familiar feature of Andalusian life in the late fall, the winter, and the early spring as the tiring trek was concluded from Salamanca, Madrid, Alcalá de Henares, Medina del Campo, Valladolid, Zaragoza, and other centers of the Peninsula. In these sheds were deposited the heavy chests and cases, which helped to swell the mounting confusion of merchandise to be loaded on the galleons preparing to sail to America in the spring and early summer. The majority of these book consignments would eventually reach Nombre de Dios on the Isthmus of Panama, or, as the sixteenth century drew to a close, Puertobelo in the same locality, or they would go to Vera Cruz in New Spain, from which places they would go forward by land and sea to their ultimate destination. A few would stop at the larger islands of the Antilles or on the northern mainland of South America.

It was a common practice for the bookseller in Spain to consign his shipment to one or more individuals known to him in these New World ports of entry. These agents then forwarded the cases to their destinations in the larger cities where the local dealers, who had originally ordered the books from Spain, disposed of them to their clientele. Frequently the owner himself accompanied his wares to the Indies, sold or exchanged them at a handsome profit, and returned to Spain. The passenger lists of the galleons invariably included these itinerant merchants whom the House of Trade permitted to travel with fewer restrictions than other members of society, and these peddlers made the arduous crossing of the Atlantic repeatedly. Some enterprising individuals in the colonies appear to have financed a visit to Spain by stocking up there with goods, especially books, which they brought back to the New World and sold at a goodly margin of profit. But probably more often it was a Spaniard bound for the Indies to make his fortune who took with him an assortment of articles, including handy-sized books, to peddle in the provinces. This type of thrifty immigrant, often a peasant, became the *nouveau riche* of colonial society, much detested by the aristocratic Spaniard and the indolent Creole living on the tribute of the conquered Indian. Now and then a town councilman or other official of Seville indulged in a bit of private speculation by shipping a case or two of easily selling books to a friend or relative in one of the overseas centers. Passengers could, however, and frequently did, take with them a box of books for their own use, in which case the titles were listed in a *memoria* rather than on a formal register. This practice was usual with missionaries and clergymen embarking for evangelical work in the New World. While most of these documents indicate purely re-

ligious works, there is often slyly buried in the list of ponderous
and formidable Latin and Spanish tomes the title of a more plebian
novel, book of verse, or even a collection of plays testifying to the
mundane tastes of the owner. But the bulk of the books shipped to
the colonies were in commercial lots sent by regular dealers and it
is important, therefore, to study the routine procedures of the
House of Trade at Seville by which the majority of printed works
started on their way to viceregal readers.

The first and indispensable step in conveying goods of any sort
to the New World was the drawing up of a *registro* or record of
each shipment which formed a part of the cargo of a given ship.
This document was a commercial instrument which also frequently
served as a bill of lading at the ports of entry. Its advantages were
obvious since it provided a clear basis for making freight contracts,
facilitated the collection of royal imposts, and rendered more difficult the prevalent abuse of smuggling. The clerical task of preparing
these manifests occupied the staff of scribes continuously during
the months before the fleets departed and, in the course of centuries, resulted in the accumulation of a prodigious mass of documents. These *registros*, however, were relatively simple in form and
followed a common pattern. Invariably and with routine piety the
sign of the Cross was placed at the top of the first sheet, and usually
in the left-hand corner or slightly below appeared an identifying
mark or brand, ordinarily a device formed by the initials of the
shipper's name, which was also stamped on all cases or bales comprising his consignment. Immediately below the Cross the first
line of the text began with a broad flourish of the pen and continued
with the required information in stereotyped phrases adapted to the
circumstances presented by the particular shipment. The characteristic nature and form of the prescribed data are easily observed in a
typical declaration covering a consignment of books to South
America in 1586:

> Register. Francisco Muñoz Centeno, who has loaded below
> deck, dry, and in good condition, five cases of books sealed
> with the seal of the Holy Office of the Inquisition of this
> city of Seville, on the ship (which may God protect) named
> *Santa Catalina*, whose master is Melchor Palomo, and which
> is moored and anchored in the port of San Lucar de Bar-

rameda, to continue, with God's blessing, its voyage with the present fleet to the realm of Tierra Firme, its General being Don Miguel de Eraso. These cases indicated below and marked with the brand here given are to be handed over and delivered at any port or place in the possession of Spain to the above-mentioned Francisco Muñoz Centeno and in the port and city of Nombre de Dios, or any other place or port of the Indies of Tierra Firme, to Alonso Ruiz or Diego Gil de Avis, General Receiver of the City of the Kings [Lima], and in the absence of both, to the person holding the power of attorney of any of them to receive the goods which the aforementioned Francisco Muñoz Centeno is sending to them on this fleet; and the one who receives them shall observe the instructions of the persons mentioned, or any one of them; they are shipped on the account of, and at the risk of, the said Diego Gil de Avis and Alonso Ruiz, copartners, in accordance with the contract executed in the City of the Kings before Francisco de la Vega, Public Notary of that City, on February 1, 1585.[3]

The wording varied, of course, according to the articles shipped, the conditions of the transaction, the ships freighted, destinations sought, and so forth, but fundamentally it was similar on all manifests. Then followed, listed in a single column, the number of cases, bales, or chests with an indication of their contents, usually in such broad classifications as hardware, wines, or textiles. At the bottom the total valuation of the consignment was noted as a basis for computing the several charges and taxes to which the goods were subject. When these were paid and, in the case of book shipments, the approval of the Inquisition was attested by a proper notation, the *registro* was presented to the Comptroller's office where one copy was kept for file and another was forwarded to the shipmaster, who usually acknowledged acceptance of the freight by signing his name to the right of the scribal Cross at the top of the first sheet.

Down to 1550 books appear to have been treated much the same as any other commodity, that is, they were listed on the manifests as so many cases of printed works, without other details. Thus, as already pointed out, the few surviving records of the first half of the century are seldom useful in shedding light on the types of literature exported. In September of that year, it will be recalled, a royal decree required that books should no longer be listed in lots but rather that the title and character of each work appear on the register. The deepening anxiety over the circulation of Lutheran writings and heresies in the Indies as well as in Spain itself had prompted this measure which, apparently, was aimed at these menaces to orthodox Catholicism more than at the light literature earlier proscribed. But compliance with this royal order added immeasurably to the paper work involved in checking a shipment of books through the House of Trade, and the effectiveness of this additional clerical labor was dubious owing to the deliberate failure of dealers to list prohibited books which they were shipping. Since the manifests of the next thirty years are missing, there is no assurance that the decree of 1550 was faithfully observed until 1583, when the records are again available. From this date on to about the end of the first quarter of the seventeenth century the *registros* show a greater adherence to the royal will, though the fragmentary and abbreviated character of these documents suggests only partial conformity. This possibly belated obedience to the midcentury command may have resulted from renewed pressure on the House of Trade officials stimulated by the Church which, after the Council of Trent, addressed itself with redoubled vigor to the task of stamping out Protestant heresies and in 1583 promulgated the enlarged Quiroga *Index of prohibited books*. Whatever the true explanation, the surviving records of the forty years or more following that date afford enlightening insights into colonial reading habits, thanks to the individual listing of short titles required by the decree of 1550.

The exact procedure employed by the House of Trade and the Holy Office in handling the consignments of books at Seville is not easily reconstructed from the existing documentation. Doubtless there were variations from time to time in the practices used, but the customary routine was somewhat as follows. When the burros had deposited their burdens at the warehouses or storage sheds of the House of Trade near the banks of the Guadalquivir, the boxes or cases of books were left opened and a list of their contents was handed over in duplicate to an official. While the headquarters of the Inquisition were located across the river from Seville in the colorful *barrio* or district called Triana, there was, apparently, a special office of this institution in the buildings of the House of

Trade itself where the inspection of books for export took place. With the manifest drawn up, the submitted list of books was transscribed and the entire document forwarded to the Holy Office. The proper official then appended a notation on the last page to the effect that "the Inquisitors of Seville commit the examination of these books to So-and-so and with his approval they will let them pass. Done at the Castillo de Triana." A slight variation in this process is indicated by a statement on a manifest covering a book shipment to Santo Domingo in 1597 which reads, "The Inquisitors of Seville give the owner of these books license to take them out of the Customs House and ship them wherever he wishes or considers convenient after they have been inspected and approved by Dr. Don Alonso Coloma, Adviser to this Holy Office."[4]

With such authorization the opened cases were presumably examined and duly checked with the list to ascertain whether any titles included appeared on the *Index*. If the examiner discovered none of the forbidden writings present he jotted the word "pase" [let it pass] at the foot of the list and then signed his name after the phrase "No son de los prohibidos" [not on the prohibited list]. Occasionally, this laconic expression was extended to read, "On these two sheets and a half there are none of the prohibited books," a statement suggesting that the practice of subsequently inserting additional pages of titles into the register was not entirely unknown. The approved cases were then closed, nailed, and stamped with the seal of the Holy Office. With this formality concluded the boxes of books were handled in the same fashion as other freight and in due course found a place in the cargoes of the outgoing vessels.

The essentially liberal policy of the Spanish Crown toward the cultural welfare of the Conquistador and his descendants in the colonies is attested by the fact that the products of the press were virtually exempt from the export taxes imposed on nearly all other goods sent to the Indies. The only direct impost on book consignments was the so-called *averia* or convoy tax made necessary by the depradations of foreign nationals on Spanish shipping. The proceeds of this source of revenue were used to equip the merchant fleets with an armed guard, a measure found indispensable since the first quarter of the sixteenth century. This charge on the colonial trade, which the unceasing activities of the pirates made permanent, varied in amount from time to time according to changing international conditions; it fluctuated between 1 and 7 percent and sometimes more.[5]

As with other goods, when this duty was calculated and paid, the register, properly certified, was transmitted to the Comptroller's office. Here a copy of the document, or a separately drawn invoice, served as an agreement between the shipmaster commanding the galleon that was to transport the books, and the shipper or owner of the goods; ordinarily, the manifest and its duplicates were considered legal instruments and sufficient documentation for all purposes. When the mounting sheaf of papers was found in order and all charges prepaid, it was marked *cargue* or *general*, the sixteenth-century Spanish equivalents of "O.K." The cargo it covered was then placed aboard ships anchored in the river or, as became the common practice, was sent down to San Lucar de Barrameda at the river's mouth where the fleet was forming. Just before sailing the registers of each ship were closed, after which no further freight could be accepted on board. The original document remained in the files of the House of Trade while the shipmaster received a sealed duplicate, which he gave bond to deliver, together with the cargo it covered, unopened and intact to the treasury officers at the port of destination. Tampering with either the register or the freight en route subjected the master of the ship to heavy penalties. Back at Seville the various manifests pertaining to a given vessel were assembled and the individual documents were sewn together to form a single volume.

As the hazards of trans-Atlantic navigation created by man and Nature, and the wealth of the Indies were both so great as to make the trade with the Spanish colonies a tremendous gamble for prodigious stakes, private exporters and shippers controlling this traffic preferred to take heavy risks by overloading the galleons, stuffing the holds beyond capacity, and piling goods high on the narrow decks, thus increasing the danger of foundering in stormy seas. The poor equipment and insufficient artillery generally provided because of a shortsighted desire to allow more space for money-making cargo added considerably to the ever-present peril of capture or destruction by marauding corsairs.

In an effort to forestall these abuses and to meet its responsibility for the safety of the New World commerce and the protection of the public interest, the House of Trade soon devised an elaborate system of inspecting and policing the lading of ocean-going fleets. A ship outward bound was subjected to a series of three *visitas* by specially appointed officials. The first of these inspections took place when the empty vessel lay at anchor in the river or at San Lucar de Barrameda. The resulting report included such details as the ship's draught and general condition, and it indicated the changes and repairs necessary before authority to sail could be given. The commanding officer of the craft was further advised regarding the rigging, tackle, anchors, supplies, and other nautical equipment that he must acquire before putting out to sea, and it was on this occasion that he was pledged under oath not to take on board any passengers for the trans-Atlantic voyage who lacked the necessary permit of the Crown or of the House of Trade.

The second inspection, for which the Comptroller's office assumed responsibility, occurred when the ship was loaded and ready to descend the Guadalquivir, or was at the mouth of this river if the cargo was put aboard at San Lucar de Barrameda. The vessel's crew, stores, armament, and general equipment were scrutinized to ascertain whether there had been compliance with the recommendations made on the first *visita*, and the shipmaster was obliged to unload any excess cargo that his eagerness for additional revenue had tempted him to accept.

The third and final check took place at San Lucar about the time that the sails were hoisted and the ship was ready to put to sea. This last inspection resembled the second, though it tended to narrow down to an effort to detect the presence of contraband or unregistered merchandise among the cargo in the crowded holds and on the littered decks. The officer in charge of this last-minute scrutiny was usually a higher official of the House of Trade who was fully empowered to compel the shipmaster to unload at his own expense any illegal goods or passengers discovered, and to confiscate any freight taken aboard after closing and sealing of the registers. When this important representative of the government bureau was satisfied that all was in proper order and that the ships were adequately seaworthy, a certificate of inspection was attached to the register of each vessel. With customary ceremonies the official then took his leave, dropping over the side into a waiting cutter which headed for the shore while the heavily laden galleon turned seaward to plough its westward course.[6]

Despite these elaborate precautions the good intentions and close supervision of the House of Trade were largely neutralized by the carelessness and deliberate corruption of its own representatives and the chicanery of the commercial and shipping interests. The three inspections prior to sailing soon became routine and ineffective, not only because of the venality of the personnel involved but also because of the manifest impossibility of making a careful check of the contents of the innumerable casks, chests and cases composing the heterogeneous cargo. A conscientious effort of this sort would inevitably be too long and vexatious for the available time of the examiners and excessively annoying to all interests concerned. In due course the practice was substituted of merely accepting the sworn statements of the pilots or shipmasters with respect to the cargoes they were carrying, and this procedure quickly degenerated into a complete nullification of the original intent of the regulations so elaborately devised. And thus it was that many of the ships comprising the annual fleets were authorized to sail in an overloaded and unseaworthy condition, their holds and decks packed with a varied assortment of profit-producing goods, including much that was contraband. The weighty boxes and cases of books, among which were more than a few prohibited titles, lying in the darkness beneath the decks or lashed to the narrow confines above them, thus started a tedious and tortuous journey which terminated for some at the bottom of the ocean and for many at the very ends of the sixteenth-century world.

If the House of Trade did not prove a thoroughly efficient organization for the control of commerce and emigration to the Spanish colonies, the care with which this organization attempted to perform its functions makes it possible to identify, for a short period of time at least, some of the many books sent across the seas to the heirs of the Conquistador. The bulky *legajos* or bundles of ship manifests remaining include a substantial number of book lists characteristically poor in details but rich in significance and insights. The manner in which these precious inventories were compiled is not wholly clear; it is possible that the titles were merely transcribed from the list submitted by the consignor or, perhaps, they were noted on the manifest as the contents of the boxes or cases were checked. If the latter procedure was followed, it seems certain that scribal clerks worked in pairs, one extracting the volumes from the container and reading off the titles while the other wrote down on the register in abbreviated form what his unfamiliarity with literature, his untrained ear, or deficient knowledge of orthography dictated to him. The results are often mystifying and present difficult paleographic problems to the modern historian. The ponderous titles of sixteenth-century books, frequently covering much of the title page of a work, were too long to reproduce completely and doubtless puzzled the industrious scribe. The latter soon fell into the habit of copying the words that he fancied he heard or that loomed large before his eyes on what seemed a reasonable assumption that they were of greater significance. Not infrequently isolated parts of a rambling title were linked together, with results which baffle the investigator today in the task of identification, a difficulty especially encountered with books in Latin. This understandable tendency might not present such insuperable obstacles to recognition if the scribes had been careful to copy the text correctly. Too often their ignorance of the ancient tongue caused the recorder to represent verbal symbols by an original phonetic spelling based on his native Castilian or, more often, Andalusian pronunciation. In some documents the spelling betrays the Italian origin of the clerk. Even Spanish titles suffered orthographic distortion at the hands of semiliterate officials. Latin works, however, were the ones which suffered the worst treatment for—proving once again that a little knowledge is a dangerous thing—a scribe with a smattering of the classical medium sometimes took it upon himself to translate the words he saw into the vernacular, occasionally with disastrous effect. At best the registers give a short title, frequently with the author's name omitted, and so abbreviated that identification is extremely difficult; useful bibliographic data, such as the place and date of publication, are invariably absent. A further hurdle for the curious reader of these books lists is the nearly indecipherable scrawl of the scribe who, perhaps, found this part of his daily routine particularly boring. The virtually illegible notations at the end of the register give strong evidence of being dashed off in great haste and indifference. Despite such drawbacks these documents are priceless records which, besides affording indications of titles shipped abroad, often tell the number of copies of each work represented and their monetary value as well.

Still other facts are gleaned from these yellowed papers. The book shipments of a single dealer, for example, varied from one to eighty and even more cases. Although small orders of three, four, six, and eight were the rule, consignments of twenty, thirty, and forty boxes or bales were by no means rare. The number of books per container differed, of course, according to the sizes of the volumes themselves, and it ran anywhere from twenty or fewer books to well over a hundred each. Hence it is not unusual to find a single shipment of more than a thousand volumes. Dated in January 1601 there is a register of one dealer which covers a total of some ten thousand books—a substantial order even in the present age of groaning presses and book-buying literacy!

A portion of the immense amount of paper work which the multiple activities of the House of Trade imposed on its staff now proves of enormous value in revealing the reading tastes of the Conquistador's descendants in the New World. As was noted in the last chapter, a fairly clear knowledge of specific titles enjoyed abroad emerges from these prosaic documents, and even a hazy perception of the degree of popularity of many works is possible. Even more significant is the evidence which these commercial instruments give of the nonenforcement of the repeated royal decrees banning "profane literature such as the lying histories of Amadis" in the Spanish Indies. Again and again the title of the very work which the authorities had singled out as the symbol of the books that they so heartily disapproved appears in the shipping manifests, thus making clear that these prohibitory decrees were of limited application and that they quickly fell in abeyance. Amadis, Palmerin and all their disciples continued to pass through the House of Trade and to invade the colonies for many decades after the promulgation of the proscriptive legislation of the Crown, and they did this with the acquiescence if not the actual blessing of the Inquisition, for the covering manifest of shipment after shipment of books, which included all kinds of romances of chivalry and profane literature, bears at the end the terse statement *no son de los prohibidos* of the Holy Office. While the examination of these lists by the inquisitorial representative was probably often cursory and perfunctory, he would scarcely have overlooked so consistently the presence of light literature in the successive consignments, particularly since popular fiction was still vigorously assailed by preachers and moralists, if his duty was to exclude it from the shipments. It is clear, therefore, that the Inquisition concerned itself only with those works definitely on its own *Index of prohibited books*, disregarding all others.

This indifference or failure of the Holy Office to enforce at the same time the earlier royal decrees, which the Church had undoubtedly endorsed, arouses some curious speculations on the current relations of the ecclesiastical and secular branches of the monarchical government in the execution of the laws in which both had a direct interest. But certain it is that the censorship of the Inquisition did *not* extend to debarring creative literature not listed on its *Index*, and that it kept a hands-off policy with respect to the lucrative book trade of the Peninsular merchants in the colonies. And it is equally certain that the House of Trade played a role in the dissemination of the products of Spanish presses in the overseas possessions of the Crown, and that by keeping detailed records— though they are now fragmentary and incomplete—it gave to posterity a precious testimony of the early diffusion of Hispanic literary culture in the New World.

BOATS AND BOOKS XI

A SHARP REPORT OF A CANNON REVERBERATED THROUGH the narrow, crowded streets emptying into the water front of Seville. It was a signal that within six hours the heavily laden galleons bound for the Spanish Indies would cast off their moorings and start southward along the twisting river on the first leg of a perilous journey.[1] The noise and animation along the wharves and throughout the busy city had increased notably during the last few days and now seemed to reach a clamorous climax. The entire population appeared to be converging on the littered docks as soldiers and sailors, swarthy and bearded, fair and beardless, and assorted civilians in colorful attire hurried through the sun-drenched alleys and streets, the air faintly tinged with the scent of orange blossoms. Everyone moved excitedly toward the river where, amidst a labyrinth of ship tackle, cordage, and sails, a dense cluster of lancelike masts pierced the cloudless blue of the sky. A scene of bustling activity met the eyes of onlookers as the last boxes, chests, and bales of merchandise were quickly stowed away and reluctant soldiers and the last tear-stained passengers, with their mountainous baggage, were hustled on board. For hours this climactic confusion of leave-taking and last-minute loading reigned until at last, slowly and gingerly, amidst a cacaphony of sharp orders, raucous shouts, and loud cursing, the little craft, one by one, swung away from the crowded docks. With bows pointing downstream they spread sails which gleamed like clear white patches in the Andalusian sunlight, and the little merchant ships, slowly falling into line, began the precarious descent of the sinuous Guadalquivir with its abrupt turns and treacherous shoals toward the Mediterranean Sea. At the head of this procession proudly moved the *capitana* or admiral's ship, bearing aloft the royal banner with the coat of arms of the sovereigns and the insignias of the General of the Fleet. A long, long voyage had begun.

These tiny vessels, which the House of Trade authorized to embark with their assorted cargoes on the hazardous crossing of the broad Atlantic, were indispensable agents in the diffusion of European culture in the New World and in the implanting of the Hispanic civilization still flourishing in nearly two-thirds of it. To sixteenth-century Spain fell the unprecedented task of discovering and charting trade routes over vaster reaches of water than the little maritime powers of the Mediterranean world had dared to imagine. Destiny had summoned the land-minded people of Castile to give the initial impetus to the greatest epic in human history— the Europeanizing of the globe. In this tremendous enterprise Iberian courage and daring pioneered the highways across the forbidding expanse of the Atlantic and Pacific oceans, and they brought to the outermost corners of the world the first contacts with the flowering culture of Renaissance Europe. Without a comparable precedent Spain improvised a system of merchant marine and set the pattern of transoceanic empire to the emerging nationalities of the Continent. Spain also acquainted them with the rewards accruing from a methodical exploitation of the hitherto undreamed resources of the expanding world. During the early period of this Europeanizing process, however, Spain, dominated more than any other colonizing power by an ethical concept, sought to bring to the subjugated populations of the New World a large measure of the intellectual, cultural, and religious gifts of Christian Europe in exchange for the material benefits derived by the homeland. To promote this material and spiritual commerce between the Peninsula and its possessions the Spanish Crown established the first regular passenger and freight service across the Atlantic, thus opening the modern age of transportation. Of interest are a few details of this pioneer shipping line which played its important part in the distribution of the Spanish conquerors' books.

The ships following in the wake of Columbus' epochal voyages usually sailed singly, but they soon found themselves exposed to the attacks of roaming corsairs sponsored in varying degrees by jealous monarchs of the Continent who thus attempted to share the

wealth of the newly found world. This situation soon gave rise to
the custom of organizing vessels into fleets for greater security,
though the practice of sending them individually was never wholly
discontinued. Surviving House of Trade records indicate that some
2,805 ships of differing tonnage departed from Seville or other
authorized ports for America between 1504 and 1555, and that
many of them sailed unaccompanied.[2] Before the end of this period,
however, merchantmen in groups were convoyed by men-of-war
of numerous classifications, and for this protection, as already
noted, a special tax, called the *avería*, was imposed. Definite, periodic dispatching of fleets began about 1543 when a renewal of
the ever-growing conflict with France made such an arrangement
essential. Regulations then provided for two fleets to depart annually, one to sail in March and the other in September, though
announced sailing schedules were never rigorously observed. These
flotillas, protected by armed ships, voyaged to the Caribbean area
where they dispersed, each vessel making its way to an appointed
destination.

Pirate aggressions against Spanish shipping increased in boldness
and frequency, however, as the colonial trade grew, with this menace particularly affecting the treasure-laden galleons returning from
the Indies. Further overhauling of the trade and navigation between
the Peninsula and its ultramarine possessions became necessary and
thus a semipermanent system was instituted in the years 1564-
1566.[3] Under the new plan two separate fleets sailed each year as
before. One, starting from San Lucar de Barrameda in April or
May, took its course to the Gulf of Mexico, dropping some of its
component ships in the Greater Antilles and at Honduras en route
to the terminal port at San Juan de Ulúa or Vera Cruz. The other
fleet, leaving the same point of departure usually in August, proceeded to the southern littoral of the Caribbean. Member ships
withdrew from the main body to put in at ports such as Santa
Marta, Maracaibo, Cartagena, and others on the mainland of South
America, while the bulk of the fleet pushed on to Nombre de Dios
(later to Puertobelo) on the isthmus of Panama. Both groups of
vessels generally wintered in the Indies and then reassembled at
Havana in March for the return voyage together to Spain. Each
fleet, however, remained a separate unit with its own convoy, gen-

eral, and rear admiral. It became the custom to refer to the ships bound for the South American mainland as the *Galeones*, and the others destined for the Gulf of Mexico the *Flota*.

As either fleet crossed the bar at San Lucar or, occasionally, at Cádiz, the *capitana* took the lead with the merchantmen following like an orderly flock of ducks. Bringing up the rear was the *almiranta*, or vice-admiral's brig, whose task was to see that stragglers did not fall too far behind. The course was laid first southwest toward the African coast and then westward to the Canary Islands, the first stop, usually a voyage of seven or eight days. There the fleets anchored a short while to take on further provisions and complete final arrangements for the crossing of the Atlantic. On leaving this archipelago the course was shifted southwest to about the sixteenth parallel of latitude, where prevailing winds carried the ships at a leisurely pace due west until the island of Deseada (Désirade), Guadaloupe, or another of the Lesser Antilles was sighted. Normally, this navigation of the open sea required twenty-five to thirty days.

These eagerly sought landmarks of the Caribbean represented the fork in the routes of the two fleets which, up to this vicinity, followed much the same course, though often the *Galeones*, departing at a different season, shifted their helms farther south and passed between the islands of Tobago and Trinidad as they headed toward the isthmus of Panama. The *Flota*, on the other hand, struck northwest after sighting Deseada and passed inside the Leeward Islands to Santa Cruz (St. Croix), Puerto Rico, and Hispaniola, or Santo Domingo, where it customarily took on fresh supplies of wood and water. While a dispersal of the fleet was then in progress, with a few merchantmen seeking harbors in the islands mentioned, the larger number of ships skirted along the southern coast of Cuba to reach the terminal port at Vera Cruz (San Juan de Ulúa).

The number of vessels comprising the annual fleets varied considerably, and it was conditioned by such factors as the current economic situation, the tonnage of the ships in service, and the fluctuating freedom of the seas from the scourge of pirates. Little precise information on the strength of the flotillas in the first half of the sixteenth century is available, partly owing to the fact that the *flota* system was not then well established. Toward the end of the century the number of craft in a given fleet varied from thirty to ninety. The "Galleons" destined for Tierra Firme, as the north mainland of South America was called, were, on the whole, more numerous, it is said, than the ships constituting the Mexico-bound *flota*. This trend is fairly well reflected in the existing registers of book shipments; the consignments to the lower half of the Western Hemisphere seem more numerous and the printed volumes thus listed represent larger quantities. Later, at the beginning of the seventeenth century, the distribution is more equal with the scales tipping in favor of the more northerly region.

Since the outgoing cargoes of Spanish and European manu-factured goods usually required more space in the holds than the silver and gold bullion and the few products such as cotton, sugar, and dyewood carried on the return voyage, the outward-bound fleets tended to be larger in size than those which headed up the Bahama channel from Havana on the homeward course. A few ves-sels of the original fleets remained in the Indies for coastal service, but often the shipping interests at Seville, seeking the largest mar-gin of profit, bought up at a cheap price old and scarcely seaworthy Mediterranean craft which they refitted sufficiently for one last voyage. These frail barks were generally loaded beyond capacity, and it is not surprising that shipwrecks and losses were appallingly common. One wonders, indeed, at the temerity of crews and pas-sengers in undertaking such a risky journey in them.

The dangers of these early trans-Atlantic voyages become more apparent when the tiny size of the sailing ships is considered. During the first half of the sixteenth century most of the ocean-going craft were not much larger than the caravels Columbus navigated on his first expedition to the New World. Rarely did a merchantman or an armed ship exceed a tonnage of two hundred; on voyages of dis-covery or exploration one-hundred-ton sailing boats were pre-ferred. After the fleet system was set up in 1543, and more especially after 1564, the tonnage of vessels increased and ships of four hun-dred and five hundred tons were common, though they seldom ex-ceeded this last figure. The causes of this restriction on the size of merchantmen plying the India trade lay in the monopoly which the Seville businessmen maintained through their *Consulado*, or Chamber of Commerce, and in the shallowness of the water on the

San Lucar bar at the mouth of the Guadalquivir River, which made the crossing of ships of more than two hundred tons burden practically impossible. When vessels of greater draught were employed the cargo was lightered to them as they lay at anchor outside the bar.

Supreme authority over the fleet at sea rested with the General, who had nearly absolute power, but actually each vessel was an independent entity associating itself with the group for the sake of its own protection. The command of a merchantman was a divided one, although the *maestre*, or shipmaster, was the officer in control. With him was a pilot who assumed entire responsibility for the navigation at sea and gave orders to the crew through a *contra-maestre*, or mate. Once in port, however, this pilot's authority and duties ceased completely. The *maestre*, on the other hand, who was often the owner or coöwner of the ship, was a general factotum who took charge of equipping and provisioning the vessel, hiring and paying off the crew and officers, making freight contracts, selling passages to passengers, and so on. He was the active representative of the shipping interests and directly identified himself with them, his nautical direction seldom going beyond indicating the general course or route to be taken at sea. The designation "captain" was limited to the commander of a war vessel which formed part of a convoy of merchantmen. Each of the latter ships was also supposed to carry a small armament of artillery and small arms. In skirmishes with pirates or sea battles with enemy craft the *maestre* of each unit was automatically the military officer or captain.

The size of the crews was variable but undermanned ships were the rule. The House of Trade issued regulations governing such matters but, like most of its legislation, they were constantly honored in the breach. An ordinance of 1522 required a vessel of one hundred tons burden to carry at least fifteen able seamen, eight apprentice seamen, and three cabin boys. Thirty years later it was stipulated that ships from one hundred to one hundred seventy tons should be manned by eighteen able seamen, eight apprentices, two artillerymen, and two cabin boys; one hundred seventy tons to two hundred twenty tons, twenty-eight able seamen, twelve apprentices, seven artillerymen, and one cabin boy; two hundred twenty to three hundred twenty tons, thirty-five able seamen, fifteen apprentices, six artillerymen, and one cabin boy. Other members of a regulation crew were stewards, coopers, carpenters, water bailiffs, a barber-physician, and the indispensable *escribano*, or notary. None was supposed to be a foreigner and precautions were taken against desertion from ships in the Indies, though these measures, too, were often ineffective. Difficulties in obtaining recruits made the law against foreigners largely inoperative and explain, in part, the prevalent crew shortage on merchantmen. Well before sailing dates it was the practice to send a crier, accompanied by drummers and fife players, into the towns and villages, chiefly of Andalusia, proclaiming the opportunities that the merchant marine offered to young men between the ages of twenty-five and thirty to see the world and earn good wages. The response was often disappointing and impatient shipmasters did not hesitate to disregard the House of Trade regulations by shipping crews that included heretics—Moorish, Jewish, and non-Catholic elements—and foreigners, as well as orthodox Christians.[4]

During much of the sixteenth century, crew members were hired on shares. At the end of the voyage the freight charges were computed and from this sum were deducted the convoy tax and an additional 2.5 percent as a special bounty for sailors rendering extraordinary service. Two-thirds of the remaining proceeds went to the ship owner, while the other third was apportioned among the crew. An entire share fell to each of the able-bodied seamen, two-thirds of a share went to each apprentice seaman, and a quarter of a share was the cabin boy's lot. No uniformity in this procedure is discernible, however, and the practice of paying wages proportionate to the various categories also operated in the same period, later becoming the general rule.

While the living conditions aboard a ship were unspeakable by modern standards, sailors enjoyed a plain fare which, measured in caloric equivalents of today, was ample in quantity if less satisfactory as a balanced diet of proteins, carbohydrates and fats. The dietary for a crew in 1560, probably typical of the sixteenth century, is as follows. The steward issued daily rations of 24 oz. of bread and 3.8 oz. of beans or chick-peas. This was supplemented on Sundays, Tuesdays, and Thursdays with 8 oz. of salt beef; on Mondays and Wednesdays with 6 oz. of cheese; on Fridays and

Saturdays with 8 oz. of salt cod. Sometimes olives, hazelnuts, dried dates and figs, and quince marmalade gave greater variety. Every day about a quart of wine, a little olive oil, and vinegar were allotted to each crew member; unrationed condiments, such as cinnamon, cloves, mustard, parsley, pepper, and saffron, helped make the monotonous fare more savory. Likewise, onions and garlic were dispensed with considerable liberality. The regular rations are estimated to have a calorific value ranging from 3,385 to 3,889 calories, which was adequate for the maintenance of the seamen. This food was eaten on wooden plates and saucers placed on a tablecloth, often spread on the deck floor; fingers were the chief implements and the cabin boys served as waiters. The *maestre* and officers had a separate table, while the passengers attended to their own needs. When wind and weather permitted, they burned charcoal and wood in the small cooking hearths or stoves, but the paying travelers were frequently obliged to content themselves with cold and uncooked victuals for days or weeks on end. The larder was often supplemented by live sheep, pigs, and fowls taken aboard at the start and consumed during the voyage. Water was doled out in small quantities daily for drinking and about a pint for washing, though this ration was reduced to the barest subsistence level if the ships were delayed by calms or by other factors during the crossing.[5]

But the trans-Atlantic fleet service did not exist merely to transport the cargoes of Spanish goods to the colonial market, though the Seville merchants doubtless derived their largest profits from this traffic. These ships also facilitated emigration to the remote parts of the overseas empire whose limits were still undefined and unknown. Again and again great exploring and colonizing expeditions were organized and departed from Seville or Cádiz for the outlying regions of North and South America, carrying hundreds, even thousands, of adventurers and settlers, along with large stocks of cattle, horses, seeds, tools, and equipment to accelerate the process of Europeanizing the recently discovered New World and beyond. Many of these undertakings ended in disaster and many of the luckless emigrants perished in shipwrecks, by famine, or at the hands of savages, unhappy victims of the lure which fact and fancy, particularly fancy, had conjured out of their imaginations and their fiction reading. But in the richer of the discovered realms where

precious metals abounded, and where sedentary Indians existed as
a great reservoir of labor, as in the viceroyalties of Mexico and
Peru, a steady flow of incoming Peninsulars and even foreigners
developed, and these emigrants swelled the passenger lists of caravels and galleons.

The fear of foreign intrusion and the desire to keep the Christianizing efforts of the Spaniards among the Indians free from the
theological confusions of contemporary Europe moved the Crown
to surround the migration to the colonies with the severest restrictions. Every passenger was required to obtain a special license or
passport, usually through the Council of the Indies, the advisory
board of the monarch. To obtain this authorization the applicant
had to give clear evidence of probity and freedom from any heretical taints, both in blood and in mind. A special register of the
House of Trade recorded for each individual such pertinent facts as
his name, age, parentage, birthplace, marital state, the ship taken,
and the port of destination. Single women were forbidden to travel
to the colonies unless they were daughters or servants of migrating
families. Married men could not leave without their wives, a restriction that even extended to the royal officials themselves, unless
special permission was granted by the Crown. This regulation was
relaxed, however, in the case of merchants who might obtain the
necessary authorization directly from the House of Trade. This
permission allowed them to remain in the Indies for three years,
and, as might be expected, it was subject to numerous abuses. The
licenses granted to ordinary passengers were valid for two years
after the date of issuance and included all members of the family,
its servants, and other dependents listed. The maximum number of
passengers that a *maestre* of a hundred-ton ship could properly accept was thirty, and he was supposed to keep his cabins and deck
clear of cargo for their comfort—another regulation frequently
flouted.[6]

Passengers received slight consideration from shippers, who
probably regarded them as a nuisance, and almost no provision for
their comfort and pleasure was made. Often these voyagers fared
far worse than the crew, for they were obliged to come aboard not
only properly armed to assist in the defense of the ship if attacked
at sea, but equipped with everything necessary for their bodily

needs, including a stock of provisions for themselves, their families, and servants. Rules forbade passengers even to sit at the ship officers' tables, and the *maestre* was specially enjoined against releasing any of the crews' supplies to his paying guests. One journeying to the colonies was, therefore, confronted with the major problem of taking sufficient bedding, food, drink, clothing, and other personal effects indispensable for himself and his retinue. Thus a staggering quantity of luggage accompanied each traveler and further cramped the limited space afforded by the small sailing ships.[7]

A document of the last half of the sixteenth century lists the supplies and goods which every passenger bound for the River Plate region should take with him. For the ocean journey the following provisions were needed: 4 hundredweight of hardtack; 1 hogshead of flour containing 28 *arrobas* (about 700 lb.); 8 *arrobas* of wine; 2 *fanegas* (about 3 bushels) of beans and chick-peas; 4 *arrobas* of olive oil; 6 *arrobas* of vinegar; 1 *arroba* of rice; 2 *arrobas* of dried fish; bacon, onions, garlic, olives, figs, raisins, and almonds.

Clothes recommended for the voyage were: a dozen shirts; three doublets or jackets; two pairs each of woolen and linen breeches; a woolen sea jacket with two pairs of woolen hose; a woolen or sackcloth short cloak; two larger woolen cloaks, one black and the other dark brown; two woolen caps, and two ordinary hats; twelve pairs of shoes, with and without laces. Significantly, perhaps, the list ends with "a half *arroba* of soap."[8]

Life aboard ship during a sixteenth-century crossing was an ordeal which might well have daunted the boldest, and an experience that it would seem no one could be induced to repeat. Yet it is clear that these hardships were endured again and again, not only by merchants consoled by large profits, but by officials, some of whom occupied sinecures in the colonial governments. Missionaries and ecclesiastical authorities traveled in this fashion often; one of the greatest of these was Father Bartolomé de las Casas, the indomitable "Apostle of the Indians" who, in his unremitting efforts to alleviate the lot of the exploited natives of the New World, shuttled back and forth some four or five times. By particular good fortune a lengthy account survives of the voyage which this famous Dominican made in company with nearly fifty members of his own Order in 1544 to Santo Domingo en route to his bishopric in Chiapas.

Only two years earlier he had returned to Spain from the Indies
discouraged by the failure to enforce the so-called New Laws
which, in large part owing to his diligent efforts, had been promulgated to ameliorate the cruel treatment of the Indians by the conquistadors. Later, on a visit to the homeland, he published his
notorious *Brevísima relación de la destrucción de las Indias* (Very
brief account of the destruction of the Indies). This special pleading in behalf of his beloved flock, in which he grossly exaggerated
their unhappy plight, did much to blacken the reputation of Spain
in the eyes of the world thenceforth and to justify the attempts of
rival nations to drive the Spaniards from their new dominions. Another notable passenger who made the voyage in this same fleet was
the widow of Diego Columbus, son of the Discoverer. Doña María
de Toledo, or the Vicereine as she is called in the record, was accompanying the remains of her great father-in-law to Santo Domingo where these sacred relics were expected to find a final resting
place in that part of the New World which his faith and enterprise
had brought to the knowledge of his fellow men. The narrative of
this historic crossing is supplied by the diary kept by a certain
Father Tomás de la Torre, one of the companions of Las Casas,
and it describes in considerable detail the experiences of the band
of missionaries from the time of their departure from their convent
in Salamanca in Spain to their arrival the following year at their
destination in the New World.[9]

On the morning of July 9, 1544 some forty-eight frocked figures, who had waited almost six months in Seville and San Lucar
for this event, hustled into lighters at the latter port and joyfully
sang litanies as they were ferried out to the *San Salvador*, one of a
fleet of twenty-seven vessels, large and small, ready to hoist its sails
and cross the sandbar at the mouth of the Guadalquivir. No sooner
had they and a few secular passengers clambered up the ship's sides
than their hardships began. Perversely, the expected wind refused
to rise sufficiently to carry the fleet out into the broad expanse of
the Mediterranean and, meanwhile, the hot sun pitilessly beat down
on the thick-robed friars who vainly sought shade on the encum-
bered deck. Little shimmering heat waves played over the deck
floor as the pitch began to ooze between its planking, and it seemed
as if all the passengers would dissolve into grease spots. The follow-

ing day, however, the pilots succeeded in taking all the vessels over the perilous bar except the poorly ballasted and overloaded *San Salvador* in which Father Las Casas and his coreligionists were uncomfortably traveling. This little bark remained obstinately wedged in the sand, and its unlucky inmates again sweltered under the hot glare of a burning sun. An offer from San Lucar to send boats to help pull the stranded ship over the sandy barrier was angrily refused by the cursing pilot and his crew, who regarded this proffered assistance as an unflattering reflection on their seamanship. The captain of the convoy accompanying the fleet sent back word that he would wait only a day or two for the *San Salvador* to extricate itself, after which time the entire squadron would proceed on its way—disheartening news to the perspiring passengers who had been placed together on this vessel in an effort to reduce the total bulk of their collective baggage. Clearly, if left behind on this occasion, they would have to wait another whole year to depart for the mission field. The disgruntled officer of the ship, who was also its owner, blamed his predicament on the land pilot whose duty was to navigate the vessels out of the river's mouth; the *maestre* was also inclined to attribute his initial bad luck to the black-robed friars on board, to whom he accorded scant courtesy, obliging them to sleep below deck where, in the suffocating holds, they were closely packed, jostled, trampled and, in general, treated almost like a cargo of Negro slaves consigned to the New World market.

These unpopular passengers suffered intolerably during the next two days as they waited to join the fleet outside the bar, but at length a strong breeze provided the impulse needed to release the *San Salvador* from its imprisonment. In these endless hours the friars were hardly able to gasp out a single litany or recite a prayer, and it was with vast relief mingled with sadness that they moved out to sea and watched the hazy line of the Spanish coast fade into the distance as the entire fleet got under way. But they quickly learned that they were merely passing from one set of discomforts to others greater. Soon the rolling swell caused the small and badly loaded vessel to pitch and toss horribly; with disconcerting promptness all but three of the friars and the Father Vicar were too violently ill to remain standing. In a little time the entire party was helpless, including the four or five neophytes whose duty was to wait on the others. Only the stalwart Vicar contrived to perform the melancholy task of placing basins and containers within reach of his prostrate companions. As the latter were unable for days to retain any food in their stomachs they grew faint, and they fell prey to a fiery thirst as they lay helplessly on the narrow, filthy deck, moaning pitifully while a merciless sun seemed determined to evaporate their dehydrated bodies. Later a few of the company experienced slight relief, but these more fortunate individuals were still too weak to aid the others lying wretchedly about, their miserable plight callously disregarded by the indifferent crew. The daily devotions of the wracked missionaries required superhuman efforts, but these devout followers of St. Dominic dared not omit these obligations altogether lest a stern Providence subject their faith and bodies to further tests. Father Las Casas, long familiar with these woes of mankind, sought to comfort and strengthen the sick with a broth concocted from the fowls he had brought aboard.

The misery of the unhappy passengers was increased by the constant fear of enemy shipping, for France and Spain were then at war. One afternoon the few travelers with energy enough to lift their heads above the deck rail beheld with dismay sixteen sails in the distance. That night all endured the agony of terror and uncertainty. With dawn, however, everyone experienced unspeakable relief when no sign of the strange vessels was visible. A more tranquil day passed and then, on the morning following, a large brig, glimpsed on the horizon, brought new alarm. This time one of the fleet's convoy gave chase and, on overhauling the mysterious craft, learned that it was Spanish. The cannon shots heard, however, threw the occupants of the merchantmen into a tense state of commotion, and the hasty moving of the cargoes below deck to free the artillery was hardly calculated to sooth the raw nerves of timorous and seasick passengers. The excitement soon subsided, fortunately, and the friars relapsed into a state of apathy and depression.

Father De la Torre wrote of sixteenth-century life on shipboard:

> A ship is a very narrow and stout prison from which no one can flee, even though he wears no shackles or chains. It makes no distinction in its cruelty to its inmates, confining

them all equally. Closely compressed into its narrow confines, heat and suffocation are unbearable. The deck floor is usually one's bed and, though some brought good mats, ours were small, hard and poor, thinly stuffed with dog hair; our bed covering was extremely wretched blankets of goatskin. . . . No one has any desire to eat and can hardly face anything sweet. The thirst one endures is unbelievable and is increased by the hardtack and salt beef constituting our fare. Water is measured out a half azumbre [about a liter] a day; wine is drunk by those who happen to have brought it. An infinite number of lice eat one alive, and clothing can not be washed because sea water shrinks it. And bad odors pervade everywhere, especially below deck, and the whole ship becomes intolerable when the ship pump is working, which varies according to whether the ship is sailing well or not. It goes at least four or five times a day in order to pump out of the hold the water that has leaked in, and this smells very foul indeed. . . . On top of this, when one feels well enough, there's no place where one can study or withdraw to himself a little on shipboard; one remains eternally seated for there is no place to walk.

And with the discomfort of the lice the chronicler might have mentioned the swarms of cockroaches common to all vessels of the period and the multitudes of insolent rats which frequently displayed a disrespectful and even aggressive attitude toward the hapless passengers.

Some of Father De la Torre's companions were never able to raise their heads even to look at the sea until they reached the vicinity of the Canary Islands, but, ironically, one of their number, Father Domingo de Ara, who was practically carried on board at San Lucar because of his ailments, recovered before almost anyone else and appeared completely restored to health and vigor by the sea air.

The prolonged nausea endured was largely the effect, it was alleged, of the incredibly bad way in which the ship was loaded. With little ballast below and most of the weight above, the *San Salvador* rolled from one side to the other while its nose plunged so deeply into the waves that the entire forward part was awash and barrels floated about the deck. Ropes were strung so that passengers and crew might move with some degree of safety from one end of the ship to the other; at all times it was impossible to cook meals. Efforts to relieve the situation by shifting the artillery about in the hold were ineffective, and the fear of capsizing was constant. The admiral of the fleet brought his galleons alongside of the *San Salvador* a couple of times a day with the intention of towing the lagging vessel, but the officer and crew of the latter, still inclined to regard any assistance as an implied criticism of their nautical skill, gave no coöperation. Pilots of other craft in the fleet displayed alarm on inspecting the badly loaded *San Salvador* and, when the passengers later reached the Canary Islands safely, they were congratulated on escaping with their lives. But Spanish laymen returning to the Indies on the other ships were disposed to believe that the real cause of the *San Salvador's* mishaps were the sins of the unpopular Dominicans in general, who had sided so actively with the Indians, and of Father Las Casas in particular, whose unremitting efforts in behalf of these conquered natives threatened the property rights and the economic power of the Conquistador. Everyone resented the fact that this lagging ship was detaining the entire fleet and, somewhat unreasonably, they visited their irritation on the unlucky friars who, it would seem, had already suffered enough for their association with the *San Salvador*. The crew openly blamed its troubles on them, and vented its spite by throwing overboard some of their passengers' provisions, carelessly breaking jars of water, and committing similar petty acts. Only the fact that another vessel had the misfortune to break its rudder shifted from the ill-starred *San Salvador* some of the onus as the fleet jinx.

On July 19 the sight of Tenerife, one of the Canaries, brought joy to all but, since the sea was rough and no shipyard was at hand there to repair the shattered rudder, the fleet pushed farther into the archipelago to Gomera. Several galleons and caravels raced to enter this harbor first and in the ensuing contest some collided, entangling their riggings to such an extent that they had to be cut away. This contretemps provoked further nervous excitement, only relieved by the sight of small boats putting out from the shore to take off the passengers. The nearness of land worked an almost miraculous cure on two of the *padres* who had lain prostrate up to this time, half dead from seasickness. With an agility that startled the others these two nausea-stricken victims almost bounded ashore. On feeling the firm earth under their feet again after the violent motion at sea, all the friars found themselves staggering on their weak legs, but so great was their relief that no one really minded this sensation.

The ten days on Gomera were restful and, on the whole, pleasant, save for a slight tiff with the vicar of the church where they were lodged. This practicing Christian disliked having his peaceful routine interrupted by an uninvited swarm of colleagues, and even Father Las Casas, a bishop, was subject to some indignities. But, for a change, the friars could enjoy regular cooked meals with plenty of vegetables, including the newly introduced potatoes from the Indies, and they could gorge themselves on the abundance of juicy grapes sagging from the arbors. Only the terrifying thought of resuming the voyage on the *San Salvador* haunted this delightful interlude, for some of the missionaries almost preferred death to a repetition of that dreadful experience. Much as the shipmaster disliked his passengers, he was unwilling to release them to other ships, fearing that their passage money could not be collected at Santo Domingo. On the other hand, the officials of other vessels in the fleet were reluctant to accept the friars, partly because their available space was already filled to capacity, partly because of the unpopularity of the Dominicans, and partly because these commanders also could not be certain of collecting passage fares at the end of the voyage. At length a compromise was worked out. The *maestre* of the *San Salvador* consented to take aboard six small boatloads of stones as needed ballast, and he permitted seventeen of the forty-eight *padres* to transfer to other units of the fleet. Then the long crossing was begun.

With a favoring wind the squadron sailed out of the harbor on Wednesday, July 30, and headed west. The *San Salvador*, properly ballasted and with its cargo well distributed, rode the waves gallantly, its few sails causing it to bound along and quickly outdistance the other more cumbrous craft, thus reversing the earlier relationship. Now it was the *San Salvador* that felt irritation at the slower pace of the fleet, obliging it from time to time to shorten sail and await the tardy arrival of the laggards. Unfortunately, there was again an unpleasant roll, and this rhythmic motion once more reduced the passengers to a helpless state of nausea. This time, indeed, not even the sturdy vicar remained standing, but in two or three days nearly everyone recovered sufficiently to be about, a situation favored by remarkably fine weather. Even the members of the crew reacted to the benign conditions and treated the clergy with far more respect than hitherto. The busy routine of prayers and religious ceremonies was possible again, and a holy day was celebrated with general rejoicing and repeated artillery salutes. There were moments of expansion when companion ships drew alongside each other; greetings were exchanged and this proximity permitted shouted conversations across the rails with other passengers. Now and then a glimpse of a bird or of clusters of sea plants aroused the hope of an early termination of the voyage. The young neophytes amused themselves by strumming guitars and singing ballads, each in his own way. Friars and secular passengers were able to withdraw with a measure of privacy and enjoy meditation or a parchment-bound volume, either devotional in character or, more often, of light fiction, poetry or history which they had carefully included in their personal baggage. Yes, life at sea could be pleasant, marred only by a monotonous diet of unsavory food and by little disturbances such as someone falling overboard, the malicious broaching of a water cask, or petty thieving. All these incidents must be expected, however, and accepted philosophically.

The shortage of liquids was, of course, a constant hardship, for the salt meat excited a thirst which the small allotments of water could never satisfy. One felt always dehydrated and sometimes injudiciously swallowed the entire daily ration of water at one swig; at other times one sipped it sparingly, never experiencing the luxury of even an instant of satiety. In mid-August the fleet ran into the doldrums, and for two or three days it was completely becalmed under the burning heat of a tropical sun; then the pangs of thirst were almost unendurable. But again youth contrived to wring some measure of enjoyment from the situation as the neophytes splashed and swam about the ship's sides in a sea as smooth as a millpond. This pleasure seemed untrammeled by the ever-present danger implicit in the favorite sport of the crew members—shark fishing. For days there was scarcely a breeze and the whole fleet seem to stand motionless like statues on a glassy and limitless pedestal, its deck planking exuding pitch in the suffocating heat.

Toward the end of August, however, appeared hopeful indications of land. Late in the afternoon of the 26th a distant cannonade among the forward ships was heard, and these sounds were interpreted as evidence that land was sighted. Sails were furled lest the vessels crash into the shore in the darkness. Sure enough, the next morning the long-desired Deseada Island of the Lesser Antilles was visible. Near it lay María Galante, and to land-starved eyes the beauty of its fresh greenness seemed superlative and remindful of the Earthly Paradise. Another calm, however, kept the fleet motionless off its shores for a half-day, and the magic spell of the isle began to diminish. A welcome afternoon breeze gently swept them onward past Guadaloupe and other islets. The unusual absence of winds delayed the expected arrival at Santo Domingo, causing the ships to glide leisurely past the Leeward and the Virgin Islands, and Puerto Rico, where individual members of the fleet began to drop out. Indeed, only twelve were left and, as water and supplies were falling dangerously low, a stop on the coast of Puerto Rico, near San Germán, was decided upon. The surliness of the pilots, impatient to reach their destination at Santo Domingo, as well as the difficulties of the tide, caused most of the remaining fleet to anchor well out to sea. Some of the passengers, however, went ashore, bringing back unenthusiastic reports of the town and several kinds of fruit. Chief among the latter were pineapples, whose taste Father De la Torre found unpleasant, reminiscent of the sour flavor of overripe melons. Much more acceptable was the fresh water which they could now drink freely and, incredibly, even wash in!

At length the remaining ships entered the mouth of the river leading to the city of Santo Domingo where welcoming cannon-shots from the shore fort greeted them. The passengers, ecclesiastic and lay alike, wearied by forty-three days at sea since leaving Gomera, joyfully hurried ashore, though not without one more mishap. The *San Salvador* narrowly averted striking a rock in the channel and was saved only by a tremendous wrenching of the tiller. A little later a near collision with the admiral's ship was avoided by a swift hoisting of sails and a quick veer to one side. But the long, tedious, and exhausting voyage from Seville was over, and one more arduous sixteenth-century crossing of the Atlantic was achieved. The remnants of the fleet pushing on to the mainland might encounter more dangers, but they would scarcely be unlike those already experienced.

A more sprightly narrative of a similar voyage nearly thirty years later, in 1573, is that of a witty correspondent, Eugenio de Salazar, who also took ship to Santo Domingo to assume a post as Oidor, or Judge, in that island. This letter contains some supplementary details which suggest that no great improvement in the trans-Atlantic service had taken place in the intervening generation.[10] This Spanish official embarked with his family from San Lucar on July 19, 1573, in the *Our Lady of Remedies*, "which," the author drily remarks, "had a better name than manners." Coming aboard from a lighter they were promptly conducted to a tiny cubicle destined to be their quarters during the entire voyage. Many of these cabins were completely closed, dark, and noisome vaults like burial niches, which were entered from beneath by a hatch. Everywhere about the ship was a tangle of ropes, cordage, and rigging which, from without, made the people on board "look like chickens and capons that are taken to market in woven reed hencoops." Scarcely had the fleet got under way when the well-known heavings of the ship, variously dubbed "the wooden horse," "the timber nag," and "the dirty bird," produced the customary effect on the passengers, whose sorry plight is described with humorous, though harrowing, realism. For three days the garrulous Judge, his wife, and children lay helpless in their tiny, foul-smelling dungeon, unable to take food or even to undress. And seldom during the forty days at sea were these landsmen free from a depressing nausea. Even when the ship was becalmed the rhythmic rise and fall on the ocean swell made the women especially cry out in sick despair, "*Ay, madre mía!* Put me ashore!"

There were endless days of dull routine, of unvaried meals of hardtack and salt meat, of constant thirst. The crew, the ships' officers, and the passengers led their separate existences. The last, unheeded and unaided, clustered about the small ship stoves, obliged to cook their food from their own stores all at the same time before the fire went out. As they consumed their unappetizing fare they sighed for the grapes of their native Guadalajara, the cherries of Illescas, or the turnips of Somo-Sierra. To drink their short ration of water it was necessary to close their eyes and lose their sense of smell and taste. Men and women, young and old, clean and dirty, all found themselves crowded together amidst unspeakable filth, without privacy for even the most intimate necessities. All night darkness enveloped them with no distraction save the reciting of creeds and prayers while the cabin boys stood watch over the binnacle. Sleep was no more than the fitful slumber of despondent souls half lulled by the beating of the waves on the ship's sides. By day it was impossible to walk about the pitching craft except when supported by an apprentice seaman on either side. Occasionally, the general apathy was suddenly transformed into alarm as a sail appeared on the horizon. The fear of pirates provoked a panic fright which some sought to hide by singing litanies; women shrieked and frantically endeavored to conceal their jewels and money before the corsairs arrived. And then the immense relief and joy that seized everyone when the sail was found to belong to a ship of the same fleet, from which they had been separated for days!

At last the incompetent pilots make rough calculations as to their location and conclude that land is near, and everyone's spirits soar perceptibly. As the vessels approach the terminal port there is a happy bustling among boxes, bags, and chests for days, and the ladies, especially, come forth in their finest array and toilet. But rarely is the happiness at the end of the voyage unmarred by such untoward incidents as collisions or near collisions as the impatient pilots excitedly attempt to bring the galleons into narrow harbors or to a safe anchorage. And the ship-bound prisoners heartily and unanimously agree, "Land for mankind, sea for the fishes!"

It was mentioned briefly in passing that life on shipboard in the sixteenth century did not entirely lack its brighter moments. The neophytes of the 1544 crossing had enjoyed themselves with guitar playing and singing, and sporting in the water when the ships were becalmed. Sufficient deck space was often cleared for cockfights as long as the birds remained uneaten, bullfights were simulated, dances and even plays were performed on a stage that never ceased to rise and fall. But more often cramped space and inclement weather made enforced inactivity the lot of all. Distractions of a sedentary character necessarily occupied more of the time than community amusements. Card games and the rolling of dice, with

associated gambling, were universal diversions, though often indulged in somewhat surreptitiously because of prohibitory regulations. But these ordinances, like so many others of the time, had
little retarding effect on shipboard, especially among soldiers. While
conversation consumed long hours for the passengers, the general
apathy induced by monotony and nausea resulted in extended periods of silence. Some might find refuge from the tedium of the
voyage in their own thoughts, but the more literate sought forget-
fulness in perusing the books included among their immediate effects. Some read aloud a current book of fiction or poetry to atten-
tive listeners, while other dipped into their volumes in solitude.
Much more time on the long crossings was spent in this fashion
than is generally realized and many literary works were thus transported to the New World in the sixteenth century and later.

Father De la Torre makes a passing reference to this distraction
in his account but, while he bears witness to the presence of books
in passengers' possession, he gives no indication of the types or titles
of reading material thus enjoyed. More specific and illuminating
information of this character is revealed by the fragmentary and
extremely terse reports made by the Inquisition authorities on the
arrival of the ships at the terminal ports. These officials boarded the
vessels before the passengers or freight were discharged and made
an interrogation—often perfunctory—concerning books, images,
and religious objects brought on the voyage. This examination was
based largely on oral questions and, if nothing of consequence was
brought to light, the *visita*, or inspection, reports were limited to a
few simple notations. Scattering records of this sort made at San
Juan de Ulúa, the port of entry of Mexico, are available from 1572
to the end of the century and, since they doubtless reflect practices
elsewhere in the Indies, the evidence they offer is of general application. These data sometimes throw interesting light on the literary
predilections of readers during the tedious Atlantic crossing.

Beginning about 1576 many, but by no means all, of these
memoranda include references to passengers' books seen or picked
up by the inquisitors during their cursory inspection of the decks
and cabins. It should be emphasized that such recording did not
indicate that the representatives of the Inquisition had confiscated or
had even disapproved of the volumes mentioned; these notations im-

plied that the books found were harmless in their eyes, and the listing merely indicated a compliance with required formalities. The
insights into shipboard reading tastes thus afforded are suggested in
the following reproductions of these brief documents:[11]

> Inspection of the Fleet of Diego Maldonado, of which Don
>   Antonio de Manrique was General, 1576.
> Ship—*Santiago*
>   Master, Andres Felipe.
>   Captain, Gonzalo Mendez.
>   Books, *Teatro del mundo, Selva de aventuras, Amadís,
>   Fray Luis de Granada,* and several of chivalry.

*   *   *   *   *

> Inspection of the ships composing the Fleet commanded by
>   General Juan de Guzmán, arriving at San Juan Ulúa in
>   September, 1585.
> Ship—*San Bartolomé,* owned by Maestre Pedro de Arbe-
>   lays
>   Captain, Nicolás de Urrutia.
>   Books, *Amadis of Gaul, Don Belianis, Flossantorum,*
>   and others, both of chivalry and devotion, and two
>   cases of books with consignee unspecified.

*   *   *   *   *

> Inspection of the ships forming the Fleet which arrived in
>   San Juan Ulúa in October, 1600, under the command of
>   General Pedro de Escobar Melgarejo.
> Flagship—*Nuestra Señora de Aranzazú,* owned by Gas-
>   par de Portu.
>   Master, Juan de Ugarte.
>   Pilot, Luis de la Cruz.
>   Books, *La Arcadia* of Lope de Vega, *Guzmán de Al-
>   farache, Exercicios* of Fray Luis de Granada, sev-
>   eral of chivalry, and prayer books. Several cases
>   belonging to His Majesty of the *Nuevo rezado.*

*   *   *   *   *

These memoranda are incomplete and their data vary greatly
in details. They supply, therefore, no basis for a statistical study.
Fairly typical is the following:

> Inspection of the ships of the Fleet which came from Spain
>   and arrived at the port of San Juan de Ulúa in September,
>   1586. General Francisco Novoa.

Ship—*Santa Lucia*, owned by Pedro de Aranda.
Notary, Martín López.
Barber, Bartolomé de Peña Aranda.
Books. They exhibited before the Commissioner. He
does not state what they were.

*   *   *   *   *

Frequently these records merely state that "odd" books, meaning those belonging to passengers and used for their diversion on
shipboard, were shown, and that so many cases, contents unspecified,
consigned to so and so were received. In neither instance are titles
given. The meager data and careless compilation of these notes indicate how casually the inquisitors performed their functions and
suggest that it was not their concern to enforce the probably forgotten decrees against admitting light literature into the colonies.
These random notations also show how ineffective was the effort
to exclude truly heretical works, since the officials apparently con-
tented themselves with purely superficial investigations.

Despite the scanty information that these *visita* reports divulge,
some of the literature which entertained sea tourists of the late sixteenth century during the weary crossings can be identified. When
weather and other conditions permitted, both the crew and the
passengers were obliged to devote certain periods each day to public
prayers and to reciting creeds and other offices of the Church services. Books of devotion, therefore, were indispensable and required
items in everyone's luggage. Most common were the *Horas* or
prayerbooks, both in Latin and in the vernacular, and mention of
these small volumes probably recurs most frequently in the inspection memoranda. Various writings by mystics of the Counter Reformation, especially Fray Luis de Granada, appear repeatedly along
with a lesser number of lives of saints and other pietistic tracts, no
one of which seems to have had a marked preference over others.

Much more conspicuous and doubtless more avidly read by
bored and uncomfortable argonauts were the *libros profanos* or lay
literature. Of these entertaining books there is a wide variety ranging over most of contemporary Castilian letters and including many
of the creative writings listed among the prevailing favorites of the
sixteenth century in Chapter IX. The representatives of the Inquisition disregarded or completely forgot reiterated royal decrees against

the "lying histories such as Amadis," as is clearly demonstrated by the inspection reports on incoming ships sent to the viceregal quarters of the Holy Office. In these brief documents the books of fiction reported as in the passengers' cabins and baggage were most often these same allegedly banned romances of chivalry. So common and universal were these tales as a means of banishing ennui on shipboard down to the end of the sixteenth century and later that the Inquisitors rarely bothered to list them by title. Generally, their notations read "many," "several," "various," "other," novels of chivalry, with details otherwise entirely lacking. The name *Amadís* was frequently jotted down in these notes but, as previously suggested, the term refers generically to all units of that novelistic cycle and it almost became synonymous with the entire chivalric genre. Other titles often mentioned are *El caballero del Febo, Oliveros de Castilla, El caballero determinado, Carlomagno y los doce pares, Primaleón*, and *Don Belianis de Grecia*. Noted more often than any of these, however, is *Orlando furioso*, presumably the work by Ariosto which appears on the *visita* reports in the original Italian and in Spanish translation. Incidentally, writings of other Italian figures, such as Petrarch, Bembo, and Castiglione, are noted. The *Silva de varia lección* and *Selva de aventuras* are among other works of fantasy, so popular in Spain and its colonies at this time, which were read on shipboard. The pastoral novel most frequently mentioned is *Diana*, presumably the famous creation of Jorge Montemayor but probably referring also to the sequels and imitations it inspired. At the close of the century Lope de Vega's *Arcadia* entertains voyagers, while more rarely the realistic masterpiece *Celestina*, attributed to Fernando de Rojas, is found, thus reflecting the same varying tastes in contemporary reading on land.

Often the inspection reports mention "chivalries and histories," suggesting that both types of literature were read by the same passengers and probably with the customary incomprehension of the line between fact and fancy which these two classes of narrative were supposed to draw. History, so-called, was a leading favorite of the Atlantic travelers and second only to the romances of chivalry—the close association is significant—though no specific title predominates on the sketchy lists. Most conspicuous, perhaps, is the *Historia pontifical y católica* which, in revised editions, was appar-

ently regarded as essential reading by many. Further testimony to
the popularity of the literary hoax *El libro áureo de Marco Aurelio*
by the good Bishop of Guadix and chronicler of Charles V, is given
by its repeated presence in these memoranda; occasionally this author's name appears as "Antonio de Guevara" without indication of
the specific work implied. Pedro Mexía's history of the Caesars is
next in recurrence, followed by scattered or isolated references to a
*Historia de Colón, Crónicas de Paulo Jovio, Crónica de España,
Guerras del Perú, Conquista de Chile, Conquista de Italia y Portugal, Conquista de México, Conquista del Perú, La cisma de Inglaterra* by Ribadeneira, *Descubrimiento de las Indias,* and a *Historia
de Malta.* Books of travel and geography might well be expected on
these shipboard lists of reading matter. Examples are the *Viaje a
Jerusalén,* the *Descripción de África* and the *Repúblicas del mundo.*
Possibly the officers of the vessels inspected had in their possession
the *Arte de navegar* by Pedro de Medina, an *Arte de marear,* a
Regla de navegación, and the *Reportorio* of Chávez.

Especially numerous are poetic works, epic and lyric, with
ballad collections increasingly evident toward the close of the century. Castilian poets such as Juan de Mena, Boscán, Montemayor,
Lope de Vega, and others are named at least once in the brief notes
of the inquisitors. Most frequently observed is the long historical
poem of Alonso Ercilla, *La Araucana,* whose successive parts are
not specified when the title is listed. Latin poets include Ovid and
Vergil particularly, though whether the books were in Latin or
in Spanish is not revealed. The *Odyssey* and the *Iliad,* literature
quite appropriate for travelers at sea, are also present. Other writers of antiquity who helped while away the tedium of sixteenth-
century ocean voyages were Terence and Cicero.

The scattering and partial *visita* reports, so perfunctorily compiled by the Inquisition commissioners, serve the same useful purpose of shedding light on the diffusion of literary culture in the
New World as do, in larger measure, the fragmentary ship registers.
If the *registros* offer convincing evidence that the holds of the little
vessels tossed about on the Atlantic's waves contained stout boxes,
chests, and bales of printed literature destined for colonists scattered
far and wide in the overseas realms of Spain, the laconic *visita* records of the Holy Office in the Indies plainly reveal that, on the

narrow decks and in the comfortless cabins of Spanish galleons, far removed from the shores of either world, the creative spirits of the Hispanic Peninsula, great and small, enthralled their shipbound audience. These hardy voyagers thus found surcease momentarily from the hardships and trials which were inevitable concomitants of participation in the pioneer stage of westernizing the terrestrial globe.

A GLIMPSE OF THE VARIED LITERATURE WHICH BE-
guiled some of the dreary hours of shipboard existence on the
Spanish galleons was offered in the last chapter. More details and a
larger number of specific titles would doubtless give a clearer picture of contemporary reading tastes on the high seas, but even these
hazy indications would probably not be available if the concern of
Spanish authorities for the preservation of the orthodox state religion had not been so intense. The profound conviction of both
the Crown and the Church that the propagation of the Catholic
faith in the newly acquired realms must be safeguarded at all costs
from the schismatic dissensions of contemporary Europe stimulated their unremitting, if somewhat unsuccessful, efforts to prevent
the circulation of heretical books in the Indies. These rulers made
earnest attempts not only to choke off the exportation of such literature from Spain itself but also to exclude from entrance to the
ports of debarkation any works of subversive character which might
evade the vigilance of the officials in the homeland. The preventa-
tive measure adopted for the American side of the Atlantic service
was a *visita*, or customs inspection, of all incoming ships. A decree
of 1556 required the treasury officers at these terminal points to
exercise extreme care in checking the cargoes of arriving vessels
with the sealed registers they brought in order to note the possible
inclusion of books on the Inquisition *Index;* any listed works discovered must be turned over promptly to the archbishops or their
duly appointed representatives.[1] The lax enforcement of this command—the fate of so many in the sixteenth century and later—soon
obliged the authorities to consider the establishment of a special
agency to perform this and other functions, since the menace of

heresy was growing alarmingly. Thus it was decided to install in the New World itself branches of the secular arm of the Church, known as the Holy Office of the Inquisition, to supervise and coordinate all activities designed to protect the purity and integrity of the one True Faith. Since this institution strove to operate by strictly legal procedures—an aspiration not generally recognized—it kept full records of its acts, some of which survive in fragmentary form. These sources of information are most accessible for the viceroyalty of Mexico, but a description of the practices observed at its seaport, San Juan de Ulúa or Vera Cruz, is probably applicable in general to the few other parts of the Indies where the ships from Spain were received.

Until 1570 the inquisitorial powers in the colonies rested mainly in the hands of the archbishops or their appointed subordinates. Prior to this date there was some censorial activity but it was, on the whole, sporadic and unsystematic. The Lutheran revolt in Europe was spreading even as the conquistadors were overrunning the New World and as the pioneer missionaries were attempting the spiritual conquest of its aboriginal inhabitants. The long-drawn-out sessions of the historic Council of Trent, which met intermittently from 1545 to 1563, were dominated by the ultra-conservative elements of the Church, and hence they failed to arrive at any formulae of reconciliation with the dissident Protestants. The great schism widened as official Spanish Catholicism clung fanatically to a rigid orthodoxy which inevitably placed it on the defensive. In an effort to purify itself within its doctrinal frame and to exclude what were regarded as pernicious influences, it resorted to practices of censorship which, on the whole, proved more potent for evil than for good. In the last of its long sessions the Council of Trent drew up a series of ten rules "as a guide and instruction for all ecclesiastics or other authorities who might thereafter be charged with the duty of literary censorship."[2] These laws applied to theological and religious works almost exclusively, though the seventh commandment dealing with "books professedly treating of lascivious or obscene subjects, or narrating, or teaching these" clearly opened the door to banning secular literature of a lighter character.

The increasing dread of Protestantism and the fear of heretical books steadily invading the overseas dominions of Spain spurred a

prompt compliance with the directives of both secular and ecclesiastical councils, but the machinery of enforcement was invariably
defective. To remedy the situation inquisitional tribunals similar to
those existing in Spain were authorized for the colonies, and they
began to operate in Lima and Mexico City on January 29, 1570 and
on November 4, 1571, respectively.[3] It was anticipated that these
local branches would be more efficient in hunting down and eradi-
cating growing evils. Books immediately claimed the special attention of the transplanted Inquisition, but only those works, it should
be emphasized, which were regarded as so inimical to the faith or to
good morals that they gained a place on the official *Index*. The
bishops in the viceroyalties had had some discretion in discharging
their duties of this sort and they were occasionally arbitrary, but
their interference with the circulation of books other than those
officially proscribed by the home office of the Inquisition in Spain
was infrequent. Indeed, these high dignitaries showed a surprising
indifference to the literature of recreation, considering the tirades
directed against it during the sixteenth century from their own
pulpits and the fact that these *"libros profanos"* were specifically
and repeatedly prohibited in the Spanish Indies by secular decrees
of the Crown.

On January 3, 1570 Dr. Pedro Moya de Contreras, then serving
as Inquisitor of Murcia in the Peninsula, was notified of his designation as presiding executive of the projected tribunal at Mexico
City. Though he started for the New World late that year, delays
of one sort or another, including shipwreck off the coast of Cuba,
prevented him from setting up this new branch of the Holy Office
until near the end of 1571. One of his first official acts was to publish a long edict which stipulated, among other matters, that booksellers and private persons receiving shipments of printed material
from Spain must present invoices or lists for the scrutiny of the Inquisition before claiming delivery. After this checking the owners
would receive instructions on the disposition they could make of
their books.[4]

This bureaucratic meddling with individual enterprise, theretofore relatively unrestricted, promptly drew the fire of a small group
of bookdealers of Mexico City. The commissioner of the Inquisition
had stopped delivery of a shipment of breviaries and missals, and

the aggrieved merchants protested that this act was an obvious in-justice and amounted to a virtual confiscation of their property.[5] This incident was symptomatic of the conflicts and disagreements which disturbed the relations of the representatives of the State, the Holy Office, and the commercial elements throughout the colonial period, and these irritations largely nullified the carefully devised efforts of authorities, ecclesiastical and secular alike, to control contraband and the black-market operations of the period. The first point of contact where friction developed was at the port of entry on the occasion of the customs inspection, which was aggravated by the separate inquisitional *visita*.

Earlier royal decrees had required specially appointed treasury officials to inspect for the Crown all incoming ships, whether single or in fleets, at the terminal ports of the Indies. No goods or persons could go ashore until this indispensable formality was completed. The sealed registers, which the shipmasters handed these represen-tatives, must be checked to see that the goods carried in the holds corresponded exactly; similarly, the passenger list served for a roll call of the voyagers aboard, all of whom must be rigorously ac-counted for. The inspectors must uncover by careful search any unregistered goods and detect any unlicensed persons seeking entry into the colonies.[6] Again and again the instructions cautioned these royal officers to perform their duties with the utmost thoroughness and care, but this need to repeat these admonitions so often is striking evidence that negligence and abuses were common. Care-lessness, indifference and, probably as often, flagrant corruption characterized the execution of these commands. The task of open-ing all the containers in the cargoes, checking their contents, and closing them again was too laborious and time consuming, and it delayed far too long the disembarkation of sea-weary travelers. The crews and officers naturally resented such excessive exertions at the end of a tiring voyage, and the merchants were disgruntled by the resulting disarrangement of their wares. And, in the end, all this bother did not stop petty thieving, fraud, or contraband. Soon the more convenient method was instituted of summoning sailors, offi-cers, and passengers on deck and of demanding from them an oral statement under oath. This procedure saved a vast amount of trouble, but it lent itself even more effectively to evasion and de-

ceit; swearing to the truth of an allegation quickly became mechanical and in no way prevented private deals by faithless officials with
merchants and peddlers on the incoming vessels. In the latter part
of the sixteenth century the President of the Audiencia of Santo
Domingo offered the Council of the Indies some suggestions for
changes in these operations which throw light on prevailing conditions. He declared that the port inspectors really limited their activities to the simple routine of administering an oath, after which
they promptly returned to the city, usually accompanied by Negro
slaves staggering under the weight of merchandise obtained on shipboard at modest prices.[7] The profits accruing from the private resale of these goods made appointments as customs officers highly
attractive. With such malpractices general, contraband trade flourished even before the Conquistador had finished his work in the
New World, and these abuses largely nullified the carefully contrived regulations governing commerce and navigation between
Spain and its colonies.

Considering the opportunities for private gain enjoyed by the
Crown inspectors and the merchants alike, the evident resentment
and hostility of both to the added inquisitorial *visita* are understandable. A parallel inspection for ecclesiastical purposes had various disadvantages. In the first place, it amounted to a division of
authority, and the treasury officials were always jealous of their
prerogatives, but more important still, it meant a menace to or, at
least, a sharing of the illicit traffic they found so remunerative. Consequently, the second and concurrent *visita* intended to ferret out
prohibited books and images thus instituted by the newly appointed
Inquisitor created a new source of conflict, wrangling, and confusion in the disorder associated with the arrival of the fleet and the
period during which the ships remained in port.[8] The effect of this
situation is reflected in the frequency with which the Holy Office
urged its representatives at Vera Cruz to exercise the utmost tact
in their dealings with their fellow inspectors, the treasury officials
of the Crown, and to take extreme care in restoring books and other
objects examined to the original cases and in such good condition
that their owners would have no legitimate cause for complaint.[9]
The fear of vexing merchants, clearly evident in these written orders
of the Inquisition, indicates that this dread institution did not enjoy

the oppressive sway over all elements of colonial society traditionally ascribed to it.

The sequence in which the two separate inspections were conducted appears to have varied from time to time, a fact doubtless resulting from the jurisdictional clashes of these two groups of officials. One of the earliest directives to the inquisitors at Vera Cruz gives priority to the secular inspection by Crown officers;[10] later, it is urged that both *visitas* be concurrent on each ship;[11] again, apparently because the two visiting delegations had gotten into each other's way the year before, a recommendation was made in 1586 that the two scrutinies take place separately, one group working on one ship while the other was fulfilling its obligations on another, so as to avoid the intemperate clashes between rival agents.[12] The unpleasantness to which the representatives of the Holy Office were subject on these occasions may even have moved them to neglect their duties at times, leaving the inspection to the Crown officers entirely. This possibility is suggested by a decree of Philip II, issued in January 1585, in which he specifically charges the prelates of the Church to require that their Provisors at the port of entry be on hand to make the examination of incoming ships for prohibited books at the same time that His Majesty's treasury officials are engaged in their inspection of the rest of the cargo.[13]

When the General of a fleet put into port his first duty was to notify the customs officers of the Crown stationed there and then stand by until their work was done. Both the secular and inquisitorial inspectors were cautioned by their respective superiors to be punctual in meeting the fleets and individual vessels so that the debarkation of passengers and freight should be delayed as little as possible—another indication of the healthy respect that the allegedly tyrannical Crown and Church had for the business elements of the colonial society over which these authorities are presumed to have exercised despotic sway. Both of the delegations put out from the shore in small boats provided by the government and soon they clambered up the sides of the anchored ships. Since the books of the Conquistador and his descendants are of primary interest here, only the routine of the inquisitorial *visita* will be described.[14]

Accompanying the deputy of the Holy Office were a notary and an *alguacil*, or constable, or occasionally a fellow official of the Inquisition who bore its emblem of authority. Into the stern cabin or some other these inspectors summoned the shipmaster, the pilot, and one or two passengers, who represented all the rest. In the absence of the latter, since some of the ships conveyed merely freight or slaves, a pair of the more intelligent members of the crew were brought together and each one of this group was constrained to answer the following eight questions and to swear to speak the truth, under penalty of the severest anathema of the Church.

1. First. From what port did the ship sail, what was the date of sailing, whose ship was it, and what was its original destination?

2. Item. In what other port of his Majesty or those of other rulers and lords did it enter?

3. Item. What people were on board, and of what nations, sovereigns, commonwealth, or lords, were they vassals; and were any of them Jews, Moors, Turks, or any of the Moriscos expelled from Spain, or heretics, Lutherans, Calvinists, or any other sect contrary to our Holy Catholic Faith?

4. Item. In case any of the above-mentioned are on board, the witness shall testify as to what things, or ceremonies, of their rites or wicked sects they have seen them perform; whether they have celebrated any fasts or maundy practices of the Jews or Moors, or said prayers, performed other rites of heretics, or maltreated Images, or argued against the Holy Catholic Faith and the Roman Church, or said anything evil about it, or against the Holy Sacraments and the power of the Pope, or against the religious orders and the ecclesiastical state, or against the King, our Lord, comparing him with other sovereigns of other religions, or whether they have eaten meat on Fridays, kept fasts and Lent, or failed to hear Mass while on land the days when the others had heard it.

5. Item. Whether any of the aforementioned or any other of the Catholics on the ship have done or said anything that may be, or appear to be, against the Holy Catholic Faith and the Apostolic Law which the Holy Roman Church has, follows, and teaches; or have blasphemed against God, our Lord, the Most Holy Virgin, His Mother, or the Saints, or against the Holy Office of the Inquisition?

6. Item. Whether on this vessel there are any possessions,

goods, or merchandise of infidels, or heretics, or rebels against his Majesty, whence they came, whose are they, and to whom are they consigned?

7. Item. Whether on board ship there are any images or figures of saints, popes, cardinals, bishops, priests, friars, and missionaries that are indecent, ridiculous, and wretchedly painted, or any forbidden books such as the Bible in any vulgar tongue, or any other books of the Lutheran and Calvinist sects and of other heretics, or any of those forbidden by the Holy Office of the Inquisition, or any others unregistered and concealed, or without license of the Holy Office?

8. Item. What books is the ship bringing duly registered, where they come from, in whose charge they are being brought, and to what persons are they consigned?[15]

The order and wording of the questions sometimes varied, and subsequent revisions of this questionnaire elaborated the phrasing of the last question. About 1572 the following change is noticed:

What books for prayer, reading or pastime are brought on the ship; whatever ones there are, the commissioners must see whether they are on the prohibited list; if they are in a foreign language, great care must be taken to ascertain what they are about; and here it should be noted that if there are Lutheran foreigners, it is their practice to bring the psalms of David in their own language which they chant at sea.[16]

Later there is another variant of this interrogation:

What cases of books are there registered or unregistered, what books are packed in cases or are found outside of them, what ones are in casks, or barrels, or mixed with other merchandise; where they were taken aboard, whether at Seville, San Lúcar, or Cádiz, or possibly at the Canary Islands, or at other ports touched; whose books are they, and for what persons in this city [Mexico] are they brought, both the registered and unregistered; if, in the replies, the inspectors are referred wholly or in part to the register, they will question further to learn whether anything more on the same subject is known.[17]

If nothing worthy of note developed out of this cross-examination, the deputy with his assistant and the notary were to search the stern cabin and others he thought necessary; he should have a few boxes, chests, or bales opened that might possibly conceal banned books or other prohibited articles since it was the "ordinary fashion of heretics" to smuggle printed volumes among legitimate goods. Obedience to this instruction doubtless irked the owners and shippers most, and their vigorous protests moved the Holy Office to instruct the agents to perform their functions with great circumspection, carefully restoring the contents of each inspected case to their original place.

The entire procedure seems ordinarily to have been exceedingly perfunctory, with the questioning a hasty, mechanical mumbling which fulfilled the letter rather more than the spirit of the regulations. Even the directing heads of the Inquisition acknowledged that a full compliance in writing "would be a lengthy and laborious task for those in charge of it" and recommended that the questions and answers be given orally; only in the event that the cross-examination produced evidence of a serious infraction was a detailed record necessary. If there was nothing untoward the scribe made a few notations of a summary character, which included indications of the place of the *visita*, the port from which the ship sailed, the date of arrival, the names of the inspectors, the *maestre*, pilot, passengers or sailors quizzed, and the gist of the information elicited. While these data were jotted down the deputy had a few cases opened and, after this cursory examination, he stated that, so far as the Holy Office was concerned, disembarkation of passengers and freight could proceed at once. The completed report in its short, terse form was then signed by the representative of the Inquisition, the shipmaster, the pilot, and the other witnesses if they were able to write, and finally the whole was countersigned by the notary.

When the inquiry brought unsatisfactory replies or suspicious findings a more extensive document was obligatory. But even where questionable literature was uncovered experience appears to have taught the Holy Office in Mexico City not to place too much reliance on the discretion of its own representatives at Vera Cruz. An edict of 1572 declared that if, on opening cases or boxes, *any* books of sacred writings, philosophy, or related subjects were noticed, the inspectors must promptly close the containers in question without attempting to read or even glance through such printed works. It was then their duty to place the seal of the Holy Office on the shipment and forward it directly to Mexico City for checking at the head office of the Inquisition before the owners could take possession. Even books consigned to other parts of the vast viceroyalty must be routed in the same way.[18]

With regard to the odd volumes picked up in the ship cabins or noted among the personal effects of the passengers, the inspectors barely mentioned them, often omitting the titles altogether, but these incidental and wholly routine notations, which were filed away in the archives of the Holy Office along with the more important evidence, offer priceless testimony to the fact that the successors of the Conquistador did actually enjoy light literature on shipboard as they crossed the Atlantic.

One other aspect of the Inquisition's instructions to its subordinates at Vera Cruz invites attention. The *visitas* in which they participated not uncommonly degenerated into more or less convivial meetings, with the shipmaster acting as host. Food was liberally dispensed and wine flowed freely. No doubt merchants on the incoming vessels contributed to these festivities for certain ulterior motives of their own. Where the fleet was large the necessity of visiting so many of its units must have been a severe test of the bibulous proclivities of the deputies and their assistants. Under these circumstances bargains and agreements of a private nature affecting the entry of books and other articles of possibly contraband character into the realm were doubtless consummated. Conceivably, the agents of the Holy Office were induced to *hacer la vista gorda*, as the Spaniards so expressively put it; that is, like their fellow inspectors of the Crown, they overlooked certain irregularities in the clearing of cargoes at the port. The stern and repeated admonitions of the chief Inquisitors to their deputies against accepting gratuities, gifts, or presents from anyone on the incoming ships amply confirm the existence of these abuses. Subordinates were expressly forbidden at the time of the *visita* to dicker or attempt to buy anything on shipboard—"not even something to eat"—for themselves or for a third party because, indeed, such an act would be "a bad example and *desedificación.*" Thus it is clear that the purposes of the inquisitorial inspection were often defeated by flagrant flouting of its regulations, and by the connivance of the representatives of the Holy Office itself with arriving passengers or crew.

Relations between the examiners and the examined were sometimes badly strained, however. During the 1585 *visita* the commissioner of the Inquisition had occasion to send for the shipmaster of *La Trinidad*. When the messenger of the dread institution came aboard to apprise its master of his errand, he found that worthy in shirt sleeves and underdrawers engaged in a friendly game of poker, or its equivalent. He was playing for stakes of silk stockings at seven pesos a pair and, as he had a hand or two more to play, this crusty seaman refused to heed the summons at once and growled that he would show up later in the afternoon. Pressed by the troubled messenger to come right away as ordered, the exasperated *maestre* bellowed loudly enough to be heard by everyone in the immediate vicinity, telling the inquisitorial emissary, with particularly lurid epithets, to get out. Such a shocking disregard of the expressed command of so august a corporation as the Holy Office was an indignity not to be tolerated, especially as this sort of thing was becoming distressingly common, and the offending shipmaster soon found himself clapped into jail and obliged to put up a heavy bail to defray the expenses of a trial. The shortage of seamen in the port, however, was great and there was a pressing need to prepare the fleet to resume its voyage—facts which possibly explain in part this mariner's independence and insolence. The urgency of the naval situation at the moment was much too severe to spare any member of the crews and, when word of the shipmaster's plight reached the General of the fleet an hour or so later, he hurried to plead personally for the release of the culprit. This high authority and the indispensability of the shipmaster's services provided irresistible pressure, and the deputy of the Holy Office promptly acceded to the General's request. When the matter was reported later to the chief Inquisitor in Mexico City, that official wrote back that the commissioner had done entirely right in jailing the disrespectful skipper; instead of locking him up for only an hour, however, he should have done so for a week! [19]

There were doubtless many similar clashes between the inspectors and the inspected, and numerous occasions when injured vanity, jealous resentment, and tactless acts on both sides caused friction and delay. Officious inquisitors, overconscious of their importance as guardians of the one True Faith, sometimes adopted an imperious manner at which equally individualistic shipmasters and pilots, accustomed to absolute command on their own vessels, did not fail to take umbrage. Well aware, too, of the manifest hypocrisy of these deputies, who were not averse to bribery in one form or another, both the crew and the passengers accorded them scant courtesy. As a consequence, arriving voyagers were sometimes subjected to petty annoyances by these pompous and too meticulous officials who searched their cabins and baggage for banned books and other contraband with excessive zeal. In 1575, for example, the deputy of the Holy Office and his assistants boarded the good ship *La Candelaria* where they found copies of prayer books and other devotional works, *Amadís* and several other romances of chivalry, a *Life of St. Francis*, and also a *Life of Julius Caesar*, which had diverted some of the passengers during the crossing. The last-mentioned volume was in the possession of a student named San Clemente, a somewhat indiscreet youth, apparently. On finding this book among the young man's personal effects the inquisitorial inspector felt called upon to emit a literary judgment on the youthful traveler's reading tastes. Departing from the ritualistic interrogations of the *visita* the official queried the student as to why he did not read something better, such as the life of St. Francis, who was a Christian? Why did he waste his time perusing a volume about Julius Caesar who had gone to hell, anyway, because, you know, that hero of ancient Rome was never baptized? This impertinent intrusion into the young scholar's reading preferences quite naturally irritated him and, not having reached full maturity, he was so injudicious as to engage in a heated argument with the censorious representative of the Inquisition. This unwise reaction to bureaucratic interference resulted in the drawing up of a judicial brief against him, in which this admirer of Julius Caesar was placed in the category of one suspect in the faith.[20] How this rash youth emerged from his embarrassing predicament the existing records do not reveal. But the reiterated admonitions of the executive officers of the Holy Office in Mexico City to their subordinates in Vera Cruz and elsewhere to perform their duties with courtesy and tact indicate that incidents of this sort did not increase the popularity of the *visita,* and that secular complaints from influential sources were so numerous that even the powerful institution of the Inquisition could not ignore them. Such excess of zeal on the part of their employees was likely to be self-defeating, particularly when it operated in conjunction with other factors tending to foster resistance to vexatious restrictions.

Between the obvious unpopularity of the Inquisition's efforts to intervene in the commercial importation of books into the colonies and the prevalence of corruption among its own servitors, it is not surprising that the precautions and measures taken to prevent smuggling were largely ineffectual. Even if, as is so often alleged, the Holy Office had sought to exclude the romances of chivalry and other forms of light fiction—which it clearly did not do—some of these books, doubtless many, would have slipped through the barriers just as forbidden works actually did. The fact that the superiors of the Inquisition issued edict after edict and command after command, demanding the utmost care and vigilance in the inspection of incoming vessels, offers convincing evidence that the attempt to suppress truly contraband literature, such as Lutheran tracts and Bibles, frequently failed. The smuggling of heretical works was continuous and even members of the religious communities themselves participated in this illegal traffic.[21]

Some of the methods by which forbidden literature slipped through the bottlenecks shaped by colonial authorities were ingenious and surprisingly modern. A letter dated October 8, 1581 at Mexico City states that single dispatch boats from Spain, which customarily did not carry registers, often transported books in casks intended for wine and in barrels of dried fruit, a common cargo permitted on these small ships. "When opened they appear to be full of filberts and other things, though inside are books."[22] Large wine containers were a specially popular means of introducing contraband printed material into the colonies. On May 9, 1608 the royal officials at Buenos Aires addressed a letter to the Holy Office at Lima, the capital of the viceroyalty of Peru which then embraced the River Plate region as well. In this document they stated that vessels from foreign ports, such as those of Flanders and

Portugal, came to Buenos Aires, bringing books and other prohibited articles "in casks and other containers." The Inquisition at
Lima replied urging energetic measures against all offenders.[23] This
use of wine containers for the clandestine introduction of banned
books in earlier centuries appears to have been reversed during the
so-called "prohibition era" in the United States when, it was reported, bottles of forbidden liquors were sometimes shipped into
the country in cases of books!

Even bolder means of introducing contraband literature into
the colonial market are occasionally referred to in the existing
records. Since binding materials greatly increased book costs, it
was a common practice in sixteenth-century Spain to place two
or three works, sometimes entirely unrelated in character, between
a single pair of covers. The units formed by such combinations
were technically known as *cuerpos de libros* and, when colonial
inspectors were careless, this arrangement facilitated the admission
of disapproved works. About 1572 instructions of the Mexican
Inquisition concerning the scrutiny of incoming book shipments
reminds those in charge of the *visita* "that in a single volume
(*cuerpo*) two or three books are bound together, and it happens
often that the first one is all right while the others are not; hence it
is a good idea to look at each one individually, both at its beginning
and end, its printer, date and author."[24]

The registers covering individual consignments usually indicated the name of the person or persons at the terminal port to
whom the shipment should be delivered. Since many months, or
even years, had elapsed between the date of the original order from
the colonies and the final delivery of the books in the Indies, the
person authorized to accept the cases might have died or be unable, for other reasons, to receive the consignment. Consequently,
one or more alternates were customarily named on the invoice. The
individuals thus designated might be the consignees themselves but
more often, especially on the Isthmus of Panama and at Vera Cruz,
which were mainly transfer points on the long and tenuous trade
routes of the Spanish empire, the receivers were agents specially
engaged in this occupation. From Nombre de Dios and later Puertobelo, when it became the terminal port on the Isthmus, pack trains

were hired to make the short but difficult journey overland to Panama City where goods were then placed aboard ships bound for the West Coast of South America.

Though most shipments reaching Vera Cruz were destined for the upland capital of Mexico City, this seaport, as the threshold of the broad realm of New Spain, offered in itself a small market for the sale of books, and this fact was sometimes an advantage in disposing of prohibited works. With sailors and foreigners from the ships swarming about the streets, a furtive exchange of smuggled objects, including books, was relatively easy to effect and difficult to detect. The Holy Office early recognized this situation and one of the Chief Inquisitor's first measures in 1572 was to instruct his associate at Vera Cruz to permit no one to offer any books for sale there without first sending to Mexico City the sworn original of the title list received from Spain. When this document had been duly checked, word was sent to Vera Cruz regarding which books could be placed on sale.[25] Eight years later this regulation was modified to prevent delays. Since the disposal of books in the port city was now considered rather slight "and nearly all are well-known and recognized romances," the head of the Jesuit monastery there, equipped with a catalogue or index of prohibited works, was authorized to pass on the suitability of books to be sold in that vicinity without need of forwarding the list first to Mexico City.

As already noted, the Holy Office in the viceregal capital soon required all consignments of books, particularly of religious character, destined to that city or to any other part of the realm, to be delivered at the inquisitional headquarters in the highland, for its administrators had found it unwise to leave the detailed examination of incoming printed works to the discretion of their own *visita* officials at Vera Cruz. Hence in the regular transportation service operating between the seaport and the capital special muleteers and teamsters were entrusted with the important task of bringing the cases of books up from the coast, since it was essential that there should be no tampering with the contents en route to Mexico City. Thus, after the seal of the Holy Office was stamped on the boxes while they were still on the arriving ships, and after they had been lightered ashore and separated from the miscellaneous freight heaped on the beach, they were balanced on the backs of diminutive, hard-working donkeys, or loaded on clumsy two-wheeled carts drawn by slowly ambling oxen. These rude vehicles were called *chirriones,* no doubt from the shrill, rasping squeal of tortured axles as the unlubricated wheels bumped, jolted, and jarred over the rough and deeply rutted roads leading to the capital. Their stolid drivers were, by extension, known as *chirrioneros.* The total of boxes and cases of books thus transported each year is unknown, but the quantity surely varied considerably from time to time. In 1584 one hundred twelve cases are recorded; at least seventy-seven were hauled up the next year, and in 1586 eighty more followed.[26] The records in each case are incomplete and the number indicated is doubtless less than the whole.

On the backs of plodding donkeys and in lumbering oxcarts the vellum-covered and paper-bound products of Peninsula printing presses made their way at last into the lovely vale of Anáhuac where, surrounded by lakes, reposed the rebuilt Aztec capital. The teamsters and muleteers brought their tired charges to a halt at last before the designated monastery or convent where trusted *consultores* of the Holy Office would examine the books so laboriously transported. This service they would render with a care and thoroughness which fluctuated greatly in the course of time, depending on circumstances. After a presumably close checking with the official catalogue of prohibited books and with the edicts subsequently issued, both by the metropolitan Inquisition in Spain and by its local branches in the New World, those volumes regarded as harmless and free of heretical taint, usually the great majority, were permitted to reach the warehouses or shops of the merchants and booksellers, chiefly in the viceregal capital but also in the larger provincial towns, who had originally ordered them a year or two before. Thus ended for many of these imported books— but not all, since some were peddled in the interior among the mining camps and stock ranches by itinerant merchants—the long pilgrimage from the scattered printing shops of the Peninsula to the tables and shelves of colonial houses and manors. Now at last the eager descendants of the Conquistador might purchase and read the copies of well-established favorites or the latest novelties from the quills of popular writers in the homeland.

The choice of colonial book buyers in entertaining literature was as wide as that of their relatives in Spain itself. Despite the long delays caused by the slowness of the means of transportation and by the bureaucratic routines of the House of Trade and the Holy Office, the time lag in obtaining copies of the most recent literary successes of the Peninsula was remarkably short. Even if these agencies, particularly the Inquisition, had sought to keep the fiction works out of the hands of the overseas readers—and, of course, early royal decrees had endeavored to do just this—resourceful bookdealers would doubtless have found means to supply the lucrative demand. That they were often able to do so even with the clearly forbidden religious and theological writings is evident from the need of the Holy Office to make periodic rounds of the city shops in an effort to detect the source of contraband literature that continued to find its way into colonial hands. Now and then bookdealers were obliged to submit inventories of their stock to the authorities of the Inquisition, and now and then one found himself in serious difficulties with this censorious corporation which, in its self-imposed task of protecting the moral and spiritual welfare of the community, took upon itself the functions of municipal police. Its officers even resorted to raids on the bookstores under pressure from Spain or from local sources, but the intervals between these forays were usually long, during which the sale of printed works of all kinds proceeded quietly as a legitimate part of the commercial activity of colonial society. The fiction, poetry, and drama of Spain's great writers stirred the hearts and minds of the Spanish-speaking peoples on both sides of the Atlantic throughout the centuries of imperial glory and national decline.

Half a century after the spectacular conquest of the Aztec empire by Cortés the heroic age was drawing to a close. Though near the rich silver mines of Zacatecas north of the capital the savage Chichimecas still exacted a high toll of Spanish blood, the work of the adventurous conquistadors, for the most part, was done; likewise, the great task of converting the more sedentary Indians undertaken by no less courageous missionaries had already degenerated, in large measure, into a routine. Nearly all that hardy generation that had subjected half a continent to the Spanish God and Monarch had disappeared from the scene, though a few venerable survivors of that epic of European expansion lingered on as solitary relics of a vanishing age. In a southern province of the Mexican viceroyalty known as Guatemala the octogenarian soldier-chronicler of Cortés' campaigns, Bernal Díaz del Castillo, who claimed to have fought in one hundred nineteen battles, still brooded over the inadequate reward for the glorious adventures of his youth so vividly set forth in his *True history of the conquest of New Spain* which was destined to remain in manuscript for another half century. Doubtless other veterans of military and spiritual conquests were rheumatically living out their days as *encomenderos* on their estates, or languishing in chilly monastery cells or, perhaps, existing in less favorable circumstances within the viceregal capital itself. Already the sons of these conquerors and first settlers were middle-aged, a generation of grandsons was reaching manhood, and a numerous group of orphans and aged widows of Cortés' soldiers were living on the King's bounty. Many of these elements of the population were vexing problems to the harassed viceroys since the indolent-minded majority preferred to presume on the lusty achievements of their sires and grandsires and seek pensions and remunerative sinecures instead of performing useful services.[1] But even the more industrious had turned chiefly to gentler pursuits than those of their martial forebears. Some administered properties bequeathed them by their conquering fathers, while others found employment in Church and State offices. In rendering a confidential report on the ecclesiastical personnel of his diocese in 1575 the Archbishop of Mexico, Pedro de Moya de Contreras, formerly the Chief Inquisitor, mentions, among other individuals, a certain "Pedro Garces, born in this country and son of a conquistador, now aged forty-three, and a worthy canon endowed with an excellent voice and skill in music; he is very honest, simple and peaceful."[2] And the Archbishop added that Garces rendered signal service by his work in training a choir. Another worthy was Esteban de Portillo, thirty-nine years old, and also son of a soldier of Cortés, who was gifted in the Mexican language and in music, and who had served as a rector and professor in the flourishing University of Mexico; and still others are mentioned by the eminent prelate. But already the antipathy between the American-born and the European Spaniard, which was to plague colonial society for centuries, was intensifying, and the Creole was emerging as a well-defined type with his frustrations and inferiority complex growing out of the discrimination in favor of the politically dominant Peninsulars. The mestizo and the mulatto elements were becoming numerous and vocal, and already the kaleidoscopic social pattern of Spanish America was crystallizing.

Physically the transformed Aztec capital, situated in a lake and subject to periodic inundations, had assumed much of the appearance and extent that it possessed throughout most of the colonial period. To the west were visible many of the graceful arches of the aqueduct designed to bring an adequate water supply from nearby Chapultepec to the city, though this important engineering work was still incomplete in 1576. On the north side of the broad central square were the excavations, started a few years earlier, for the foundations of the vast cathedral whose construction occupied nearly a century. Already the viceregal palace lined the east side of the plaza, while on the south, opposite the cathedral site, stood the buildings of the Ayuntamiento and the Cabildo. Convents and other ecclesiastical structures as well as imposing private residences had risen within the slowly expanding confines of the city. Scattered about the central blocks were vacant lots serving all too often as convenient repositories of accumulating refuse and filth, thus seriously threatening community health. A few years later, when Archbishop Moya de Contreras acted as viceroy of the realm, he ordered the owners, under penalty of confiscation and resale, to build high fences around these empty spaces within six months.[3]

As already suggested, the size and character of the population of Mexico City had changed considerably during the decades following the Spanish capture, and the racial texture of the capital had grown more complex. An uncertain number of Indians, numerically the largest element, lived miserably about the periphery of the center reserved for Spanish families, and these unhappy natives provided much of the domestic help and menial labor of the city. In the whole viceroyalty of New Spain the white population was approximately 30,000, only about one-tenth of whom resided in the capital.[4] For the non-Indian inhabitants in the archbishopric of Mexico, whose jurisdiction, of course, extended beyond the city limits, there are approximate figures for the decade 1570-1580 which indicate the heterogeneous composition of the population in and about the viceregal capital. Since the Conquest the number of Negroes had steadily increased until, about 1576, it exceeded that of the Spaniards themselves. The latter totaled 9,495 as against 10,595 blacks, while there were 1,050 mulattoes and some 2,000 mestizos.[5] To the viceroy Martín Enríquez, the social effects of the rapidly growing Negro element constituted the gravest problem of the realm. Though these Africans furnished the most dependable labor supply, they created special difficulties. In the first place, the resulting miscegenation produced a dangerous increase in mulattoes who, as extramarital offspring, were invariably raised by their mothers, and thus grew up without masculine restraint. Lacking all discipline, they preferred laziness, idleness, and viciousness to learning a craft. Tougher and more insubordinate than the mestizos, they were a constant threat to public order, the Viceroy affirmed. The Negro slaves, he observed, were more acceptable to the Indian women as mates than their own men, and the blacks were quite disposed to contract such unions since by law their progeny were born free. Consequently, the Viceroy urged his king to decree that such children should also be declared slaves.[6]

By 1576 Don Martín Enríquez de Almanza, the fourth of the long series of viceroys sent to colonial Mexico, had completed two-thirds of his twelve-year term. Abler than most sixteenth-century administrators, he had found his exalted office no sinecure, and he was already requesting Philip II to relieve him. The tremendous domain over which he presided, including the recently conquered Philippines, presented problems too complex for one man, however capable and energetic, to cope with. Communications with the distant archipelago were difficult to maintain. Ships were lost during the long Pacific crossing and many passengers and crew died en route. It was necessary to draft in Mexico settlers needed in the Philippines, a measure which caused audible grumbling against the tyranny of the viceregal government. Closer to New Spain the bordering seas were plagued by bold corsairs, and within the realm vexations were unceasing. The Chichimeca Indians hovered about the silver mines daily killing Spanish inhabitants and running off livestock; thus the flow of the precious metal required by Philip II for his ambitious schemes in Europe was threatened. Many Spaniards, made restless by a half-century of pillage and lawlessness, were little disposed to settle down and hence the ideal of internal peace and order remained an unrealized aspiration. Rivalries of religious orders, bickering prelates, quarreling magistrates, and wrangling petty officials of his own government, all seeking special privileges and rewards, added to the Viceroy's troubles. Besides the complicated affairs of state he was "expected to be the father of the people, the patron of the monasteries and hospitals, protector of the poor,"[7] and the task was far too exacting for his waning strength.

But topping all misfortunes, that year of 1576, were two disasters, one personal to the Viceroy and the other general. In the early spring death deprived him of the consoling companionship of his wife and, almost at the same time, there descended upon New Spain the most devastating of the many plagues that afflicted colonial Mexico. Called by various names of Aztec origin, it attacked the Indians only; the symptoms were a severe headache followed by an increasing fever which seemed to consume the tortured bodies of the victims. Before the seventh day death usually ended the patients' torment. So widespread and virulent was this pestilence that an estimated two million natives perished before the rains brought relief the following year. Late in 1576 the Viceroy reported to the King:

> This year has been very arduous in this land because of the great lack of rain and the excessive heat; a severe plague has struck among the Indians who have died in great numbers and they are still dying because, though it is the end of October when there are frosts and it becomes cold, it is still hot. But, as it is not quite so hot now, the Indians are getting better, and I hope to God that, if it cools off, it will bring great relief to them.[8]

Both he and the Archbishop worked to the extent of their knowledge to combat the plague, but the disease irremediably ran its fatal course. The best physicians of the land held consultations but their collective wisdom was too puny to conjure away the blight that lay upon the land. Priests and friars joined the doctors and the barbers in applying the chief remedy prescribed by the science of the day—bloodletting—and no doubt these well-intentioned efforts contributed to the high mortality of the afflicted Indians. As a gesture the helpless and bewildered Viceroy exempted the unhappy aborigines during the period of the disaster from the tribute they owed as subjects of the Spanish Crown.

Despite these multitudinous difficulties Enríquez contrived to keep the economic wheels in motion and even to promote the educational welfare of the realm. Though the scourge had crippled the industrial life of the viceroyalty by producing a shortage of man power, particularly in the mines, he managed, somehow, to ship to Spain in 1576 silver valued at 1,111,211 pesos, the largest total since the Conquest.[9] But the Viceroy's efforts were not limited to increasing the revenue of the royal treasury. In a letter to Philip II he had written: "Since I came here I have always favored learning as one of the most important things and have urged all the religious orders to have schools." And it was true that he had worked hard in behalf of education and learning in New Spain. He had displayed a sympathetic interest in the prospering University, founded over twenty years before, which now counted on its faculty some of the

most distinguished scholars of the time, and with his encourage-
ment a number of schools and seminaries were founded. The noble
intention of the Spanish Crown to bring literacy and learning to its
Indian subjects was weakening, but it still remained an ideal. The
supply of truly dedicated missionaries to send to outlying provinces
for this work was always inadequate, and the need was pressing for
local institutions to prepare them. This situation had contributed
recently to an extension of Jesuit activities into New Spain, a development which served, however, to increase the tension existing
among rival orders, particularly the Franciscans. During the decade
of the 1570's the Jesuits established several schools destined to be
influential, for which scholarships were granted through the intervention of the Viceroy. In 1576 the Cabildo of Mexico City was
requested to appropriate funds for prizes to students in the Jesuit
seminaries and, after considerable deliberation, this municipal body
gave 100 pesos toward the purchase of books as incentives to
worthy students.[10]

The story of Spain's exploitation of the material wealth of its
American colonies has obscured the more beneficial aspects of its
rule, which included a genuine concern for the spiritual and physical welfare of its subjects. The systematic if crude and ineffective
efforts to combat the fearful plague of 1576-77 are a reminder that
only six years before Philip II had sought to increase a scientific
knowledge of medicine and protect public health by bringing medical practice under state control. In 1570 he had appointed general
physicians and issued extensive instructions governing the medical
profession in the New World. The chief of these men of science
was a *protomédico*, whose primary obligation was to assemble all
possible data on herbs, trees and plants of medicinal value. Detailed
reports on the cultivation and utilization of such flora were required, along with specimens.[11] Philip II's first appointee to this
office, Dr. Francisco Hernández, a native of Toledo and one of his
own personal physicians, was still in Mexico in 1576. This learned
gentleman spent seven years at his scientific task, traveling constantly and enduring great hardships in quest of material for a
natural history of the realm. So ardent was his zeal that, although
his salary was modest and the need for his medical services urgent,
particularly during the months of the plague, he gave no time to

medical practice and refused a fortune in fees which his profession
and distinction would have permitted him to acquire. By 1576 he
was completing some sixteen volumes of text and drawings of plants
and animals studied, together with the results of many experiments
performed in the local hospitals to demonstrate the efficacy of certain specifics. Unfortunately, only a few extracts of this valuable
work, in which Dr. Hernández invested so much time, money, and
health, were destined to appear in print.[12]

Still others in Mexico were making important contributions to
medicine in 1576. Father Agustín Farfán, an Augustinian friar, who
became a professor of that science in the Royal University, was
spurred by the pestilence desolating the country to produce his
Brief treatise of medicine, published in 1579 and famous as the first
work of its kind to appear in the viceroyalty. Of even greater contemporary fame in the capital, however, was Dr. Juan de la Fuente
who, during the worst of the plague, summoned his colleagues into
conference and performed an autopsy on one of the Indian victims
of the mysterious disease. Two years later he was the first to fill
the newly established chair of medicine in the local University.[13]

Another physician of the city was a surgeon named Juan Unza
whose story might have been taken out of the romantic tales read
by the Conquistador. A Basque of noble birth he had, somehow,
committed a murder and then retired to a hospital in Extremadura
where he acquired remarkable skill as a doctor. Wishing to expiate
his crime through suffering martyrdom, he came to New Spain and
joined the Franciscan order in Mexico City, where he lived a life
of extreme austerity and acquired an almost mythical reputation
for marvellous cures. When, as sometimes happened, his efforts
proved unavailing and his patient died, he was wont to impose upon
himself the cruelest flagellation to atone for his possible carelessness in failing to cure the deceased!

Such were some of the individuals practicing the ancient art
of Galen and Hippocrates in the Mexican capital that year of 1576,
but medicine was not the only science with devotees. In the nearby
Colegio de Santa Cruz de Tlaltelolco, founded to educate the Indian
charges of the Crown but now falling upon evil days, there lived a
grand old man, the first great anthropologist of the western hemisphere and a contemporary of conquistadors. Still presiding over his

beloved Indian charges, this venerable Franciscan and humble scholar, Friar Bernardino de Sahagún, was devoting much of his time to the laborious task of copying parts of his monumental *History of ancient Mexico,* a priceless record of the customs and rites of the Aztecs, whose compilation had engaged him and his assistants a third of a century or more. Arriving in New Spain with a group of nineteen Franciscan monks in 1529, he promptly interested himself in every phase of the native civilization so recently conquered. Studious and patient, he thoroughly mastered the Nahuatl or Aztec speech, in which he preached and wrote. After a varied experience he began his great history, employing a corps of bilingual and trilingual students of his college to assist him. Carefully organized and divided into twelve books, the great work, written in Aztec, slowly grew, being revised and recopied again and again. The superiors of his Order complained loudly of the high cost of the project, and the full burden of copying and translating his opus fell upon the aging scholar. Finally, in this very year of 1576, as a result of a letter from the Archbishop to the King, the new Commissioner General of the Franciscans, Friar Rodrigo de Sequera, brought instructions from the Council of the Indies to send a Castilian version of the whole twelve books to Spain.[14] Thus during the current year and the two following the aged Friar Sahagún patiently translated and copied the enormous manuscript which was doomed to remain unpublished for over two centuries, though Herrera, Torquemada, and other historians later drew freely from this vast storehouse of information. Only long after the end of Spanish rule in Mexico did this pioneer scientist gain a merited recognition.

There were other men of learning steeped in the languages and lore of the Indian civilizations in New Spain also at work in 1576 and later, but their findings, though conscientious and thorough, hardly compared to the quality of the research which the gentle friar, Bernardino de Sahagún, left to posterity. The Spanish government, often so remarkably enlightened, was shortsighted in placing barriers to the publication and diffusion of these scientific studies which offer incontrovertible evidence of the intellectual attainments of its nationals in the New World of the sixteenth century.

Still another useful, if less important, manuscript was ready for the press at this time in New Spain, though destined to wait long centuries before even a part was printed. This work was a *Chronicle of New Spain* written by the official historian of the city, a famous Spanish Latinist and professor in the universities of Spain and Mexico, Francisco Cervantes de Salazar. Born in Toledo about 1515, he had been a disciple and friend of great humanists such as Alejo de Vanegas and Luis Vives and, like them, he had railed unavailingly at the novels of chivalry which had intoxicated the generation of the conquistadors. In Spain he had published a series of Latin dialogues, which were continuations of similar compositions by Hernán Pérez de Oliva, Luis Mexía, and Luis Vives, and one of these was dedicated to Hernando Cortés, the Conqueror. After coming to Mexico about 1550 and teaching in its new university, he published for the use of students three other Latin dialogues which are important documents for the sixteenth-century cultural life of the viceregal capital. In the first the University of Mexico, its physical appearance, teachers, and customs are described to a newcomer from Spain and, in commenting on its distinguished faculty, Cervantes de Salazar does not fail to compliment himself highly. Two citizens of the capital serve as loquacious cicerones to a visitor in the remaining two dialogues, in which the points of interest of the center and outskirts of the city are extoled with much descriptive commentary designed to impress the stranger.

Numerous other works flowed from the quill of this important Renaissance figure who, it appears, was never quite satisfied with his academic honors and never quite ceased to aspire to further eminence in the Church. In a confidential communication written in 1575 the Archbishop gave an unflattering verbal sketch of the aging writer's personality. "Canon Francisco Cervantes Salazar is sixty years old, with twenty-five in this country to which he came reputed as a great Latinist, though with age he has lost some of this. . . . He likes to be listened to and praised, and he is partial to flattery. He is fickle and changeable, and has no very good reputation for chastity or morality; he is ambitious for distinction and is convinced that he will be a bishop, and they joke him about this. . . ; he is no churchman, nor one to be trusted with responsibility."[15] These somewhat acidic comments on the friend and disciple of

Vives and other great humanists of the Spanish Renaissance appear
to be among the last made during his lifetime, for his death occurred
soon after.

A half-century after the Conquest a different trend was perceptible in the literary production of Mexico. The more utilitarian
forms, such as the chronicles, the speculative and scientific works,
manuals, catechisms, grammars, and vocabularies of Indian languages, were gradually yielding to verse, the drama, and the more
conventional belles-lettres. Except for an occasional historical narrative secular in character, most of the earlier literary activity was
carried on by serious-minded friars earnestly seeking to indoctrinate
the natives. To a large extent the cultivation of letters was still in
the hands of ecclesiastics, but a new generation had come into being,
one more numerous and less devoted to the strict, ascetic life of
the pioneer missionaries. More settled conditions tempered religious
fervor and a disposition to imitate the refinements of the homeland
was evident. Though the spirit of the Renaissance was beginning
to falter in Spain under the pressure of the Counter Reformation,
its strength was renewed in the land called New Spain, at least
temporarily, expressing itself in contemporary art, architecture, and
literature. Poets and dramatists were plentiful in Mexico in the last
quarter of the sixteenth century—so much so, indeed, that the most
celebrated of them, Fernán González de Eslava, had a character in
one of his plays say, "So you're becoming a writer of couplets!
You'll not earn much as a poet, for they're more plentiful than
manure here."

The increasing stability and wealth of the realm created an
ampler leisure and a wider literacy, while attracting cultivated
minds from Spain. About the middle of the century one of the
most gifted poets of the motherland, renowned for his love lyrics,
Gutierre de Cetina (1520-1557?), had come to Mexico where he
died, leaving, however, an influence on colonial verse that remained
for decades. In this year of 1576 another Spanish poet, Juan de la
Cueva (1550?-1610), soon to play an important role in the evolution of the national theater, was momentarily residing in the viceregal capital and writing verse extoling the beauties of the city "which
is in a lake, built on the water like Venice. . . ."[16] He reports
metrically:

> Seis cosas excelentes en belleza
> hallo, escritas con C, que son notables
> y dignos de alabaros su grandeza.
> Casas, calles, caballos admirables,
> carnes, cabellos y criaturas bellas
> que en todo extremo todas son loables,

indicating alliteratively that, among objects of extreme beauty noted in this New World center, he included its horses and its women. But in a sonnet to his own brother, the Inquisitor, whom he accompanied to New Spain, he betrayed his homesickness for his native land, to which he returned in 1577 after a three-year absence.

Whether Spanish or Mexican born, most of these versifiers were mere dilettantes, and their extraordinary number points up the change that had come over the city and its environs since the triumph of the Conquistador. One or two, however, had talent and deserve more than passing mention. The first important poet born in New Spain was Francisco de Terrazas (1525?-   ?), the eldest son of a conqueror of the same name who had been Cortés' *mayordomo*. This writer was so outstanding in his own time as to win recognition from no less a genius than the author of *Don Quixote*. In his *Canto de Calíope* Cervantes acclaimed him as "a new Apollo," while on his death a hyperbolic epitaph was written likening this Creole bard's literary achievements to the valorous feats of Cortés. A wealthy lord of numerous towns in New Spain, Terrazas was the acknowledged leader of the literary circle of the capital. Little more is known about him, but surviving specimens of his poetic talent justify in some measure the high encomiums heaped upon him. His acquaintance was intimate with Latin, Italian, and Castilian poets, and about the year 1576 he composed perhaps the most exquisite sonnet of sixteenth-century Mexican poetry, in which he imitated and excelled the Portuguese classic Camoens. His vein was lyric but he did not fail to essay the epic so popular during the age in which he lived, and the fragments of his *Conquista y Nuevo Mundo* entitle him to a place among the successful cultivators of the genre. In Terrazas' octaves describing the adventures of Jerónimo de Aguilar, the shipwrecked Spaniard whose services as interpreter were so invaluable to Cortés, there is power and simplicity of expression notably lacking in many of the epics so fashionable in the sixteenth century and later.

Better known in the literary history of Spanish America is the friend and relative of Terrazas, the Spanish-born Fernán González de Eslava (1534-1601?), the first important dramatist of the New World, who arrived in 1558. After his death an admiring friend collected and published sixteen of his dramatic productions, mainly short allegorical plays called *Coloquios* (Colloquies). Were it not for an episode causing considerable stir in Mexico City in 1574, little else concerning this playwright would be known. As this incident offers some entertaining sidelights on the social and political life in the capital during the rule of Viceroy Enríquez, it deserves a little space.[17]

One of the commonest features of Spanish colonial administration was the symbolic conflict of Church and State represented in the persons of the Archbishop and the Viceroy. It was a tradition established almost as soon as civil control replaced the military rule of the Conquistador, and no small part of the political activities of the community emanated from this perennial rivalry. Both high officials were jealous of their prerogatives, and their proud and touchy dispositions easily involved them in jurisdictional disputes. Viceregal society, religious and lay, took sides in these quarrels, and passion sometimes flamed at white heat. The twelve-year period of Enríquez was no exception. Both he and the Archbishop Moya de Contreras were able, strong-minded, and capable administrators, and a clash of personalities was inevitable. Moya de Contreras' energy and success in establishing the Holy Office in Mexico had brought him succession to the archbishopric on the death of its previous occupant in 1573, and it was the celebration of his assumption of this high office which touched off a scandal that rocked the capital for many weeks.

Ever since the Conquest the Church's power and wealth had steadily increased and its leaders, usually enjoying longer tenure of office than the viceroys, were often able to resist successfully any intervention in its affairs by secular authorities. Already the Church was acquiring vast estates and this process had advanced so far that Philip II ordered Enríquez this same year of 1576 to give a detailed accounting of the property controlled by the clergy and to forbid further acquisitions. Such a commission was hardly calculated to further coöperation between the secular and ecclesiastic wings of the government. A little earlier the Viceroy had alienated even his own supporters by seeking to carry out royal instructions to impose an exceedingly unpopular sales tax. Possibly seeing in the resentment of the commercial elements an opportunity to embarrass his opponent, the Archbishop wrote to the President of the Council of the Indies, whom years before he had served as a page, and complained of the Viceroy's actions in this connection. Just as the installation festivities of the new Archbishop were beginning in December 1574, Enríquez received a letter of reproof from the presiding officer of the Council of the Indies. Since the Viceroy had merely obeyed orders in imposing the unwelcome tax, he was understandably surprised and irritated by this rebuke. Sensing that Moya de Contreras had some responsibility for the censure received, Enríquez acted with deliberate rudeness during the ceremony of bestowing the *palio* on the new Archbishop which custom compelled him to witness.

It was the fashion of the time to relieve the solemnity of religious pomp by rounding out such exercises with entertainment of a lighter sort. For this purpose a play entitled *Desposorio espiritual entre el pastor Pedro y la Iglesia Mexicana* (The spiritual marriage of the shepherd Peter and the Mexican Church) was performed, specially written by Juan Pérez Ramírez, the talented son of another conquistador. Light and humorous skits for the amusement of the populace were customary between the acts of the more serious drama, and in one presented on this occasion the Viceroy fancied that he detected some barbed and unflattering references to himself. The festivities were prolonged and three days later the performance of another play took place, this time a work of González de Eslava entitled *Un coloquio en la consagración de Dr. D. Pedro de Moya de Contreras* (A colloquy on the consecration of Dr. D. Pedro de Moya de Contreras). This was a highly laudatory allegory designed to fulfill the accepted didactic purposes of contemporary drama, with a cast chiefly representing such abstractions as Faith, Hope, Charity, and the Mexican Church. Like its predecessor it had comic skits interspersed between the acts, and one of these short pieces was a farcical arraignment of the detested sales tax. It was recited with immense gusto by a mulatto comedian whose broad humor and crude satire provoked prolonged and

raucous laughter from the audience. Still smarting under the repri-
mand of his superiors in Spain, the Viceroy was sure that he saw the
handiwork of the Archbishop in the selection of this particular
entr'act and he promptly wrote to the President of the Council,
bitterly assailing Moya de Contreras and sourly declaring, "I might
forgive him all the other short skits, but this one I couldn't stomach."
After dispatching this letter he abruptly ordered the suspension of
any further performances.

Meanwhile, possibly uneasy, the Archbishop prepared his own
defense before the same authority. Among other things he asserted
that the comedies had been approved by the Inquisition censor,
Friar Domingo de Salazar, soon to become Archbishop of the
Philippines, and that no one else saw the objections in them that the
Viceroy did. A few days later he sought to strengthen his position
by drawing up a notarized account exonerating himself of any
blame and transferring the responsibility to the censor and to the
authors, Juan Pérez Ramírez and González de Eslava. By this time
the entire city was aroused and was noisily taking sides. The climax
soon came in the form of an insulting *pasquin* or lampoon posted on
the door of the main church, which laid the full blame for the hated
sales tax upon the innocent viceroy.

This libel was more than Enríquez could bear and, backed by
the Audiencia, his advisory body, and ignoring ecclesiastic immuni-
ties, he arrested as the possible authors of the *pasquin* the poet,
Francisco de Terrazas, González de Eslava, and others associated
with the performance of the second play. Thrown into jail and
with the proximity of the torture rack to remind him of its awesome possibilities, the forty-year-old dramatist was required to
make a declaration concerning his participation in the recent festivities. When the text of his play was shown him he acknowledged
its authorship at once, quickly adding, however, that the Inquisition
had approved it. He disclaimed any connection with the offending
skit performed with his play and categorically denied any responsibility for the libel against the Viceroy. His innocence, on the
whole, was fairly clear, but the fact that he was a known adherent
of the Archbishop probably accounts for his detention until January 5, 1575, seventeen days later. These highhanded procedures
of the Viceroy were, apparently, more successful in keeping the

relatively small community of Spaniards and Creoles at a fever heat of excitement than in identifying the true culprits. Both principals in the controversy reported their sides of the story at great length to Philip II and his Council of the Indies and in due time these officials took action. To Moya de Contreras was administered a strong rebuke together with an injunction to act with more docility in the future, while Enríquez was curtly advised that some of his acts were not in keeping with his high office.

The notoriety resulting from the incident probably caused the leading dramatist of New Spain no permanent embarrassment for he continued to write prolifically. Though similar in some respects to the *autos sacramentales*, or religious plays, whose literature the greatest dramatic geniuses of Spain, Lope de Vega and Calderón, were to enrich, González de Eslava's *Coloquios* are frequently remarkable for their natural dialogue, simple plot, and comic touches. Usually symbolic in character and designed to convey the theological lessons which the Church wished to teach, often well-drawn and realistic types, using the contemporary speech of Mexico, mingled with the more allegorical figures. This playwright celebrated secular as well as religious occasions with his dramatic compositions, as the titles indicate. The return of López de Legaspi's companions from their explorations of the Philippines in 1565 was thus commemorated, as was Enríquez' construction of seven forts along the road to the Zacatecas mines to protect communications with the capital from the marauding Chichimecas. Perhaps the Viceroy was appeased by González de Eslava's allegorical play praising his measures taken to combat the terrible plague in 1576. In this drama the leading parts were figures representing Pestilence, Wrath, Clemency, Health, Zeal, Temporal Remedy, and Wisdom. These plays are probably less to the taste of posterity than the more mundane productions of this colonial dramatist, of whom, unfortunately, only one brief skit survives.

The foregoing accounts of various aspects of life in the Mexico City of 1576 show clearly that the tone of community existence had changed in the fifty years since the Conquest. The streets that once echoed solely to the rattle of armed soldiery now felt the tread of teamsters' carts, of the carriages of wealthy dignitaries, and of the feet of peaceful civilians. The hardy generation of adven-

turers, for whom feats of arms were the measure of manly achievement, was now succeeded by one more sedentary and effete which
preferred literary and commercial success. The sword was yielding to the quill as an instrument of material advancement, and a
familiarity with letters and learning was becoming a surer guar-
antee of social preference than military skill. If the passive literacy
of the conquistadors had largely limited their reading to the popular
novels of chivalry, their sons and grandsons were acquiring a more
mature taste and a preference for the more artistic expression of
Renaissance literature which was accompanied by a desire to imitate
these classic models in works of their own. Literature had become
a pursuit rivaling and even surpassing in public esteem the dangerous
career of arms, and this shift of interest paralleled the multiplication
of convents and monasteries. Thus an enlarged market for books
of a more varied nature was created. A printing press was established as early as 1539, but at no time was it permitted to compete
seriously with the sale of printed works from Spain whose importation was protected, as already noted, by a monopoly granted by the
Crown.

The primary function of the local presses—for others were subsequently set up—was to facilitate the work of evangelization by
the Church among the Indians through printing the catechisms, dictionaries, grammars, and pietistic literature needed by the missionaries. In 1576 two presses were in existence in Mexico City, but only
three books appear to have come from them that year, and these
were purely utilitarian. All bore the imprint of Pedro Balli, a bookseller by profession who, apparently, had begun work as a printer
two years before. A certain Pedro Ocharte, of French origin, owned
the other printing press and had published books since 1563. Recently, however, he had been in serious difficulties with the Inquisition and for the time being his activities had ceased. The relative
idleness of the presses resulted, apparently, from a royal decree
issued late in 1573 forbidding the printing of breviaries and prayer
books in New Spain, thus depriving the printers of their chief
trade. In September 1575 the Viceroy had reassured his monarch
concerning the enforcement of this particular decree by declaring
that ". . . with respect to the printing presses, there are two here
and, except for a few unimportant things, the doors are kept well

locked on them."[18] Also residing in Mexico City at this time was another member of the craft, the Italian printer Antonio Ricardo, who, after operating a press from 1577 to 1579, moved to the viceroyalty of Peru where he established the first printing shop in Lima.

In view of the relatively small number of Europeans in the viceroyalty of New Spain the quantities of books imported were remarkably large, and the booksellers surprisingly numerous. Bookstores as such probably did not exist in the capital at this time except, perhaps, in the case of printers who combined the manufacture and sale of their products in a single establishment. Dealers in assorted goods, who often lived at the back of their shops, frequently included imported volumes among their wares; others acted somewhat as brokers, disposing of consignments received from time to time in job lots to other merchants. How many individuals in Mexico City were engaged in this apparently lucrative business is uncertain, but the evidence of scattered documents of the period suggests that their number was considerable. Transient dealers and peddlers arrived on every fleet, and books were numbered among the effects for sale in the New World, because these wares commanded much higher prices in the colonies than in the homeland, their bulk was small, and the margin of profit was gratifyingly large. These facts account for the heavy smuggling of printed works that went hand in hand with the legitimate trade.

This constant influx of books helped build private collections, which were numerous both in Mexico City and elsewhere in the realm. The many convents and monasteries assembled substantial libraries, while the wealthy, both secular and ecclesiastic, eagerly acquired additional tomes to occupy some of their abundant leisure and to adorn their homes. That great and scholarly professor, Friar Alonso de la Veracruz, who founded the Colegio de San Pablo about 1575, also had the distinction of establishing the best library in the realm; according to contemporary accounts, it contained works on all known disciplines, arts, and languages. Spain itself was scoured for the latest and the oldest printed works which were shipped with maps, astrolabes, and other instruments for his collection in Mexico.[19]

Precise data on this early traffic in books are rarely found in contemporary documents thus far discovered, which fact gives peculiar importance to the scribal records relating to two business transactions of 1576 recently unearthed in Mexico City. Their exceptional interest lies in the book lists that they preserve. While intrinsically they are merely commercial agreements governing the disposition of limited quantities of imported volumes in the local market, they offer extraordinarily revealing glimpses of the book trade in a New World outpost of European culture hardly a half-century old. A study of these presumably typical sets of titles gives a fairly clear idea of the kinds of printed works which practical-minded merchants deemed salable during the rule of the viceroy Enríquez. The first of these documents concerns a collection of 341 volumes, while the second, dated later in the year, covers an order for 1,190.[20]

At an unspecified hour on July 21, 1576, six individuals appeared before Antonio Alonso, a public scribe with a stand on the central square of Mexico City, to legalize a promissory note. Three came merely to affix their signatures as witnesses to the agreement between the other three. A certain Pablo García, resident of the viceregal capital, had formed a partnership with a public notary named Pedro de Trujillo to purchase from Alonso Losa, a local bookseller, a miscellany of 341 books, plus maps, woodcuts, and drawings of sacred and secular subjects. Rapidly drawn up, this commercial instrument gave the individual price and title of each work, the latter in so brief a form as sometimes to defy identification.

The time allowed for repayment reflects the slowness of transportation and communication of the period. One third of the modest sum involved was due in seven months, or at the end of February 1577; another third a year later, and the final instalment fell due on the last of February 1579. The interest rate is undisclosed. The document likewise fails to name the place where the books would be sold. In view of the extended period allowed for discharging the obligation, these volumes were possibly intended for a market in the provinces rather than in the city itself.

Some 121 titles are represented in the 341 volumes, usually by one or two copies each; a few by four, six, eight, or a dozen, the last being the highest quantity noted. Though not all works are identified, about half of the total are clearly theological tomes, manuals, or pietistic writings for which the clergy offered so large a public. This professional literature filled much of the shelf room of convent and monastery libraries where it sometimes survived the ravages of centuries in such numbers as to leave the erroneous impression that colonial society regaled itself with no other literary fare. Indeed, some prejudiced historians have even asserted that this kind of reading material was the only one permitted by Spanish authorities, their judgment being influenced by the fact that so many of these musty, unused volumes remain today. It is exceedingly doubtful, however, that the lay public of New Spain in 1576, or at any other time, spent much of its leisure immersed in these rather forbidding pages or, for that matter, that the clergy limited itself exclusively to the same. The other half of the titles listed are nonreligious in character and probably found their way into the possession of purchasers less concerned with Church affairs. If this latter group of books is roughly subclassified as secular nonfiction and belles-lettres, approximately two-thirds fall into the first division and the remainder in the second.

Medicine is predominant among the sciences. A translation of the *De materia medica* of Dioscorides, the Greek physician of the first century whose treatises were authoritative up to the Renaissance period, links the healing art with the time of Hippocrates. Of related interest are the two copies of a famous work of pharmaceutics, the *Exposición sobre las preparaciones de Mesue*, by Antonio de Aguilera, an exegesis of a work by a ninth-century Arabic doctor of Harun Al-Raschid at Bagdad called Juan Mesue, to whom legend attributes the method of using gold for fillings in teeth. So great was the reverence for his pharmaceutical preparations that they were almost the dogma of sixteenth- and seventeenth-century Spanish practitioners. Other works of medical lore present are two copies each of an anatomy by Charles V's personal physician, Bernardino Montana de Monserrate, and another by a similar attendant of Philip II entitled *Libro de problemas* (Book of problems). Still another opus of this character and of special interest to purchasers in Mexico in 1576 was the *Secretos de cirugía* (Secrets of surgery) by Pedro Árias de Benavides, a Spanish doctor who had traveled extensively in Guatemala and New Spain studying the medical practices of the Indians, which he described in this book. At one time this gentleman had served as director of the general hospital in the viceregal capital.

Other sciences are represented by a miscellany, including a work on military tactics, an almanac (*chronografía o repertorio*), a single copy of Gabriel Alonso de Herrera's classically written treatise on agriculture drawn from Latin and Greek authors with modern adaptations, and two books on music. Law, its theory and practice, is represented by a collection of royal ordinances of Castile, Simancas' treatise on primogeniture, Soto's famous *De justitia et jure*, Villasante's gloss of the laws of Taurus, a guide for judges (*Dechado de jueces*), and six copies of a manual for scribes. Political science has its place in the list with Boccaccio's *Caída de príncipes* (Fall of princes), the first treatise of this Italian writer translated into Spanish. A guide to commercial practices is Mercado's *Tratos y contratos de mercaderes y tratantes*. Its author had taken the habit of his religious order in Mexico and only the year before the date of this book list had died at sea while returning to his duties.

History, geography, and natural science claimed a few titles, usually a copy or two of each. Early Christian history is recorded in the *Historia ecclesiástica* (Ecclesiastical history) of the fourth-century bishop, Eusebius, while chronicles of Dominican and Augustinian orders tell of later activities. More numerous are purely secular accounts of events. The popularity of contemporary history seems evidenced by the dozen copies of a chronicle of Don Juan de Austria (*Batallas de don Juan*), the engaging half brother of Philip II and the hero of the Battle of Lepanto where Cervantes was crippled. This quantity might be contrasted with the lone copy of a Latin chronicle of his thirteenth-century ancestor, Don Fernando. Historical outlines were acceptable in the Mexican market of 1576, judging by Valerius Maximus' account of Rome, Carthage, and other peoples "in their order of vices and virtues," and the two copies of a similar treatment of the realms of Spain by Philip II's current librarian, Esteban de Garibay. An item of direct bearing locally was the copy of a work in Italian, *Historia de la India Mexica* (History of Mexican India). There is a translation of the *Collectanea rerum mirabilium* by a third-century Roman writer, Caius Julius Solinus, a curious assembly of notes on the products, customs, etc., of geographic areas derived from Pliny's *Natural history*, also on the 1576 list.

Philosophy and theology were often fused in an age when the problems of good and evil primarily preoccupied the greatest minds, and a thorough analysis of this important reflection of the Renaissance in contemporary Spanish America requires a broader documentary base than is permitted the historian by the number of book lists thus far discovered. One item in the 1576 promissory note of Pablo García and his partner Pedro de Trujillo must, however, be mentioned, for there is a special significance attaching to the presence of two copies of the *Ocho Partes* by the foremost humanist of the century, Erasmus of Rotterdam, on this book list of post-Tridentine Mexico. Less completely than is so often affirmed had the repressive influence of the Counter Reformation swept the name and influence of the author of *In praise of folly* into oblivion in the Spanish-speaking world. As this particular document and later ones show, the writings of Erasmus not actually on the *Index of prohibited books* were openly and freely shipped to the Spanish Indies where they were read without visible hindrance.

Of less importance were the *Coloquios matrimoniales* (Matrimonial colloquies) of Pedro Luján, the Sevillian moralist who also fathered the mediocre romance of chivalry *Don Silves de la Selva*, though the half dozen copies of his treatise on "how to be happy though married" indicated a larger demand than for the work of Erasmus just cited. An equal number is noted of another didactic work, *Libro de la verdad* (Book of truth), an array of two hundred dialogues between Truth and Man on the subject of the sinner's conversion. Surprisingly enough, it was written by Pedro de Medina, author of the most famous book on navigation of the century.

Quantitatively, purely creative literature has a small representation, but again the Renaissance taste is reflected in the classic letters of antiquity. Notably present are those writers of Roman Spain who contributed so greatly to the glories of the so-called Silver Age of Latin literature. Conspicuous is the name of that brilliant epic poet, Marcus Annaeus Lucan, said to be second only to Vergil himself. Presumably the work listed merely as "Lucan" refers to that long historical poem on the conflict of Caesar and Pompey, *Farsalia*, which won permanent acclaim. Other writers listed are Martial, whose gay, satiric, and cynical *Epigrams* exerted an influence on the picaresque novels of Spain, and, inevitably, Seneca with his revered tragedies. Four copies of the comedies of Terence further reveal the interest in classic drama of the Mexico City of González de Eslava, while unspecified writings of Horace and Suetonius also find a place in the prosaic promissory note of 1576. The two copies of Ovid's *De amatoria* suggest that the austerity and gloom associated with Philip II had not descended on all his subjects abroad.

The more recent creative writers of Spain were also in evidence, though in limited variety and numbers. On the whole, they tend to reflect a sixteenth-century fondness for apologues, anecdotes, epigrammatic tales, and proverbs. Possibly *"Proberbios del Marques"* refers to the first collection known in Europe of these terse bits of wisdom from popular speech, made by the distinguished fifteenth-century poet, the Marqués de Santillana. A later writer, recently deceased in 1576, Juan de Mal Lara, is represented by several titles, including his widely read *Vulgar philosophy*, a potpourri of apologues, proverbs, witty sayings, and short stories, and his more didactic works such as the *Rudimentos o principios de gramática* (6 copies), *Principios de retórica* (12 copies), and *In syntaxin scholia* (6 copies). Mal Lara also composed a number of plays and tragedies, like Juan de la Cueva still in Mexico City who, before his departure to the New World, had been a member of the literary academy held in the Seville home of the author of the *Vulgar philosophy*. Other items of interest on the book list of 1576 were these popular collections of fantastic and eerie absurdities, *Jardín de flores curiosas* by Antonio de Torquemada and the *Silva de varia lección* by the more celebrated Pedro de Mexía, Charles V's chronicler. The perennial favorite Guevara's *Libro áureo de Marco Aurelio* is present in a modest two copies and an equal number of his less known *Montecalvario*. As for the novels of chivalry so dear to the Conquistador, this 1576 book list gives the erroneous impression that the vogue was completely past already, for the only representatives of this genre were two copies of the synthetic *Cavallería christiana* of Jaime de Alcalá. If the sons and grandsons were still reading the melodramatic fare of their sires—and some of them surely were—neither list of 1576 can serve as proof; on the whole, these succeeding generations seem collectively to have acquired a more discriminating taste, though many individuals had by no means renounced the predilections of their elders. And finally, to conclude this summary of the books which figured in the business deal on the plaza of Mexico City that July day of 1576, there remains only to mention such reference works as a dictionary, a few treatises on grammar and rhetoric, including the ever-present *Arte de la lengua* of Nebrija and the less familiar *De elegantia lingua latine* of Lorenzo Valla.

The second document which sheds light on the book-buying preferences of Mexico City in 1576 offers possibly greater interest, because of the larger quantity and variety of works listed, and because it records an order of books to be imported from Spain.[21] Since the dealer, who happens to be the same Alonso Losa of the earlier transaction, presumably wished titles with the readiest sale in his market, his list reveals in a general fashion the best sellers of the moment. On December 22, 1576 the Mexican merchant had a promissory note notarized to a leading bookdealer of Seville, Diego de Mexía, through the latter's business associate, Pedro Calderón, then in Mexico City. The amount pledged was "2,065 gold pesos at eight silver reales per peso" for 1,190 volumes. As usual the form of the titles is the briefest, but frequently more details are given than in the earlier document. Ordinarily each item is listed with the price per copy in pesos or reales and the kind of binding, whether vellum, calfskin, wooden boards, or cardboard. Occasionally the size—folio, quarto, or octavo—are specified and, more rarely, the place of publication. This last appears chiefly in works from foreign presses, particularly those at Lyons, Paris, and Rome, and the press of Plantin at Antwerp, a fact of special interest since the international character of the book trade at this time is revealed. Even more significant, these indications demonstrate that, contrary to beliefs still prevailing, sixteenth-century Spanish America was able to acquire the finest products of European as well as Spanish book manufacturers.

Throughout Alonso Losa's book order varying quantities of the same title are listed, with the total of a single work reaching as high

as a score or two. Many of the names on the earlier document of
the year reappear, testifying to the current acceptability of these
books in the local market. This second book list of 1576 is typical
with respect to the predominance of ecclesiastical literature, which
accounts for some 50 to 60 percent of the titles. However, except
for a few manuals and guides for the training of the clergy, such as
Pedro Martir Coma's *Directorium curatorum o institución de curas*,
of which twenty-two copies were ordered, only one or two each
are desired of works in this class. Many are exegetic or polemic in
character, with a sprinkling of catechisms and sermons. Of particular interest is the item of twenty Bibles in varied editions, some
to come from the presses of France and Antwerp. Though the
Protestant revolt had so alarmed Philip II's Spain that this self-ap-
pointed guardian of the Faith had sought to combat its heresies by
strengthening the Inquisition in the Peninsula and by extending it
to the overseas possessions, yet a Mexican merchant could still import and sell with relative freedom foreign as well as Spanish editions of the Holy Scriptures in his colonial market. No fewer than
one hundred twenty-five Bibles were known to be circulating in
Mexico City in 1573,[22] and presumably there were many more in
1576. Losa's order of this date included not only the twenty copies
of the Bible, but two more of the New Testament, two concord-
ances, and a miscellany of commentaries on the Four Gospels. It
may be assumed, of course, that the clergy were the dealer's clientele for these books, but the absence of visible interference in placing orders for such sacred literature is significant. The task of translating the Holy Word into native languages and of diffusing it
among the inhabitants of the New World was steadily proceeding
despite the deepening shadow of intolerance and persecution cast
by the Counter Reformation.

Philosophy more secular in character is mainly represented by
a few sets of Aristotle's writings, the *Dialecticas* of Titelmen, and
seven copies of the *Reina Saba*. That pioneer of higher learning in
Mexico, Alonso de la Veracruz, who had assembled a magnificent
library, had also published important commentaries on Aristotle
and other scientific writings on the presses of Mexico and Spain,
and these are represented on Losa's book list by an order of a copy
of his *Cursus actium*. The name of the foremost Spanish humanist

of the century, Juan Luis Vives, also appears, but without indication of specific title, a common practice on most colonial book lists. This lack of detail inevitably evokes speculation as to the exact work implied, particularly in the present instance in which the order is for twenty-five copies.

Just as theology and philosophy tended to blend in sixteenth-century learning, so did philosophy and science overlap. A perusal of Losa's order reveals fewer titles in the last-mentioned category than were present in the lot turned over in July to García and Trujillo. Medicine is represented by only one copy each of *Idea medicina*, Antonio de Aguilera's *Praeclarae rudementorum medicinae*, and the *Problemas* of Villalobos; natural science, by four copies of the *Físicas* of the Jesuit Córdoba, and by one copy of a similar work of the more famous scholar, De Soto. Fuenllana's treatise on guitar playing is noted in two copies, and there is one of the well-known work of Herrera on agriculture. Jurisprudence and law claim larger quantities and variety of titles. Of particular note are the dozen copies of the *Censuras del derecho*, and half as many of the law code of the colonies, the *Recopilación de Indias*. Of a more theoretical character are Decio's *De regulis juris*, De Soto's *De justitia*, and Jacobi Menorchus jureconsultis, with three copies each of the first two, and one of the last. Practical treatises are present in twelve copies of Mercado's *Tratos y contratos*, noted on the earlier book list, and Monteroso's long-standard guide for public scribes.

The field of belletristic literature offers a considerably larger variety of titles on the Losa order list than in the case of the García-Trujillo transaction. Since the Mexican dealer of the later document wished to import these works from Spain, it is likely that his list reflected his practical knowledge of the reading preferences of the viceregal public. A cursory inspection of this list clearly reveals that the characteristic tastes of the Spanish Renaissance were current in the contemporary New World, and that the sons and grandsons of the Conquistador were well within the orbit of that great intellectual movement. In the viceroyalty of New Spain, too, there was an eagerness to discover the ancient world, more particularly the history and letters of classical Rome. If Aristotle and other great minds of ancient Greece had strongly influenced philosophy and science in both Spain and Mexico, the historians, rhetoricians, and poets who had contributed to the glories of the Rome of antiquity were holding similar sway over humane letters. Quantitatively the most conspicuous names on Losa's book order among Roman writers of history are Salust, Justin and Julius Caesar. The first of these, with title of work unspecified, has a total of thirty-five copies, a dozen of which are requested in Spanish translation, pasteboard covers; these last are priced at four reales; the remaining twenty-three are requested in the Lyons edition, selling for one real less per copy. Possibly these books are the *Vida de Yugurta* or the *Conjuración de Catalina*, or both. Similarly, the order calls for thirty-one copies of "*Justinos*," possibly Justin's famous revision of Trogo Pompeyo's *Historia universal;* nine of these are specified as editions printed in Lyons. Caesar's *Comentarios* are included, eighteen copies of the Latin original, and a half dozen of the Spanish translation. There is also a solitary copy each of "*Julio Caesar historia*" and of the *Fastos Romanorum.* Of incidental interest are the dozen copies of the *Antigüedades judaicas* by the Jewish historian Josephus Flavius. Matching the earlier list, there is a single copy of the *Historia eclesiástica*, a famous account of the early church by the Bishop of Cos, Eusebius (267-340 A.D.). Save for Illescas' *Historia pontifical*, Zurita's *Anales de Aragón*, and a *Historia de mar y tierra* by Pedro de Salazar, later history is disregarded.

Considerably larger on Losa's order is the representation of the rhetorical and creative writers of classical Rome, both in the variety of authors and in the number of copies desired. The individual titles requested are both in Latin and in translation, and often from presses outside of Spain. Of the twenty-six copies of Cicero's *De officiis*, for example, sixteen were specified as from Antwerp and ten from the Plantine press. And the twenty-one copies of the epistles of this great orator, which offered incomparable models to later writers and threw so much light on the closing times of the Roman Republic, were to come from Paris and Lyons at prices ranging from three to twenty-six reales. Two three-volume sets of the *Orations* in octavo, and a solitary copy of a work indicated merely as "Cicero," are also included. Of related interest is an item of twelve copies of a *Quejas de Pompeo al Senado.*

Latin poets, however, outnumber the prose writers, with Vergil numerically well in the lead. There are thirty-three and thirty-four copies respectively in Latin and in Spanish, merely indicated as "*Vergilios.*" Again foreign editions, particularly from the Lyons press, are desired. Martial, whose scintillating epigrams were listed on the earlier document, was also much in demand among the sophisticated book buyers of Mexico City in 1576, for twenty-five copies bound in pasteboard figure in the Losa order. Ovid's *Metamorphoses* are wanted to the extent of nine copies, and also Seneca's tragedies. Other writings of antiquity or pseudo antiquity are the two copies of Apuleyo's *Asno de oro* and three copies of Guevara's omnipresent *Libro áureo de Marco Aurelio.*

More scattered and diversified on this second book list of 1576 are the representatives of Castilian literature, but particularly interesting as a reflection of contemporary reading tastes in Mexico City. The fifteenth century is symbolized by the dozen copies of the first collection of popular proverbs in Europe made by Íñigo López de Mendoza, better known as the Marqués de Santillana, who had ushered in the Italian sonnet as a metrical form and thus anticipated one of the favorite forms of Spanish Renaissance poetry. Could his well-known scorn of the popular ballads account for the fact that there was but one lone copy of *Romances viejos* included on Losa's list? Four copies are listed of another important representative of fifteenth-century lyric verse, Jorge Manrique's moving couplets on the death of his father, destined to find a place in every anthology of Castilian poetry and to be rendered into English with inimitable grace by Longfellow.

Even more significant, perhaps, was the order for eighteen copies of that masterpiece of Castilian letters, second only to the still unwritten *Don Quixote*, the *Tragedia de Calixto y Melibea*, listed by its better-known title *Celestina*. This great example of Spanish realism, of which twelve copies were to be of the Antwerp edition, finds itself in the equally famous company of that first picaresque novel *Lazarillo de Tormes*, and underscores the almost complete absence of the contrasting literature of chivalry. But this version of the realistic tale of *Lazarillo* was undoubtedly the one which Church censorship had toned down considerably and which came between the same covers with Torres Naharro's play *Propaladia.*

It is, perhaps, a coincidence that these two documents on the book trade of Mexico in 1576 should indicate such a surprising lack of the fantastic literature of chivalry; aside from one copy of the Italian prototype of this genre—*Orlando furioso*—there was but a single volume of the same insipid *Cavallería christiana* noted on the first list. Later records show that there was still a profitable market for the adventures of Amadís, Palmerín and their followers in New Spain and in other parts of sixteenth-century Spanish America, but here these heroes are notably absent. The presence of the *Celestina* and *Lazarillo* on the later book order might lead one to suppose that the trend away from sentiment was well under way a generation before *Don Quixote* appeared to destroy with laughter the lingering popularity of the chivalric romance, but the much larger number of cloying novels of bucolic amours, of which Jorge Montemayor's celebrated *Diana* is the foremost example, quickly removes this misconception. This title recurs again and again on Losa's list, usually with an indication of "first," "second," and "third" parts, thus referring probably to the original work of Montemayor and its sequels by other hands. Adding up these various items there are twenty-one copies of the first part, twelve specified in pasteboard covers and nine in boards, from Antwerp, all priced at four reales each; only six in boards and at the same price are wanted of the second part, while eleven of the third part in pasteboard covers at three reales each are ordered. These pastoral novels reach a grand total, then, of thirty-eight copies, one of the largest quantities listed.

Other familiar works find their place in modest numbers. There are seventeen copies of the popular *Floresta Española*, by Santa Cruz de Dueñas, whose fables, legends, and apothegms continued to divert readers on both sides of the Atlantic. And last, but certainly not least, are the dozen copies of Erasmus' *Apothegms* showing, as the earlier list of the year had done, that the great humanist of Rotterdam could still bring something of his understanding and wit to the far-off colonies of Spain, even when the tide had turned against his broad tolerance and humanity.

On the whole, the great lyric poetry of sixteenth-century Castilian literature is but modestly sampled by Losa's book order. The recurring items *"Boscanes a lo humano"* (twelve copies in boards, at five reales) and *"Boscanes a lo divino"* (fifteen copies in pasteboard covers, at the same price) doubtless refer to the two collections of poems just off the presses of Alcalá and Granada (1575) by Juan Boscán Almogaver, generally credited with introducing the Italian meters into Castilian poetry; with these were published some verses by his accomplished contemporary Garcilaso de la Vega, whose almost faultless metrical compositions will forever be classic in Spanish letters. Of related interest are the two copies of Montemayor's *Cancionero,* presumably the collection of profane verses by the author of *Diana,* since his religious ones included in the original two-volume edition unfortunately fell under the ban of the Inquisition.[23]

As in the case of the preceding book list of the year Losa's order contained scattered items for reference works related to belles-lettres, mainly grammars and dictionaries. That hardy perennial of the sixteenth century and most of the colonial period, the *Arte de la lengua* of Nebrija, reappears with a respectable total of twenty-eight copies, while the companion dictionary by the same scholar is represented by a half-dozen. Corresponding works in four or five languages, presumably editions of the important Calepino compilations, are present in small quantities, to which may be added the two copies of a *Vocabularium ecclesiasticum.*

These two little documents relating to trivial commercial transactions recorded in Mexico City that plague-ridden year of 1576 are no more than tiny cracks projecting a very dim and insufficient light on the cultural life of a long-forgotten generation that lived out its days in the viceregal capital of New Spain and its environs. Faint and imperfect as are these glimpses, they illumine one little corner of the intellectual life of the transplanted civilization of Spain during its great moment in history. These lists of books serve, also, as an indication of the remarkable progress that the Spaniards had made in little more than half a century in transforming the center of a primitive native empire into a city of culture and refinement comparable to those of many Spanish and European municipalities. In hardly more than a generation the rough community of extrovert conquerors had almost wholly given way to a society lending its highest esteem to works of the spirit and the mind.

THE REPEATED PLEAS OF VICEROY MARTÍN ENRÍQUEZ to be relieved of his responsibilities in the conduct of the affairs of New Spain were at last heeded by his monarch in Madrid. But if this capable public servant entertained hopes of retiring to a well-earned rest in the homeland after his exceptionally long term of office, he soon learned that Philip II was not yet willing to spare the services of one of his most conscientious administrators. Another vice-sovereign, Francisco de Toledo, who had also labored long years in the New World, had asked to be discharged from his obligations for reasons of health, and to this request the king saw fit to acquiesce. Thus the post of viceroy of Peru, already deemed of greater importance than that of Mexico, became vacant, and to this lofty position the tired and aging Enríquez was promoted. Years before, a precedent had been established when the first viceregal administrator in the New World, Don Antonio de Mendoza, was transferred from Mexico City to Lima, where it was his fate to die in office; and in this latter respect, too, Enríquez was to emulate his predecessor.

The realm that he was thus chosen to rule was truly enormous, for it extended from Panama in the north down the rugged backbone of the Andes to the Strait of Magellan in the south where Philip II was then making a futile effort to plant a colony and thus guard that gateway to the Pacific; and from the west coast of the continent, which Pizarro and his companions had conquered a half-century before, it reached to the Atlantic seaboard, where a second and successful attempt was just concluded to found Buenos Aires as a sentinel at the back door of the viceroyalty on the River

Plate. With the union of Portugal and Spain in 1580 under Philip II Brazil had become a part of the Spanish empire, and the entire continent of South America was Spanish. Thus the extent of the territory which Viceroy Enríquez ruled briefly from 1581 to his death in 1583 was far more vast than that of Mexico over whose destinies he had presided so long and so well.

Much of this limitless region remained unknown despite the incredible explorations that followed the conquest of Peru, and strange legends of varied origin still lured adventurers into the mysterious hinterland of the continent. The lost settlement of the Caesars was enticing expeditions south into Patagonia, while the quest of El Dorado continued in the north. It was to Viceroy Enríquez at Lima that Agustín de Ahumada, the brother of the great mystic of Ávila, who shared Santa Teresa's youthful fondness for the novels of chivalry, addressed his letter in 1582, asking permission to organize an expedition to locate a nearby El Dorado, "the land richest in gold and people ever seen." [1] That these dreams, still haunting the minds of men late in the sixteenth century, continued to derive something of their inspiration from the literature of fantasy is indicated by a Lima book list of 1583.

By that year viceregal Peru had emerged from the turmoil and anarchy of the first decades after the conquest and Lima, its capital which Pizarro had founded in 1535, was settling down to its appointed destiny as the administrative core and cultural arbiter of a vast empire. The rival factions of conquerors, who had lived by the sword in their bloody quarrels over the control of the rich hinterland, had, for the most part, perished by that weapon and in their place were soberer elements engaged in the more prosaic tasks of the economic exploitation of the land and the religious conversion of its inhabitants. Violence had yielded to these gentler activities, and more orderly habits of civilized life, which even included extensive reading of books, now prevailed. The "City of the Kings" was, in reality, transformed from a lair of brutal ruffians wrangling over the spoils of conquest to the most important cultural center of the entire southern continent. Already it enjoyed considerable literary activity of its own and, judging by a book order of that year, it claimed a public which demanded the best and most recent products of Spain's printing presses.

This evolution was greatly accelerated in 1569 by the arrival in Peru of the great, if somewhat humorless, administrator, the Viceroy Francisco de Toledo, whose decisive character and organizing genius brought to an end during his twelve-year rule the period of incessant strife throughout the realm.[2] With the crushing of the imperial family of the Incas the conquest of the Indians was virtually completed. By establishing the absolute and unquestioned sway of the Spanish Hapsburgs, thus compelling lingering dissident elements among the Peninsular conquerors to acknowledge a power above that of their own greed and ambition, this great proconsul of Philip II gave the viceroyalty of Peru the pattern and form of colonial government which endured almost unchanged for more than two centuries.

With peace came prosperity and leisure for some, as the rich silver mines yielded up their treasure. Though this increasing wealth inevitably tended to be concentrated in the hands of the steadily growing numbers of Spaniards pouring into the realm, some measure of economic well-being filtered through to the now considerable Creole element and even to the heterogeneous population of Indians, Negroes, and mixed elements forming a complex society with a solidifying hierarchy of castes and classes. By 1583 the general prosperity appears to have mitigated, at least in the towns of the viceroyalty, the hard lot of the lowly and exploited Indians. A decree of the following year strictly forbidding the natives, male and female, to wear silken garments, cambric shirts, velvet shoes, silk slippers, or gold and silver ornaments, on penalty of confiscation, suggests that many of the natives possessed the means of aping the manners and dress of their white overlords.[3] Indeed, such apt pupils of the conquerors were the Indians that they were already threatening to outdistance the Spaniards in a marked preference for gay attire and an associated indisposition to perform manual labor!

By 1583 the dominant influence of the Church on spiritual, intellectual, and social life, which was maintained throughout the entire colonial period, was plainly evident. Members of the multiplying religious communities were displaying an understandable preference for the comforts and refinements of the capital as against the hardships and isolation of work in the barren heights of the Sierra where dwelt the majority of their Indian charges. Thus, to an enlarging leisure class of laymen were added many of the clergy who were more devoted to idleness than to contemplation, and more addicted to political activities in the capital than to proselyting in the wilderness. This group, literate and leisured, already constituted a profitable market for booksellers of Lima who endeavored to provide their trade with the most recent and desired writings of Spanish authors, whether light fiction or ponderous theology. The more earnest members of the Church were also, of course, important customers, particularly at this time when the Counter Reformation was bringing forth the great literature of the mystics and the apologists. In that very year in Lima a great prelate, later canonized, Don Toribio Alfonso Mogrovejo, was instilling renewed enthusiasm in the colonial Church for its mission of Christianizing the native wards of the Spanish Crown. This great figure, a layman of Spain suddenly transformed by some strange alchemy into the Archbishop of Peru, had come to his diocese in 1581 where his practical piety, austere life, and unremitting devotion to his duties were to gain lasting veneration for his name in Peru and inspire at least one colonial playwright to compose a respectful *comedia* based on his life and work.[4] One of his first acts was to summon to the Third Church Council of Lima in 1582 bishops from such vast distances as those represented by the dioceses of Panama, Nicaragua, Popayán, Quito, Cuzco, Chuquisaca, Santiago de Chile, Tucumán, and Paraguay for the purpose of regulating ecclesiastical affairs and facilitating missionary work among the Indians by the preparation of manuals, catechisms, and books of devotion in the native languages. This great assembly was still in session late in the year 1583.[5]

Cultural life in the Lima of 1583 had already assumed the hue and quality that long made it a leading center of transplanted Spanish culture in the New World. Despite some competition from the monasteries and a recently founded Jesuit *colegio*, the University of San Marcos, authorized by imperial decree in 1551, was now, after some early hesitation, firmly established as an important seat of higher learning and was attracting to its faculty some of the finest intellects of Spain and Peru. The most conspicuous of these was the celebrated Jesuit scientist, philosopher, and teacher, Father José de Acosta, who took an important part in the proceedings of the Third

Church Council in Lima while occupying the Chair of Scriptural Writings at the University. It was during these years in Peru that he composed the first two books of his famous *Historia natural y moral de Indias*.[6] This work was the first attempt to make a systematic and scientific account of the physical geography and natural history of the American continent, and its success earned for its author the designation "the Pliny of the New World." Moreover, Lima and the viceroyalty of Peru had, by 1583, their own pleiad of poets who, whatever their merits—and these are far from clear— were numerous enough and sufficiently vocal to be heard and praised in the far-off motherland. Indeed, they even received the plaudits of Spain's greatest literary genius, a certain Miguel de Cervantes who inserted in his pastoral novel *La Galatea*, first published in 1585, a poem called *Canto de Calíope* in which he lists with praise the names of eleven bards in Peru apparently known to him.[7]

By 1583 the opulence of the City of Kings permitted a more lavish indulgence of the universal taste for elaborate public spectacles; the populace was no longer content with the crude performances of *autos sacramentales* which it had witnessed on Corpus Christi day and on other religious occasions ever since the Conquest. Moreover, it was ripe for the more secular form of drama then on the eve of its great development in Spain and soon to reach Peru. The immediate demand for more tasteful and artistic representations of sacred themes during religious festivals was met in 1582 by a self-styled *maestro del arte cómico*, who supervised the extraordinarily solemn and impressive performance of the Corpus Christi play of that year. This individual, whose name was Francisco de Morales, possessed exceptional skill as a theatrical director which he soon transferred to the secular theater in Lima.[8] It was he who gave the viceregal capital its first *corral de comedias*, or showhouse, and it was he who awoke the *limeño* public to the possibilities of a new diversion destined to become the passion of all classes of colonial society. Who knows that the copies of the "*comedias de Lope de Rueda*" that a bookdealer of Lima ordered from Spain that year of 1583, were not to serve as script to this theatrical *empresario* and his company of players in the practice of their art?

A still more significant indication of the cultural majority to which the viceregal capital of Peru was attaining in 1583 was the introduction of the printing press. Even as a bookseller was making out his large order for volumes to be imported from Spain that year an Italian printer, Antonio Ricardo, recently arrived in Lima, had set up his shop and was probably at work arranging type for the first printed work produced in the realm, the *Doctrina christiana y catequismo*, though royal authorization of a press in the viceroyalty had not yet been received. One of the accomplishments of Archbishop Mogrovejo and the Third Church Council, still in session in Lima, was the preparation of a catechism, and it is known that the actual printing of this work began well in advance of the receipt of the Royal Decree of Philip II dated August 7, 1584, granting the Piamontese printer the sole right to exercise his technical profession in the viceroyalty of Peru.[9]

But if Lima had published no books of its own by 1583, it had long been receiving printed literature of all kinds from the mother country. Even amidst the clamor and violence of civil strife of the early days of the city's existence some of its citizens found sufficient repose and freedom from distraction to read books, including such banned literature as the universally popular romances of chivalry. Only eight years after Pizarro had founded the capital on the banks of the Rimac River the Audiencia of Lima received strict orders to prohibit the entry into Peru of any of these *"libros de historias profanas,"* the reading of which was regarded not only as a waste of time but positively harmful.[10] Yet notarial records soon after this date give clear indications that, among the varied assortment of books in the possession of laymen and clerics alike, there was a goodly representation of such *"historias profanas"* as that of *Amadis of Gaul.* Printed literature of all sorts was, therefore, found in Lima long before that city had settled down to the peaceful monotony which characterized so much of the colonial period.

In the years leading up to 1583 the capital continued to receive fresh increments of Spanish adventurers, many well educated and of aristocratic origin, while the wealthy but politically powerless Creole class and the clergy increased in numbers. These elements, together with a few others who had been taught to read, gave the viceregal capital a larger literate public than that possessed by some of the cities of Spain, and profit-minded merchants of Lima, like

those of Mexico City, quickly found it to their advantage to include substantial orders of printed volumes among the many manufactured wares imported from the mother country. In this connection a record preserved in the National Archive of Peru at Lima is
of unique interest, for it is a list of books to be purchased in Spain
rather than an invoice or receipt of a shipment sent. Its special value,
therefore, lies in the insight it offers into the current tastes of the
limeño book buyers at the time it was drawn up. The document in
question is an agreement of Juan Jiménez del Río, a bookseller of
"la muy noble y muy leal ciudad de los reyes," made on February
22, 1583, with a certain Francisco de la Hoz who was about to
depart for Spain, under which the latter obligated himself to bring
back to Lima on his return from abroad a considerable quantity of
books whose titles are listed and whose specifications as to binding
are indicated. Such a business arrangement was common enough in
the colonial days when the hazards of importation were so great;
merchants usually found it expedient to entrust such commissions
to agents personally known to them and frequently gave their
representatives full power of attorney. In drawing up the list of
volumes to be purchased there is little doubt that the bookdealer,
Jiménez del Río, set down the titles for which he had received
requests from his trade or which he had found by experience met
with the readiest sale among his clientele. It is fair, then, to consider this collection of works as those which, in the Lima market of
1583, were the acknowledged best sellers, and as such they throw
some light on the state of culture existing in the viceregal capital at
that time. Though there is no evidence that the books in question
were actually brought back to Lima, it is reasonable to suppose that
the order was filled in whole or in part. Whether this was the case
or not, the agreement between Juan Jiménez del Río and Francisco
de la Hoz, with its attached book list, loses none of its value as an
index of the literary tastes of the *limeño* book-buying public in
that year of grace 1583.[11]

An analysis of the book order presents difficulties not encountered in other colonial documents studied relating to shipments and
inventories of printed works. The total number of volumes represented, for example, cannot be clearly stated since sets of works in

an indeterminate number of volumes were ordered, and Hoz was authorized to purchase any continuations or other writings by certain authors. A fair estimate of the total is, perhaps, a little under 2,000 books, to which should be added the twenty reams of *menudencias*, that is, some 2,880 booklets and loose sheets containing lives of saints, narrative ballads, short sentimental tales, children's stories, almanacs, and so on. Details of price are lacking but more data than usual are offered on types of binding and place of publication.

Of particular interest is the variety of literature indicated by the approximately 135 titles in the list (in some cases separate parts of a given work appear as separate items), and also by the short pieces in the *menudencias*, since both clearly refute, if any refutation is still necessary, the oft-repeated and long-credited assertions of historians, critics, and others that Spanish authorities sought to keep out of the colonies any literature save that of approved theological character. Jiménez del Río's order called for the varied types of works which had already been available in the Lima market and for which he found a continuing demand among his customers. A cursory examination of the titles ordered should therefore convince the most skeptical that the expatriated Spaniards, Creoles, and other literate elements of colonial society had access to and could enjoy the same books as did the majority of their kinsmen in contemporary Spain itself; moreover, a striking similarity of literary preferences is noted. It will also be found that the list offers, on the whole, a representative selection of sixteenth-century literature, though it is remarkable for the relatively small percentage of purely religious works included. If, for the sake of convenience, the titles are again distributed into three arbitrary classifications (in some cases a difficult and misleading operation), namely, (1) ecclesiastical works, (2) secular books (nonreligious nonfiction), and (3) belles-lettres, the comparative ratios are surprising. In Jiménez del Río's order the proportions are approximately 24 per cent for belles-lettres, 32 per cent for nonfiction, while ecclesiastical writings comprise about 44 per cent, or less than half of the whole order. With the city full of prelates and dignitaries from remote parts of the continent attending sessions of the Third Church Council at Lima, it is a little curious that the bookdealer did not find it necessary to replenish still more his stock of theological and religious works.

Of greater significance is the fact that more than half of the titles which Jiménez del Río found that his trade wanted were of the character of those which, according to some historians, were accessible to colonists only as contraband. The fact that a Lima bookseller made public his intention of ordering novels of chivalry that were banned in early decrees by recording his agreement with Francisco de la Hoz before a royal notary is clinching evidence that the law was a dead letter—which circumstance again suggests the danger inherent in basing the writing of history on extant legislation.

A discussion of the first of the three categories adopted for the grouping of the titles in Jiménez del Río's order, namely, the strictly religious and theological works, is omitted since at no time has there been a question of their admission into the colonies and today there is probably less interest in this branch of literature. Suffice it to say that the writings of such great mystics of the Counter Reformation as Fray Luis de Granada and Fray Luis de León are conspicuously represented in this list of books found to be selling well in the Lima market of 1583.

Of the more humanistic secular works history is best represented, though the diversity of titles is not impressive. The two works of which most copies were desired relate to the Catholic religion; two others tell of the wars in Africa; another is a chronicle of Spain; and another appears to be an account of the victory of Juan de Austria over the Turks at Lepanto. The absence from the list of any available history of the Indies suggests a curious lack of interest in their own world on the part of *limeño* readers.

Works of jurisprudence, law codes, and manuals present a larger variety, though quantities ordered are small. The most notable title representing the first-named group is undoubtedly the *De justicia et jure* of the great Salamancan professor, Domingo de Soto, a colleague of Father Francisco de Victoria and almost as renowned. This work was regarded as one of the greatest of its time in the philosophy of law and, like other titles by this author, should be counted more properly among the philosophical writings included in Jiménez del Río's order. It is of interest to recall in passing that it was this same Domingo de Soto who presided over the famous controversy between Las Casas and Sepúlveda and who sided with the "Apostle of the Indians" in his defense of the natives. The treatises of Felipus Decius, Antonio Gómez, and Parladorios, frequently noted on later book lists, had a sale in the Lima of 1583 along with the famous *Siete partidas* of Alfonso the Wise, and a law code of Castile. Doubtless the copies of canonical and civil law were indispensable reference works in the viceroyalty of Peru. Manuals or guides, called *Práticas*, for the instruction of aspiring advocates and scribes also had a moderate sale, particularly that of Monterroso, which appears on most book lists of the period and of which its author, by a royal degree of 1569, enjoyed an exclusive monopoly of the sales in the Indies in 1583.[12]

Among the sciences, medicine and related subjects are best represented, though a strictly limited number of copies of each title was ordered. The *De succedaneis medicamentis* of the physician and botanist Juan Fragoso, surgeon of Philip II; the *Libro de medicina* of Bernardus de Gordiono, a fifteenth-century Spanish doctor; the *Libro o práctica de cirugía* of Joannes de Vigo; and a work of the fourteenth-century physician, Guido de Chauliac or Chaulien, long considered a great authority and famous for his description of the Black Plague in 1348, with a commentary by a later Spanish doctor, Juan Falcó or Faucon, are the works requested. Only one other science (using the word in the more modern, technical sense) is represented by an important work, that of navigation, on which Pedro de Medina's *Regimiento de navigación* was the standard authority in the sixteenth century. The often-reprinted and translated *Examen de ingenios para las ciencias* of the philosopher Juan Huarte de San Juan, who thought deeply on the problems of the relations between the physical and the moral, enjoyed a greater sale in the Lima of 1583 than the more technical scientific works.[13] This title will be noted again and again on later lists.

Philosophy is such an all-embracing term that numerous works already indicated under other disciplines should be included here, notably those of Domingo de Soto. Fitting a narrower definition are a few titles, particularly the writings of Saint Thomas Aquinas and the commentaries on them and on those of Aristotle by such

pure Thomists as Bartolomé de Medina and Francisco de Toledo.
A more eclectic philosophy is found in the works of that Renaissance humanist, Alejo Vanegas.

Most of the foregoing volumes must have appealed to a small
and select group of Jiménez del Río's customers. Less abstract and
more utilitarian literature, such as miscellaneous texts and reference works, found a wider sale, judging by comparatively large
quantities of individual works ordered. It is not clear which of the
many writings of the famous Erasmist, Juan Luis Vives, is requested in the item "100 *luis biuas*", but it is reasonable to suppose
that it refers to his *Instrucción de la mujer cristiana*, the accepted
guide for the proper training and education of young ladies. In the
Indies anxious colonial dames were doubtless eager to rear their
daughters according to the approved fashion of the Peninsula and
this manual was doubtless an answer to their prayers and a recommendation of their ecclesiastical counselors. In any event, the little
volume sold in such quantities as to place it inevitably among the
best sellers of the time. Incidentally, if the identification of this
mysterious item is correct, there are strict injunctions in this book,
as will be recalled, against the reading by young ladies of some of
the very same titles, such as *La Celestina* and certain novels of
chivalry, which Jiménez del Río was including elsewhere in his
order.

Another work of utilitarian character enjoying a wide sale
during most of the colonial period was the famous Castilian grammar of Antonio de Nebrija, the *Arte de la lengua castellana*, first
published in 1492. A study of all extant shipping records, invoices,
and inventories might well prove that more copies of this work
went to the Spanish Indies than those of any other single work.
That Jiménez del Río found it among his best sellers in 1583 is
indicated by the order for fifty copies. This work was doubtless
serving in the diffusion of Castilian in the New World and was
acting as a needed check against syntactical peculiarities which
were already creeping into the transplanted Spanish of Peru and
of other parts of the Western Hemisphere where the language of
Castile was used. Dictionaries, almanacs, and calendars are miscellaneous items of secular nonfiction appearing in the list.

The assortment of belles-lettres in Jiménez del Río's order offers a better index of what was widely read in viceregal Peru and is, perhaps, a more accurate reflection of the leisure reading habits of sixteenth-century Spain and Spanish America. The first and best of the long romances, *Amadís de Gaula*, was still among the favorites in Lima, though the adventures of one of his emulators, *Belianis de Grecia*, appears to have enjoyed wider esteem. Of interest is the bookdealer's comment that only the first and second parts of this novel were desired, since plenty of the third and fourth were to be had in the Lima market. On the whole, if Jiménez del Río's order is an index of the best sellers of 1583, the choice of romances of chivalry does no great honor to the critical discrimination of the *limeño* public.

Next in succession is *Lepolemo o el Caballero de la Cruz* which, though regarded charitably by a later critic,[14] was quickly consigned, it will be recalled, to the bonfire of Don Quixote's library. The inferior *Príncipe Felixmarte de Hircania* had sufficient appeal to be included in the order along with a request for any sequels that might have appeared subsequently. Bespeaking its exceptional popularity throughout the Indies are the twenty copies of Contreras' *Selva de aventuras*, the sentimental tale that gained the distinction of being one of the few works of imagination placed on the *Index of prohibited books* by the Inquisition. And lastly, it is apparent that Spanish versions of the Italian chivalric epics of *Orlando* gave pleasure to Peruvian readers of 1583.

But the public of the viceregal capital could also appreciate the best creative literature of the mother country, as is shown by the inclusion of the dialogued novel *La Celestina*, still regarded as second only to *Don Quixote* in Spanish letters. Another masterpiece, *Lazarillo de Tormes*, the first of the picaresque novels which Spain gave to world literature, was similarly esteemed in the Lima of 1583. And Guevara's celebrated *Libro áureo de Marco Aurelio*, which enjoyed equal favor with *Amadis of Gaul* and *La Celestina* in the popular taste of sixteenth-century Spain, reflects this distinction in contemporary Peru.

In a language as musical as Spanish, poetry in all its forms rivaled and exceeded in popularity the prose fiction already mentioned. Ballad collections, lyric and narrative verse often predominate in colonial lists of belles-lettres, though in this respect the Lima order

of 1583 is less typical. The omnipresent *romanceros* are here limited
to a nonnational group, probably the Carlovingian cycle, though
the *Cancionero* of Jorge Montemayor and the works of Castillejo
and a version in *octavas* of the story of the Cid reveal a sounder
taste for national themes and verse. The only indication of the
limeño public's interest in literature concerning its own part of the
world and of local inspiration are the twelve copies of the first two
parts of Ercilla's epic of the campaigns against the Araucanian
Indians of Chile, *La Araucana*. This apparent indifference to local
themes and preoccupation with Spanish and European literature
characterize the entire colonial period and illustrate the complete
spiritual and literary as well as political and economic subordination
of the colonies to the mother country.

Spanish drama in 1583 had hardly entered upon its great period,
its *siglo de oro*, but already it was adumbrated even in Peru, by the
reading of *comedias* of Torres Naharro and Lope de Rueda. Soon
this literature of diversion would eclipse completely that of the
romances of chivalry and hold a more permanent place in the affections of Spaniards and Spanish Americans alike.

In the miscellaneous assortment of essays, short tales, etc., the
Lima order again reflects contemporary tastes of Spain. The redis-
covery of classic poets and essayists of antiquity has recognition
in the *epístolas* of Cicero and Ovid, and the epics of Vergil and
Homer. Timoneda's popular *Patrañuelo*, a collection of twenty-two
patrañas, or anecdotes or stories, also claims a place among the best
sellers of Lima along with the curious miscellany *Silva de varia
lección* and the *Entretenimiento de damas y galanes*.

Not without interest are the brief side lights of Jiménez del
Río's order on the types of binding in which *limeño* book buyers
preferred their reading matter. Ordinary trade books came bound
in plain vellum, which apparently resisted the hard wear to which
they were subjected in the colonies. Fiction works, which doubtless passed frequently from hand to hand, were invariably bound
in this material, though occasionally, as in the case of common religious writings, the order called for half the number of copies in
vellum and the other part in paperboard covers, usually with gilt
floral designs upon them. Larger folio volumes, ponderous theological tomes for the most part, were usually requested in wooden

boards, sometimes covered with calfskin, occasionally by leather with colored, figured designs, and with book clasps. The smaller items, the *menudencias*, were likewise bound in vellum, though exception might be made of the *coplas*, which were found to be acceptable when folded and stitched like pamphlets.

The notarized agreement between the Lima merchant Juan Jiménez del Río and the Spain-bound Francisco de la Hoz may well have seemed to the scribe who recorded it that day in February of 1583 a rather insignificant, routine instrument of no interest to others than the two individuals concerned. But to the scholar, rummaging in the archives nearly three and a half centuries later, this inconsequential document is a precious relic of the past, casting its bit of light on the cultural life of viceregal Peru in the great period of the sixteenth century and furnishing an index to the literary tastes of its capital less than half a century after its founding by the illiterate swineherd and intrepid conquistador, Francisco Pizarro.

ONE MAN'S LIBRARY, MANILA, 1583 XV

At THE HEIGHT OF PHILIP II'S REIGN THE PHYSICAL dimensions of the Spanish empire dwarfed those of any other that the world had known, including ancient Rome. When the Duke of Alba made Portugal a vassal of the Castilian monarch in 1580, Spain not only added Brazil to its New World dominions, thus bringing all South America under its aegis, but acquired rich islands and strategic footholds in the Far East which supplemented its own holdings in that remote part of the globe. The Crown claimed as its own not merely the entire Western Hemisphere, but also the Pacific Ocean, the latter as a new and grander *mare nostrum*—a Spanish lake. Philip II vainly sought to seal off the entrance to it from the east with an ill-fated colonizing expedition to the Strait of Magellan, while his new ownership of a similar waterway at Malacca, of the Molucca islands, and of ports on the Asiastic mainland gave him control of the approaches from the West. Previously a series of maritime explorations, beginning with Magellan's famous voyage and culminating with that of Legaspi in 1564, had annexed to the swollen empire of Spain the strategically located archipelago of the Philippines, named for the reigning king. Just as the Spaniards had pioneered the first freight and passenger line across the Atlantic, so did they also establish the first regular service of this sort across the Pacific. As the fleet sailed yearly out of Seville, the single "Manila galleon," beginning in 1565, made its vastly longer voyage annually, navigating between Acapulco in Mexico and Manila on Luzon.[1] Considering the slow and clumsy means of transportation of the age, the effectiveness of the system of trade and communications that the Spanish government set up between

its far-flung possessions is little short of amazing. A rudimentary
maritime commerce was already operating in the Pacific with
Manila as an entrepôt, and it was bringing such distant regions as
China and Peru in touch with each other. While head of the South
American viceroyalty, Don Martín Enríquez reported the safe
arrival at Callao of a vessel which the Governor of the Philippines,
Don Gonzalo Ronquillo, had dispatched with a cargo of chinaware,
silks, iron, blankets, wax, spices, and even some badly needed artillery. The viceroy of Peru indicated that these goods from the
Asiatic mainland and islands had sold very well in the local market,
all of them, in fact, "except the cinnamon which has a poor sale because it isn't good." This movement of commodities to and fro
across the endless wastes of the Pacific did not fail to include such
items of a settled existence as the products of European printing
presses, a fact which is confirmed by a surviving book list of 1583.

About a quarter of the way through a volume of yellowed Inquisition papers preserved in the General Archive of the Nation at
Mexico City are seven thin, brownish folios, possibly of Chinese rice
paper.[2] In quality and appearance these sheets differ considerably
from the other manuscript pages bound with them, of which practically all relate to matters in New Spain. Caught in the binding
before the first of these folios of contrasting texture and color is a
scrap of white paper with the brief legend:

> January 1583. Documents on various matters sent by the
> Commissioner of Manila to the Inquisitors at Mexico City.[3]

On both sides of the first sheet are listed in rapid but legible hand
some fifty-four short titles of books. All but one of the first eleven
names are preceded by the Spanish articles *un* or *unos;* the rest,
except for the plural "books for children" and "primers," appear
without any indication of quantity. It seems likely, therefore, that
this collection was a small, personal library, mainly of single copies,
which fact soon moved the listing clerk to omit further numerical
designations with the remaining items. Surmounting the first page
of this document is the customary sign of the Cross, under which
appears the cryptic caption:

Memoria de los libros sigtes q traygo yo trebiña—1583.

No other notation appears on either side of the sheet, and the documents following offer no clue to the identity of "trebiña" (or possibly treviño),[4] or to the circumstances attending the compilation of this interesting list of printed works. It seems safe to deduce, however, that this particular document relates to a collection of books brought half around the world to Spain's most distant possessions less than two decades after the effective occupation of the Philippine Islands by the Adelantado Legaspi, and barely a dozen years after the bold capture of Manila from Mohammedan hands by Spanish conquistadors.

For the study of the diffusion of literary culture in the sixteenth century this relatively short list of books is one of the most interesting that Spanish colonial archives have yielded. Its exceptional character lies chiefly in the high percentage of fictional and secular writings, contrasting with the purely religious works dominating most early book lists. If one adopts again the convenient though somewhat unreliable distribution of titles under the headings: (1) belles-lettres, (2) secular nonfiction, and (3) religious writings, the proportion of 60 to 70 per cent or higher usually found for the last named group passes over to the first two categories of this Manila inventory. To be more specific, belles-lettres are represented by some twenty-three titles, or 43 per cent of the total, a remarkably high percentage; there are eleven different works classified as secular nonfiction, or about 21 per cent of the whole, leaving only about nineteen titles to the usually predominant religious writings, or 36 per cent, hardly more than half the proportion normally noted on colonial book lists. But of greater interest than these statistics are the books themselves.

Taken as a whole this selection of literature is a valid reflection of contemporary tastes and, save for a few lapses, suggests that the unknown Trebiña was a gentleman of considerable discrimination. Particularly interesting is his choice of belles-lettres, the largest single group, in which he maintains a fairly even balance between prose and poetry. Some four or five titles include the now shopworn but still popular romances of chivalry, but they are hardly representative of this literary fashion at its prime. *La historia de los nobles cavalleros Oliveros de Castilla y Artus d'Algarbe* and the

Historia del emperador Carlomagno y de los doze pares de Francia
are mere novelettes or long short stories which, however, claimed
readers to the end of the colonial period. The remaining works of
this character on the Manila list of 1583 are in verse and hence less
typical. The *Caballero determinado* is presumably the version of
Olivier de la Marche's work *Chevalier délibéré* so often noted on
contemporary lists. Another verse rendition of this French novel
of chivalry was made by Jerónimo de Urrea, who prepared a translation of Ariosto's *Orlando furioso*, also present on the Trebiña list.
Of similar metrical form was the *Caballero de la clara Estrella* composed in royal octaves by Andrés de Losa.

But the prose accounts of the glamorous exploits of *Amadís de
Gaula, Palmerín de Inglaterra*, and the innumerable progeny of
these heroes are notably absent from the personal library of this
traveler to the Philippines, a fact that suggests the possibility that
the vogue of this fiction was waning in 1583, but that contrasts with
the book order sent that year from Lima. By then, however, the
adventurous knights had already yielded much ground to their un-
armed and even less realistic rivals, the love-stricken shepherds of
the current pastoral novels. Such false idealization of rural life as
is offered by these narratives of bucolic amours in a mixture of
delicate verse and refined prose made them even more escapist than
the earlier romances of chivalry, but this circumstance did not lessen
their hold upon the reading public toward the close of the sixteenth
century. The copy of the tender and tearful *Arcadia* by the Italian
Sannazaro, which had appeared in Spanish translation in 1549, indicates that the unidentified Trebiña shared this taste with his generation. Even before Sannazaro's work was available in Castilian its
best qualities had been incorporated into the eclogues of that refined poet of Spain, Garcilaso de la Vega, whose name appears
twice on the Manila book list, and the success of both these writers,
particularly in the aristocratic circles of the Peninsula, created a
demand for the Spanish pastoral novel. The first to meet it, as
already stated, was Portugal-born Jorge de Montemayor with his
celebrated *Siete libros de la Diana*, published about 1559. On the
Trebiña list appears the item "Diana, Prima, 2a, 3a, 4a", which
doubtless refers to this famous work and its continuations. In 1564
Alonso Pérez, a physician and also a friend of Montemayor, by then

deceased, brought out a second part of the *Diana*, a prolix and pedantic narrative with obvious borrowings from Sannazaro and Ovid. Less certain, however, is the identity of the remaining parts, though the third is possibly the more readable *Diana enamorada* by Gaspar Gil Polo, published in Valencia the same year as the *Segunda parte*. In the famous scrutiny of Don Quixote's library, it will be recalled, the parish priest recommended that Montemayor's *Diana* be spared from the flames because of its excellent prose "and because it had the honor of being the first of such books," though he urged the excision of certain magic elements and most of the verse that it contained. Regarding the sequels by Pérez and Gil Polo his convictions were clear. "Let the *Diana* of the Salamancan," he said, "accompany and increase the number of the condemned volumes in the yard, but keep Gil Polo's *Diana* as if it were by Apollo himself!" The fourth part indicated on the Manila list of 1583 is possibly the *Clara Diana a lo divino* of Bartolomé Ponce, just published the year before. In this work the author sought to achieve what was attempted with respect to the reading of chivalric romances, that is, to elevate public taste by a pious imitation of the fiction which had attained such formidable popularity. But the evidence is slight that these religious substitutes counteracted the influence of the pastoral best sellers of the time.

Despite the unabating attacks of the moralists, which were shifting from the Amadises to the Dianas, the demand for unadulterated sentimentality grew, a trend that the Manila list clearly reflects. The *Teagenes y Clariclea* from the *Historia Etiopica* of the Greek novelist, Heliodorus, the Spanish version of which was made in 1554 from a French translation of the original, thus enjoyed a revival; it was represented probably by the Salamanca edition of 1581 in the Trebiña collection. Another work by an ancient writer on this list was the *Asno de oro* of the Numidian philosopher, Lucius Apuleius. Similarly episodic, it offered an entertaining potpourri of the miraculous, the ludicrous, the voluptuous, and the horrible along with the charmingly sentimental story of Cupid and Psyche. Incidentally, it was about to supply Cervantes with inspiration for Don Quixote's furious combat with the wineskins at the inn. To be noted is the recurrence of the highly moral *Selva de*

aventuras of Jerónimo Contreras, later to adorn the *Index of prohibited books.*

Hardly less acceptable to the public than the foregoing were
the collections of apothegms, anecdotes, and short stories which
offered their readers between the covers of a single book a wide
variety of diversion and instruction. Trebiña's list included several
works of this type, the best representative being that gem of fourteenth-century Castilian letters, the *Conde Lucanor o libro de
Patronio* by Juan Manuel, whose fifty interesting tales furnished
sources to such literary geniuses as Cervantes, Calderón, and Shake-
speare. The less valuable but widely read *Floresta española*, a somewhat similar aggregation of anecdotes and stories, also finds a place
on the Manila list. And the gracefully written but rather absurd
collection of brief tales, incidents, and dialogues, Antonio Torquemada's *Jardín de flores*, which won unmerited success, was also
carried to the Philippines in 1583.

In poetry the Trebiña of the book list displays more discriminating taste, barring perhaps the versified romances of chivalry. In
transporting this small library to the ends of the earth, presumably
for his own solace and refreshment, he had chosen the writings of
some of the best poets of his own century and earlier. While enjoying the innovations of the so-called Italianate school he still appreciated the old Castilian meters, judging by the copy of a
Romancero, probably a collection of old ballads, and particularly
by the moving *Coplas de Jorge Manrique a la muerte de su padre.*
Another fifteenth-century poet, the Valencian Ausías March, likewise inspired by the subject of death, is also represented in this
Manila library, presumably in the Castilian translation of Jorge de
Montemayor, published only a few years before, in 1579. The old
metric forms are also preserved in the *Inventario* of Antonio de
Villegas, a follower of Cristóbal de Castillejo, the worldly cleric
who championed the traditional meters against those introduced
from Italy. But the real renown of the *Inventario* rests on the appended part that its author did not write, the charming prose tale
of the Moorish lovers, Abindarráez and Jarifa, and their generous
treatment by the high-minded Spaniard, Rodrigo de Narváez.
Though less mawkishly sentimental than the contemporary pastoral

novels (the tale had also appeared with Montemayor's *Diana*), its popularity doubtless owed much to the current vogue. Though it was widely read in the sixteenth century, the inclusion of the *Inventario* in the Manila list is one of the few instances noted in colonial records.

In 1583 the popular drama of Spain was about to enter its great period, but the prolific genius of Lope de Vega had not yet fully fashioned the most typical product of the Golden Age—the Spanish *comedia*. By then, however, his acknowledged forerunner, the goldbeater of Seville turned playwright and barnstormer, Lope de Rueda, had already played his part and passed from the boards. Subsequently, an enterprising bookseller of Valencia, Juan de Timoneda, to whom Spanish letters owe much, had brought out an edition of these early plays in prose and verse, a copy of which was transported to the Philippines by the Trebiña of the document. Thus, as early as 1583, the works of Lope de Rueda, who had brought the theater to the common people of Spain, had reached the antipodes as well as Mexico and Peru.

For once Antonio de Guevara's *Libro áureo de Marco Aurelio* does not appear on a list, but this popular writer is represented by his *Epístolas familiares*, which were eighty-five in number and dealt with a wide diversity of subjects in scarcely simple or "familiar" language. The owner of the Manila collection seems to have chosen this work, as he did so many others in his library, with a view to having the widest variety of themes and materials in the limited number of books that he could carry on his far journey. Another omnibus volume of light and varied character, *El honesto y agradable entretenimiento de damas y galanes* (The proper and agreeable entertainment for young ladies and gentlemen), was not quite so "proper" as its name proclaims. Its first edition appeared in 1583 at Granada, and its presence in this Philippine collection in the very same year is a startling indication of the rapidity with which books hot off the press reached the farthest limits of the contemporary Spanish-speaking world.

Turning to the small group of secular nonfiction, the titles present show no marked predilections of the possessor, though the majority may be vaguely classified as philosophic and scientific works. Two well-established treatises on medicine and surgery sug-

gest that they were included as practical references for one residing at a remote outpost where professional medical assistance could
hardly be expected. The *Cronología o repertorio de los tiempos* by
a former cosmographer of the House of Trade at Seville indicates
that the traveler to the Philippines shared the universal respect in
which this work was held in sixteenth-century Spain. But of greater
significance than the works just mentioned was the *Examen de ingenios para las ciencias* of Huarte de San Juan, noted, it will be
recalled, in the Lima order and certainly one of the most influential
books of its time. The author was the first to set forth the theory
of the interrelation of psychology and experimental physiology.
As a pioneer work, first published in 1575, it aroused in translation
profound interest throughout Europe and had a serious effect on
contemporary thought. The inclusion of a copy of this work in a
private library at Manila only eight years after its publication is interesting evidence of the intellectual caliber of some of the Spaniards who followed hard upon the heels of the conquistadors. The
quality of the owner's mind, is, perhaps, further revealed by what
appears to be a Spanish translation of *Della instituzione de tutta la
vita de l'uomo nato nobile* by the contemporary Italian philosopher,
Alexander Piccolomini, one of the first to treat Aristotelian philosophy in a romance language. This effort to democratize philosophic discussion brought down upon the author's head the condemnation of critics, lay and ecclesiastical, and he was denounced
as a heretic. Another indication of the unknown Trebiña's broad
interests and appreciation of fine writing is offered in the *De la
diferencia de los libros que hay en el universo* (On the differences
in the books that there are in the world) of the learned Alejo
Vanegas. Less convincing testimony of this sort, perhaps, is the
Coloquios matrimoniales, a fictional guide prepared by Pedro
Luján, who had earlier written some of the dullest and most absurd
of the novels of chivalry.

History in its broader aspects find no place in this assortment of
books, and the only representative of this discipline is an account of
an isolated event which shook Christian Europe, the surrender of
the Isle of Rhodes to the Mohammedans under Soleiman in 1522.
Both Garcilaso de la Vega and Boscán, the Spanish poets for whom
the Trebiña of the book list shows partiality, took part in the futile

effort to relieve the siege of the Christian Knights by the Turks, and possibly this fact explains the presence of the lone volume of history in the Manila collection. The remaining miscellany of secular nonfiction is composed of an *Arte de canto llano*, revealing the owner's concern for one aspect of music, some unnamed "books for children," and primers.

Regarding the purely religious works included little need be said, since this type of literature is of slight general interest today. As already suggested, the proportion of works in this category on the Manila list is one of the smallest encountered on the book lists of the period; moreover, few of those present are strictly theological or exegetical in character. The majority are devotional writings such as the *Meditations of St. Augustine*, the *Contemptus mundi* of Thomas a Kempis, and the *Tratado de la oración y meditación* of San Pedro de Alcántara. The mystical *Audi, filia, et vide* of Juan de Ávila is present, which fact is of some interest because its earlier editions had been gathered up by the Inquisition.[5] Occasional works of piety in verse also form a part of this Manila library, such as the *Parto de la Virgen*, translated into royal octaves from the Italian of Sannazaro, the author of the lachrymose *Arcadia*.

An over-all view of this compact library taken to the Philippines in 1583 leaves an impression that the owner sought to assemble a group of books small enough to be included among his personal baggage on a long journey, and sufficiently diversified in character to meet the needs of his body, mind, and spirit during a prolonged residence at a place far removed from his cultural sources of supply. The episodic nature of much of the creative literature selected and the variety offered by the contents of the nonfictional works both suggest the desire of a gentleman of some culture to provide himself with reading material for every mood. It is true, of course, that the omnibus character of many of these selections, as well as the apparent partiality for writings of Italian influence, faithfully reflect the literary preferences of the closing decades of the sixteenth century in Spain and elsewhere, but the special choices recorded on this Manila book list betray a certain deliberateness in bringing together the maximum variety of literary staples in a small larder.

But who was the owner of this curious collection of volumes, and in what capacity did he find himself in the far-off Philippines

so soon after their conquest? The answers to these questions are
not apparent. A search among records thus far available has failed
to cast any light on the identity of the "trebiña" of the book list,
or even reveal anyone bearing that name at that time in the Philippine islands. What the owner's position in this remote archipelago
was is equally obscure. The predominance of secular writings on
the list and the devotional, rather than the theological, character
of the religious books included may indicate that he was a layman
and not a member of the clergy. Neither the quantity nor the quality of the volumes reported suggests that he was a dealer or a merchant; practically all titles are represented by one copy only, and
the choice of literature strengthens the conviction that this collection of books was the property of a person of considerable taste
and discrimination. Possibly the owner was an official of the Crown
in Manila who had brought his family with him, a conjecture which
might explain the presence of children's books and primers on the
list—and perhaps of the *Coloquios matrimoniales* as well. Whatever
"trebiña's" identity, the survival of the document recording the
literary works which he had brought with him offers clear proof
that, despite the oft-cited prohibitory legislation against *libros
profanos*, at least as early as 1583 some of the best and most representative of Castilian literature found its way into the most distant
lands on which the conquistadors unfurled the banner of Spain, the
Philippine islands.

What was the character of the Manila of 1583, from which its
Commissioner of the Inquisition dispatched this curious book list
to his superiors at Mexico City? To what sort of outpost of empire
had Spanish literary culture thus penetrated? In a few brief years
the Adelantado Legaspi and his lieutenants, Goiti and the youthful
Salcedo, as dauntless as any of the conquerors who had earlier
served Cortés and Pizarro, had achieved one of the most swift and
complete conquests in Spain's stirring annals. Within seven years
of Legaspi's arrival in 1565 Spanish soldiers had overrun almost the
entire archipelago of the Philippines and added it to the possessions
of the Crown, and subsequently the process of consolidation had
continued, with these remote islands forming a part of the viceroyalty of Mexico.[6] By 1583 practically all the territory there ef-

fectively occupied by Spain during the next three centuries was
already pacified, though some incidental mopping-up activities
were in progress, such as the elimination of the Japanese invaders
from the neighborhood of Cagayán on the northern tip of the
island of Luzón, and the planting of new townships.[7] Already
Spanish authorities, both secular and ecclesiastic, were thinking of
the archipelago, particularly the strategically located city of Manila, as a bridgehead for the immeasurably vaster conquest of China
and the Far East. The union of the kingdoms of Spain and Portugal in 1580 under Philip II had made Manila in fact the capital of
an enormous empire in the East Indies stretching from Goa in
India to Macao in China, and a powerful control center of a po-
tentially fabulous oriental trade.

In that very year of 1583 the Governor of the Philippines and,
even more significantly, the Bishop of Manila, had addressed earnest
pleas to their monarch at Madrid urging him to drop his multifarious
projects in Europe in favor of the immensely greater opportunities
offered by his newly acquired title and rights to the Portuguese
possessions. Bishop Salazar, known as "the Las Casas of the Philippines" because of his defense of the natives against the ruthless
conquistadors, betrayed his imperialistic leanings when he declared
in a special letter of entreaty dated June 18, 1583, that, although for
twenty-three years he

> . . . had supported the contention of nearly all learned men
> in Spain, and even in the Indies itself, who condemned the
> conquering of the Indian peoples, since his arrival in the
> Philippines where he had consulted with well-informed and
> God-fearing persons, he had changed his mind.[8]

He then outlined an ambitious plan by which China might be won
for Christendom—and for Spanish trade. This project was one of
the rare subjects with which he was in agreement with the secular
governor, who also sent a letter two days later stating that 8,000
Spaniards and a fleet of twelve or thirteen galleons would suffice to
take over the entire Chinese empire.[9] Prudent Philip II apparently
did not share this optimism, though it was evident to him that
Manila was becoming a rich entrepôt for the lucrative commerce of
the Far East. The governor at Manila had·dispatched a well-laden

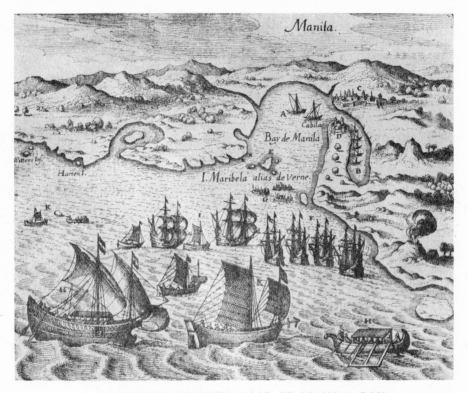

A SIXTEENTH-CENTURY MAP OF MANILA BAY

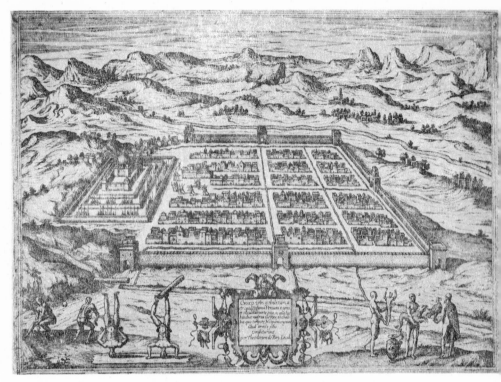

EARLY SEVENTEENTH-CENTURY CUZCO

ship to Peru, with a view to opening trade with that viceroyalty, and already the traffic with Mexico was proving so profitable that rival merchants there and in Spain were beginning to bring pressure on the Crown to impose strict limitations on the volume of goods permitted on the cumbrous Manila galleon which plowed its lonely course across the vast reaches of the Pacific Ocean.

In 1583, however, this prosperity had not fully developed, and the affairs of the Philippines and their capital were momentarily in a precarious state. Some seven hundred Spaniards lived in Manila amidst an undetermined number of natives,[10] but these European elements were, for the most part, restless and unprincipled adventurers seeking quick wealth at the expense of the conquered. Those who held *encomiendas* of Filipinos were taking their luckless tributaries out of the fields and putting them to work in the mines and galleys, thus creating a food scarcity which threatened the existence of Spanish overlord and native serf alike. The spirit of revolt was smoldering, and some of the Filipino chieftains were conspiring with the Datu of Borneo to oust the Spaniards from the islands. Governor Ronquillo was aiding and abetting this shortsighted exploitation by the *encomenderos* while at the same time imposing prohibitive taxes on the local trade with Mexico and with the Chinese merchants called *sangleyes*. When the latter arrived in their junks, they were herded together in a single dwelling, separated from the other residents of the city, and placed under a special warden with arbitrary powers. This official often obliged the hapless Chinese to sell their goods far below value, or even robbed them of their wares entirely, subsequently shanghaiing the Orientals for service on the Spanish galleys. This shameless treatment was discouraging the very trade which held so great a promise of profit for the Spaniards themselves.[11] To the correction of these and other abuses the recently arrived missionaries, headed by Bishop Salazar, vigorously addressed themselves, thus initiating the friction between secular and ecclesiastical authorities destined to vex so much of Philippine history during the long centuries of Spanish rule.

This conflict between the representatives of Church and State half the world away from the centralized control of Madrid was disadvantageous to the Bishop, who was outnumbered by acquisitive laymen, but his repeated complaints to Philip II resulted in some measures which made the year 1583 important in the annals of the Philippines. To curb the arbitrary power of the Governor and the excesses of the *encomenderos* a royal decree of May 5, 1583 established the Royal Audiencia of Manila with jurisdiction not only over the entire archipelago but extending to "the mainland of China, whether discovered or yet to be discovered,"[12] thus preparing for the possible expansion to continental Asia that the worthy Bishop was recommending. The following year the appointed officials arrived and this judicial agency began to function.

Even earlier in 1583 another institution was authorized, possibly to strengthen the hand of Bishop Salazar. This was a branch at Manila of the Inquisition of New Spain, and to the newly designated Commissioner instructions were issued under date of March 1, 1583.[13] Possibly the Trebiña book list represents one of the first acts of this official of the Holy Office on assuming his duties in the Philippines. Thus in this historic year important institutions of the Spanish governmental system were formally authorized or set up in the fringe of islands lying off the coast of Asia.

But more unexpected incidents were taking place at the Philippine capital in 1583. Governor Ronquillo died on February 14, after serving less than three years in office.[14] Poor health and personal difficulties had beset him constantly during his brief term and doubtless hastened his end. His passing brought destruction to the city whose affairs he had administered so arbitrarily. While the funeral services were in progress at the St. Augustine monastery, wax tapers placed on the huge catafalque, which reached nearly to the ceiling, ignited the timbered roof of the structure and the flames, fanned by a strong wind, quickly consumed the entire building, from which only the Holy Sacrament was rescued. The conflagration spread to the nearby bamboo huts thatched with the tinderlike *nipa* leaf, and in the space of two hours most of the city was reduced to a mass of charred and smoking ruins. All public buildings were destroyed, including the main church and its precious organ, the hospital, the bishop's residence, the warehouse stocked with goods for transport to Mexico, the fort, the armory and its magazines with all the powder and munitions on hand. So intense and voracious were the flames that they even melted most of the cannon and artillery that the Spaniards sorely needed for the defense of the city.[15] Thus, in addition to being threatened with starvation, most of the population was suddenly homeless, and the capital was nearly helpless to resist attack.

Prompt action, both by the new governor, Diego de Ronquillo, nephew of the deceased executive, and by the clergy, brought fairly rapid recovery from the disaster. Conspicuous in the pressing task of reconstruction, which occupied the rest of 1583 and succeeding months, was the energetic Jesuit, Antonio de Sedeño, who first taught the Filipinos to quarry and shape building stone, to mix mortar and lay these blocks; similarly, he taught them to manufacture the first tiles and bricks used in the old city of Intramuros,[16] and it was he who built the first limekiln. His talents as a contractor and builder were not limited to ecclesiastical structures but extended to drawing the plans and laying the foundations of the first stone fortress on the shore front for the protection of the city.[17] In these endeavors church and secular officials collaborated effectively, and in 1583 many of the buildings which were to constitute early colonial Manila rapidly took shape. This coöperation did not, unfortunately, extend to other spheres, and the difficulties which kept the governor and bishop at odds continued until the arrival of the Royal Audiencia.

In such a remote outpost, where living conditions were still rude and harsh, where security from the hazards of nature was slight, where the threats of Japanese and Chinese pirates were constant, where natives sullenly plotted revolt, and where a handful of Europeans sought to implant an occidental civilization in a widely scattered archipelago, meanwhile extracting the maximum material gain from the process, it seems almost incredible that there was any place or time for books, whether of light or solid literature. Yet fragmentary evidence, of which the Trebiña document is a small part, clearly points to their presence in Manila at this early date. The records of the House of Trade at Seville indicate that substantial sums were allotted to Bishop Salazar and the clergy accompanying him to the Philippines to pay the costs of transportation of a large number of books.[18] That these volumes actually reached Manila is apparent from the reference contained in the bishop's letter to Philip II of June 18, 1583 regarding the destruction of " a very good library" in the fire which consumed his living quarters.[19] Doubtless many other printed volumes had arrived by that year and continued to do so. One clause of the Chief Inquisitor's instructions written in Mexico City for the new Commissioner at Manila suggests that books were a regular part of the cargo of ships reaching the far-off Philippines. It read as follows:

> One of the most important reasons for inspecting the ships is the books, especially the boxes which come as cargo. The royal officials and magistrates of his Majesty who reside in those ports shall send the said boxes to the Commissioner of the Inquisition without opening or taking out any books from them. The Commissioner shall open them and examine the books, comparing the titles with the General Catalogue [of prohibited works]. And after seizing such as he finds are prohibited, he will give the rest to the owners. To this end the Commissioner shall make known to the royal officials of the city and to those who reside in the ports the ordinance which accompanies this document; and this applies even when the said boxes of books have previously been examined by another inquisitor."[20]

Though the book list here studied leaves many questions unanswered, and its almost complete lack of detail is tantalizing, the survival of this short document through more than three and a half centuries adds small but eloquent testimony to the wide diffusion of Spanish literary culture throughout the expanding world of the sixteenth century. Even more clearly does it show that, however far from the homeland the conquistadors' swords might take them, and into whatever vicissitudes their destiny might lead them, close upon the heels of these conquerors, even to the very antipodes, followed the creative spirits of Spain, great and small, through the medium of those silent disseminators of ideas—printed books. When the tremendous expansive power of sixteenth-century Castile reached out to the distant Philippines, Spanish law and Spanish letters, as the vanguard of European civilization, had completely encircled the terrestrial globe.

ON THE MEXICAN BOOK TRADE, 1600 XVI

At THE CLOSE OF THE SIXTEENTH CENTURY IT WAS already apparent that the glorious period of high adventure and stirring conquest in the New World was ended. Spain had clearly passed the zenith of its power and the era of tremendous expansion was over. Weakened by difficulties in all parts of its over-extended empire, the motherland was obliged more and more to limit itself to consolidating gains already made, thrusting forward here and there, as in New Mexico, a defensive frontier against the foes, both internal and external, who threatened its holdings with increasing boldness. In New Spain the generation of conquerors and first settlers had passed away and their descendants were being pushed from their inherited positions of privilege and from their feudal *encomiendas* by a throng of latecomers from Spain, for the most part fortune hunters, canny merchants bent on exorbitant profits, and parasitic favorites or sychophants of the successive viceroys usurping the remunerative offices of the realm and possessing themselves of sinecures. By the end of the reign of Philip II America had become for the Peninsula, as Cervantes expressed it, "the refuge and haven of all the poor devils of Spain, the sanctuary of the bankrupt, the safeguard of murderers, the way out for gamblers, the promised land for ladies of easy virtue, and a lure and disillusionment for the many, and an incomparable remedy for the few." The drain on the royal coffers caused by the activities of an idle bureaucracy was further increased by the annual appropriation of more than 40,000 pesos for pensions to the supplanted and indigent families of the Conquistador whose services the debt-ridden monarchy could not wholly forget.[1] That hardy type, the sturdy fighter, ever alert to defend his rights and those of his royal master, who never slept without his weapons near at hand, was now no more. On the contrary, the Crown, fearful of disturbances and even of insurrection in the Indies, had forbidden the manufacture of arms in the colonies and had severely limited the importation of them from the homeland. The fitting out of expeditions to penetrate the outlying provinces of New Spain and other parts of the Indies, the Philippines and elsewhere, was stripping the viceroyalty of its defense against external enemies and its own multiplying and restless elements.

And there were perceptible changes in the spiritual and intellectual climate of the realm. As the consolidation of Spanish civilization in the New World progressed towards its fullest realization in the seventeenth century, every aspect of life in the Mexican capital of 1600 seemed to reflect the baroque tendencies which were beginning to predominate in the arts. On all sides appeared a strange juxtaposition of opposites together with an intermingling of contrasting extremes which wove a complex pattern of intricate detail. In architecture, in racial composition, in social structure, and even in ethics striking appositions were replacing the relative simplicity of Renaissance forms in these varied manifestations of human existence with a bewildering kaleidoscope of slums and palaces, of grogshops and seminaries, of greed and spirituality, of science and superstition, of beauty and squalor. The ornateness, the complexity, the vitality, the opulence, and the picturesqueness so commonly associated with the baroque phenomenon were represented in the myriad facets of viceregal society as the new century opened.

In 1600, Mexico City was still expanding and changing physically. The rude, fortlike houses of solid masonry built soon after the Conquest had long since been demolished, and in their places were the mansions of the rich with façades displaying a complicated ornamentation of *tezontle*, tiles, and bronze. The old, primitive church, built soon after the Conquest on the great central square, had given way to the slowly rising mass of the new cathedral, and everywhere the monasteries were erecting magnificent churches and temples reflecting the anti-Renaissance tendencies that would dominate the artistic expression of the seventeenth century. These structures seemed to stand in opposition to the ugliness and filth which lingered on from the earlier city and increased as the population grew. The many canals of the lake-ringed municipality were choking up with the refuse dumped into them, thus rendering difficult the navigation of the canoes and small boats which brought supplies from the mainland. The environing *barrios,* or districts, were likewise cluttered and crowded, constituting a continual menace to public health. The main avenues and streets of the vice-regal capital were thronged with the variegated elements of the population who took delight in the colorful religious processions of the Corpus Christi, the *mascaradas,* or pageants, the tourneys, and the *autos de fe* of the Inquisition. But even the wretched huts of the Indians lying beside the imposing palaces of the aristocrats did not mar, in the eyes of visitors, the superficial splendor of the city, and excellent poets were singing paeans, as did Bernardo de Balbuena in his colorful *La grandeza mexicana,* in praise of the colonial metropolis.

Not only newcomers from Spain were swelling the number of inhabitants, but also others from the nearby provinces of New Spain who preferred the increasing refinements of the capital to the rigors of frontier life on the ranches and in the mines. In characteristic juxtaposition with the privileged white classes ostentatiously flaunting their luxury and wealth was a large and menacing proletariat composed of the most varied stocks and races which swarmed about the streets and barrios. Indians, Negroes, mulattoes, mestizos, and heterogeneous mixtures, renegade Spaniards, and even foreigners constituted this restless group whose multiplying numbers caused the authorities considerable uneasiness. There had been riots and Negro revolts in the realm along with milder local disturbances. Indeed, the African elements had shown a greater capacity for resistance to their white masters and for extracting economic advantage from their hard lot than had the more numerous Indians who, since the collapse of their first struggle against the Conquistador, had become abject vassals shamelessly exploited in innumerable forms of forced labor and social neglect. The Negroes were displaying surprising astuteness and adaptability in their condition of servitude, which was not so rigorous that it was impossible for them to purchase their freedom by diligent effort; the grave concern of Viceroy Enríquez a quarter of a century earlier regarding these manumitted slaves still troubled his successors. As overseers of Indian labor gangs the Negroes proved even more ruthless than the Spaniards, while the Indian women continued to show a marked preference for them as mates. By shrewd perception and bare-faced effrontery some of these Negroes had caused the cost of living in Mexico City to soar to prohibitive heights through a system of racketeering which their emulators in North American cities centuries later might envy. Each day as the Indians entered the causeways of the capital with supplies from the surrounding country, they were met by Africans and mulattoes, sometimes as many as five hundred, who obliged the natives to sell all their produce to them at nominal prices. Having thus cornered the food supply of the city, these unauthorized middlemen resold the fruit, vegetables, meat, and firewood in the markets and on the public squares to the domestic servants of Spanish households at four times their cost and more. Bakers, innkeepers, and the general public as well found themselves compelled to buy solely from these racke-teers, for this *recontonería*, as it was called, was so well organized and so firmly established that the viceregal and municipal authori-ties were helpless to cope with it.[2]

But among the white ruling classes graft and corruption on an even larger scale afflicted the social, civil, and economic life of the realm. The practice of selling public offices to private bidders was sanctioned by the Madrid government, which was desperately seeking to increase the royal revenue, and inevitably the purchasers valued their posts mainly as a means of acquiring prestige or, worse still, as an opportunity to line their own pockets. Each new viceroy, whose term of office was usually about four years, arrived from Spain accompanied by a swarm of favorites and hangers-on whose condition as European-born Spaniards gave them special advan-tages over the Creoles born in the colonies. When these white Mexicans did not view the intruders with downright hatred, they bitterly felt as one of their number, Francisco de Terrazas, a gifted poet of the period, wrote[3] concerning his native New Spain:

> Madrastra nos ha sido rigurosa
> y dulce Madre pía a los extraños.*

*To us she has been a stepmother harsh and severe,
To those from abroad a mother merciful and gentle.

The division of these two sectors of the white ruling class, clearly perceptible in 1576, had by 1600 widened and deepened to an unbridgeable abyss. Arrogantly and with brazen indifference to the rights of the Conquistador's heirs, these new conquerors were seizing the wealth and power of the Indies to build quick and prodigious fortunes. By threats and intimidation this class of *nouveau riche* was acquiring the land that had been left to the Indians for cultivation. As a result of these forced sales at low prices, the unhappy descendants of the Aztecs were sinking into utter misery and suffering an alarming decline in numbers, both of which conditions accentuated the juxtaposition of extreme affluence and poverty.

And slowly but surely the larger estates won by the Conquistador were changing hands as the daughters of the Creole possessing class eagerly accepted marriage with Spanish fortune hunters whose European birth gave them a social distinction denied the American-born white. One of these adventurers, Mateo Rosas de Oquendo, a satiric poet residing in Mexico City in 1600, described his own kind with sardonic humor when he wrote[4] that these Peninsulars

> Todos son hidalgos finos
> de conocidos solares...
> ¡Como si no se supiera
> que allá rabiaban de hambre!*

Indeed, the custom of impecunious European noblemen of seeking to recoup their fortunes by union with American heiresses is hallowed by long tradition, for many of the Oidores and other high officials from Spain contracted marriages with the daughters of prosperous colonial merchants. The latter gladly bestowed large dowries in return for the advantages, both social and practical, of having influential members of the viceregal government within the family. In 1600 the high rate of these nuptial inducements had become so staggering that only the richest magnates could afford them; the less prosperous citizens were finding it impossible to marry off their daughters advantageously, with the result that the

---

*All profess to be fine gentlemen
of well-known noble families ...
As if one wasn't aware
that back home they were furiously hungry!

increasing numbers of convents and monasteries of Mexico City were filled to overflowing with nuns.

By 1600 the Church had lost most of the proselytizing zeal that had animated so many of its great spirits during the Conquest and the period immediately following, and already the clergy had abandoned much of the enormous task it had assumed of incorporating the Indian vassals as equal citizens into the body politic of the nation through education. From this dynamic policy it was shifting to the static post-Tridentine mission of preserving the accepted dogmas of the Faith against the inroads of heretical attack. Already the puritanism had relaxed which the great mystics of the Counter Reformation had stimulated. The materialistic trend, clearly visible a quarter of a century before, during the rule of the viceroy Enríquez, had continued and now the colonial Church was fabulously wealthy, having already under its control half of the land of New Spain. Churches, cathedrals, and monasteries were multiplying rapidly and the clergy constituted a disproportionate element of the total population. Some of these consecrated men were still actively promoting the work of conversion and education, but the majority were leading lives of doubtful social utility.

But this large leisure class, both secular and ecclesiastical, thus artificially created gave rise to one important and significant by-product—a remarkable preoccupation with and a cultivation of intellectual and artistic expression which, modified by local conditions, was a bright reflection of contemporary Catholic Europe. Already the process of transplanting Hispanic civilization to the New World had so far advanced as to insure permanence and to transform these remote regions into westernized outposts of the European continent. In Mexico City as in Lima much of this cultural activity revolved about the universities, which had grown rapidly in prestige and importance since their founding a half-century before; the monasteries and seminaries established by the various religious orders were also flourishing centers of learning which sometimes acted as competitive agencies of intellectual dissemination. With extraordinary fidelity colonial thought and literary trends followed those of the Peninsula, and these overseas subjects of the Crown had nearly as many cultural advantages as had those residing in the homeland. In this propitious atmosphere

of New Spain one of its native sons, Juan Ruiz de Alarcón (1581?-
1639), soon to become one of the foremost dramatists of Spain's
great literary age, could imbibe the rich lore of Renaissance learning with much the same ease in the University of Mexico as he did
later at Salamanca, to which he departed in 1600 to complete his
education.

The cultivation of belles-lettres, so clearly perceptible in 1576,
continued to flourish in the viceregal capital. González de Eslava,
who had written many allegorical plays and short skits, was probably still alive in 1600, though he was near the end of his life.
The literary luminaries of a quarter of a century before would
soon be, if they were not already, eclipsed by newer figures, a few
of whom were to win enduring fame in Spanish letters. Foremost,
of course, was the great playwright already mentioned, Ruiz de
Alarcón. Of lesser stature, but hailed as "one of the greatest of
Castilian poets" by an eminent critic, was Bernardo de Balbuena
(1561?-1627), who was Spanish born but who spent most of his
life in New Spain. In 1600 he was still a provincial parish priest but
about to come to Mexico City; there in due course he wrote some
of the most important poetic works produced at the beginning of
the baroque age in Spanish America, including the colorful pane-
gyric of the viceregal capital, *La grandeza mexicana*, already mentioned, a pastoral novel, and a vast epic in 5,000 *octavas reales*,
entitled *El Bernardo o Victoria de Roncesvalles*. Another and far
more pedestrian epic, *El peregrino indiano*, recounting the conquest of Mexico, had just appeared in 1599. Its author, Antonio
de Saavedra Guzmán, a Mexican-born son of an early settler, had
labored seven years in its composition and had completed the long
poem on shipboard while sailing to Spain. And there were those
who penned festive and satirical verse, such as Rosas de Oquendo,
already quoted, and others who remain anonymous.

A book list of 1600[5] presents striking proof that the liberal tendencies of the sixteenth century were not so effectively crushed
in the colonies as is commonly believed, and that the intellectual
currents of thought of Catholic Europe flowed concurrently and
with relative freedom in the New World. This document also offers unique insight into the high degree of culture then obtaining
in Mexico. Almost every field of contemporary knowledge is rep-

resented in its more than 678 items, the old and the new, progress and retrogression, science and superstition and charlatanism appearing, like so many other features of viceregal life, in strange juxtaposition. All this, of course, merely proves that sixteenth-century New Spain was but an outpost of Europe. The titles of the works listed give a surprisingly inclusive picture of the crosscurrents of late Renaissance thought, and the number of Italian writings represented is truly extraordinary. To those who have proclaimed the "darkness" that fell on intellectual life, particularly in the Spanish Indies, after the institution of censorship by the Inquisition, it will come as something of a surprise that, even as early as 1600, the provisions of the *Index Quiroga* (1583) were so poorly enforced that works specifically condemned there, such as those of Erasmus, Apuleius, Génébrard, Alberto Pío, Polydorus Virgilius, and Javellus, came in this shipment of books whose invoice bore the customary approval of the inquisitorial censor. The exceptional diversity of this book collection and the remarkable light that it sheds on the intellectual interests of Mexico at the end of the century of Conquest warrant a more extensive analysis than other similar documents have received here.

On the good ship *La Trinidad* of the *Flota* departing for New Spain in 1600 under the command of General Pedro de Colón Melgarejo, Luis de Padilla, *"vecino de Sevilla,"* dispatched an undetermined number of cases of books to Martin Ibarra at San Juan de Ulúa to be sold for cash or on credit. The invoice of this shipment was drawn up with rather more care than was customarily displayed by the clerks of the time, and it includes frequently such useful bibliographic data as the existence in a given work of notes or commentary, with the commentator's name, the presence of *figuras finas*, the language in which the work is written, the volume number, and, at times, even the publisher. Remarkably few errors were made in listing by the scribe who, to judge by his confusion of *c*, *s*, and *z* in spelling, was an Andalusian. The more important titles are divided into broad classifications for brief discussion.

Of the 115 odd titles which may be classified as theological and ecclesiastical works, the greater part are without special interest here. The absence of the great Spanish mystics and the general scarcity of works of pure devotion suggest that the colonial priesthood was interested rather in the formal, expository and polemical aspects of Catholic Christianity. Typical, perhaps, of the spirit of the times are the *Summae Silvestrinae* of Silvestro Mazzolini, the *Advertentiae theologiae scholasticae* of Vellosillo, and the *Fortalitium fidei* of Alfonso de Espina.

With such works the *curas de almas* of New Spain might well have remained content, easing their consciences with the thought that their flock had little need of learning. However, such was not the case; interest in the philological aspects of biblical criticism is attested by six entries listing biblical texts in Greek or in Hebrew, with or without Latin translation.[6] There are commentaries on Genesis, the Pentateuch, Joshua, the Psalms, the Song of Solomon, the Book of Kings, and various Prophets.[7] Similar interest is shown in the case of Périon's study on the lives of the prophets, Valtanas' *Concordancias*, Bustamente's *De animantibus scripturae sacrae*, and Vallés' *De iis quae scripta sunt physice in libris sacris*. The polemic aspect of Christianity, both practical and theoretical, appears in the inquisitors' manuals, the attacks on Luther by Dobneck and on Erasmus by Alberto Pío, in addition to the *Haeretici descriptio* of Alardus, a similar work of Du Préau, the *Contra Alchoranum . . .* of Dionysius de Rickel, and Guerra de Lorca's *Cateches pro advenis ex secta mahometana*. No less polemical and equally theoretical—in sixteenth-century Mexico—must have been the works *contra judaeos*, of which there are three. The recent *cause célèbre* of the Portuguese Jewish family Carvajal, of whom several members perished in *autos de fe* in Mexico, underlines the significance of these items. On the whole, the ecclesiastical titles of the list reveal—with the exception of the philological and expository interest noted—a picture in exact agreement with what was to be expected, namely, a consolidated post-Tridentine church.[8]

In the field of philosophy, sixteenth-century currents are even more faithfully reflected. First, there is the traditional medieval note, represented by Boethius, the *Ars magna* of Lull, and the interest in dialectics; then the neo-Platonic interest of the Renaissance[9] is shown by three Platonic texts, by Plotinus, Iamblicus, Philo Judaeus, Maximus Tyrius, and Montañés' commentary on

Prophyry. For the Renaissance proper, there are Ficino, Pico della Mirandola, León Ebreo, and Bembo.

Closely connected with this current is that of the Jewish Kabbala and, by way of natural extension, that of the theurgic and extravagant philosophies and superstitions of the sixteenth century. Petrarch, two centuries before, had had the good sense to laugh at the astrologers.[10] But Pico della Mirandola, influenced by the mystical elements in Plato, and seeking in the Jewish Kabbala the tradition of the original revelation granted to man,[11] developed a "theosophy" which sought "to penetrate the mysteries and grasp the occult forces of nature and to lift the veil from the face of God."[12] The same mystic spirit, imbued with the new scientific hope of controlling Nature, turned to white magic, to spells and charms as a means of making her subservient to human desires. Hence the search for such fantasies as the philosopher's stone, elixirs of life, and fountains of youth, which excited the uncritical mind of the Conquistador but also had some bearing on the development of chemistry, astronomy, botany, and medicine.[13] Works of this sort are numerous on the list, from the *De mysteriis Aegyptiorium* of Iamblichus to Pico's *Conclusiones philosophicae cabalisticae et theologicae*, with nineteen other titles. By way of contrast are the *Reprobación de la astrología judiciaria* and the *De haereticis et sortilegiis* of Paulus Grillandus.[14]

The esoteric doctrines of the Kabbalists sought to achieve human happiness by subjugating nature to man's desires but not all thinkers in the sixteenth century were so optimistic. According to the latter, happiness could be achieved only by subduing human desires to the stern realities of the universe. The list reveals that this neo-Stoicism makes its appearance in sixteenth-century Mexico as well as contemporary Europe, for among the titles are Seneca, *De vita beata*, Lipsius' *De constantia*[15] and his *M. T. Ciceronis Consolatio . . . De quo judicium Justi Lipsii subjunctum*. With these can be placed Marcellino's *Il Diamerone, ove . . . si mostra la morte non esser quel male che'l senso si persuade*.

Another great current of thought in the sixteenth century stems from Aristotle and his followers, the latter being mostly neo-Scholastics,[16] although such neo-Aristotelians as Vicomercatus and J. C. Scaliger are represented on the book list.[17]

But most important of all philosophic currents in the sixteenth century is that of the eclectics, who broke away from the authorities of the past and prepared the way for the new science and for modern thought. Pomponazzi is represented only negatively by the work of his opponent Niphus,[18] but there are Cardan's *De sapientia* and Scaliger's attack on his *De subtilitate*. Though not free from superstition, Cardan strove to explain all things naturally. On the list he went to Mexico in company with Sextus Empiricus, the late Greek skeptic who so influenced Montaigne that he placed nine of this author's maxims on his study walls. He also goes to New Spain with the nominalist Gómez Pereira, whose *Antonina Margarita* anticipated certain aspects of the teaching of Descartes;[19] with Bernardino Telesio, who in his *De rerum natura* endeavored to reform natural science by freeing it from Aristotle and the ancients, basing it on observation; and with Nicholas Copernicus, whose *De revolutionibus orbium coelestium* in 1543 may be regarded as ushering in the modern age.

In the last-mentioned title philosophy has joined hands with natural science and this calls for a consideration of the scientific works on the *registro*. Again is noted an indiscriminate juxtaposition of the old and the new, the good and the bad. Of all sciences the first to emerge in the Renaissance was botany because of its connection with the healing arts,[20] and the list includes the ancient botanists, modern commentators such as Andrés de Laguna[21] and the works of the great sixteenth-century herbalists, Mattioli and Fuchs. The latter particularly, together with his master, Brunfels, made an epoch in the history of botanical iconography.[22] Finally, an interest in the flora of the Indies is apparent in Juan Fragoso, *Discursos de las cosas aromáticas ... de la India Oriental*, and in José de Acosta, *Historia natural de las Indias*.[23] The mystical note, already mentioned in connection with Pico della Mirandola, also appears here in the work of Giovanni Battista della Porta and of Acosta. Mystical tendencies are likewise observable in medicine, with numerous works of medical "secrets" by Porta himself,[24] by Paracelsus and by Fioravanti.[25]

The works of the ancient physicians are still studied, as are those of their sixteenth-century followers such as Trincavellius, but the ancients also have their opponents in the persons of Manardo and Fernelius. Pre-Vasalian anatomy is represented by Massa, and in Paré appears a genuine scientist, the founder of French surgery. Another first-class physician was Conrad Gesner (pseudonym Evonymus), whose works were on the *Index*. Fracastoro holds first place in the sixteenth century among students of the phenomena of epidemics, and no less distinguished is Brasavola. The *Gynaeciorum sive de mulierum affectibus*, edited by Caspar Wolff, is the first collection of gynecologic treatises ever published.[26]

In mathematics, astronomy and physics there are, first, the usual works of the ancients, Euclid, Archimedes, and Apollonius of Perga; then, the medieval treatises of Boethius, Hasan Ibn Hasan, Alfonso the Learned, Vitellio, Sacrobosco, and Campano.[27] Renaissance astronomy is represented by Peuerbach, corrector of Ptolemy, by his pupil Regiomontanus, author of the oldest complete treatise on trigonometry published in the West, and by Reinerus Gemma, whose reputation as an astronomer caused him to be consulted by Charles V. Interest is shown by the list in meteors and comets and in such mathematical exercises as squaring the circle.[28] Finé's absurdities in this effort were corrected by Pedro Núñez.

Reformers of the calendar are Gauricus, and Clavius, known as the sixteenth-century Euclid, and chief assistant to Gregory XIII in this reform. Other distinguished scientists, in the strictly modern sense, are Benedetti, who seconded Galileo's researches on falling bodies; Pedro Ciruelo, who reformed the theory of astronomical refraction; Guidubaldo del Monte, the friend and protector of Galileo, who won for him the support of his brother Cardinal del Monte; Erasmus Reinhold, who offered the first application of the theories of Copernicus; and last and greatest, Copernicus himself.

Geology is represented by Albertus Magnus, whose work on minerals and metals was distinctly ahead of his time; by Besson, inventor of a theory for discovering subterranean springs; by Fracastoro, who held with Leonardo da Vinci that fossils were once living organisms; and by Georgius Agricola, the principal physical geologist of the sixteenth century. The interest in mining and metallurgy, to be expected in Mexico, is attested by Pérez de Vargas' *De re metalica* and by the often-noted *Quilatador de plata, oro y piedras* of Juan de Arfe. Applied science appears also in various works on the astrolabe, in Finé's studies on clocks and on measurements, in Arfe *De varia commensuracion para la escultura y architectura*, in Mizauld's study on meteorology, and in various works on military science, agriculture, and animal husbandry.

Commentary on the items coming under the broad heading of humanities may appropriately begin with bibliography, of which there is one comprehensive work, *Della libraria Vaticana*. A somewhat similar interest is shown in Jacobus Middendorpius, *Academiae celebres in universo terrarum libri duo*. Logically follow encyclopedic works which, though distinctly medieval in origin, were the best that the age afforded. They are Vincent de Beauvais, a work not superseded until the eighteenth century; and Bartholomaeus Anglicus, whose *De proprietatibus rerum*, though composed about 1250, was still well known to Elizabethans.

Geography, rather than being a natural science, was an adjunct of the history of belles-lettres. The only contemporary geographer of standing is Peter Apian, in the revised edition of Gemma Frisius. For the ancient world there is Pausanias, Dionysius Periegetes, and Solinus, whose *De memorabilibus mundi* indicates what the bookdealer considered the taste of his trade in this field to be.

Ancient history has a wide array with Xenophon, Herodotus, Diodorus Siculus, Quintus Curtius, Arrianus, Sallust, Caesar and the pseudo-Berosus. There are general histories by Génébrard, Arias Montano, St. Antoninus Forciglioni, and others. For Spanish history there are the *Crónica general*, that of Ocampo, the *Decades* of Nebrija, Valtanas' account of the conquest of Granada, and López de Gómara's history of the Indies, which had so strongly influenced one Conquistador, Bernal Díaz del Castillo, that he wrote his memoirs. Related historical works are the *Nobleza de Andaluzia* of Argote de Molina, Mainoldus' account of the titles of the Spanish king, and others. There are four works on Italian history; two each on French, Austrian, and Hungarian; and one each on Albanian, Turkish, and Chinese. Allied fields are political science, law,[29] biography (Plutarch, Diogenes Laertius, Giovio), archaeology (Egyptian, Roman), and numismatics.

In the general field of belles lettres, as other lists show, Spanish colonists were avid readers of literary or purely creative works. In the present *registro*, however, they appear more as serious students of literature and languages. Impressive evidence is offered in such items as the *Nomenclator* of Junius and the *Sex linguarum dictionarius*, eight Hebrew grammars, three copies of Clenardus' Greek grammar, that of Budé, and two Greek-Latin dictionaries, and particularly the *Arte y vocabulista arábigo* of Pedro de Alcalá and the Syriac grammar of Caninius. Adequate mastery of the Latin language would appear to have been taken largely for granted, since not a single copy of the usually omnipresent *Arte* of Nebrija is included in the shipment, though two other grammars are represented. On the other hand, there are Salinas' study on the pronunciation of the ancients, collections of inscriptions, and works of more general classical erudition. One each of Latin-Italian and Spanish-Italian and two Latin-French dictionaries are listed, together with Alunno's *La fabrica del mondo . . . tutte le voci di Dante, del Petrarca, del Boccaccio. . . .* There are two copies of Andrés de Paza's *Del antiguo lenguaje de España*, a French grammar, and the *Arte y vocabulario de la lengua del Pirú*.

Interest is apparent in the principles of rhetoric and poetics, in Aristotle, Quintilian, Minturno, Scaliger,[30] Rengifo, the *Dialogus Ciceronianus* and the *De conscribendis epistolis* of Erasmus. With these should be grouped Brouchier's critique of Lucian, Parrhasius on Claudian, Cardona on Sannazaro, Guastarini on the *Gerusalemme liberata*, and the *Discorsi* of Torquato Tasso himself.

Some twenty-nine titles represent Greek literature from Homer to Lucian, Heliodorus (four copies each), and Eristathius. These were all translations in Latin, French, Spanish, or Italian, and only one was accompanied by the Greek text.

Latin literature has thirty-two titles, of which nineteen are poetic texts: Vergil, 3; Horace, 3; Ovid, 4; the elegiacs, 3; Silius Italicus, 2; Martial, 1; Claudian, 2; and one anthology. As a companion to the poets there is the mythological dictionary of Natalis Comes.

Titles of neo-Latin literature are somewhat fewer, with a total of twenty-two, including Petrarch, Folengo, Alciati, various collections of apothegms and adages, collections of epistles by Erasmus, Budé, and Sepúlveda; and the collected works of Bembo, Fracastoro, Pontano, Poliziano, Eneas Silvio and Ringelbergius.

Purely creative Spanish literature numerically has a minor representation on this book list, totaling only twenty-seven if the *Lyrae heroycae* of Núñez de Coria, a heroic poem composed in Latin on the exploits of Bernardo del Carpio, is included. This, together with the *Paso honroso* of Pineda and Olivier de la Marche's *Chevalier délibéré* in Spanish garb, give evidence that the Conquistadors' favorite fiction still had a demand, though a seemingly slight one. Perhaps the presence of that antidote, Jaime de Alcalá's *Caballería cristiana*, confirms this fact. The *Hermosura de Angélica* of Barahona de Soto and Ariosto's *Orlando furioso* may be regarded as occupying a middle ground between the *libros de caballerías* and the sentimental and pastoral literature which succeeded them in popular favor. Others representative of the later taste are Cervantes' *Galatea*, Lope de Vega's *Arcadia*, the *Pastor de Iberia* of Bernardo de la Vega, the *Enamorada Elisea* of Covarrubias, and the *Habidas* of Arbolanche. Not unrelated are the rarely noted *Inventario* of Villegas, the anonymous *Cuestión de amor*, published together with San Pedro's *Cárcel de amor*, the *Diálogo de amor* of Juan de Encinas, and Diego Gracián's translation of the *Arrêts d'amour* of Martial d'Auvergne.

Picaresque novels and the *Celestina* are notably absent from this list, although many copies of Mateo Alemán's *Guzmán de Alfarache* are known to have reached Mexico this same year. The printed *comedia* had not yet come into its own and only the *Comedias y tragedias* of Juan de la Cueva represent the dramatic genre. Poetic works, however, are fairly well represented by seven items —Aldana, Espinel, Lobo Lasso de la Vega, Lomas Cantoral, López Maldonado, Montemayor, and Sayago.[31]

The contemporary interest in Italian literature which this list reflects more clearly than most is plainly visible in the prose writings of Boccaccio, two copies of Sannazaro's *Arcadia*, two of the *Asolani* of Bembo, and one each of the dialogues of Sperone and of the Cortegiano. The works of Muzio and A. Piccolomini's

Dialogo . . . della bella creanza delle donne reveal an interest in manners. Alciati's Latin emblems have their Italian parallels in the works of Cammilli, Giovio and Ruscelli. Remaining prose works are in the nature of the miscellanies so well received in the sixteenth century: Doni, Calmo, and Guicciardini.

Italian dramatic literature includes the *Egloga pastoril* of Lilia,[32] Dolce's *Il capitano*, his collected comedies, and *Comedias varias en lengua italiana*, undoubtedly Ruscelli's edition. Titles of poetry are much more representative, with two copies of Dante; Petrarch, in both Italian and Spanish; Tibaldeo (?);[33] the *Orlando furioso*, and its continuation by G. B. Pescatore. Other works: the *Opere toscane* of Alamanni, Ruscelli's anthology, *I fiori delle rime . . .*; a similar collection of *Stanze* by Dolce and Terminio; the *Rime* of Bernardo Tasso, Torquato Tasso, Anibal Caro, and Lodovico Martelli and, finally, the *Epigrammi toscani* of Girolamo Pensa.

This exceptionally rich and varied book list included also a few items relating to the arts. Juan de Arfe's *De varia commensuración para la escultura y architectura*, already mentioned among the works of applied science, also comes under this heading. There are two oustanding writers on lute music—Esteban Daza, and Luis de Narváez, who introduced into Spanish music for the *vihuela* the new principle of variation or *diferencias*.[34] A much greater writer in the fine arts was Francesco Colonna, whose *Hypnerotomachia*, published by the Aldine Press in 1499, is one of the most attractive products of the Italian Renaissance; it is an allegorical novel of love in which the slight plot is merely a pretext for a hymn of praise to *"la beauté et l'art antiques."*[35] In this year of 1600 it bore across the Atlantic, to the land of the Aztec pyramids, its vision of the grandeur and glory of Greece and Rome.

This remarkable list of the books which a certain Luis de Padilla dispatched from Seville provides indisputable evidence of the high degree of culture to which the intellectual life of Mexico City had attained at the close of the sixteenth century, and these volumes, taken as symbols of the erudition of the elite, offer extreme contrasts when considered in juxtaposition with the crass ignorance, superstition, and intolerance characterizing the mass of the population of the viceroyalty. But, of greater significance, this curious document demonstrates with crystalline clarity that the intervening ocean did not isolate this capital or, indeed, any other colonial center, from the main currents of contemporary European thought. On the contrary, it indicates convincingly that there were men of solid culture and catholic interests residing in the New World who were intimately concerned with the same moral and scientific problems which preoccupied the most brilliant minds of the late Renaissance in Europe. This scribal record of a shipment of printed works can, indeed, serve as a sober corroboration of the seeming hyperbole of these descriptive verses which Bernardo de Balbuena wrote a few years later about the splendor of the capital of New Spain:

> Aquí hallarás más hombres eminentes
> en toda ciencia y todas facultades
> que arenas lleva el Gange en sus corrientes:
> Monstruos en perfección de habilidades,
> y en letras humanas y divinas
> eternos rastreadores de verdades. . . .*

*Here thou wilt find more eminent men
in every science and discipline
than the grains of sand born by the Ganges' currents;
and, likewise, prodigies of perfection in accomplishments,
in letters, humane and divine,
and eternal seekers after truth. . . .

THE *PICARO* FOLLOWS THE *CONQUISTADOR* XVII

Ｓｔｕｄｅｎｔｓ of the literature of spain's golden age are familiar with a curious parallelism in the circumstances associated with the writers and the production of the two greatest novels of the period, *Don Quijote de la Mancha* of Miguel de Cervantes and *Guzmán de Alfarache* of Mateo Alemán. Despite the coolness which apparently characterized their personal relations[1] there are striking similarities in the conditions affecting the literary careers and masterpieces of the two novelists. Both men found life a constant struggle against poverty and eked out a precarious living from poorly compensated government posts; both served terms in debtor's prisons, where their greatest works may have been conceived if not actually written in part; both found little happiness in domestic life; both derived much fame but little fortune from the popularity of their chief works; both received the compliment of a spurious sequel of their masterpieces by pseudonymous emulators and were thus spurred to bring forth authentic second parts of their respective novels; and both sought opportunities to better their lot in the Spanish Indies, though only Alemán actually crossed the ocean to the viceroyalty of New Spain, where he died in obscurity. A further, and less generally appreciated, aspect of this parallelism is the spontaneous and enduring acclaim accorded both famous novels in the overseas possessions of Spain in America. If, as will presently appear, the greater part and quite probably the entire first edition of the *Quijote* was shipped to the New World in 1605, *Guzmán de Alfarache*, from 1600 on, appears to have reached those distant shores in even greater quantities and to have enjoyed, particularly during the years immediately after its first publication, even greater sales in the Indies than did Cervantes' masterpiece. Throughout the remainder of the colonial period these two great novels retained a reading public probably exceeding that of any other work of prose fiction.

In a measure, Alemán shares with Cervantes the distinction, if that is the proper term, of destroying the obviously waning popularity of the literature that had done so much to stimulate the Conquistador and his immediate successors, for the *pícaro*, or rogue, was, as a modern writer aptly puts it, "a sort of *Amadís de Gaula* upside down, an antihero."[2] The chief protagonist of picaresque fiction was devoid of idealism and predisposed to a somewhat cynical parasitism which he much preferred to any honest toil. He accepted stoically and without illusions the grim reality of existence, and by trickery and petty thieving he extracted a precarious living from the society in which he found himself. "His most lofty aspiration is to get enough to eat . . ." and "he reveres not his king and lady, but his stomach." The pícaro was, indeed, the very reverse of the chivalrous knight, and virtually the only trait that these contrasting fictional characters had in common was a restless desire to move about the world, driven on by some subconscious urge. The episodic, loosely knit plot of the idealistic tales is repeated in the sardonic recital of the adventures of shrewd and heartless rogues who crudely reveal the foibles and hypocrisies of the society through which they roved. As the novels of chivalry portrayed and glorified an unreal world, the picaresque narratives, usually told in the first person, dwelt on the ugly and the sordid and, by satirical exaggeration, presented a caricature of contemporary life. The earlier *Lazarillo de Tormes* (1554) had set the pattern, later so widely imitated in Spanish and European letters, but it was Mateo Alemán's masterpiece at the end of the century which clearly defined the new novel form and first used the term *pícaro* in identifying this literary type. His work was, indeed, a sort of parody of the chivalric fiction with which the more sophisticated readers were already surfeited.

Guzmán de Alfarache's birth, like that of most *pícaros*, was slightly irregular and not of a character to reflect great credit either upon himself or upon his parents. His father was a Genoese merchant who established himself in Seville and contracted a union

with the young widow of an elderly gentleman. At the age of fifteen the orphan Guzmán was obliged to seek a living and launched
upon what proved to be a notably shady career in the highways and
byways of Spain and Italy. His first adventures took place in country inns where he experienced firsthand the wiles practiced by their
proprietors on unwary customers, particularly in the disguised
dishes they served. An alleged omelet, which might more properly
be called an "egg poultice," made the unhappy lad violently ill. A
friendly muleteer later gave him a lift and the two, together with a
couple of friars, put up at another roadside tavern. Quite by accident, while searching for his missing cloak, Guzmán detected the
innkeeper's attempt to pass off some mule flesh as veal, and the ensuing melee was broken up by the police.

After more encounters on the road, interrupted by long moral
disquisitions and intercalated stories—the latter technique was similarly employed by Cervantes in the first part of his *Don Quixote*—
Alemán brings his *pícaro* to Madrid where Guzmán soon acquired
the manifold vices of the low life of that city. His associates were
beggars and gamblers from whom he learned an extensive repertoire
of frauds and card tricks. As a scullion in the household of a nobleman, he found among his fellow servants a ready outlet for his passion for gambling, and to recoup his heavy losses he mastered a facile
knack of pilfering small articles about the house and of deceiving
the cook in various ways. Disaster inevitably overtook him and he
lost his position. A trusting apothecary commissioned Guzmán to
deliver a quantity of silver to a merchant and with this booty the
now conscienceless rogue made his way to Toledo as a well-
dressed young man. At the Cathedral he struck up an acquaintance
with a very attractive lady who invited him home to supper. Elated
at his conquest, Guzmán ordered a sumptuous meal at his own expense, but the sudden arrival of an alleged brother forced him to
witness the enjoyment of the banquet by the scheming pair from
the concealment of an inverted bath. Guzmán then found it expedient to depart hastily from Toledo, and he decided to enlist in
a company of soldiers bound for Genoa where he planned to look
up his father's relatives. After further misadventures he reached
the Italian city, though in rags and badly down on his luck. The
family of his sire had no desire to accept their vagrant kinsman and

had him tossed in a blanket by four evil spirits who allegedly haunted the chamber in which he was lodged.

From Genoa Guzmán moved on to Rome where he became a member of the highly lucrative guild of beggars which had reduced alms-seeking to both a science and a fine art. It had perfected methods of simulating the most dread diseases and bodily malformations which infallibly evoked the pity of passers-by, particularly in the vicinity of church entrances, and the professional mendicants thus derived substantial incomes. Guzmán had the good fortune to attract the attention of a very compassionate Cardinal of the church who took him home and summoned the most famous surgeons of the Eternal City to treat the *picaro's* apparently diseased leg. The rogue revealed his fraud to the physicians but prevailed upon them to enter into a combination with him by which they could collect high fees from the kindly church official. Though the cure thus arranged proved long and costly to the Cardinal, his delight on Guzmán's complete recovery after several months moved him to take the young charlatan into his domestic service as a page. The light-fingered proclivities and the passion for gambling of the misguided youth eventually brought about his undoing, and the long-suffering Cardinal dismissed him from his household. And thus Guzmán passed from one employment to another and, in the course of the sequel to this long novel, he traveled from city to city of Italy. Finally, after numerous misadventures, he returned to Spain where the knaveries of this consummate rogue at length earned him a harsh sentence of servitude in the royal galleys. This severe penalty at last brought repentance and, on his aiding the authorities in the discovery of a mutiny, the picaresque tale closes with a promise to grant this antithesis of Amadis of Gaul his freedom.

Such in brief is the narrative, interlarded with much extraneous material, which attained a popularity on both sides of the Atlantic rivaling that of the earlier romances of chivalry. So enthusiastic was the reception accorded Mateo Alemán's work that over twenty editions appeared within a few years, and it was promptly translated into various languages. This leisurely tale of the seamy side of life, written in a simple, natural style, seems grossly tedious today, and it is a little hard to comprehend the ardor of the book-buying public of the time for its pessimistic reflections of life, its lengthy phi-

losophizing, and its interminable interruptions in the form of intercalated stories. It may be because of the modifications which its
predecessor, *Lazarillo de Tormes*, had suffered at the hands of the
Inquisition, that Alemán found it expedient to freight *El pícaro*, as
the novel was popularly called,[3] so heavily with moral platitudes
and wearying disquisitions. Possibly the readers liked these didactic
passages, but it is more likely that they realized that the author had
necessarily written with one eye on the Holy Office, and therefore they patiently endured these digressions for the sake of the
genuine entertainment that they derived from the *pícaro's* adventures, somewhat as a modern radio audience submits with relative
passivity to the saccharine and mellifluous "commercials" of broad-
casted programs. But, whatever difficulty the twentieth-century
reader may encounter in relishing the prolix account of Guzmán
de Alfarache's adventures, the book shipments of the first decade
of the seventeenth century and long after give ample testimony to
the warm welcome bestowed upon this literary creation in the contemporary New World.

Though the first edition of *Don Quixote* reached the Spanish
Indies in the year of its publication, as will appear in the next chapter, there is no available evidence that *El pícaro* arrived so soon after
leaving the press. This delay may be explained by the fact that the
ship manifests of 1599 survive in an exceedingly fragmentary state,
though they are hardly worse than those of other years. A better
explanation, perhaps, is that the first editions of that year came off
the presses too late to catch the annual fleets leaving in the late
spring or early summer.

But if *El pícaro* missed the boat in 1599, much evidence is at
hand to suggest that this delay was compensated for by the large
number of copies shipped the year following. Scarcely a manifest
of 1600 covering consignments of books fails to include "*Libros
del pícaro*" in lots of a dozen, a score, or a hundred and more, the
majority of which went to Mexico City. Diego Mexía, a prominent
dealer of Seville, dispatched nine copies to a certain Diego Navarro
Maldonado and twenty-four others to Pablo de Ribera, the latter
a bookseller of the viceregal capital. The largest single shipment
noted was one by Don Diego Núñez Pérez, a councilman of Seville,
to his brother in New Spain that same year on *La Trinidad*. This

consisted of *three hundred* copies of "*Pícaros y por otro n^e Guz-*
mán de Alfarache," the sole item on the invoice and valued at 40,800
maravedís.[4] But, with only a fraction of the *registros* of 1600 still
surviving, the exact or approximate number of copies of Alemán's
masterpiece shipped to the New World that year can not be ascer-
tained.

The current best seller was found in the deck cabins as well
as in the holds of trans-Atlantic galleons, and there it helped to
while away the tedium of the long voyage. On his arrival at Vera
Cruz on October 23, 1600 a youthful passenger of the good ship
Nuestra Señora de Aranzazu, Juan de Ugarte by name, a native of
the Valley of Horozco in Vizcaya, submitted to the customary
questioning of Inquisition officials who boarded each incoming
ship before its freight, human and otherwise, was discharged. In
reply to the query concerning books in his possession he reported
that "to amuse himself he was bringing a book entitled *La Arcadia*
of Lope de Vega and another, *Guzmán de Alfarache*."[5] Another
passenger aboard *La Caridad* also reported a copy of Alemán's
work brought for the same purpose,[6] and an examination of the
complete *visita* or inspection report would doubtless reveal many
more copies thus transported that year.

Further proof of the exportation of volumes of *El pícaro* from
Spain to its Indies seems hardly necessary, but meager data are
available for succeeding years and offer added testimony. Though
no single order in the existing records of 1601 included so large
a quantity as the three-hundred lot shipped the year before by the
Seville *regidor* Núñez Pérez, *Guzmán de Alfarache* is found in
varying numbers on most book lists. One shipment of that year,
accompanying a passenger bound for Puertobelo, totaled nearly
ten thousand volumes, one hundred fourteen of which were copies
of *El pícaro*.[7]

By 1603 "*Libros del pícaro, parte segunda*" began to appear on
the *registros*. These were in all probability copies of the false continuation which a certain Juan José Martí, writing under the name
of Mateo Luján de Sayavedra, brought forth in 1602, and this
spurious sequel accompanies further copies of the *Parte primera*
sent to the colonies. The incomplete records of the following years
supply little additional detail but they justify the assumption that

substantial consignments of *Guzmán de Alfarache*, together with Alemán's subsequent *Vida de San Antonio de Padua*, and later the true *Segunda parte de la vida del pícaro*, continued to reach the Spanish Indies.

When in 1605 copies of *Don Quijote* began to make their appearance in the lists it might be supposed that the popularity of the picaresque novel was promptly eclipsed, but the evidence at hand does not suggest this. While enthusiastically welcoming the great work of Cervantes, colonial readers evinced no lessening of their appreciation of *Guzmán de Alfarache*, if the evidence of the ship manifests is accepted. Large as the initial consignments of *Don Quijote* were in the year of its first publication, the copies of Mateo Alemán's writings were even more numerous. On a *registro* of April 15, 1606, for example, it is recorded that a relative of the author, Juan Bautista del Rosso, who had had considerable financial participation in the publication of *Guzmán de Alfarache*, dispatched to Puertobelo three cases containing 292 copies of *La vida de San Antonio de Padua;* a little later he consigned 102 more copies of the same work to Cartagena de Indias in the galleons, while in the *flota* sailing for San Juan de Ulúa in New Spain he sent three cases containing 490 copies of the authentic *Segunda parte del pícaro*.[8]

That the *Quijote* gave the *coup de grâce* to the moribund novel of chivalry has long been accepted as an article of faith in literary history, but there is good reason to believe that the large shipments of *Guzmán de Alfarache*, as already suggested, had done much to wean colonial readers from the type of literature which Cervantes burlesqued. Even in the last decade of the sixteenth century there are indications in the shipping lists of a decline in interest in the fantastic tales which had so long entertained readers on both sides of the Atlantic, but after 1600 there is a pronounced falling off in the number of chivalric works among fiction books shipped. When *Don Quijote* began to accompany *Guzmán de Alfarache* to the New World these two heroes quickly vanquished *Amadís* and *Palmerín* as well as their innumerable descendants.

In successive years the fleets continued to bring further copies of Alemán's writings to supply the profitable colonial market, and one of these annual armadas, that of 1608 composed of seventy vessels, brought the author himself to the viceroyalty of New Spain along with the great Mexican dramatist, Ruiz de Alarcón, though these two outstanding figures of the *siglo de oro* were not passengers on the same ship. Back in 1582 Alemán, then thirty-four years old, had taken steps preliminary to procuring passage to the New World, but he did not, for reasons unknown, complete arrangements.[9] Again in 1607 Alemán, now nearing sixty and his economic plight seemingly hopeless despite the extraordinary success of his novel, took the necessary measures to depart for New Spain where he might count on the favor and influence of a cousin, Dr. Alonso Alemán, a successful lawyer of Mexico City and a professor in the local university. This time the proper credentials were obtained for himself, three of his children, a niece and two servants, but the menacing activities of Dutch pirates moved the head of the *Casa de Contratación* at Seville to suspend the sailing of the fleet that year, thus obliging the impatient Alemán to postpone his departure until 1608.[10]

When the ships of this *Flota* dropped anchor at San Juan de Ulúa on August 19 of that year the representatives of the royal treasury and of the Holy Office presented themselves for the usual customs and inquisitional inspections. The decks and cabins were, apparently, examined with somewhat more than the ordinarily perfunctory care on this occasion. The author of *El pícaro Guzmán de Alfarache* had, seemingly, been entertaining himself on the ocean voyage with, or at least had in his possession, a copy of a recent work of his fellow craftsman, Miguel de Cervantes, entitled *Don Quijote de la Mancha*. Although this currently popular novel had been permitted to enter the viceroyalty of New Spain quite unmolested in the first year of its publication and later, for some unaccountable reason the inspector for the Holy Office saw fit in this instance to appropriate the distinguished traveler's copy and forward it to his inquisitorial superiors in Mexico City. Through the good offices of the Archbishop, however, it appears that Alemán soon recovered the confiscated volume, for on the report rendered by the overly zealous commissioner there is a marginal note stating that "the book was returned at the request of his Illustrious Reverence, Don Francisco García Guerra, to its owner, Matheo Ale-mán, accountant and servitor of His Majesty."[11]

Concerning other incidents of this crossing of the Atlantic and the subsequent years in Mexico, little is known beyond the very meager data vouchsafed by the author of *El pícaro* himself in his later treatises on Castilian orthography and on the life of his bene-factor, Archbishop García Guerra. The *Ortografía castellana* was published in Mexico City in 1609, while his last known publication, the *Sucesos de don fray García Guerra, Arzobispo de México,* ap-peared in 1613.[12] He was reported as still living in 1615, but the exact date of his death remains undetermined.[13]

If few of the documents shedding light on the annual shipments of Alemán's works to the colonies are now extant in Spain, records testifying to the actual circulation of his writings within the New World are even more scanty and fragmentary. Rarely are clear in-dications obtainable of the sale and distribution in the viceroyalties of the works of Spain's greatest creative writers, though the re-peated shipments of such literature from Seville are indisputable. A small but illuminating scrap of evidence of the interest of colonial Peru in Alemán's best-known books is offered by a promissory note discovered among the notarial records preserved in the National Archive at Lima. This simple document is an agreement made in that city on February 13, 1613 by Juan Flores Chacón, a mer-chant, to pay one Juan de Sarria, a bookdealer of the viceregal capi-tal, the sum of 740 pesos and 4 reales for a total of about 155 volumes.[14] Sixty percent of the total number of books, whose titles are appended to the promissory note, are works of Mateo Alemán, chiefly *Guzmán de Alfarache.*

Lima at the time of this simple transaction was a thriving city, still the administrative and cultural center of the greater part of the southern continent. Its population was about twenty-five thousand, of which approximately twelve thousand were Spanish, ten thousand were Negroes, while Indian and mixed elements composed the re-mainder.[15] The rich silver mines were yielding generous treasure, and discoveries of new deposits of precious metals were frequently reported. These fortunate circumstances facilitated the amassing of ample fortunes, provided a still larger leisure class than was presented in 1583, and had stimulated commericial activities in the viceregal capital to such a degree that, on the very day that the public notary recorded the agreement of Flores Chacón and Sarria concerning a batch of books by Alemán and others, the Viceroy officially inaugurated the *Consulado de la Universidad de Mercaderes*, a sort of Chamber of Commerce, with regulations similar to those of the highly important Consulado at Seville.[16] This economic well-being, so long enjoyed by Lima, had fostered even further the growth of large religious communities, and had attracted many educated scions of Spanish aristocracy and a number of intellectuals and creative writers from the mother country. All these diverse elements afforded a profitable market to the book business, and gave an impetus to less uplifting diversions as well. As in New Spain, the abundant wealth encouraged laxness in the overpopulated convents and monasteries of the viceregal capital, and prosperous laymen sought pleasures which moved the diocesan synod, at a meeting that year of 1613, to take vigorous measures against immoral abuses clearly apparent in the social life of the city. The *corrales de comedias*, for example, were approaching the height of their popularity as theatrical companies from Spain performed the works of famous *siglo de oro* playwrights to enthusiastic audiences. Some actresses were, unfortunately, prone to add to the appeal of this form of amusement—and, incidentally, to the gate receipts—by also introducing to the *limeño* public an early version of the modern strip tease.[17]

But the opposite extremes, which so often characterize the Spaniard and his ways, were also represented in the Lima of 1613. In one of the cells of the convent of the Third Order of St. Dominic there languished a frail nun, Isabel Flores y Oliva (1586-1617), who had won wide repute for saintliness and who, later in the century, was to be canonized as Santa Rosa de Lima, the patron saint of the Americas. And only a few years before a venerated Dominican, Diego de Hojeda (157?-1615), had written in a convent of the city the best sacred epic in the Spanish language, *La Cristiada*, which has been likened to Milton's *Paradise lost*. Only the year before some ecclesiastical misunderstanding and injustice had divested this saintly poet of his office as Prior of the Convento del Rosario and exiled him to Huánuco, thereby hastening his death.[18]

Unimportant in itself, the promissory note of Juan Flores Chacón to Juan de Sarria in the Lima of 1613 is a significant bit of evidence of the thriving book trade of the capital. Its interest lies chiefly in the predominant number of Alemán's books in the appended list. Of the total of some 155 volumes representing thirty-seven different titles, seventy-four are copies of *Guzmán de Alfarache* and nineteen of *La vida de San Antonio de Padua*. In other words, the copies of *El pícaro* constitute almost one-half of the entire lot of books for which Flores Chacón gave Sarria his personal note. Nearly all other titles on the list are present in only one or two copies; a few old standbys of the book trade, such as the *Arte de Antonio* (Nebrija) reached as high as ten copies each. It seems fair, therefore, to interpret the presence of so large a number of copies of a single work as some indication of the salability of the picaresque novel particularly and as further evidence of the wide and sustained popularity which this moralizing tale enjoyed in early Peru. Alemán, living obscurely that year of 1613 in the great viceroyalty of New Spain and publishing his last work there, was doubtless wholly unaware of this transaction and its implied tribute to his genius. And it is equally unlikely that he enjoyed any royalties or returns from the sale of the seventy-four copies of his masterpiece and of the nineteen copies of his pious *Vida de San Antonio*. This seems all the more certain when one notes the modest value they represented in the promissory note. The ninety-three volumes by Alemán are worth only 69 pesos and 6 reales, each copy apparently appraised at 6 reales. Deducting this sum there is a balance of 670 pesos and 6 reales (figuring the peso at 8 reales) as the total valuation of the remaining sixty-two or so books on the list. Even without royalties to pay, Alemán's works would seem to have been obtained at an exceptionally low price.[19]

The other titles offer little of special interest. The list is typical in that religious works have a large representation, the greatest number of copies falling to the *Manual de diversas oraciones y spirituales exercicios* of the renowned Fray Luis de Granada. The ten copies of the *Arte* or Latin grammar of Antonio de Nebrija are further evidence of the omnipresence of this text in colonial records and of its widespread and sustained use throughout the period. Zurita's *Anales de Aragón* and Herrera's *Historia de Portugal* may be singled out as examples of secular nonfiction, to which should be added, perhaps, the readable *Viaje entretenido* of Rojas Villandrando. Besides *Guzmán de Alfarache*, so impressively represented, belles-lettres can count one copy each of the *Romancero general*, of Guevara's *Epístolas familiares*, of that miscellany of Pedro Mexía, *Silva de varia lección*, and of the *Transformaciones* of Ovid, together with *"unas historias etyopicas"* of Heliodorus.

The name of one partner in this transaction, the Lima book-dealer Juan de Sarria, will recur conspicuously in the next two chapters, for there is little doubt that the merchant who turned over the seventy-four copies of *El pícaro* in exchange for Juan Flores Chacón's promissory note was the same person who was instrumental in bringing the first copies of *Don Quijote* to readers in South America seven years before, when, it appears, he was just entering upon his business career. For this accident of association a youthful bookseller may claim a fortuitous glory in the annals of literary history, since it was his happy destiny to facilitate, though unwittingly, the introduction and distribution of two of the greatest masterpieces of Spanish literature into the remote vice-royalty of Peru.

DON QUIXOTE INVADES THE SPANISH INDIES XVIII

WHEN THE COMMANDERS OF THE ANNUAL FLEETS sailed from Spain to the Indies in the spring and early summer of 1605, one bound for Mexico and the other for Tierra Firme or South America, these gentlemen were probably unconscious of serving as instruments for the introduction into the New World of one of the greatest literary works of all time, *Don Quijote de la Mancha*, written by a certain Miguel de Cervantes Saavedra and just off the press. Stowed in the holds and tucked away in the passenger cabins of many vessels of the two *flotas* was quite possibly the entire first edition of this famous novel journeying to the lands of the Conquistadors' descendants. Just how many copies of this masterpiece went overseas on this occasion will probably never be known, owing to the extremely fragmentary state of the existing bills of lading of the galleons which sailed the Spanish Main. The surviving records at Seville indicate that quantities dispatched in 1605 varied from "three books of Don Quixote de la Mancha printed at Madrid. By Juan de la Cuesta" which a "Juan de Saragoza" sent on the *Nuestra Señora del Rosario* to Juan de Guevara at Cartagena,[1] to the 262 copies consigned to San Juan de Ulúa on the *Espíritu Santo* for Clemente de Valdés, a resident of Mexico City.[2] Another substantial shipment was Diego Correa's, who forwarded two cases of books, including 100 copies of *Don Quijote*, to Antonio de Toro, their owner, at Cartagena on the *Espíritu Santo*, probably another ship bearing the common pious name.[3]

But the enjoyment of the great "book of the year" in the New World did not have to wait until the contents of the heavy boxes reached their destinations and were sold to a scattered clientele; it began on the high seas. When the vessels anchored in the port of entry the customs officials came aboard as usual, and the few available *visita* reports of 1605 made at Vera Cruz show that copies of *Don Quijote* were found in the passenger cabins, where they had doubtless served their owners well in beguiling the tedium of the voyage. Thus, as the islands and shores of the Indies drew nearer, cramped and weary voyagers mingled the delights of Cervantes' immortal pages with the joy of anticipation of the crossing's end.

To whom properly belongs the distinction of first introducing the greatest masterpiece of Spanish literature into the Western Hemisphere is a matter which, perhaps, can never be precisely determined, but the names of individuals appearing on the few surviving *visita* reports of 1605 made at San Juan de Ulúa may be put forward as possible candidates. On September 28 of that historic year two Franciscan commissioners of the Holy Office, Fray Francisco Carranco and Fray Andrés Bravo, summoned a notary of one of the ships for the customary interrogation. This individual declared that his name was Alonso de Dassa, that he was a native of Monte Molina, and that he was thirty years old "more or less." He had come on board *La Encarnación*, commanded by Captain Gaspar de Maya, which had touched at Cádiz after leaving Seville. From July 12, when they set sail from the Atlantic port of Spain, they had made no other stop except at Guadalupe to take on fresh water, and en route no sails, friendly or hostile, were sighted, and they had had no dealings with people other than those within the fleet itself. On the sixth question concerning books, Alonso de Dassa reported that "for his own entertainment he was bringing the First Part of *El pícaro, Don Quijote de la Mancha, Flores y Blancaflor;* and for his prayers he had a *devocionario de fr. Luis*, a 'S. Joan Chrisotomo,' and a *Book of hours of Our Lady*." He prudently disclaimed knowledge of anything of a forbidden nature on board. Captain Maya of the same ship gave his age as fifty, his home town as Seville, and stated that he, too, had a copy of *Don Quijote* and a *Book of hours* which, he understood, were not banned works.[4]

On the *Nuestra Señora de los Remedios* Juan Ruiz Gallardo, twenty-six years of age and hailing from the "Villa de Ayamonte," announced that he had amused himself on shipboard by reading *Don Quijote de la Mancha* and *Bernardo del Carpio*. On the *San*

Cristóbal, another Sevillian, Alonso López de Arze, twenty-five years old, acknowledged bringing a copy of Cervantes' latest novel to read and some collections of ballads, which worldly literature was balanced by a devotional work of Fray Luis de Granada.[5] These and other copies of *Don Quijote* included in the personal baggage of their owners were, in all likelihood, the first to reach the mainland of New Spain and begin its conquest by the Knight of the Sad Countenance.

If it is clear that these few loose copies of the great novel found in the ship cabins actually did reach the New World, it can not be stated with certainty how many of the indefinite number carried in the holds of the small vessels were equally fortunate, for the fleets of 1605 suffered fairly severe losses before dropping anchor in the terminal ports of the mainland on the American side of the Atlantic. The earlier squadron bound for Tierra Firme and Panama made a late departure from Seville, on May 15. It consisted of thirteen galleons for Cartagena and the Isthmus, two more for Santa Margarita, and one each for Santa Marta, Río de la Hacha, Puerto Rico, and Santo Domingo.[6] One of the galleons heading for Panama was wrecked in crossing the treacherous bar at the mouth of the Guadalquivir, while four others were lost off the coast of Santa Margarita with all their cargo, which probably included part of the precious first edition of *Don Quijote.* Later *La Trinidad* sank in the vicinity of Havana with but few of its personnel escaping.[7]

The later, Mexico-bound *Flota* also had a measure of bad luck, both at the start and when its voyage was well advanced. Its forty-three vessels got under way on July 12; twenty-five were bound for New Spain, three for Honduras, two for Campeche, and one each for Puerto Rico, Santo Domingo, and Havana.[8] These thirty-three ships departing from Seville were subsequently joined by ten more at Cádiz. On a black and tempestuous night shortly after leaving San Lucar de Barrameda the large *almiranta,* with orders to touch at Honduras, was struck by lightning near the port of Trujillo and sank with all but eleven of its 101 passengers and crew.[9] It was also reported that well out to sea the *Flota* was assailed by eight enemy sloops. Though it was successful in sinking two of its attackers and capturing two others in this engagement, one of its heavily laden merchantmen was lost with all but twenty

on board.[10] Presumably still other copies of *Don Quijote* carried in
the cabins and cargo of the unlucky craft disappeared with it, thus
narrowing still further the total number of the first edition to reach
the Spanish Indies that year.

With many of the shipping registers of 1605 now missing from
the archives and with an unknown number of copies of Cervantes'
novel lost at sea in the series of maritime disasters of that year, it is
hardly possible to ascertain either the quantity originally shipped
from Spain, or that eventually reaching the hands of readers in
America. It might be hoped that colonial archives of the Hispanic
nations of the New World would yield documentary evidence of
the actual arrival of a specific book shipment recorded in the surviving registers of the House of Trade at Seville, and thus supply
a complete documentation which would demonstrate beyond cavil
the unhampered circulation of printed literature among the Conquistador's descendants. Such instances are rare indeed, but in at
least one this link is established clearly and unmistakably. By a
happy coincidence, it relates to a shipment including seventy-two
or more copies of the first edition of *Don Quijote*, which safely
made the crossing of the Atlantic in the year of its publication. The
fortunate discovery some years ago in the National Archive of Peru
of a *recibo*, or receipt, covering a consignment of books at Lima
makes it possible to trace the course of a large part of one substantial book shipment from its deposit at the House of Trade in
the Andalusian capital to its safe arrival over a year later at the seat
of the viceroyalty of Peru.[11] It is thus feasible to offer a fairly detailed account of the vicissitudes experienced by the gallant knight
and his squire when they first invaded the continent of South
America.

On or about March 26, 1605, an enterprising bookseller of
Alcalá de Henares in Spain, Juan de Sarria by name, brought into
Seville on donkeyback sixty-one cases of his wares which he wished
to forward to his business associate in far-off Lima, an individual
known as Miguel Méndez. There was an assorted stock of volumes
in these boxes, but the precise number, unhappily, can not be stated
because the manifest sheets covering the first twenty cases are missing from the register.[12] This unfortunate lacuna in the record pre-
cludes a determination of the total copies of *Don Quijote* which

Sarria shipped that spring, but the remaining part reveals that the cases numbered from 21 to 40 contained forty copies of Cervantes' masterpiece, and that those from 41 to 61 raised the total to sixty-six. The Lima receipt of this Sarria consignment lists only forty-five cases, for not all those transhipped at Panama had yet arrived at their destination, but this large fraction of the whole included seventy-two copies of *Don Quijote*. Thus it is evident that the first twenty cases of the original sixty-one, whose record is missing from the register still preserved at Seville, contained at least six *Don Quijotes* and very likely many more.

After the procedures at the House of Trade, described in an earlier chapter, were completed, the entire consignment of the Alcalá de Henares bookdealer was, apparently, placed on board a merchantman bound for Puertobelo which bore the euphonious, if commonplace, name *Nuestra Señora del Rosario*. As already noted, the Tierra Firme fleet raised anchor in the middle of May and departed for the Spanish Indies, making its customary first stop at the Canary Islands. A leak in one of the vessels, the *Espíritu Santo*, which, according to its register, carried at least one hundred copies of *Don Quijote* among its cargo, caused considerable delay. It was, therefore, well after June 5 when this outlying archipelago disappeared over the stern as the fleet resumed its westward course.[13] Fortunately, the *Nuestra Señora del Rosario* was not among those galleons which went to the bottom off the coast of northern South America near the island of Santa Margarita and, in due course, it put in at Cartagena and, finally at the terminal port of Puertobelo. There the long-awaited appearance of the fleet was most certainly the great annual event and a signal for a momentary awakening from the lethargy and tropical torpor in which this trading center drowsed during most of the year. Its streets and water front swarmed with the perspiring and colorful overflow of its greatly increased population.

Among the transients on hand at Puertobelo to welcome the incoming ships was the son of the bookseller of Alcalá de Henares, Juan de Sarria, *hijo*, whom the document describes as "younger than twenty-five and older than twenty-three." He had come to the Atlantic port of the Isthmus to take delivery of the book consignment whose transfer overland to Panama City, transshipment

to Callao, the port of entry of Lima and Peru, and final delivery
into the hands of his father's partner in the viceregal capital were
entrusted to his care.

Puertobelo, ordinarily a small cluster of houses with a drab
governor's residence, a rude hospital staffed with two parish priests,
and a recently completed fort, the Castillo de San Felipe, had func-
tioned as the western terminus of the transatlantic freight and
passenger service between Spain and its South American colonies
for only a little over a decade when young Sarria appeared there,
probably late in the summer of 1605, to receive the copies of *Don
Quijote* and other volumes in the shipment from his father. Earlier
the less salubrious locality of Nombre de Dios farther to the east had
served as the anchorage place of the fleets, but considerations of defense from pirate attacks, particularly after Drake's successful
forays, as well as of health, had contributed to a shift to the only
real harbor on the Atlantic side of the Isthmus. The main expanse of
water front at Puertobelo was a good two miles in length and half a
mile wide, with a deep and sandy bottom coming almost to the
shore's edge; ships could enter and leave readily regardless of the
direction of the wind, and they were assured safe shelter from
storms. The Spanish government had been spending 60,000 pesos
a year to erect the necessary buildings, and at a cost of some 62,596
pesos annually it was maintaining a garrison of fifty soldiers, whose
supplies and equipment came mostly from Peru, in the Castillo de
San Felipe to guard against the surprise attacks by the highwaymen
of the sea.[14] Only a short while before, in 1602, an English rover,
William Parker, had managed to sack Puertobelo, and constant
vigilance was imperative. Timber, stone, and fresh water were
abundant in the vicinity, but the terrain was marshy and the steep
range behind the town, together with the lay of the port itself, prevented free ventilation by cooling breezes. These conditions helped
to breed fevers of high mortality, especially when the scanty population was abruptly augmented by the throng of officials, merchants, artisans, and hundreds, even thousands, of soldiers and
sailors from the anchored galleons at the time of the annual Puertobelo fair.

This latter institution was initiated at Nombre de Dios about
1575 to facilitate at this meeting place exchanges of goods from

Spain and Peru. After the removal to the new site the fair flourished
during nearly a century and a half. More than a distributing center
for merchants of the surrounding area, the famous Puertobelo's
function was that of an entrepôt for the entire Spanish-South
American trade which, in a certain sense, was international. All the
commerce of the west coast of the southern continent and even
that of the Río de la Plata region on the lower Atlantic seaboard,
was required by Spanish law to pass through Panama. Thus the
merchants of Peru, mainly Lima, enjoyed in a vast region a virtual
monopoly which was almost as exclusive and as profitable as that of
their counterparts in the Spanish Peninsula itself. By an agreement
between these Spanish and Peruvian businessmen, duly sanctioned
by the Crown, the Peninsular exporters could trade on their own
account only as far as the Isthmus. Hence the representatives of
the merchants of Spain—in reality, those of Seville and Cádiz—
bringing manufactured articles from the mother country, such as
fabrics, hardware, glassware, wine, books, and paper, met the corresponding agents of the Peruvian traders at Puertobelo in order to
effect an exchange of these products for the precious metals from
the mines and for other commodities such as sugar, tobacco, and
vicuña wool of the viceroyalty brought up to Panama on coastal
vessels. These two groups of merchants were organized as guilds
with definite rules and regulations governing their relations. At
the time that *Don Quixote* first passed through Puertobelo in 1605
the import and export duties were netting sums between 150,000
and 170,000 pesos whenever the fleets came in, which, of late, had
not been regularly.[15]

The Atlantic galleons customarily stopped at the more health-
ful and protected port of Cartagena until word reached them that
the Peru fleet had arrived at Old Panama City. They then proceeded on to Puertobelo. Meanwhile, on the Pacific side of the
Isthmus seamen and Negroes unloaded the treasure and goods from
Peru and transported them across the intervening land on *recuas* or
pack-trains of mules and on *bongos* or large dugouts down the
Chagres river. In Puertobelo the few townspeople rented part or
the whole of their houses at exorbitant rates, and temporary huts
and barracks were erected on the compounds and nearby fields in
an effort to meet the housing shortage as the heterogenous throng

gathered for the fair. The cost of lodging and food rose to incredible heights and all values and services suffered a heavy inflation during the two weeks that the occasion ordinarily lasted.

The first step in the procedure of the Puertobelo fair was the customary inspection of the registers and cargoes of the incoming ships by the royal officers who had come from Panama City for this purpose. When they were satisfied that the merchandise was properly registered and that no contraband was included, the order to unload was given. Thereupon, under the supervision of these same officials, the general of the fleet and the *alcalde* of Puertobelo, slaves and seamen began the arduous task of transferring the goods from the holds and decks of the anchored vessels to sledges, on which the heavy cases and bales were dragged to the shelter of tents made from the ships' canvas and set up along the water front and in the public squares. There the owners or their agents identified their consignments by the distinguishing marks on the cases, which were also drawn on the invoices. Meanwhile, a commission composed of representatives of both the Spanish and the Peruvian guilds met as a sort of office of price administration or stock exchange to establish the rates at which the various kinds of commodities would be traded, and these quotations were publicly posted. Faithful adherence to these exchange rates appears to have been the rule on these annual occasions.[16]

Such were the necessary preliminaries of the Puertobelo fair and during the next fortnight, later extended to a longer period, the houses, shops, stalls, streets, and squares of the port town bulged with boxes and bales of commodities which changed hands and were gradually loaded onto mules and into small river boats. Lying scattered about were heaps of ingots of silver and other precious metals in full public view and, apparently, without fear of theft. Everyone had surrendered to an orgy of barter, including the sailors of the galleons who offered sweetmeats and other tidbits brought from Spain for sale in tiny booths or stands.

Into this animated scene, then, came the young man, Juan de Sarria, to claim the sixty-one cases of books, including the first copies of *Don Quijote* to arrive in this part of the world, and to pay for them in behalf of Miguel Méndez, the Lima merchant by whom he was employed. When he had found these boxes, which were probably piled one upon the other under the shelter of a tent made of ship's sails, and had fulfilled the indispensable legal and commercial requirements, he set about the task of transporting this rather considerable consignment of printed volumes across the Isthmus whose terrain was much too rough and broken to permit the use of carts or wheeled vehicles.

Before the arrival of the fleet at Puertobelo, Sarria had doubtless dickered with one or more of the several owners of mules engaged in conveying freight, and he had probably already made preliminary arrangements for the transfer of his father's wares to Old Panama City. This form of service was, in fact, one of the most important industries of the district and some thirty-three citizens of the isthmian city were engaged in this occupation. It was an arduous one, calling for considerable strength and skill, both in lifting the heavy cases and in balancing them properly on the backs of the diminutive animals to which they were ingeniously strapped. The vigor of the few Indians of the locality was unequal to the demands of this heavy task and the *arrieros*, or muleteers, attending these *recuas* had long been burly Negro slaves who possessed the hardened physiques and the muscular dexterity required to load the merchandise and keep the cantankerous beasts moving forward along the narrow and, in places, precipitous trail. Approximately 300 of the Africans were thus engaged when Sarria arranged for the transportation of his books. Some of the goods were thus brought directly across the Isthmus, while others were piled into barges which proceeded slowly along the coast from Puertobelo and then ascended the Chagres River to the depot at Las Cruces, where they were loaded on the backs of waiting mules and carried to the Pacific side at the Old City of Panama. In the whole region at the time of the Sarria shipment the thirty-three individuals engaged in this freight-moving business had a total of 850 mules. The number of these beasts of burden operating in the various pack trains varied from 75, which was the largest, through 55, 40, 30, 25 and less; the smallest, apparently, used only five animals.[17] As a result of the need for this means of transportation, mule breeding was one of the leading industries of the region, particularly in the small towns of Nata and Los Santos not far from the Pacific terminus, but the best stock was imported from Nicaragua.

The two routes across the Isthmus formed a sort of triangle, of which the one swinging southwest along the seacoast and then turning up the tortuous Chagres River constituted two sides.[18] It was a difficult journey beset with perils of shallows, rapids, sudden floods, and sunken logs, and usually required about two weeks' time, depending on the condition of the stream. The latter was navigable to Las Cruces, which was about five leagues from the Pacific Ocean, and the remainder of the crossing was by muleback. A settlement had grown up at this junction where a large warehouse in charge of a public official was established to store goods in transit and this service netted the government as high as 10,000 pesos a year, though a decline in trade had recently brought this sum nearer to 4,000 pesos.

The second route, known as the Gorgona trail, struck overland in a southerly direction and the eighteen to twenty leagues separating Puertobelo and Old Panama could ordinarily be covered in four days with stops at inns, but parts of this way were exceedingly dangerous. On leaving the site of the fair on the Atlantic side the pack trains passed through the squalid quarters of the slaves called "Guinea;" then, skirting the Cascajal River, they began the abrupt ascent which carried them over the highest part of the continental divide. Long years after Sarria's time it was reported that the passage was

> . . . steep and narrow, in many places almost perpendicular [so] that we were obliged to ascend climbing with our hands and feet . . . we sunk up to the knees in mud . . . at other times the whole party seemed to be lost in the windings of the road, cut deep into the side of the mountain.

Concerning another range nearly a thousand feet high a later traveler declared:

> It was impossible to keep on the mules without breaking [one's neck]. . . . Some part of this road is not above two feet broad, having precipices on each side four or five hundred feet deep, so that by the least slip of a mule's foot, both itself and the rider must be dashed in pieces.[19]

Even in the less hazardous stretches, constant vigilance was required in crossing the rain-drenched jungles and numerous swift

streams where a stumble or slip might irreparably ruin books and
other perishable wares by wetting. It was over this route, apparently, that young Sarria had chosen to bring the first copies of *Don
Quijote* to reach South America, and it appears that something in
the nature of the mishap just mentioned befell a part of his consignment of sixty-one cases. In the *recibo* dated at Lima on June 5, 1606
which bears his signature, Sarria reported that several boxes got
wet between Puertobelo and Old Panama and he was obliged to
take out the damaged volumes on his arrival at the Pacific side and
repack them separately. He was inclined, however, to lay the
blame for this misfortune at the door of the packers in Spain who,
he asserted, had not done their work well, rather than upon the
difficulties of the Gorgona trail. These water-soaked books numbered ninety-one in all and the list of titles, which is duly inserted
into the record, reveals that only one of the precious copies of *Don
Quijote* suffered from immersion. The majority of the works included were a wide diversity of religious writings together with
copies of *La hermosura de Angélica*, a half-chivalric novel by Barahona de Soto, of the diverting *Viaje entretenido* of Rojas Villandrando, of some epistles of Cicero, and some *Romanceros* or ballad
collections, the latter the most numerous item contained in the case.

When Don Quixote and Sancho Panza passed through Old
Panama for the first time in their adventurous careers encased in
the packing boxes of the Sarria shipment, the city on the Pacific
side of the Isthmus, founded some eighty-six years before, was experiencing a decline in its fortunes.[20] Primarily a transfer point for
the trade between Spain and its vast holdings in South America, the
prosperity of this center depended largely on the annual fleets from
the Peninsula which, in recent years, had arrived in smaller numbers and at intervals of two, and sometimes, three years. Moreover,
some of the normal traffic was by-passing the Isthmus altogether
by going from the mother country to Peru by way of New Spain.
And it was also alleged that the China trade, funneled through
Manila in the Philippines, was drawing off some of the silver of
both Mexico and Peru to purchase the textiles and chinaware of the
Far East. As a result unemployment was rising in the shrinking
population of the isthmian city, and the pack trains and the barges

on the Chagres River could hardly be kept busy seven or eight months of the year.

The site of Old Panama was anything but attractive. Lolling on the edge of the Pacific, whose shifting sands were fast filling up the exposed harbor, it was immediately backed by low, swampy country which soon terminated in a mountain range on the north and craggy, forbidding hills to the east. On the west side a small stream separated the city from the little town of Nata. Occupying a frontier position between two oceans, its inhabitants lived in continual dread of attacks by enemies both external and internal. Piratic aggressions were common, and lurking in the surrounding highlands were *cimarrones*, or fugitive Negro slaves, who made travel in the interior and life on the outlying ranches a source of uneasiness; though frequently hunted down, these runaways were rarely captured. And the climate left much to be desired; it was hot, humid, and dank, with almost continuous rainfall throughout the winter. The moisture quickly rusted tools, weapons, muskets, and lances, and there was nearly always a shortage of these articles which had to be imported from Spain. Usually in December fresher breezes swept in, tempering the heat somewhat, and produced a more comfortable temperature until about the end of April. Despite the excessive precipitation and the soaked condition of the district generally there was no water within the confines of the city suitable for drinking, cooking, or even for washing clothes. Negro water carriers hauled a supply from ravines a half league away and they sold it in the streets at a half *real* a jugful. To the east and west of the city were brief stretches of fertile soil, but much of the surrounding country, especially toward the north, was hilly and sterile.

In 1607 a remarkably detailed report was prepared concerning Old Panama and its vicinity which offers a fairly complete description of the locality about the time that Sarria, Jr., passed through with his copies of the first edition of *Don Quijote*. The anonymous compiler is very precise in some of his facts and figures and a few of these will be utilized. The city itself, lying like a recumbent L along the water front, extended exactly 1,412 paces east and west, ending at the Convento de la Merced, and 487 paces from the sea inland; two unnamed rivers, one of which dried up part of the year, formed its boundaries. The chief avenue along the shore, called the *Calle de la Carrera*, was paralleled by three others, all of which were crossed by seven muddy streets starting at the beach and pointing inward toward the hinterland. Besides the blocks of miscellaneous wooden, story-and-a-half, tile-roofed houses of Europeans thus formed, there were three public squares, the main one, on which the principal church and some of the public buildings faced, lying in the corner of the L, and two smaller ones. These dwellings numbered 322, only eight being built of stone; the five convents had gardens or orchards and were the only habitations that gave a touch of charm to the untidy community with its quagmires and pools of greenish, stagnant water. Surrounding this drab core of the city was a ragged periphery of squalid, grass-roofed shacks which sheltered the much larger Negro population and a few poor whites.

The decline in commercial activity had reduced the inhabitants to one-third the number of earlier days. The 1607 census reveals that the male Europeans totaled 548, of whom 495 were Spaniards and the remainder a sprinkling of Portuguese, Italians, Flemish and Frenchmen; 215 were married, 277 bachelors, and 56 were widowers. The corresponding female element was smaller, being only 303, and there were 156 children under the age of ten. The only educational activities were, apparently, in the hands of a few Jesuits who taught Latin for 300 pesos a year, and a schoolmaster teaching reading and writing who had his house rent free. Only twenty of the citizens owned horses, the true symbol of social and economic eminence.

These whites were greatly outnumbered by the 3,721 Negro slaves who, dwelling in the thick cluster of huts and lean-tos fringing the city and still speaking their African dialects, had long replaced the Indian aborigines; the latter survived only in three tiny and scattered villages inland, and hence the *encomienda* system characterizing the Spanish social organization in so many parts of America was nonexistent in the Isthmus.

The chief occupations of this community at the crossroads of the Spanish world were bartering, freight hauling, and shipbuilding. Agriculture was not sufficiently developed to maintain the settlement and much foodstuff was imported from Peru. It was essen-

tially a community of middlemen who dealt not only in manufactured articles from Spain but also in the merchandise and food-
stuffs which came up the west coast of South America more frequently from the rich Peruvian viceroyalty. These imports included flour, sugar, molasses, chick-peas, starch, olives, soap, foot-
ware, canvas, and shipping tackle as well as the silver and other
products of the mines. The slow-moving coastal shipping took
back lumber, building stone, tanned hides, and newly arrived Negro
slaves as well as the manufactures of Europe. This business was in
the hands of some twenty brokers who conducted their negotia-
tions mainly in their own homes. There were, besides, about twenty-one shopkeepers in the retail trade of the city.

Next in order of importance economically were the pack train
and freight service on the Chagres River, which together employed nearly a third of the population, black and white. The
abundance of timber made shipbuilding one of the minor industrial
activities, but this was hampered by the necessity of importing so
much of the rigging and caulking materials from Spain. As a result only two or three vessels, of from 60 to 175 tons, were turned
out each year. Fishing did not seem to pay enough to warrant the
effort, but the coastwise shipping down the coast to Buenaventura,
Guayaquil and Callao, and north as far as Nicaragua was fairly
profitable. There was virtually no maritime service as far north
as New Spain, however.

When at last Sarria's pack train trooped into the miry streets
and steamy atmosphere of Old Panama with his sixty-one cases intact if slightly damaged by the wetting received on the trail, his
troubles were by no means over. To defray the heavy handling
charges of his large shipment across the Isthmus he was obliged to
sell eight of his boxes and their contents, thus reducing his total
to fifty-three. Though it appears that he gave a strict accounting
of this transaction, the record has not been found and it is impossible to state whether copies of *Don Quijote* were included in
the sale. And now the problem of transportation down the coast
to Callao and Lima must be faced. The open harbor had silted up
to such an extent that vessels of fifty or sixty tons could no longer
enter, even at high tide; occasionally, they anchored a league off
shore, and goods were lightered back and forth, but more often

they put into the deep-water, if somewhat exposed, harbor of Perico located in the little group of islands about two leagues south of the city. It was, therefore, both inconvenient and expensive to load cargo on the coastal ships at Old Panama.

The busy season coincided, of course, with the arrival of the Spanish fleet at Puertobelo, and Sarria had reached the Pacific terminus when freight space was scarce and rates had doubled. At other times of the year, in contrast, it was often difficult to fill the holds and there was a corresponding drop in the cost of shipping. Generally, goods in packing cases such as books were charged twelve or thirteen *tomines* per twenty-five pounds from Panama to Lima. Possibly the young man entrusted with the care of the consignment of copies of *Don Quijote* and other works was unable to obtain shipping space for his remaining fifty-three cases, or possibly he decided to wait on the Isthmus until cheaper freight rates were in force. Whatever the circumstances, he apparently did not deliver the books in Lima until the middle of the following year. Presumably he had met the Spanish galleons at Puertobelo in the early fall of 1605 and, although the voyage down the west coast of South America took many weeks and even months, the interval between that date and June 5, 1606, when the receipt was drawn up at the viceregal capital, suggests a lengthy stopover at Old Panama or somewhere en route. Perhaps Sarria, Jr., sought to reduce the inconvenience of this delay to his father's partner in Lima by turning over eight of his fifty-three cases to a cousin in Panama, Gregorio de la Puerta by name, who had acquired some space on the *Nuestra Señora del Rosario*. When he received this advance shipment, Miguel Méndez, the merchant in Peru, could begin unloading his new stock on the market while the remaining forty-five cases were in transit. If this was, in fact, young Sarria's idea, he was probably surprised and chagrined to learn, when he later arrived with the bulk of the consignment, on the *Ave María* and the *Nuestra Señora del Carmen*, that his plan had miscarried, for neither his relative nor the eight cases had yet put in an appearance at Lima. Hence, of the original sixty-one cases, he could take receipt for only forty-five, and no record has since come to light of the missing sixteen, which undoubtedly contained a certain number of copies of Cervantes' masterpiece. But it is clear from the lengthy document signed by Juan de Sarria and Miguel Méndez before a public notary that June day in Lima that at least seventy-two priceless copies of *Don Quijote de la Mancha* had come to delight readers for the first time in the remote realm of Peru almost a year and a quarter after a bookseller of Alcalá de Henares had deposited them at the House of Trade in Seville.

Legend has it or, perhaps, *tradición,* to use the term that the gifted Peruvian writer, Ricardo Palma, gave to his historical anecdotes, that the first copy of *Don Quijote* to reach Lima was one brought down in a galleon from Acapulco in New Spain to the Count of Monterrey, Viceroy of Peru. Sent by one of his friends in Mexico, it allegedly arrived late in December of 1605 and found that vice-sovereign gravely ill. One of the visitors at his bedside was a Dominican friar, Diego de Hojeda, subsequently famed for his Milton-like religious epic poem *La Cristiada,* and upon him the dying ruler of the viceroyalty, too ill to read the novel which came so highly recommended, bestowed his gift. Thus this precious volume passed into the library of the Dominican convent and there presumably it remained until 1855 when it disappeared without a trace. In March 1606, the account continues, six other copies came to Lima directly from Spain and passed into the possession of aristocratic personages of the capital.[21] Conceivably, there is a basis for this tale which Ricardo Palma recounts, and possibly in this manner Don Quixote did first invade this part of the world. Sarria's apparent delay in bringing his book consignment may well have caused him to lose priority in introducing Cervantes' famous work to Peru, but Palma's story rests on nothing firmer than the hearsay report of that genial raconteur, who rarely let strict historical fact interfere with the telling of a good yarn. Until more solid evidence of a documentary character is forthcoming, the six dozen copies which the Sarrias, father and son, introduced in mid-1606 represent the first authenticated delivery in the Peruvian viceroyalty of the immortal narrative of Don Quixote's adventures. Into whose hands these precious copies subsequently fell, the record does not say. All that can be stated with assurance is that not all the seventy-two copies were disposed of among the *limeño* public. At least nine of them were repacked in boxes and carried once again on donkeyback, this time to Cuzco and its vicinity in the high Sierras of the Andes. Thus it appears that not more than sixty-three of these copies remained in Lima itself.

The *recibo* lists case by case the entire forty-five of the shipment and indicates a grand total of 2,895 volumes with varying quantities of each title, each of which is written in extremely abbreviated form, together with the price per copy in reales.[22] Like most such colonial inventories, this lengthy document invites analysis and commentary. While its singular value lies in the unmistakable evidence it offers of the arrival at the viceregal center in mid-1606 of a substantial number of copies of *Don Quijote*, it would be manifestly unfair to omit consideration of the vastly larger quantity of other representative works included. Handiest are the three general categories previously adopted: belles-lettres, ecclesiastical literature, and miscellaneous secular writings. As usual, there are uncertainties in the identification of the shortened titles, and the statistics emerging are inevitably rough approximations.

The 2,895 books represent some 163 different works; about 12 per cent of the total of both volumes and titles are readily classified as creative literature of entertainment. In quantity *Don Quijote* easily tops this class, though the comparatively inexpensive ballad collections are a close second in number. The one copy each of *El caballero del febo* by Esteban de Corbera and *Don Florisel de Niquea* by Feliciano de Silva offer a contrast to the relatively large number of Cervantes' great novel, and again the student of literary history is tempted to perceive a confirmation of the oft-reiterated assertion that the Knight of the Sad Countenance did indeed give the *coup de grâce* to the declining vogue of the romances of chivalry which had so long claimed devoted readers in Spain and its Indies. Certain it is, in any event, that after 1605 book shipments to the colonies included almost none of them. As pointed out elsewhere, the presence of *Don Florisel de Niquea* may be due as much to its pastoral as to its chivalric elements. Of passing interest is the fact that the author of this fiction is linked to the history of Peru through his son, Diego de Silva, one of the conquerors of the Inca empire, who once resided for some time in Cuzco. There he had the distinction of serving as godfather at the confirmation of the first genuinely American writer, the half-caste Inca Garcilaso de la Vega, famous for his *Royal commentaries of the Incas.*

Only slightly behind Cervantes numerically in the Sarria consignment was that other great contemporary, Lope de Vega, who is represented by five different titles in a total of sixty-three books. The most significant of these was the lone copy of *Comedias de Lope de Vega*, probably the first edition of the collection of a dozen plays which was also a literary event of the historic year of 1605, for it portended a fundamental change in the reading habits of the colonists during the next two centuries. The bulky novel and un-dialogued verse were still the preferred reading matter of the Conquistadors' descendants in 1606, but comedies printed in *sueltas,* or loose copies, as well as in groups were soon to become the chief fictional fare of colonial readers and theatergoers.

The predominance of ecclesiastical literature in the shipment causes no surprise, of course, and its character reflects only too clearly the two basic types of literary production of the Counter Reformation, namely, theological studies in Latin which served to expound and define Catholic dogma to the clergy, both secular and regular, and the works of religious instruction or devotion in the vernacular designed to reach the lay membership. The demand for writings of this sort often resulted in such large orders for a single work that, while some 57 per cent of all titles were ecclesiastical in nature, fully 75 per cent of the total number of books in the Sarria assortment fell into this class. These included sermons, catechisms, religious manuals, lives of saints, books of devotion, works of exegesis, and the poetry of the mystics such as Luis de Leon and Luis de Granada. It might be mentioned in passing that the twenty-eight copies of the *Conceptos espirituales* of Alonso de Ledesma suggest the early introduction into the Indies of the *conceptismo* which was to plague the poetry of the colonies as well as of the mother country during the rest of the seventeenth century and later.

These pietistic and theological writings, then, were the stock in trade on which booksellers leaned heavily in conducting their business and from which their largest returns were derived. Among the titles on the Sarria receipt were works printed under contract to the Alcalá de Henares dealer, and there were others which he had purchased outright from the authors. The ten copies of the *Flos Sanctorum* by Francisco Ortiz Lucio appearing on the *recibo* were probably a part of the edition that the elder Sarria had obtained through an agreement made in Madrid in 1603,[23] while notarial records indicate that the *Devocionario y horas* by the same writer, of which thirty copies came in the shipment to Lima, was bought with rights of publication by this merchant in Madrid on November 26, 1605 for the sum of 2,000 reales.[24] On January 1 of the same year and hence in time for the shipment to Peru made that spring Sarria, Sr., signed a promissory note for 1,085 reales in favor of an Augustine friar, Pedro de Vega, for sixty-two of the latter's *Tabla de los Salmos, Part III*, twenty-nine of which were among the contents of the forty-five cases delivered in Lima.[25] And doubtless other titles listed represent similar investments of the Peninsular merchant.

The group of miscellaneous secular works is of greater general interest. Numerically, it is a trifle larger than that of belles-lettres and constitutes about 15 per cent of the entire shipment. But if the proportion of volumes is small compared to those of ecclesiastical literature, the variety of titles offers a less sharp contrast. Of the 163 or so titles in the consignment, about 49 works or 30 per cent can be credited to this classification. These figures again suggest that theology was not the sole interest or intellectual activity of the more serious readers in the viceroyalty of Peru; though religious literature tended to predominate, it did not exercise such an exclusive monopoly of the colonial mind as has been commonly believed. These secular writings included works on medicine, veterinary science, books on precious stones, volumes on law and its practice, history, biography, geography, philosophy, grammar, almanacs, etc., much as other early book lists had shown.

As in other instances, it is likely that writings of the first and last classes, that is, belles-lettres and miscellaneous secular works, though fewer in number than the second group, enjoyed a wider reading and appreciation as they passed from hand to hand than did the theological treatises, whose appeal was to a more professional public. What should be stressed in connection with all categories in Sarria's shipment, as in others observed, is that many of the titles had recently appeared in Spain for the first time. This clearly indi-

cates that the colonists not merely received works whose vogue in
the Peninsula was well established or even dying out, but could
obtain from their local dealers the most recent publications being
read in the homeland and could thus keep abreast of contemporary
thought and literary fashions. Furthermore, the inclusion of a part
or the whole of Cervantes' latest book that spring of 1605 offers
convincing proof that such works were commonly sent to the
overseas possessions of the Spanish Crown even before they were
generally available to the public in Spain. So profitable was the book
trade in the colonies that it was, apparently, the ordinary practice
to hustle the first printing of a volume off the press and on to
Seville in time for the departure of the annual fleets to those outlying parts of the empire.

Among other things, the study of these related documents in
Seville and in Lima concerning the particular consignment of sixty-
one cases of books shipped by Juan de Sarria, *padre*, points to the
conclusion that the distinction of being among the first, and perhaps the very first, to introduce into Peru the princeps of the best
of all novels, *Don Quijote de la Mancha*, belongs to the enterprising dealer of Alcalá de Henares who dispatched them from Spain;
to his son, Juan de Sarria, *hijo*, who conveyed them from Puertobelo to Lima; and to Miguel Méndez, bookseller and merchant of
the viceregal capital, who sold them to his trade.

DON QUIXOTE IN THE LAND OF THE INCAS XIX

THE SLOW, PLODDING PACK TRAINS PAINFULLY CLIMBing from Lima on the arid coast of Peru through the still more arid wastes of sand and rock to the chill heights of Cuzco, ancient seat of Incan power in the lofty Andes, were the sole means of transportation of the domestic trade in Spain's richest province of the New World. On this arduous journey, variously indicated as from 140 to 184 leagues in length and often requiring from one to two months of travel,[1] the merchants of the viceregal capital sent a goodly portion of their wares, mainly manufactured goods from the mother country, for sale at a handsome profit among the Spaniards and other prosperous inhabitants of remote towns and mining centers in the interior. That many of these isolated subjects of the Spanish Crown were literate and even possessed intellectual interests is clearly evident from the fact that substantial quantities of printed books were among the merchandise thus laboriously transported. Further activities of young Juan de Sarria, so recently arrived in Lima with the forty-five cases of these wares, plainly show that the opportunity to read all types of secular as well as ecclesiastical literature was by no means limited to the fortunate dwellers in the New World centers of culture, but it was also well within the reach of those expatriates who sought riches in the distant villages and rough mining camps of the interior. Additional documents pertaining to the son of the Alcalá de Henares bookseller throw further light on the early peregrinations of Don Quixote de la Mancha and his practical-minded squire, and they supply evidence of the prompt invasion of the Andean heights by these two adventurers so lately arrived on the Pacific shores of South America.

The firm of Méndez and Sarria, like most others, did not restrict its commercial activities to the local market of Lima, but pushed the sales of its goods with considerable vigor in the outlying parts of the vast realm of Peru as well. Scarcely had Sarria, Jr., made delivery of the consignment of books brought down from Puertobelo when he attached his signature to receipts for two smaller allotments of the same merchandise which he was pledged to transport to and sell in Cuzco and other parts of the highlands. Indeed, on the day following his official act of turning over the large shipment to his father's partner in Lima—that is, June 6, 1606—he signed agreements to convey and sell in the hinterland two batches of printed volumes. The larger, totaling approximately 438 books, were to be disposed of inland if possible, and the entire proceeds would go to the firm. Possibly with the object of stimulating the young salesman's spirit of enterprise, the second and smaller consignment of eighty-two books was entrusted to him on different terms. These volumes the younger Sarria was to sell in Cuzco and its vicinity in behalf of, and at the risk of, the partners, but with the understanding that he should receive one-half of the profits resulting from the venture. The two notarized records setting forth these stipulations, the titles of the works involved, and the price of each have fortunately survived.[2]

The viceregal city of Lima in 1606, with its population of about 25,000 people, was the busiest mart of trade in the southern continent and possibly in the entire Western Hemisphere during the early decades of the seventeenth century. Whole districts in the vicinity of its central square were given over to merchandising activities which yielded such spectacular returns that virtually everyone participated in the local trade in one way or another. Some dealers were said to have goods to the value of a million pesos, while there were many others with smaller, though still substantial, fortunes. So large were the liquid assets of these wealthy merchants that many were sending their surplus funds to Spain or Mexico, even as far away as China and the Far East, to be farmed out as loans at high rates of interest. The lure of money-making was so pervasive that the nobility of the city, including the Viceroy and, it was whispered, even the Archbishop, were engaged in trade, though all these dignitaries allegedly scorned such sordid occupations. This lucrative avocation was pursued surreptitiously, of course, and through suitably discreet intermediaries. Liberal credit terms, from one to three years, were extended, and buying on the installment plan appears to have been common.[3]

The most animated district of the capital was along Merchants' Street, which cut a narrow swath southward through the arcades and structures massed on that side of the central square. The forty or more shops lining this congested thoroughfare offered their customers the richest and most varied wares from all parts of the world. Leading westward off the plaza and toward the seaport of Callao was another important business artery known as Mantas Street, along which were numerous stores, shops, and stalls. Here the establishments of the craftsmen, such as candlemakers, iron-mongers, and coppersmiths, tended to congregate; paralleling this narrow thoroughfare was the more famous street of the silver-smiths, given over almost entirely to the *talleres* of skilled craftsmen who fashioned a part of the precious metal of the Andean mines into marvellously wrought objects of luxury. The flow of silver from the mountain heights through the viceregal capital on the coast seemed as constant as that of the life-giving waters of the nearby Rimac River descending from the same source and, at times, it amounted to a flood. In this very year of 1606, when Don Quixote visited the cordillera of the Andes for the first time, a tobacco peddler had accidentally come upon a rich vein of silver in a hill on the road to fabulous Potosí, and already the settlement of Oruro, in what was later Bolivia, was being laid out in the vicinity of a seemingly inexhaustible mine.[4] These great expectations were amply vindicated, for this mining community high in the Altiplano re-mained one of the chief sources of the highly prized metal during all the centuries of Spanish rule.

The records fail to reveal on which of Lima's busy streets the firm of Méndez and Sarria conducted its business, but one may hazard the guess that it was on Mantas street where numerous book-sellers of the capital plied their trade. Whatever the exact location, it is probable that the two assortments of books which young Sarria was to take on the long journey into the Peruvian highlands, including at least nine copies of Cervantes' great novel, were loaded on the backs of submissive mules just off the city square separated from the river by the low mass of the viceregal palace. Almost every day, it seemed, pack trains got under way, some composed of as many as seventy or eighty animals, each ten of which were attended by an Indian or Negro *arriero*, or muleteer. Emerging from the city these caravans moved slowly southward along the dusty, well-beaten trail, and soon plunged into the sandy wastes along the coast.

The first day's journey usually ended at a little village named La Cieneguilla from the shallow stream that watered the tiny, verdant valley surrounding it. This hamlet, four leagues (roughly twelve miles) from Lima over level terrain, was situated just beyond the crumbled ruins of the ancient holy city of Pachacamac, which stared bleakly out to sea. From the pleasant coastal oasis of La Cieneguilla the rude highway rose sharply to the chilly *punas*, or upland deserts, sometimes skirting along the edges of awesome precipices, sometimes plodding through craggy ravines. Occasionally, the stony monotony of the landscape was broken by a drab Indian village whose wretched inhabitants eked out a comfortless existence, and now and then a fleeting glimpse of herds of agile *vicuñas* and *huanacos* on distant slopes relieved the weariness of rock and sand. At night, travelers and muleteers took shelter, if there was room, in the *tambos*, or crude inns, irregularly scattered along the way, or huddled together in a cave when they could. Not infrequently, all shivered in the penetrating chill of the open plain or ridge under the star-studded sky.

The first substantial settlement after leaving Lima was Huancayo, situated some forty leagues away on the Mantaro River at an altitude of about eleven thousand feet and in a relatively fertile basin. The pork and bacon produced in this vicinity during the early seventeenth century were reputed to be the best in the realm, while its chickens and eggs were consumed with relish in Lima itself. Wheat, corn and fruit prospered in this mountain fastness, and its community, which supported two monasteries, was the chief food-producing center for the nearby mining camps. Fourteen Indian villages lay scattered about this relatively populous depression, and the large and well-stocked inn of the European town brought joy to the hearts of foot- and saddlesore travelers.

The trail from Huancayo to Cuzco passed through some of the most rugged parts of the Peruvian highlands and it offered a gruel-

ing test of endurance to animals and humans alike. After crossing
the river by a stone bridge the rough road rose four times to mountain passes above thirteen thousand feet and dropped as many times
to below sixty-five hundred,[5] subjecting the venturesome travelers
to that peculiar sense of anxiety, often accompanied by nausea and
violent headaches, of the dreaded *soroche*, or mountain sickness.

At intervals trails branched off to remote mining camps or to
such important settlements as Huancavelica, the great mercury-
producing center, where there were two thousand houses occupied
by Spaniards and three thousand more sheltering the Indian workers, and Castrovirreina, fourteen leagues farther on with its silver
deposits and five hundred or more dwellings.

Though the trail climbed steadily to dizzy heights, it paralleled
the southward course of the Mantaro River, which at times resembled in the distance a tiny silver thread twisting through craggy
canyons; again the narrow highway dropped to the very edge of
this stream near Huamanga, later called Ayacucho and scene of the
final battle for independence, where its waters were spanned by a
precariously swinging rope bridge. Here it was necessary to shift
the heavy cases and packs from the backs of the mules to the
shoulders of Indian and Negro burden bearers and swim the mules
to the opposite shore, particularly when mountain floods rendered
fording impossible. Huamanga was approximately the halfway
point between the two chief cities of Peru—Lima and Cuzco—and
its relatively pleasant climate and comfortable conditions offered
travelers and beasts a welcome respite.

Further arduous ascents and descents led past impressive monuments of ancient Indian civilizations and over streams crossed by
primitive rope bridges, and finally brought the pack trains to the
towering cliff bordering the swift-flowing Apurimac River. A sheer
drop to these turbulent waters was accomplished by a series of
four hundred steps gouged out of the living rock which descended
to a plank bridge that shook ominously under the tread of each
passer-by. Cieza de León, a sixteenth-century chronicler, had commented on this spectacular part of the road built by the Incas. "Let
those who may read this book and who may have been in Peru consider," he wrote, "the road that runs from Lima to Jauja through
the cragged sierras of Huarochiri and the snow-covered mountains

of Pariaca, and those who hear them will judge whether what they saw is not even more remarkable than what I write; and besides this let them remember the cliff that drops down to the Apurimac River."[6] At this point the animals, which had been slowly guided down this precipitous staircase, were discharged of their burdens and conducted, one by one, by the muleteers who sweated under the weight of the freight transferred to their own backs. So terribly dangerous was this part of the overland journey that Lima merchants usually purchased special insurance to cover losses occurring there. Despite the perils and hardships of negotiating such risky crossings, these trails were used constantly by a swarm of Spanish merchants and peddlers journeying with their wares, including books, images, and objects of art, from one isolated population cluster to another in the barren but wealth-producing cordillera. The provisions and goods which they brought were exchanged for the plentiful silver pouring out of the mines, and this traffic yielded profits which quickly built up respectable fortunes and richly compensated the enterprising dealers for their incredible hardships. Many of these perambulating middlemen were notorious for their swindling and mistreatment of the Indians, which fact moved provincial officials to forbid them to settle down in the aboriginal communities.

The final stage of the wearing journey was relatively comfortable and free of danger as the trail dipped more gradually into the fertile bottom land of the basin in which Cuzco was located, and soon a pleasanter prospect of green pastures, wheat fields, and truck gardens greeted the eyes of the travelers. The more level highway led past the imposing relics of the sumptuous buildings of vanished civilizations of the highlands and, at long last, it ended in the bustling center of the former Incan capital where the thin, tired, and dusty pack train and its worn attendants made the long-anticipated halt.

Cuzco in 1606, when Don Quixote and Sancho Panza first beheld its hidden splendor, was rated the finest city in the great viceroyalty of Peru after Lima. It rested in a sort of bowl among the hills, and the fertility of its surroundings, the multitude of fruit trees, and the abundant vegetation did not fail to arouse the enthusiasm of travel-jaded visitors both from the outlying mining camps in chilly, harsh, and bare mountain pockets at still higher altitudes and from the coastal deserts; all were prone, momentarily at least, to liken this ancient city and its setting to an earthly paradise. This center of the Altiplano held a population of three thousand or more Spaniards and over ten thousand natives, distributed among four large parishes. Its liveliest section was around the two large central squares, which were separated by a street given over to a variety of shops and stores. In these emporiums the latest goods imported from Europe were on display, along with a glittering array of objects revealing the extraordinary skill of local silver-smiths. In the center of the two flanking plazas were the more in-formal markets and stalls of the Indians, mainly women, who stolidly exposed for sale bits of silver, silken gloves with golden ornamentations, and similar articles mingled with coca leaves, jerked beef, and other products of the land. The imposing Cathedral and the Jesuit convent loomed up on the first of the squares, and near them were the Franciscan and Dominican monasteries. On the west side was the similar establishment of the Mercedarians, the prison, and the impressive offices of the well-paid *corregidor*, and the mu-nicipal *cabildo*. Here, too, were the many benches of the public scribes. Along the streets leading to this two-ply hub of the city were the massive structures of the well-to-do, their nearly blank, forbidding walls, fronting on the narrow thoroughfares, broken by small windows with iron gratings and by a large portal sealed by a heavy, studded door, over which the proud escutcheons of the inmates stood in bold relief. Scattered about the city were fountains of water to delight the thirsty eyes and parched mouths of travelers so long accustomed to arid peaks and desolate plains. In this remote corner of the world, so difficult of access, had Don Quixote and his squire made their appearance so soon after emerging into the ken of man in the Spanish Peninsula many thousand miles away.

A study of the titles of books thus sent to Cuzco in young Sarria's care permits some interesting deductions. Since a consider-able number of the works mentioned are not found in the records of the forty-five cases of books which he had just brought down from Panama, it is evident that the two collections were assembled, in part at least, either from other shipments received the same year or from older stock on hand. Whether these variations in the kinds of reading material loaded on the pack train and bound for the interior sprang from differing demands of the trade in those remote centers, or whether the dealers availed themselves of an opportunity to unload in the provinces titles which had proved less salable in the viceregal capital, are questions which can not be clearly answered. It is possible that the second and smaller group, for which Sarria, Jr., was to receive 50 per cent of the proceeds, was composed of older stock. However, the inclusion of two copies of *"comedias de lope de vega,"* presumably the first *Parte* of the plays of the great Spanish dramatist published for the first time in 1605, argues against this theory. The other two fictional works on the list, *Celestina* and the *Pícaro (Guzmán de Alfarache)*, may well have been efforts to clear the shelves of old orders.

In order to make a brief examination of the types of book which were sold and presumably read in Cuzco and its vicinity the usual practice is followed of dividing the works represented into three general classifications, that is, belles-lettres, secular, and ecclesiastical literature. Though numerically the last-mentioned group constitutes about three-quarters of both collections (the clergy were, of course, the chief consumers of books), discussion will be limited mainly to the first two classes.

What strike one's attention first, perhaps, in the larger consignment for Cuzco are the works of pure imagination, in particular the nine copies of *Don Quijote de la Mancha*. The latter were undoubtedly brought to Peru in the shipment which young Sarria had received in Puertobelo and probably formed a part of the first edition of Cervantes' masterpiece. Thus it seems certain that at least nine copies of the princeps, of which so little was known for two centuries, found their way in 1606 to the ancient seat of the vanished Incan empire high in the Andes of South America.

Lope de Vega, in this same consignment, is represented by three titles—two prose works, *Arcadia* and *El peregrino en su patria*, and one in verse, his less secular *Isidro*—totalling thirteen copies in all. But the two copies of the *comedias* of Lope[7] in Sarria's second batch, as already indicated, are the most significant item because of the tremendous influence that this type of literature was to exert on the leisure reading habits of the colonies in the years following.

The lone copy of *Don Policisne de Boecia*, published in 1602 and generally considered the last of the long series of novels of chivalry before *Don Quijote*, may represent an effort to unload on the possibly less surfeited reading public of the Sierra the type of fiction which was already less palatable to the more sophisticated bookbuyers of Lima. The small number of romances of chivalry noted on most book lists of the opening years of the seventeenth century indicates that the popularity of this genre had nearly vanished before the appearance of Cervantes' great work even in the far-off colonies.

Antonio de Guevara's *Libro áureo de Marco Aurelio*, which had enjoyed so much public favor throughout the sixteenth century, was still among the best sellers in Lima and the Peruvian hinterland, while Rojas Villandrando's readable *Viaje entretenido* and a somewhat emasculated *Lazarillo de Tormes* claimed an audience in the same realm.

Secular literature offered to the Cuzco market included philosophical classics such as Boethius' *Consolation of philosophy*, and Juan de Torres' *Filosofía moral de príncipes*, chronicles of Charles V and Alphonso the Wise, histories of Spain by Mariana, of the Indies by Gómara, as well as Pérez de Hita's ever popular *Guerras civiles de Granada*, geographies such as Rebullosa's *Descripción de todas las provincias y reynos del mundo*, and treatises of a scientific or practical nature on veterinary science, surgery, manuals of instruction for lawyers, scribes, and other public officials, almanacs, etc.

Overshadowing all other works, of course, were ecclesiastical writings which, besides ponderous theological and exegetical treatises, tracts, sermons, and books of devotion, also included quantities of poetry of a distinctly pious nature. In both of the assortments which Sarria was taking to Cuzco the stock was preponderantly of that character, yet it may be pointed out again that the Latin tomes and religious works probably did not reach as large a public as the much smaller quantity of fictional literature. Even the clergy were known to be addicted to the less respectable forms of literary expression and the relatively few copies of purely imaginative writings doubtless passed from hand to hand—which probably explains their extreme rarity in the books of the period that have survived the ravages of time.

An examination of the titles on the two book lists suggests a few statistics which are offered without claim to complete accuracy. Some works have not been identified, a few are indicated conjecturally and may belong to other categories than those arbitrarily set, and the use of "*unos*" in indicating the number of copies in one instance renders exact figures impossible of attainment. Nevertheless some interest may lie in the following statements.

The first group of about 438 volumes, representing some 123 titles, gives for belles-lettres 13 per cent of the total number of copies and 10 per cent of all the titles; secular literature claims 11 per cent of the copies and 21 per cent of the titles; and ecclesiastical works represent 76 per cent of all copies, but 69 per cent of the titles.

In the second and smaller group the percentages are similar. Of the approximately eighty-two copies representing thirty-five titles, belles-lettres fall to 9 per cent of the total copies and 18 per cent of the titles; finally, ecclesiastical works again tower with 76 per cent of the copies and 73 per cent of the titles. These percentages do not vary greatly from those obtaining in the records of other book shipments of the period.

It is noted that the prices placed on the books intended for the Cuzco market tend to rise sharply over those indicated in the receipt for the forty-five cases of books just received from Spain. Considering the additional freightage involved, the increased cost of books in the Sierra is not, of course, surprising. But one is struck by numerous inconsistencies and what appears to be a somewhat capricious marking up of prices. These differences are further complicated by the monetary units in which the values are expressed. The receipt for the forty-five cases from Spain signed by young Sarria and Méndez in Lima gives prices in *reales* (records of the original shipment at Seville, unfortunately, give no indication of cost), but the documents covering the two smaller assortments bound for Cuzco and vicinity express the value of each copy, sometimes in reales, sometimes in pesos, and more often in *patacones*,

apparently a slang term for pesos. Assuming that the latter unit was
the equivalent of eight reales,[8] which was standard for the silver
peso at that time, the prices for the Cuzco customers were stepped
up from 25 per cent to considerably over 100 per cent above those
prevailing in Lima, though in one or two instances the same amount
is indicated for both markets.[9] The copies of Lope de Vega's *Arcadia*, for example, are listed at 12 reales in Lima and for Cuzco,
while *La hermosura de Angélica* rises from 12 reales to 2 *patacones*
(16 reales?), and the *El peregrino en su patria* jumps from 8 to 20
reales. A copy of *Don Quijote*, which is listed at 24 reales in the
viceregal capital, costs the *cuzqueño* some 4 *patacones* (32 reales?).
The *Filosofía moral de príncipes* of Juan de Torres is marked up
from 50 reales per copy in Lima to 9 *patacones* or 72 reales in Cuzco
and vicinity. These examples are probably sufficient to illustrate the
price differentials at which Sarria, Méndez and Company, merchants
of Lima, offered their wares to their widely separated trade. But
more important than these economic considerations is the clearly
indicated fact that Spaniards, Creoles, and others reading the
sonorous language of Castile were not denied access to the best and
most representative literature of the motherland even though their
destinies carried them to the most outlying frontiers of Spain's vast
and far-flung empire.

Both in Spain and abroad the success of Cervantes' novel was
immediate and its popularity manifested itself in various forms.
Not only did repeated editions appear in the first year of its publication, but as early as June 1605, and only a few months after it began
to come off the press of Juan de la Cuesta at Madrid, masqueraders
delighted to rig themselves in the garb of Don Quixote and Sancho
Panza in celebrating the birth of a royal prince at Valladolid. Contemporary accounts of similar festivities at Zaragoza in 1614, Córdova in 1615, Seville in 1617, Baeza, Salamanca, and Utrera in 1618
tell of representations of the gaunt Knight of the Sad Countenance
on his equally gaunt nag, of Sancho Panza, and even of Dulcinea del
Toboso, which hugely amused the onlookers. By 1617 these fictional characters had inspired a comic skit entitled *The invincible
deeds of Don Quixote de la Mancha* which was performed on the
Madrid stage. But before this date the humorous fame of the roving

pair had crossed the borders of the Spanish Peninsula. The first English translation appeared in 1612, and the year following a figure dressed as Cervantes' hero took part in the gaiety attending the arrival at Heidelberg of Frederick V, Elector of the Palatinate, and his bride, Elizabeth Stuart, daughter of James I of England. And in 1621 the guild of silversmiths paraded through the streets of Mexico City in the likenesses of a long line of knights-errant, last and most modern of which was Don Quixote himself, attended by his trusty squire and his ladylove, Dulcinea.[10] In these earlier years the profounder significance of the immortal characters created by Cervantes remained unrealized by the public who saw in their bizarre misadventures only a clever burlesquing of the long-famous knights of chivalry.

The comic renown of these literary creations had made them familiar to crowds in the cities of Europe and on the streets of the viceregal capital of New Spain across the sea well within two decades after the first appearance of the novel, but even more remarkable is the fact that it reached much sooner into the heart of the Inca land of South America and there took visual form in less than three years from the same event. Of equal interest is the possibility of a direct connection between a physical impersonation of Don Quixote and his associates in the mountain fastness of Peru toward the end of 1607 and the load of books, including the nine copies of Cervantes' masterpiece, which the apprentice bookseller, Juan de Sarria, had laboriously transported to these parts the year before. This engaging supposition is suggested by the chance survival of a curious descriptive narrative, published early in the present century, of a program of festivities held in the mountainous region through which Sarria's pack train had so recently passed. This possible relationship may justify a brief account of the incident.[11]

The monotony of life in the colonies of Hispanic America was frequently relieved, in smaller communities as well as in the viceregal centers, by a variety of diversions, in most of which all classes participated. Probably the most prevalent entertainment of a popular character was a public procession featuring costumed figures and decorated floats. On solemn and religious occasions the sacred images in glittering raiment were brought forth from churches and temples to dazzle the eyes of the faithful who lined the festooned

streets; on more festive holidays there were parades of a strictly
secular character. Sometimes the objects of reverence were mingled
with more mundane spectacles in a lengthy program of festivities
celebrating an event such as the birth, marriage, coronation, or
similar happening in the life of royalty or of its duly appointed
representatives in the viceregal governments. The entry of a vice-
sovereign upon his new duties, his birthday, or other felicitous incidents in his domestic and public career were opportunities for an
often tedious series of gaieties, many of which marked the survival
of medieval pageantry and chivalric exercises in Spanish cultural
activities.

Only a few months before Juan de Sarria reached Lima with his
substantial shipments of books from Spain the Count of Monterrey,
Viceroy of Peru, had died in office. On receiving this news the
reigning monarch, Philip III, designated the Marqués de Montesclaros, then serving as his vice-sovereign in New Spain, as successor
to the same high office at Lima. There was some delay in issuing the
formal notice, however, and it appears that official word of the new
appointment did not reach Peru until about the middle of 1607, or
well over a year later. Soon thereafter the news of the appointment
spread throughout the interior of the realm, including an obscure
mining camp named Pausa in the highland province of Parinacochas,
now a part of Ayacucho. This small community lay on a barren,
open plain near high-yielding veins of silver and copper. The mines
were worked by some fifteen hundred Indians, but the European
contingent of this frontier settlement numbered no more than
twelve families. The presiding magistrate was a *corregidor* appointed annually; the incumbent was a man named Pedro de
Salamanca.

Possibly it was this official's hope to ingratiate himself with the
newly arriving Viceroy and thus extend his own term of office in
this lucrative, if outlying, post by organizing a somewhat elaborate
celebration of the elevation of the Marqués de Montesclaros to the
viceregal palace at Lima. Whatever his motives, he arranged for a
festive *Juego de sortija*, or Joust of the Ring, at Pausa, ably assisted
by a certain Cristóbal de Mata, ordinarily a resident of Potosí, by a
mestizo, Román de Baños, by the local parish priest, Father Antonio
Martínez, and by a youthful and lively Spaniard, hailing from Cór-

dova in the old country and known locally as Don Luis de Gálvez, who was to impersonate Don Quixote de la Mancha for the first time in this remote corner of the New World.

The *Juego de sortija* was basically a contest of skill in running a lance or spear through a small metal ring while riding a horse at full speed. Starting from an agreed line the mounted contestants, with lance couched, charged at full tilt, each in turn, at a suspended circlet, sometimes held in the mouth of an artificial swan or in the hand of a symbolic figure erected for the purpose,[12] and this tiny opening each sought to penetrate deftly with his knightly weapon. A descendant of this ancient pastime is, doubtless, the practice, still observed on merry-go-rounds at country fairs, circuses, and shore resorts, of snatching brass rings from an inclined slot as riders whirl about on their wooden steeds. In 1607 the game of *correr la sortija* was a closer survival or continuation of the chivalric exercises of the Middle Ages whose colorful pomp and pageantry were slow to lose a grip on the enthusiasm of a people fond of display. Whatever tendency there was to relegate these picturesque spectacles to the past had been retarded by a century of reading glamorous romances of chivalry and sentimental pastoral tales whose verbal pictures of the times "when knighthood was in flower" cast a hypnotic spell over their devotees. Amadis and his congeners were frequently depicted as engaging in these medieval contests, and more recently the exceedingly popular novel *El pastor de Fílida* by Luis Gálvez de Montalvo was rekindling a passion for staging *juegos de sortija*, for the climactic incident of that pastoral narrative was such a spectacle described in considerable detail.[13]

The form and manner of presenting these functions varied slightly in details, but a traditional pattern is discernible in most of the descriptions that have come down. Primarily a sport of the aristocracy, entertainment of this sort was usually provided by a wealthy nobleman for the ladies and gentlemen of his own circle. As the sponsor, patron, or president of a tournament of this type, he organized the program and provided two sets of prizes. One went to the successful contestant in each match, and the other to those adjudged as deserving special distinction for their gallant appearance and dexterity, for the most ingenious costume or elaborate float presented on the occasion, for the most brilliant marksmanship in piercing the ring, and, finally, for the cleverest bit of verse painted on the ornamented placard that each competitor bore. The awarding of these general prizes was the concluding event of the program.

By a *cartel*, or poster, ceremoniously tacked upon a conspicuous tree or other prominent place several days in advance of the tournament the *mantenedor*, or sponsor, announced that he and a companion were prepared to meet all comers or challengers, technically known as *aventureros*, who might wish to try their skill against them in a Joust of the Ring. Those who chose to enter the lists were obliged to put up prizes of their own which went to the *mantenedor* or his assistant if either of the latter won the match; on the other hand, if the challengers won, they would take the trophy provided by the patron. All awards were made by duly appointed *jueces*, or umpires, though often the prizes for general excellence, bestowed as the final act of the tournament, were left to the arbitrament of the feminine onlookers. Besides the prizes which the *aventureros* must offer, they were also obligated to appear in mask and costume as part of a pageant or an original skit. Ordinarily, the inviting host specified the rules to govern the contests, and the entrants indicated their acceptance of the conditions thus imposed by signing their names in the space allotted for this purpose on the *cartel*. It was the fashion to enter the lists under a fictitious title, usually taken from chivalric literature, such as "The Knight of the Flaming Sword." The masquerade which each contender organized usually represented some legendary hero, pagan god, abstract virtue or vice, or more or less allegorical figure, with the accompaniment of attendants suitably arrayed and a decorated float; an indispensable element of this bizarre equipment was a placard indicating the identity of his *invención* in a few neatly worded verses. These collateral features transformed the simple contests of skill in piercing the *sortija* into a carnivallike pageant which doubtless delighted the assembled guests even more than the exhibitions of manual and equestrian dexterity.

The regulations of these tournaments set forth in the *cartel* varied considerably according to the whim or inclination of the sponsor. They stipulated, for example, that the *mantenedor* was free to lengthen or shorten the fiesta in accordance with the number of entries, the minimum number of the *aventureros* necessary, and the value of the prizes which the latter must offer to enter the lists; those who came without previously signing the *cartel* were debarred from participation until all the official entrants had competed, unless the failure of one or more to appear made substitutions desirable; and the contestant whose foot slipped out of his stirrup, who dropped his reins, or tangled his spurs, was declared ineligible for the prize; instead, he was usually awarded a tumbler or pitcher of water to drink as a sort of booby prize. If a competitor's lance glanced over the top of the ring support, he could not try again unless some compassionate damsel in the stand, designated by the *mantenedor*, deigned to grant the unlucky marksman the boon of her permission. *Aventureros* wishing to demonstrate their skill in more than one match in the tournament were required to present themselves on succeeding occasions in completely different disguises and *tableaux*. Such, then, were typical conditions imposed by the organizers of these courtly exhibitions.[14]

Ushered in by a fanfare of trumpets the patron of the tournament and his aide, brightly attired and cavorting on spirited and gaily caparisoned mounts, appear before the assembled guests with a placard in verse heralding their willingness to meet any contenders in a trial of skill. After further ceremonious flourishes the pair advance to the umpire's platform and orally announce their purpose. Presently the first challenger presents himself in mask and costume, bearing a sign with the *letra*, or short stanza, explaining his impersonation. When he and his attendants have played their carnival role, the *mantenedor* and he take their places, on horseback and with poised lance, on the predetermined line, and each in turn digs spurs into the flank of his mount and charges at the target. Three times this operation is repeated, and the one scoring best in the judgment of the umpires is awarded the prize of the other. Imitating the chivalrous practices of the medieval knightly jousts, the winner gallantly bestows the trophy won by his prowess upon a lady seated on the platform reserved for her sex. In measured succession all the *aventureros*, now competing with the *mantenedor* and now with his assistant, repeat the same ceremonious pattern with variations until the panel is complete.

This program is usually timed to end at sunset, when the judges

summon the *mantenedor* to bring forth his prizes for the special
distinctions of the tournament. The evaluating of the best performances in marksmanship and in the masquerade customarily lay
within the province of the umpires, but the selection of the contestant making the most gallant appearance in the matches and composing the wittiest verses for his placard—these brief metrical effusions were sometimes regarded as the *pièce de résistance* of the banquet of entertainments—was graciously left to the vote of the ladies
in the audience. Most pleasing to masculine vanity was the designation as the most *galán*, since this distinction indicated that he was
the most pleasing in the eyes of the opposite sex. Moreover, the
award was frequently a handsome, gilded sword, though sometimes
he was given a beautifully decorated mirror in which he might
behold his own triumphant charm. For the most ingenious and
original *invención*, as the pageant tableau was called, the prize might
be a light lance or, perhaps, a gold chain, or similar object. The best
marksman of the tournament became the possessor of a golden ring
symbolizing the nature of his skill, while the most inspired placard
verse was rewarded with a plume of peacock feathers or a delicate
jewel. The giving of these awards concluded the program of entertainment.

It was in such a spectacle that Don Quixote and his trusty squire
made their first visual appearance in the land of the Incas and, quite
probably, in the New World, late in the year of 1607. By some odd
quirk of fortune that eccentric idealist, which Cervantes' genius had
so recently created, chose to manifest himself in the flesh for apparently the first time in the ultramarine possessions of Spain in a
highland plain of Peru as desolate and as bleak as the terrain of his
own dismal La Mancha in the Peninsula. As already noted, the historical personage directly responsible for this curious happening
was the otherwise unimportant individual, Don Pedro de Salamanca,
one time *corregidor* of the mining community at Pausa. Possibly it
was his addiction to the chivalric and pastoral fiction of the day,
conveniently supplied by itinerant book-peddlers such as Juan de
Sarria, *hijo*, that suggested a pageantlike *juego de sortija* to him as
an appropriate way to honor the appointment of the new viceroy
at Lima. And perhaps it occurred to him that, if a descriptive ac-

count of the occasion reached that lofty servant of the king, the result of presenting a fashionable *divertissement* of this sort might prove personally very advantageous indeed. At any rate Don Pedro de Salamanca carefully organized these festivities which took place, apparently, in the late spring of 1607, that is, owing to the reversed seasons of that part of the world, in October or November. Enlisting the aid of others in the small community and inviting guests from round about, the *corregidor* brought a bright touch of medieval color and magnificence to the drab settlement in the Andean Sierra.

The function was inaugurated by the time-honored custom of posting the *cartel* in the village square under a canopy of crimson velvet, a ceremony in which forty costumed horsemen participated. This ritualistic announcement of the jousts occurred ten days in advance of the date set to *correr la sortija*, and during this period nine *aventureros* affixed their signatures in the proper place, thus indicating their intention of competing for the prizes. Each one had adopted a picturesque pseudonym, many of which were of easily recognizable provenance. Those listed were "The Fortunate Knight," "The Knight of the Sad Countenance," "Stout Bradaleon," "Belfloran," "The Antartic Knight of Luzissor," "The Dreaded Madman," "The Knight of the Woods," "The Knight of the Dark Cave," and "The Gallant Gentleman of Contumeliano."

At the appointed hour on the tenth day Don Pedro de Salamanca, as the *mantenedor* who now termed himself "The Knight of the Flaming Sword," opened the tournament proper. With a flourish of trumpets, cymbals, and flageolets he entered the enclosure, clad in black raiment trimmed with gold and wearing a hat with a long, waving plume. He was mounted on a spirited horse with a pearl-studded saddle and before him rode an escort of a dozen horsemen, while at his side were four grooms in uniforms with yellow stripes. Accompanied by this impressive retinue, he paraded majestically about the suspended ring in the middle of the compound. Near this target was a table displaying the prizes of gleaming silver and, only a little distance from them, were three carpeted platforms. The ladies were seated on the one to the right, while the two on the left were occupied respectively by the three *jueces,* or umpires, and by various clergymen invited for this festive occasion. More plebian elements stood or squatted at a distance, forming a broken circle.

The *corregidor* of Pausa adopted a somewhat irregular procedure by playing two roles at his Joust of the Ring. Having first displayed himself as *mantenedor* before the admiring eyes of his guests, he dismissed his mounted entourage and alighted at a tent draped with figured silk and crimson velvet and pitched at one side of the enclosure. In a brief time he reëmerged in the guise of Stout Bradeleon, the first contender in the lists. By preconcerted arrangement Cristóbal de Mata, his aide, also appeared in an elaborate comic masquerade, doubtless intended to put the spectators in a happy mood at the outset. The theme of this carefully staged pageant was the common one of presenting the pagan god Bacchus surrounded by a swarm of votive disciples in varied states of inebriation. Don Cristóbal played his part with relish, appearing in the conventional garb of the tippler's divinity and astraddle of a huge cask made of wicker and trimmed with grapevines and an array of bloated wineskins, the whole carried on the backs of alcoholic devotees wearing gay caps with doctoral tassels attached to indicate their advanced degree in the baccanalian faculty. With a wreath of vine tendrils about his head, a measure in one hand, and in the other a tankard from which he poured out the wine to a swarm of reeling, howling, and laughing topers, this carnival Bacchus rode noisily about the compound to the delighted shrieks of the feminine onlookers and the benevolent smiles of the clergy. Wild-eyed Indians in gaudy costumes pounded drumlike tamborines and emitted shrill cries, thus adding to the hilarious din. If there was doubt in anyone's mind regarding the meaning of this frenzied scene, it was quickly effaced by the placard on the cask by which its chief actor confessed in meter that:

> I am Bacchus, the son of Venus,
> and he who avoids me,
> makes frigid himself and my mother.

When at length this merrymaking began to weary the onlookers, the *corregidor,* temporarily doffing his mantle as *mantene-*

dor for that of the *aventurero*, Stout Bradaleon, and his mate, Cristóbal de Mata, still in the role of Bacchus, took their positions at the designated line on horseback with lance in hand, and alternately they lunged at the hanging ring three times. Both contestants showed skill in these efforts, but the judges decided that the winner was Don Pedro, who bestowed his prize, with gallant diplomacy, on the wife of the visiting *corregidor* from the neighboring province of Condesuyo.

The incidents associated with the other matches need not be described since they are of the same general pattern. The leading magistrate of Pausa reassumed his office as *mantenedor*, and alternating with his companion, who kept the disguise of Bacchus, he met the various challengers, a number of whom united in a joint masquerade featuring card players and gamblers. Later there was a full-scale tableau simulating the splendor and the glory of the Inca civilization, enlivened by a series of songs and dances called *taquíes*. But the crowning event of this festive occasion was the very latest novelty from the homeland, the appearance of a new knight of chivalry who was fast laughing his famous predecessors out of existence. He was the chief protagonist of a mirth-provoking novel by a writer of some renown. If memory did not deceive, the rather funny title of the book, taken from its leading character, was *Don Quijote de la Mancha*, which individual, somewhere in its pages, dubbed himself "The Knight of the Sad Countenance." The local wit of Pausa, Luis de Gálvez, hailing originally from Córdoba, had entered the lists, it was known, under this humorous title, and the gathering awaited his entry with intense expectancy. The misadventures of the woeful knight were already a common topic of conversation among them and, because his impersonator on this occasion enjoyed something of a reputation locally as a comedian, the audience was sure that the most would be made of this new material.

It was well along in the afternoon of that day late in 1607 that the Don Quixote of popular imagination emerged from the pages of the novel to appear in person for the first time in an out-of-the-way corner of the world. Let the anonymous chronicler, as an eyewitness, relate in his own words this historic event in the literary annals of the New World.

At this juncture there appeared in the enclosure the Knight of the Sad Countenance, Don Quixote de la Mancha, depicted so naturally and so like his description in the book that it was an extraordinary pleasure to see him. He was mounted on a decrepit nag quite similar to his Rocinante, and was garbed in some very ancient hose, a rusty coat of mail, a helmet surmounted by a heavy plumage of rooster feathers, a collar nearly three inches high, and a mask giving a very real likeness. Accompanying him were the parish priest and the barber, appropriately clad as squires, the Princess Micomicona described in his narrative, and his faithful squire Sancho Panza, comically attired, astride his crudely saddled ass with well-stuffed saddlebags behind and the helmet of Manbrino. Sancho was serving as both a groom and a lance-bearer for his master, who was impersonated by a gentleman from Cordova renowned for his keen sense of humor, named Don Luis de Córdova, though known in these parts as Luis de Gálvez. At the time of these festivities he had come as a judge from Castrovirreina and now he presented himself in the enclosure, amidst gales of laughter from the onlookers, displaying his placard which read:

> 'I am the fearless Don Quixote
> who, though subject to misfortunes,
> is firm, and brave and bold.'

His squire, represented by a very witty fellow, requested permission of the judges for his master to compete in the *sortija* and, as his prize, offered a dozen strips of shammy-skin. Since he was so badly mounted and because the clumsiness was deliberate, his three lance thrusts went wide of the mark. The award, therefore, went to his opponent, the pagan god Bacchus who, with comic gallantry, presented his trophy to an old woman in the audience, a maidservant of one of the ladies present. Sancho then recited some witty couplets but, since they were a bit off-color, they are not recorded here.[15]

The afternoon still permitted time for three more *aventureros* to appear, each with his own *invención*, preceding the trial of skill with the *sortija*, until lengthening shadows brought the still incomplete festivities to a close. The final and indispensable act of bestowing the awards for special excellence in the tournament was illuminated by a multitude of torches fitfully dissolving the darkness which had descended upon the gay scene. While the ladies

through the generosity of the *corregidor* of Pausa, the umpires de-
were refreshed by a light repast served to them in this half-light
bated their decisions. The masquerades and everyone's participation
were so successful, the affable chronicler records, that fair judg-
ments were hard to reach. But they agreed unanimously that, for
fidelity of detail and the spontaneous laughter evoked by his representation, the Knight of the Sad Countenance clearly took the prize
for the best *invención* of the afternoon. On receiving this award,
which was four yards of purple satin, the impersonator of Don
Quixote, hugely enjoying his success, facetiously handed the rich
cloth to Sancho Panza with instructions to present it to Dulcinea
the next time that he was fortunate enough to see her. When the
remaining awards were distributed—on the *corregidor*, Don Pedro
de Salamanca, as *mantenedor*, the umpires tactfully conferred the
distinction of making the most attractive appearance of the occasion
—the festivities ended. As the unnamed reporter of the event put
it in concluding his account, "With this act the program came to a
close; it was so excellent that it might have taken place in Lima
itself. The only thing needed was a larger audience, but the quality
of the few ladies present amply compensated for the lack of
quantity." [16]

This curious description of a ring joust, held in the Altiplano
of Peru hardly more than a life span from the time that Pizarro's
conquering expedition first entered that region, offers striking evidence of the completeness with which social and cultural aspects of
contemporary Peninsular life were reproduced even in the most
outlying portions of the sprawling Spanish empire. But what is of
greater interest in this *relación*, which has so oddly survived the
passage of centuries, is the positive proof of the widespread reading
of Spain's creative writers in the most remote parts of the New
World. It bears witness not only to the universal diffusion of light
literature throughout the Spanish speaking world, but to the short-
ness of the time lag in its distribution. The pageantlike festivities
that Don Pedro de Salamanca organized in the mining camp of
Pausa, far removed from either Lima or Cuzco, clearly demonstrate
that, even in such raw surroundings, he or people of his acquaintance had firsthand knowledge of at least two currently popular
novels imported from the homeland. The recital of the events

which featured the *Corregidor's juego de sortija* at Pausa reveals
patent imitations of a similar diversion described at length in the
final pages of the widely read *El pastor de Fílida* by Luis Gálvez de
Montalvo. The comic tableau of Bacchus and his bibulous disciples,
for example, is of direct inspiration from this pastoral narrative, even
to the point of borrowing verses from it for the placards. And when
Don Luis de Gálvez (did he take his adopted name from the author
of the pastoral novel?), on receiving the prize for his highly successful impersonation of Don Quixote at Don Pedro de Salamanca's
ring joust, presented his trophy with mock gallantry to an aged
female servant sitting with her mistress among the guests, he was
merely emulating a similar act recounted in this same fictional work.

Of even more obvious inspiration on this occasion, of course,
was the masterpiece of Cervantes. First published less than three
years before, it supplied the theme for the prize-winning skit of the
Cordovan Luis de Gálvez in an obscure mining camp of Peru. And
the emphasis in this New World masquerade on the purely comic
aspects of Don Quixote and his squire reflects all too accurately the
contemporary failure in Spain itself to appreciate the profounder
meanings inherent in these chief protagonists. But this picturesque
incident, which served to relieve the monotony of existence in the
harsh and forbidding surroundings of the little community high in
the Andes, may well have been a by-product of the bookseller's
excursion into the Peruvian hinterland the year before. It may be
that one of Juan de Sarria's nine precious copies of the first edition
of *Don Quijote de la Mancha* had played a role in facilitating this
early American impersonation of Cervantes' immortal knight so
soon after the latter's appearance in the novel.

THE LITERARY LEGACY XX

Cortés, pizarro, balboa, alvarado, de soto, and Coronado—to pronounce these and many more names of the Spanish poets of action is to recite whole stanzas of the heroic epic of the westernization of the world. These sixteenth-century conquerors and explorers were the pioneers of a tremendous historical movement, beginning over four centuries ago, which has brought European civilization and technology to every part of the earth. Their exploits in the first stages of this vast process are legendary, and were performed despite a poverty of resources and a lack of technical aids such as were possessed by those who later carried forward their efforts. Columbus had but three clumsy caravels, of less than one hundred forty tons burden, with which to discover the Western Hemisphere, and Magellan was scarcely better equipped to circumnavigate the globe; Cortés, with four hundred soldiers and sixteen horses, conquered Mexico, while Orellana's small band crossed the Amazon jungle on its great waterway in improvised barks; and Cabeza de Vaca, with a bare handful of companions, survived disaster to wander through thousands of miles of unexplored country on foot and without the elementary necessities of existence. Almost the sole accouterments of all these adventurers were indomitable courage and will power. That generation of heroes were frontiersmen in time, in space, and in spirit. They lived on the borderland between the medieval and the modern ages, they struggled in the hidden depths of unknown continents, they fought along the front lines of clashing faiths and cultures. Though strongly conditioned by the ethical and collective traditions of the Middle Ages, they were men of action who incarnated the new Renaissance spirit of individualism; they were, in short, a dynamic blend of medieval superstition and modern curiosity. This amalgam of opposites seemed to fit them peculiarly for the historic mission of initiating the mighty task of Europeanizing the entire habitat of mankind. They combined a proselyting zeal with the crassest materialism, and in their stupendous enterprise they were men of iron dominated by an almost childlike credulity, which facilitated an acceptance of the marvelous, and inspired in them a romantic, almost poetic, vision of life. In their psychological drives they were not notably unlike their fellow Europeans, as pointed out in the first chapter, but in the subjective qualities of spirit and imagination the Spanish conquerors, momentarily at least, were sharply distinguished from their continental associates. The elements of exaltation and illusion in the spectacular subjugation of the New World by the Hispanic peoples gave an original and unique touch to the great saga of European expansion which the subsequent participation of other nations never quite equaled, a fact which makes the first chapter in the long annals of westward movement one of the most stirring. As a modern writer puts it, "imagination was the life-giving sap of the European world in America"[1] and, it may be added, this quality played a potent role in the rapid domination of vast new continents by a few thousand men in little more than two decades.

The visionary mind of the Conquistador, which endowed him with such unparalleled vigor, resulted from varied stimuli of recognizable and obscure origins. This is not the place, however, to attempt again to map the surface streams and the hidden springs which fed this subconscious pool of energy, and but one of its probable sources is here singled out for consideration. There can be little doubt that a factor in creating the fantastic illusion of the Conquest in the minds of so many participants was the multitude of fables, myths, and legends that so completely possessed their imaginations. It is not necessary to enter into the controversy about whether the strange notions of the Conquistador were inspired solely by the fancies of natives encountered in the New World, or only by the classical lore that he carried with him. The truth undoubtedly lies in a combination of both. A vague similarity of aboriginal themes to conceptions brought over caused certain beliefs, perhaps, to flourish more than others among the white invaders. This slight overlapping possibly explains the persistent quest of the Fountain of Youth, the Seven Enchanted Cities, the El Dorado and, notably, the Amazons. But, in general, the Spanish conquerors merely projected or superimposed their own myth-inspired inventions on the Indian fables and superstitions which came to them in garbled translation and in the poorly comprehended responses to their queries. The Europeans were the heirs of a wealth of medieval and classical legends transmitted by storytellers, through popular ballads and, now still more vividly and pervasively diffused, through the printed books so recently made accessible to them. By this last medium their minds were flooded with the magical lore of the Middle Ages, of the Orient, and of the ancient world, served up to them in old and new guises by enterprising writers of romances of chivalry, of sentimental novels, and of eerie tales. Imaginations thus surcharged easily accepted the marvelous and readily found confirmation of their wildest fancies in any rumor reaching their ears from whatever source. Light literature, then, was unconsciously helping to shape historic events, and it assuredly played an important, if a subjective and impalpable, role in this first act of the drama of expanding Western civilization. Moreover, the Conquistador's addiction to fiction brought the habit of secular reading to the remotest portions of the earth at the very moment that Occidental institutions and laws were transplanted there. Concurrently, and perhaps preceding the introduction of theological and religious literature for the spiritual conquest of these outlying regions, came the books of diversion for laymen.

By following hard on the heels of the invaders during the military phase of the Conquest, the merchants promptly supplied the demands for these goods, and after the rapid subjugation of the native populations the number of these tradesmen multiplied greatly to meet the growing requirements of adventurers and settlers pouring in from the Peninsula. In a short time booksellers in scattered parts of Spain were hustling the latest novelties from their presses to Seville in time to catch the annual *flotas* to the Indies, thus virtually eliminating the time lag for colonial readers thousands of miles away. Even a work published in Madrid or Zaragoza might reach Manila on the other side of the world in the same year of its printing, and residents of Mexico City might receive copies of it within a few months, even weeks. The brisk trade in books overseas was a lucrative monopoly that nullified the halfhearted efforts of Spanish monarchs, inspired by moralists and the clergy, to prohibit the exportation of lighter forms of literary expression which rendered the distinction between fact and fiction so hard for the Indian neophytes in their study of Castilian and Latin. Their Spanish masters would not be deprived of the company of their favorite writers and books by any royal whim! Historians have long been prone to put too much faith in written laws and to compose their learned treatises from such prohibitory legislation without troubling to investigate its effectiveness. This procedure is particularly unreliable in the case of the Spaniard whose extremely individualistic character begets a certain perversity by which he may bow superficially to authority but declines to obey it. This attitude is summed up in the well-known phrase, "*Obedezco, pero no cumplo.*" Hence the error of the long-standing conviction that the imperial decrees of the early sixteenth century, which were not aimed primarily at the white overlords, were successful in rigidly excluding the "lying histories" and profane literature generally from circulating in the Spanish colonies during the colonial centuries.

Nor was the Holy Office of the Inquisition, whose restrictive influence on the intellectual and cultural life of the viceroyalties has been grossly exaggerated, a serious bar to the relatively free distribution of secular books in those distant regions. The repressive activities of this censorious agency were largely limited to works formally listed on the *Index* or against which edicts had been subsequently issued. Rarely did these proscriptions operate against the creative literature which entertained the general reading public or against lay works of nonfiction. The Holy Office labored primarily to preserve what it fancied was the purity of the Catholic religion and morals against heresy and the schismatic influences of the Reformation, and if it took action against any work of profane letters, it did so because it detected there something regarded as subversive of the True Faith or of Christian morality. Toward many secular writings, whose ethical character was dubious, the Inquisition displayed remarkable indulgence, though occasionally, like all other human institutions, it was inconsistent.

Too much stress has been placed on the inquisitorial *visita* or inspection of incoming vessels in the ports of the New World as an effective means of debarring the entry of books into the vice-royalties. Its alleged efficiency has created the myth that all but approved religious books came into the colonies only as contraband. This police measure of the Holy Office was not directed at the literature of diversion or secular instruction but at the heretical writings of Lutheran and Protestant dissidents which it was charged to keep out. But even in this effort it hardly succeeded, owing to the evasion of Spanish merchants and pilots on the arriving fleets and to the carelessness and venality of its own agents at the ports of entry. And there is evidence that the directors of this secular arm of the Church were keenly sensitive to the loud complaints and sometimes vociferous protests of the merchants in the Peninsula and in the colonies against such interference with a gainful traffic in books. Again and again the inquisitorial inspectors were cautioned to exercise the utmost care in opening and closing the cases of goods examined on the incoming vessels so as not to provoke the ire of these businessmen. Clearly the Holy Office was not regarded, by some contemporaries at least, with the dread and awe with which posterity has invested it, and it is evident that, had the Crown or the Inquisition itself wished to seal off the New World possessions from the intellectual ideas and creative literature of Catholic Europe—which was not the purpose of either—the acquisitiveness of commercial elements would have thwarted this effort. That such obscurantism was not the intent of Peninsular authorities is amply confirmed by the unimpeachable documentary testimony of shipping invoices preserved at Seville and of inventories of books received found in the archives of the former colonies in America.

The demonstrated fact of the relatively unimpeded circulation of secular and entertaining literature during the sixteenth and seventeenth centuries in the Hispanic New World poses a number of questions. These enigmas doubtless account for the reluctance of many to accept the clear implications of the evidence presented and for the tendency to continue asserting that Spain imposed harsh restrictions on the intellectual life of its dependencies, particularly with respect to the distribution and reading of books. Why, for example, have almost none of these imported works of

fiction survived in modern Hispanic America? Why, if all the
writings of Spain's great literary age were available to its subjects
overseas, did they not stimulate a richer production of literature
in the former colonies? Why, if novels were so readily accessible
to book buyers in the viceroyalties, is there no authentic representative of this genre composed in America during the three centuries of Spanish domination? And what, if any, were the enduring
effects of the free circulation of books during this same period?
Satisfactory answers to these and other queries that might be made
require detailed investigations that lie outside the scope of this account, but some observations may be made.

At first glance, it would seem certain that, if the novels of
chivalry and other popular literature of the century of conquest
and later were shipped in such large numbers and were admitted
so readily into the Spanish Indies, surely a few copies of these early
editions would have escaped the ravages of time to offer their
corroboration. Yet it appears that, of those countless volumes
which crossed the ocean to stimulate and entertain the colonists,
not one has survived. A diligent search in the libraries and private
repositories of Spanish America forty years ago indicated a total
lack of early imprints of the great works representing the Golden
Age of Spanish literature. "Any book antedating 1700 is a *rara avis*
in these convents," was the substance of the report,[2] and even those
of the eighteenth century were infrequent. Since that time few if
any conventual or personal libraries have yielded such bibliographic
treasures, and the prospects for the future are scarcely more hopeful. What, then, was the fate of the thousands of novels, plays, and
collections of poetry which most certainly came into the hands of
the Conquistador and his descendants?

Most of the volumes of this literature of diversion were undoubtedly subjected to even harder wear than was the lot of those
that circulated in the Peninsula. As already suggested, the exiled
Spaniards and their American-born offspring must have welcomed
these artistic creations of Spanish genius which brought them something of the homeland, the sun of culture and civilization that
lighted their world. In the hearts of most the longing to return or
to visit Spain became a hope deferred, solaced only by these printed
transmitters of its spirit. Undoubtedly, these books passed from

hand to hand in the colonies and in time were thumbed out of existence. Indeed, this was the fate of nearly all the romances of chivalry in the Peninsula itself. Many of the shorter works, such as *Roberto el diablo*, *La doncella Teodor*, *Los Cavalleros Tablante de Ricamonte*, *El caballero Clamades*, reached colonial readers without covers in pamphlet form like the majority of the later comedies, and their life was inevitably brief. The slight respect in which authorities held this literature caused the destruction of many of the copies for the paper they contained, since a shortage of this commodity in the viceroyalties was chronic. Add to this the havoc of moisture, dust, and bookworms, the destruction by earthquakes, particularly in Lima, and the repeated inundations of Mexico City, the great center of viceregal culture, and it is not strange that none has survived, even in the larger cities and towns where a real reverence for books might be expected.

A consideration of the subsequent history of these countries of Spanish America will explain the disappearance of many books fortunate enough to outlast the earlier periods. The bitter struggle for independence, which was really a civil war, the succeeding turbulent revolutions, the flight of Spanish and Creole aristocratic families during and after the break with Spain, the destruction of public and private libraries, the secularization of convents and monasteries, the quartering of troops in these religious institutions and in other public buildings where records and books were preserved, all contributed most effectively to wipe out these cultural relics of the old order. When so few early editions survived in Spain itself, it is small wonder that these treasures of the bibliophile vanished so completely in the distant lands of Spanish speech where even greater political instability has been the rule.

Less easy to summarize are the reasons which account for the failure of a steady flow of books of nearly every kind from the Peninsula to stimulate a richer literature from the pens of colonial writers. It is well to recall at the outset, however, that if the cultivation of letters in the viceroyalties seems feeble, in quantity and quality it greatly exceeded the output of contemporary English and French settlements elsewhere in the Western Hemisphere. And if the inspiration of the inhabitants of early Spanish America was greatly inferior to that of the mother country, the difference was

far less extreme than in the case of the colonial dependencies of the
other European nations. The cultural dominance of the Peninsula
in the Hispanic New World was, of course, absolute, and literary
manifestations, as in the other subordinate areas of America, were
bound to be imitative there. More than elsewhere, however, the
creative spirits of the viceroyalties made important contributions to
the common culture of the motherland. In the sixteenth century,
long before the English settlements at Jamestown and Plymouth,
the best prose chronicles in the Spanish language were written by
men associated with the New World. These narratives began with
the conquistadors themselves. The famous *Letters of Cortes to
Charles V*, the *True history of the conquest of New Spain* by
Bernal Díaz del Castillo, the accounts of Cieza de León, and Agustín de Zárate relating the vanquishing of the Incan empire in Peru,
and many others, constitute a rich literature, to which must be
added the *Royal commentaries* of that first genuinely American
writer, El Inca Garcilaso de la Vega. *La Araucana*, by Alonso de
Ercilla, an active participant in the Conquest, is generally conceded
by critics to be the best historical poem in Castilian. Wholly inspired by the poet's experience in Chile, it was partly composed
there. Likewise produced in the viceroyalty of Peru was the best
religious epic in that language, *La Cristiada*, by Father Hojeda. In
the last half of the seventeenth century a Mexican Creole nun, Sor
Juana Inés de la Cruz, living out her days in a convent of the capital of New Spain, wrote the most inspired lyric verse of her time
in the Spanish-speaking world. These figures and their works made
colonial literature something more than a stunted branch of the
vigorous letters of the motherland, a fact which is explained, in
part at least, by the free circulation of books throughout the Spanish Indies and the consequently easy access that viceregal writers
had to the inspiration of the great literary spirits of Spain.

The abundance of printed works at hand could not alone, however, create an indigenous literature in the colonies. The Creoles
and other articulate members of society faced more serious obstacles, of a psychological and practical nature, to the development
of self-expression than the distance from Peninsular colleagues,
which was, to some extent, bridged by books. Temperamentally,
the descendants of the Conquistador were unsuited for the sustained

effort which the mastery of any art medium requires even in the gifted, and with rare exceptions they were content to be mere dilettantes. This defect of character stemmed largely from the social and cultural conditions of their environment and heritage. American-born whites and mixtures were, in large measure, denied participation in the governmental and ecclesiastical affairs of the viceroyalties, and the avenues to ambition were largely cut off since the highest offices in these realms invariably went to Peninsular Spaniards. The traditional attitudes of scorn toward manual labor and the monopolistic control of commerce in the hands of Europeans placed technical occupations beneath the dignity, and business activities beyond the reach, of the Creole landed gentry. Under these circumstances enforced idleness seemed an inescapable lot, and their lives were too often frittered away in frustration and vice. The cultivation of letters served merely as a personal adornment; even in Spain itself it was hardly a career. The low esteem in which the Creole elements were held by the hated newcomers, and the undeniable superiority of the creative spirits of Castile in all fields of art, engendered a profound sense of inferiority in these American-born descendants. Though their proud natures reacted passionately to this situation, its seeming hopelessness generated an apathy hardly conducive to persistent effort. Their literary exertions, therefore, were mainly limited to occasional verse, pretentious and shallow for the most part, and pompous prose which clothed its vacuousness in strained figures of speech and a latinized diction.

Even when a writer of talent and industry felt the urge to undertake a work of deeper significance and greater solidity, legal and economic difficulties were likely to hamstring him. For the publication of most manuscripts prepared in the colonies it was necessary to obtain a license from authorities in Spain. Aside from the long delay involved in fulfilling this requirement—and it frequently took years—the original work forwarded to the Peninsula was exposed to loss at sea in transit and the even greater hazards of bureaucratic red tape in the Council of the Indies. If, after this expense and trouble, the author was fortunate enough to secure the desired authorization while still living, he had the alternatives of hiring a Peninsular printer to publish his manuscript, or of bringing it back to a colonial print shop. If he chose the first arrangement, as was often the case, he had no check on its progress through the press or opportunity to read proof; if he decided on the second expedient, there were grave problems. Though the presses set up in the viceroyalties not infrequently produced admirable specimens of the typographical art, their function was essentially that of job printing for the communities they served. Originally established to assist the evangelical work of the missionaries by printing catechisms, primers, tracts, and similar literature, they also published more secular works, such as public notices, almanacs, descriptions of festivities, laudatory biographies of local celebrities, particularly clergymen, and occasionally books of genuine significance. The costs of printing, however, were prohibitive, a condition aggravated by a recurrent scarcity of paper, and only wealthy institutions and individuals could ordinarily commission the books which came off the colonial presses. When at last the determined and financially able Creole writer saw his work in print, sales were unlikely to reimburse him for his monetary expenditure, and his published literary effort invariably suffered in both price and esteem as it competed with the much preferred importations from Spain.[3]

These almost insuperable barriers do not necessarily reflect a hostile attitude on the part of the Crown toward the intellectual endeavors of its subjects overseas; rather, their continued existence responded more directly to the desire of Peninsular booksellers to protect a well-paying monopoly from colonial competition. The monarchs in Madrid, chronically hard pressed for revenue, dared not oppose the restrictive tendencies of its merchant class, and the Church generally chose not to antagonize that group. In the light of the severe handicaps that the writers and scholars in the colonies thus experienced, the quantity and quality of the literature of the period are remarkable. The tenacity and hardihood of the Creole authors to which this production testifies were, in some instances, stimulated by the very diffusion of Peninsular books among these colonial writers, who prepared many manuscripts which ultimately disappeared or have not yet been unearthed.

The preceding chapters have shown that the novel in its various forms regularly poured into the Spanish Indies throughout the sixteenth century and later. The romances of chivalry accompanied the first conquerors, and in the following decades these narratives came in almost incredible numbers. Well before their popularity had seriously waned the didactic fictions of Guevara, and particularly the sentimental and refined tales of shepherds and their lassies, had captured the fancy of an ever-widening audience. As the end of the century of expansion approached these artificial stories began to be slightly cloying to their readers and novels of a more realistic and satiric character appeared on the book lists with increasing frequency. *La Celestina, Lazarillo de Tormes* (in a subdued version), *Guzmán de Alfarache* and, finally, *Don Quijote de la Mancha*, magically combining the elements of the chivalric, the pastoral and the picaresque, almost crowd out the long-standing favorites. This uninterrupted streaming of novelistic literature into the colonies surely reflected a constant demand for this kind of reading entertainment, and it would seem that the presence of so many examples of this genre in private hands might have spurred some talented descendant of the Conquistador to essay a similar work. Colonial society already offered exploitable material for an imitation of the life stories of rogues so common in Spain. If there were such authors in any of the viceroyalties, no true novel of any sort is known which belongs to the three centuries of colonial literature.

The reasons set forth above to explain the relative paucity of viceregal letters are, of course, of equal application to the novel, a medium certainly calling for sustained effort, and possibly no further explanation is needed. One other factor, however, is generally thought to account for the low stature of colonial writing and the absence of novelistic literature. The Inquisition, which allegedly discouraged the circulation of books, is likewise accused of stifling all manifestations of intellectual life in the colonies, save that of orthodox theology, and, by its assumed vigilance, of excluding any echoes of the ideas then agitating contemporary Europe. Thus compelled to silence, so runs the theory, the imaginative colonial did not dare to write novels, stories, essays or histories, but took refuge in baroque prose and verse which substituted verbal virtuosity for content.[4]

It is not an inviting role to appear as an apologist of the Holy Office, particularly where so many impressions of this institution are conditioned by conceptions similar to those set forth in Edgar

Allan Poe's "The Pit and the Pendulum," but the glimpses of its operations noted in earlier chapters of this book suggest that the verdict of posterity on the Spanish Inquisition is harsher than the facts wholly warrant. To place so much of the blame for the lack of novels in the colonial era on this institution is to overlook the important fact that the greatest epoch of Spanish letters, the age that witnessed the flowering of the genius of Cervantes, Lope de Vega, and Calderón, coincides with the most vigorous period of the Holy Office in the Peninsula, and historians generally agree that its branches in the American colonies were much milder agencies than the parent organization in Spain. The inquisitors in Mexico City, Lima, Cartagena, and elsewhere, of course, shared the hostility of other ecclesiastics, moralists, and even secular leaders of thought against the universal practice of reading novels, but they took no drastic measures to stop the habit. It is abundantly clear that this form of fiction continued to be read everywhere in the Indies as in Spain itself. The negative attitude of Spanish humanism toward this special kind of creative writing was based on a purely intellectual concept of the mission of literature. To great thinkers like Vives, dominated by an ethical pragmatism, fiction was valid only when it served objective truth. In a word, it must be instructive. Rather than entertain idly, it should enlighten, it should bear witness to the validity of moral values. Hence the long disquisitions on proper conduct, which now seem so tedious, in the picaresque novels. Clearly, the romances of chivalry and the pastoral narratives served none of these didactic purposes; their appeal was purely emotional and even erotic, and they taught no moral. Their popularity therefore aroused the bitter antagonism of such humanists towards all manifestations of this literary genre.[5] The clergy and the moralists, however, rarely had recourse to the agencies at hand for suppression—the *Index of prohibited books* and the Inquisition—however vehement and impassioned their denunciations. This is a fact to be kept constantly in mind. The few fictional works officially proscribed by these means were often seemingly innocuous tales and some that were deliberately concocted as antidotes and with the express purpose of undermining the enthusiasm for the very literature that so sorely irked the humanists. Spanish authors of the Golden Age doubtless felt themselves somewhat inhibited by the uncompromising opposition of the clergy and the ever-present possibility that their work might run afoul of the censorship of the Holy Office. Like the Creole nun Sor Juana Inés de la Cruz, in her famous letter to the Bishop of Puebla, they wanted no rumpus (*ruido*) with the Inquisition, but whatever apprehension these writers may have experienced, it was not sufficient to paralyze their inspiration, and from their pens came some of the greatest works of their time.

The failure to cultivate the novel in colonial literature results from a number of causes, but the most important was not the repressive influence of the Holy Office. A more direct factor, in all probability, was the commercial and economic pressure exerted by Peninsular dealers. Why should colonial writers be encouraged in any way when those of Spain were in such great demand everywhere? Peninsular presses could hardly keep up a supply of the editions required of the home-grown authors, and profits were very satisfying. But of greater significance was the fact that, shortly after the beginning of the seventeenth century, the novel as a popular medium gave way to a reading vogue of an entirely different sort. Coinciding with the introduction of *Don Quijote de la Mancha* into the colonies late in the year 1605 there appeared the first of the published collections of Lope de Vega's comedies called *Partes*. These three-act plays were the most characteristic products of Spain's *siglo de oro* and, as the dramatic writings of other playwrights took form in print, they soon supplanted the bulky prose narratives in the popular affection. Shorter in length, cheaper in price, and more flexible and varied in the delight afforded by its dialogued verse, this dramatic literature not only became the preferred reading of all, in the colonies as well as in Spain, but it influenced contemporary customs, manners, and habits of speech. The novel continued to be read but its sixteenth-century appeal was gone, and as a literary form it declined in Spain perceptibly. In the viceroyalties, where public taste so closely and so promptly reflected that of the homeland, the incentive for undertaking long narratives disappeared completely. Those descendants of the Conquistador who felt an urge to create fiction turned to the theater as an outlet.

Though the colonial letters of Spanish America failed to include an authentic novel, they did present numerous examples of what might be conveniently termed prose with novelistic elements. In general, such works were ostensibly composed with a didactic purpose. These narratives frequently made use of devices characteristic of fiction, such as anecdotes, intercalated incidents more or less relevant, and dialogues, supplied by the writer's imagination. Many works fall more or less into this category, and the contemporary influence on them of the novels and plays so readily accessible to the colonial authors is unmistakable. In some instances the narrative so closely approximates a novel that it may be regarded as the precursor of the later development of that genre in Spanish American literature. The inspiration of the chivalric romances is not as evident as other novelistic forms, perhaps, though the verve and the descriptions of certain events in Bernal Díaz del Castillo's *True history*, such as the battle of Otumba where a handful of Spaniards allegedly routed a horde of two hundred thousand Aztec warriors, are reminiscent of the chronicles of Amadis with which that soldier-author was familiar.[6] More easily detected is the influence of the Dianas and other pastoral fiction in such rudimentary novels as the *Siglo de oro en las selvas de Erífile* (1608) of Bernardo de Balbuena, and the *Sigueros de la Virgen* of Francisco Bramón (1621).

Much less artificial and closer to Spanish genius were the picaresque novels with their satiric sketches of types and customs, and the reflection of these episodic narratives is more apparent in colonial writings. A fairly large number of works produced in widely separated parts of the Hispanic New World betray their filiation. *El cautiverio feliz* of Francisco Núñez de Pineda Bascuñán (1607-1682), for example, vividly recounts the author's life as a captive among the Araucanian Indians, but the work, like Mateo Alemán's *Guzmán de Alfarache*, is marred by tiresome moral reflections and other irrelevant matter. *El Carnero* of Juan Rodríguez Freile (1636) is a gossipy chronicle of seventeenth-century Bogotá replete with tales of witchcraft, the sardonic humor of soldier-rogues, and spicy love stories mingled with pedantic theological allusions. And the *Infortunios de Alonso Ramírez* (1690) by Sigüenza y Góngora, relating the misadventures of a Puerto Rican's journey around the world, is a short work sometimes regarded as

the forerunner of the Mexican novel. Still other narratives that
found their way into print could be cited but the list may be closed
with a reference to *El periquillo sarniento* of Fernández de Lizardi
(1816) which, appearing at the end of the colonial period, is the
first work to merit the distinction of being called a novel and bears
an unmistakable relationship to the Spanish picaresque tradition.
Clearly, none of these curious works was written in isolation from
contemporary and earlier literary influences of Spain, and all plainly
reveal the inspiration of Peninsular works which came to the
colonies through the unhampered circulation of books brought
by the profit-minded enterprise of merchants on both sides of the
Atlantic.

The last of the questions raised regarding the importation of
secular and fictional literature into colonial Hispanic America concerns the enduring effects of this diffusion of literary culture on
the Conquistador's descendants in those parts today. So much time
has elapsed and so many later influences have been at work that the
determination of the heritage left by these early transmitters of
ideas is a difficult undertaking. Such an investigation goes beyond
the limits of this book, which seeks only to demonstrate the reality
of the circulation of printed works in the sixteenth-century New
World. A few comments are offered, however, to indicate that the
dissemination of printed literature throughout the Spanish-speaking
world of that period is not of purely antiquarian interest.

The Spanish empire of the House of Austria was essentially a
Romanized empire. It did not content itself with merely acquiring
colonies useful for the economic aggrandizement and political prestige of the mother country but, following the great example of
Rome, it sought to give to the subjugated inhabitants of the conquered lands its own institutions, culture, religion, and language;
it strove to incorporate subject peoples into the body politic and
social of the ruling portion of the empire. Spain wished to His-
paniolize the vanquished Indians, ultimately to transform them
into citizens of the great commonwealth and liegemen of the
Crown, enjoying equal rights with all other subjects. Hence the
remarkable efforts of the first decades after the Conquest to
Christianize the aborigines, teach them Latin and Castilian, and
train them in the arts and crafts of Western civilization. Despite

the glaring shortcomings of this vast endeavor, of which jealous rival nations have made too much, Spain established in an incredibly brief time, considering the transportation and communication facilities of the age, an extraordinary unity among the widely dispersed regions it occupied, a unity of customs, culture, and language which remains virtually intact to the present day. The printed books that poured into these areas in increasing quantities from the Conquest on contributed in no small measure to this unification of the Spanish American mind and spirit. The New World colonies of Spain were a vast school in which all pupils read the same texts and were stimulated by the same ideas and ideals coming to them through these channels. Throughout the length and breadth of the continents the ways of thinking, of feeling, and of imagining had an identical source, a common storehouse of legends, myths, themes, and ideas which were drawn upon in the invention of local stories, ballads, and diversions. This collective fund was the medieval and renaissance lore of Catholic Europe, brought from the earliest times by the printed page as well as by oral means and passed from mouth to mouth among the unlettered. This universal patrimony of even such widely separated communities of Hispanic America as, for example, New Mexico in the United States and Tucumán in Argentina, is demonstrated again and again by the discovery of parallel folkloric themes, fables, and riddles in the traditions and popular verse of the humble descendants of the Conquistador. And some of these curious survivals show unmistakable evidence of inspiration by the chivalric literature of the sixteenth century. Spain was clearly the door through which passed these and so many other literary motifs of Europe and Asia noted in the primitive poetry of remote areas of Spanish America. As one investigator declares: "However inadequate the analysis of the book lists on the ship registers, we see that the collections of verse thus brought to the New World are the very ones of whose contents we find vestiges in the oral tradition of Tucumán, and surely all America as well."[7]

The unobstructed circulation of practically all books, save those of Protestant heresy, of course, was an effective aid in implanting the language of Castile as the universal idiom of Spanish America.

The lands discovered by Columbus were regarded as the property of the Crown of the central provinces of the Peninsula and hence the speech of that part of Spain rather than others became the official medium of communication. The enthusiastic reading of fiction books in Castilian throughout the New World possessions of Spanish monarchs served to implement this linguistic policy and to restrict the adulteration of the common language by the regional dialects of nationals from other parts of the mother country who, in time, were permitted to emigrate to the American colonies. With relatively slight modifications this particular form of Spanish remains basically the generalized medium of expression of the modern Central and South American republics, except Brazil. Among uneducated inhabitants of these countries today, especially those living in isolated parts, the continued use of archaic syntactical constructions, words, and phrases furnishes a living record of the speech habits brought by the Conquistador, and many of these peculiarities can be traced to the romances of chivalry and other popular literature familiar to those early adventurers and first settlers.[8]

In other ways the chivalric and sentimental novels, which constituted so large a part of the sixteenth-century reading fare, have left their mark in Spanish America four centuries later. In a previous chapter it was suggested that the ceremonious courtesy still characterizing the cultured representatives of the Spanish-speaking world on both sides of the Atlantic may stem in part from the influence of chivalric ideals which came through the tales of knight-errantry and possibly the pastoral novels. This literary vogue, lasting more than a century, did not end abruptly in the laughter which Cervantes' masterpiece evoked. In the years following Don Quixote's appearance on the scene many of these romantic narratives held a place in private libraries, and the idylls of shepherds and their lassies, the *Dianas* and the *Galateas*, were still a part of the reading of cultivated gentlemen to the very end of the colonial age.[9]

The chivalric tale of greatest longevity in Spanish America was, apparently, the *Historia de Carlomagno y los doce pares*, of French origin. Its first edition dates from 1525 at least, and references to it by members of conquering and exploring expeditions are reported soon thereafter. And the schoolmaster of *El periquillo sarniento*, the action of which novel takes place in the late eighteenth century, warned his pupils, it will be recalled, against reading this particular book, thus testifying to its prolonged popularity. Recently a folklorist of Tucumán, Argentina found very old editions of this story in many houses in the country districts of that province. "In our travels in search of *cantares*," he reports, "we have had occasion to meet around a hundred persons of whom might be stated what Don Leopoldo Lugones said concerning an old man in his *Guerra Gaucha:* 'In 20,000 nights he had read with unwearied enthusiasm one single book, *The history of Charlemagne and the twelve peers of France.*' "[10] A distinguished student of folklore in Puerto Rico likewise designates this romance of chivalry as the one of widest influence and states that "in cheap editions it has been reprinted and sold so much in Spain and in all countries of Spanish speech that, even at the present time and in the humblest shacks in Puerto Rico, copies of this novel could be found."[11] Themes, incidents, and characters of this narrative recur again and again in the conversations of older people in many parts of Spanish America who were nurtured by it, and in the folk ballads which they still recite. And in the same kind of popular poetry handed down from one generation to another in Mexico, Chile, Peru, Argentina, and Puerto Rico there are identifiable motifs likewise found in the classical literature of Spain such as *La Celestina* and *Guzmán de Alfarache*. Still others of an amatory, religious, picaresque, and even obscene character betray a recognizable filiation from earlier Castilian works, thus establishing a link between the medieval and renaissance literary traditions of the past with those of today among unsophisticated inhabitants of Spanish America.[12] In a somewhat tenuous fashion these survivals bear witness to the early circulation of books in colonial times.

These vestigial remnants of an age long past are rapidly disappearing; in another generation they may have vanished. Though incomplete, fragmentary, and dispersed, like the *registros* of book shipments to the New World which point to one of their original sources of inspiration, these humble literary descendants, like the simple, uncultivated people who transmit them, are the posterity which testify to the existence of illustrious progenitors. Spain, in the period of its political and cultural grandeur, did not give merely her men in the pioneer task of bringing much of the New World into the light of Western civilization, but something more enduring; she gave generously those symbols of her creative genius— her books.

BIBLIOGRAPHY

A BRIEF BIBLIOGRAPHY

The books and articles listed here constitute an introduction to the subject. For additional material, see the References which follow.

Bataillon, Marcel, *Érasme et L'Espagne. Recherches sur l'histoire spirituelle du XVIe siécle* (Paris, 1937).

Bayle, Constantino, S.J., *El dorado fantasma* (Madrid, 1943).

Blanco-Fombona, Rufino, *El conquistador español del siglo XVI* (Madrid, 1922).

Blom, Franz (ed.), *R. P. Tomás de la Torre, Desde Salamanca, España, hasta Ciudad Real. Diario de viaje, 1544-1545* (Mexico City, 1945).

Bonilla y San Martín, Adolfo, *Luis Vives y la filosofía del Renacimiento* (Madrid, 1929; 2 vols.).

————, *Libros de caballerías* (Madrid, 1907-1918; 2 vols.).

Carreño, Alberto M. (ed.), *Gonzalo Gómez de Cervantes. La vida económica y social de Nueva España al finalizar el siglo XVI* (Mexico City, 1944).

Cartas de Indias (Madrid, 1877).

Castro y Bravo, F. de, *Las naos españolas* (Madrid, 1927).

Cejador y Frauca, Julio, *Historia de la lengua y literatura castellana* . . . (Madrid, 1915-1922; 14 vols.).

Colección de documentos inéditos para la historia de España (Madrid, 1842-1895; 112 vols.).

Diffie, Bailey, *Latin American civilization: colonial period* (Harrisburg, Pa., 1945).

Fernández de Castillejo, Federico, *La ilusión en la conquista* (Buenos Aires, 1945).

Fernández del Castillo, Francisco, *Libros y libreros en el siglo XVI* (Mexico City, 1914).

Fernández Duro, Cesáreo, *La armada española* (Madrid, 1895-1903; 9 vols.).

Furlong, Guillermo, S. J., *Bibliotecas argentinas durante la dominación hispánica* (Buenos Aires, 1944).

Gandia, Enrique de, *Historia crítica de los mitos de la conquista americana* (Buenos Aires, Madrid, 1927).

García, Genaro, *Documentos inéditos o muy raros para la historia de México* (Mexico City, 1905-1911; 35 vols.).

García Icazbalceta, Joaquín, *Documentos para la historia de México* (Mexico City, 1858-1866; 2 vols.).

————, *Bibliografía mexicana del siglo XVI* (Mexico City, 1886).

Gayangos, Pascual de, *Libros de caballerías*, in *Biblioteca de autores españoles* (Madrid, 1931).

Gestoso y Pérez, José, *Noticias inéditas de impresores sevillanos* (Seville, 1924).

Green, Otis H., and Irving A. Leonard, "On the Mexican book trade in 1600: a chapter in cultural history," *Hispanic Review*, vol. 9 (1941), pp. 1-40.

Hamilton, Earl J., "Wages and subsistence on Spanish treasure ships, (1503-1660)," *Journal of Political Economy*, vol. 37 (1929), pp. 430-450.

Hanke, Lewis, "The development of regulations for conquistadors," in *Contribuciones para el estudio de la Historia de América. Homenaje al Dr. Emilio Ravignani* (Buenos Aires, 1941).

Haring, Clarence H., *Trade and navigation between Spain and the Indies* (Cambridge, 1918).

———, *The Spanish Empire in America* (New York, 1947).

Icaza, Francisco A. de, *El "Quijote" durante tres siglos* (Madrid, 1918).

Jones, Tom B., "The classics in colonial Hispanic America," *Transactions of the American Philological Association*, vol. 70 (1939), pp. 37-45.

Lanning, John Tate, *Academic culture in the Spanish colonies* (New York, 1940).

Lea, Henry Charles, *The Inquisition in the Spanish dependencies* (New York, 1908).

Lee, Bertram T., and H. C. Heaton, *The discovery of the Amazon according to the account of Friar Gaspar de Carvajal* (New York, American Geographical Society, 1934).

Leonard, Irving A., *Romances of chivalry in the Spanish Indies with some registros of shipments of books to the Spanish colonies* (Berkeley, 1933).

———, "Best sellers of the Lima book trade, 1583," *Hispanic American Historical Review*, vol. 22 (1942), pp. 5-33.

———, "*Don Quixote* and the book trade in Lima, 1606," *Hispanic Review*, vol. 8 (1940), pp. 285-304.

———, "On the Cuzco book trade, 1606," *Hispanic Review*, vol. 9 (1941), pp. 359-375.

———, "*Guzmán de Alfarache* in the Lima book trade, 1613," *Hispanic Review*, vol. 11 (1943), pp. 210-220.

———, "Conquerors and Amazons in Mexico," *Hispanic American Historical Review*, vol. 24 (1944), pp. 561-579.

———, "One man's library, Manila, 1583," *Hispanic Review*, vol. 15 (1947), pp. 84-100.

Lohmann Villena, Guillermo, *El arte dramático en Lima durante el virreinato* (Madrid, 1945).

Madariaga, Salvador de, *The rise of the Spanish American empire* (New York, 1947).

Maudslay, A. P. (tr.), *Bernal Díaz del Castillo. The true history of the conquest of New Spain* (London, The Hakluyt Society, 1908-1916).

Means, Philip Ainsworth, *Fall of the Inca Empire* (New York, 1932).

Medina, José Toribio, *Escritores americanos celebrados por Cervantes en el Canto de Calíope* (Santiago de Chile, 1926).

————, *Biblioteca Hispano-Americana* (Santiago de Chile, 1898-1907; 7 vols.).

————, *Historia del tribunal del Santo Oficio de la Inquisición en México* (Santiago de Chile, 1905).

Menéndez y Pelayo, Marcelino, *Orígenes de la novela* (Madrid, 1905-1915; 4 vols.).

————, *Historia de los heterodoxos españoles* (Madrid, 1911-1932; 7 vols.).

Montesinos, Fernando, *Anales del Perú* (Madrid, 1906; 2 vols.).

Núñez Cabeza de Vaca, Álvar, *Naufragios y comentarios* (Buenos Aires, Mexico City, Colección austral, No. 304, 1942).

Pacheco y Cárdenas, *Colección de documentos inéditos de descubrimientos, conquistas . . . en América y Oceanía* (Madrid, 1864-1884; 42 vols.).

Paso y Troncoso, Francisco del, *Epistolario de Nueva España* (Mexico City, 1939-1942; 16 vols.).

Pereyra, Carlos, *Las huellas de los conquistadores* (Madrid, 1942).

Pérez Pastor, Cristóbal, *Bibliografía madrileña* (Madrid, 1898-1907; 3 vols.).

————, *La imprenta en Medina del Campo* (Madrid, 1895).

————, *La imprenta en Toledo* (Madrid, 1887).

Portillo y Díez de Sollano, Álvaro de, *Descubrimientos y exploraciones en la costa de California* (Madrid, 1947).

Putnam, George Haven, *Censorship of the Church of Rome* (New York, 1906-1907; 2 vols.).

Putnam, Ruth, and Herbert I. Priestley, *California: The name* (Berkeley, 1917).

Quesada, Vicente Gaspar, *La vida intelectual en la América española durante los siglos XVI, XVII y XVIII* (Buenos Aires, 1910).

Raleigh, Sir Walter, *Discovery of Guiana* (London, Hakluyt Voyages, vol. 7, 1927).

Recopilación de leyes de Indias (Madrid, 1756; 4 vols.).

Rodríguez Marín, Francisco, *El "Quijote" y Don Quijote en América* (Madrid, 1911).

Rodríguez Prampolini, Ida, *Amadises de América. La hazaña de Indias como empresa caballeresca* (Mexico City, 1948).

Rodríguez Villa, Antonio, *El emperador Carlos V y su corte, según las cartas de D. Martín de Salinas, embajador del infante D. Fernando (1522-1539)* (Madrid, 1903).

San Martín, Juan de, y Alonso de Lebrija, *Relación del descubrimiento y conquista del nuevo reino de Granada, años 1536 a 1539* (Madrid, Sociedad de bibliófilos españoles, 1916).

Schevill, Rudolph, "La novela histórica, las crónicas de Indias, y los libros de caballerías," *Revista de Indias* (Bogotá), época 2ª, Nos. 59-60 (1943), pp. 173-196.

Serrano Redonnet, Antonio E., "Prohibición de libros en el primer sínodo santiagueño (Tucumán)," *Revista de filología hispánica*, vol. 5 (1943), pp. 162-166.

Spence, Lewis, *Legends and romances of Spain* (New York, 1920).

Taylor, Paul S., "Spanish seamen in the New World," *Hispanic American Historical Review*, vol. 5 (1922), pp. 631-661.

Teitelboim, Volodia, *El amanecer del capitalismo y la conquista de América* (Santiago de Chile, 1943).

Thomas, Henry, *Spanish and Portuguese romances of chivalry* (Cambridge University Press, 1920).

————, "The output of Spanish books in the sixteenth century," *The Library* (London, Sept. 1, 1920), pp. 69-94.

Ticknor, George, *History of Spanish literature* (New York, 1854; 3 vols.).

Torre Revello, José, *El libro, la imprenta, y el periodismo en América durante la dominación española* (Buenos Aires, 1940).

————, *La fundación y despoblación de Buenos Aires (1536-1541)* (Buenos Aires, 1937).

————, *Orígenes de la imprenta y su desarrollo en América Española* (Buenos Aires, 1940).

————, "Merchandise shipped by the Spaniards to America (1534-1586)," *Hispanic American Historical Review*, vol. 23 (1943), pp. 773-781.

Veitia Linaje, José de, *Norte de contratación de las Indias occidentales* (Seville, 1672).

Velasco Ceballos, Rómulo, *La alfabetización en la Nueva España* (Mexico City, 1945).

Zárate, Agustín de, *Historia del descubrimiento y conquista de la provincia del Perú . . .*, in *Biblioteca de autores españoles* (Madrid, 1862), vol. 26, pp. 459-574.

Zepeda Rincón, Tomás, *La instrucción pública en la Nueva España en el siglo XVI* (Mexico City, 1933).

REFERENCES

REFERENCES

CHAPTER I

1. Washington Irving, *The life and voyages of Christopher Columbus to which are added those of his companions* (New York, 1860; 3 vols.), vol. 3, introduction, p. xv.

2. Bartolomé de las Casas, *Brevísima relación de la destrucción de las Indias* (abridged edition of the *Biblioteca enciclopédica popular*, 77, Mexico City, 1945), paragraph 16.

3. W. G. Gosling, *Life of Sir Humphrey Gilbert* (London, 1911), quoted in Howard Mumford Jones, *Ideas in America* (Cambridge, 1944), p. 243, note 32.

4. Jones, *op. cit.*, p. 54.

5. *Ibid.*

6. Arnold J. Toynbee, *A study of history* (abridgement by D. C. Somervell, New York and London, 1947), p. 413.

7. Of interest in this connection are the comments of J. Bayard Morris in the introduction to his translation of *Hernán Cortés, Five Letters* (London, 1928), p. xxxiii:

Between the Spaniards who conquered the New World and the buccaneering Englishmen of Elizabeth's reign who successfully robbed them of a large portion of its spoils there was indeed little to choose. The methods of Cortés in Mexico differed little from those adopted by the English in North America, in India and in New Zealand during the succeeding centuries. . . .

8. Sir Walter Raleigh, *The history of the world* (London, 1786; 2 vols.), vol. 2, p. 575.

9. See Salvador de Madariaga, *Christopher Columbus, being the life of the very magnificent Lord, Don Cristobal Colón* (New York, 1940), p. 80; Samuel E. Morison, *Admiral of the Ocean Sea, a life of Christopher Columbus* (Boston, 1942; 2 vols.), vol. 1, p. 76.

10. See Emma H. Blair and James A. Robertson (ed.), *The Philippine Islands, 1493-1803* (Cleveland, 1903-1909; 55 vols.), vol. 33, pp. 27-29.

11. Irving, *op. cit.*, p. xii. A more traditional interpretation of the Spanish conqueror is given in Rufino Blanco-Fombona, *El conquistador español del siglo xvi* (Madrid, 1922), *passim*.

CHAPTER II

1. One of the best discussions of the Spanish chronicle is that of George Ticknor, *History of Spanish literature* (New York, 1854; 3 vols.), vol. 1, chaps. 8, 9, 10.

2. See Julio Cejador y Frauca, *Historia de la lengua y literatura castellana* ... (Madrid, 1915-1922; 14 vols.), vol. 1, p. 412.

3. Summaries of the plots of *Amadis of Gaul* and other romances of chivalry are given in Lewis Spence, *Legends and romances of Spain* (New York, 1920).

4. Marcelino Menéndez y Pelayo, *Orígenes de la novela* (Madrid, 1905-1915; 4 vols.), vol. 1, p. ccxxiii.

5. The following useful table of sixteenth-century novels of chivalry is reproduced from Henry Thomas, *Spanish and Portuguese romances of chivalry* (Cambridge Univ. Press, 1920), pp. 147-148:

1508	Amadís de Gaula	1534	Lidamor de Escocia
1510	Sergas de Esplandián	1534	Lucidante de Tracia
	Florisando	1535	Rogel de Grecia
1511	Palmerín de Oliva	1540	Valerian de Ungría
1512	Primaleón de Grecia	1542	Philesbian de Candaria
1514	Lisuarte de Grecia	1544(?)	Palmerín de Inglaterra
1516	Floriseo	1545	Cirongilio de Tracia
1517	Arderique	1545	Crisalián de España
1518	Clarián de Landanis		Florando de Inglaterra
1519	Claribalte	1546	Silves de la Selva
1520	Leoneo de Ungría	1547	Belianis de Grecia II
1521	Lepolemo	1550	Floramante de Colonia
1522	Clarimundo	1551	Rogel de Grecia II
1522	Clarián de Landanis II	1556	Felixmarte de Hircania
1524	Clarián de Landanis III	1562	Espejo de Príncipes
	Reymundo de Grecia	1563	Leandro el Bel
1526	Lisuarte de Grecia II	1564	Olivante de Laura
	Polindo	1576	Febo el Troyano
1528	Lidaman de Ganayle	1579	Belianis de Grecia III
1530	Amadís de Grecia	1581	Espejo de Príncipes II
	Florindo	1587	Duardo Segundo
1531	Felix Magno	1589	Espejo de Príncipes III
1532	Florambel de Lucea	1602	Clarisol de Bretanha
	Florisel de Niquea		Policisne de Boecia
1533	Platir		

6. There is a genealogical table of the Amadis heroes in Pascual de Gayangos, *Libros de caballerías*, in the *Biblioteca de autores españoles*, vol. 40, p. xxxviii.

7. A genealogy of the Palmerín cycle is given in Gayangos, *op. cit.*, p. xlv.

8. See note in Diego Clemencín (ed.), *El ingenioso hidalgo don Quijote de la Mancha* . . .(Madrid, 1833; 8 vols.), vol. 2, p. 457.

9. Thomas, *op. cit.*, p. 149.

10. Charles V had a copy of *El caballero determinado* in its original French with illuminations, and also the Castilian version of *Hernando de Acuña*, likewise with illuminations, when he retired to the monastery at Yuste. Cf. William Sterling, *The cloister life of the Emperor Charles V* (Boston, 1853), pp. 316-317. It appears likely that his son Philip II reverently preserved these relics of his father, judging by the "Libros de diversas facultades de la testamentería de Felipe II, 1600" in *Documentos para la historia de España* (Madrid, 1877), vol. 68, pp. 486-488, where two copies are listed, one evaluated at 8 reales, and the other at 16.

11. Salvador de Madariaga, *Guía del lector del Quijote* (Madrid, 1926), p. 50.

12. Thomas, *op. cit.*, p. 80.

13. Archer Huntington, *Catalogue of the library of Ferdinand Columbus* (New York, 1905). John B. Thacher, *Christopher Columbus, his life, his work, his remains* (New York, London, 1903-1904; 3 vols.), vol. 3, pp. 422-453.

14. Juan de Valdés, *Diálogo de la lengua* (Madrid, 1928, *Clásicos castellanos* ed.), pp. 168, 172.

15. E. Allison Peers, *Studies in the Spanish mystics* (London, 1927; 2 vols.), vol. 1, p. 8.

16. Ricardo Rojas, *Historia de la literatura argentina* (Buenos Aires, ed. 2, 1924-1925; 8 vols.), vol. 1, p. 84.

17. "La vida de la Santa Madre Teresa de Jesús . . . por ella misma," in *Biblioteca de autores españoles* (Madrid, 1861), vol. 53, p. 24.

18. Gaston Etchegoyen, *L'amour divin. Essai sur les sources de Sainte Thérèse* (Paris, 1923), pp. 44-46.

19. Francisco de Ribera, *Vida de Santa Teresa* (Barcelona, 1908), p. 99.

20. The text of this letter is reproduced in Rubén Vargas Ugarte, *Manuscritos peruanos en las bibliotecas del estranjero* (Lima, 1935; 3 vols.), vol. 1, p. 245.

21. Thomas, *op. cit.*, pp. 152-153.

22. *La Florida del Inca* (Madrid, 1723), libro II, parte I, p. cxxvii.

CHAPTER III

1. Diego Clemencín (ed.), *El ingenioso hidalgo don Quijote de la Mancha* . . . (Madrid, 1833; 8 vols.), vol. 1, p. xiii.

2. Francisco Rodríguez Lobo, *Corte en Aldea y Noches de Invierno* (Valencia, 1798 [First edition in 1619], pp. 18-20, quoted in M. Menén-

dez y Pelayo, *Orígenes de la novela* (Madrid, 1943), vol. 1, pp. 370-371.

3. Quoted in Henry Thomas, *Spanish and Portuguese romances of chivalry* (Cambridge, 1920), p. 153.

4. See George Ticknor, *History of Spanish literature* (New York, 1854; 3 vols.), pp. 251, 253; Rufino Blanco Fombona, *Los conquistadores españoles del siglo xvi* (Madrid, 1922), p. 231.

5. Ticknor, *op. cit.*, p. 250.

6. Thomas, *op. cit.*, pp. 64-65.

7. See notes in Clemencín, *op. cit.*, vol. 1, pp. 110 ff.

CHAPTER IV

1. Particularly useful for this chapter is Ruth Putnam and Herbert I. Priestley, *California: The name* (Berkeley, University of California Publications in History, vol. 4, no. 4, 1917), *passim*. Also of interest is Leonardo Olschki, "Ponce de León's Fountain of Youth: History of a geographic myth," *Hispanic American Historical Review*, vol. 21 (1941), No. 3, pp. 361-385.

2. Cf. Silvio Zavala, *Los intereses particulares en la conquista de la Nueva España* (Madrid, Facultad de derecho, Universidad Central de Madrid, 1933), *passim;* Volodia Teitelboim, *El amanecer del capitalismo y la conquista de América* (Santiago de Chile, 1943), *passim*.

3. Sir Walter Raleigh, *History of the world* (London, 1786), vol. 2, p. 478.

4. Celeste Turner Wright, "The Amazons in Elizabethan Literature," *Studies in Philology*, vol. 27 (1940), No. 3, pp. 433-456.

5. Cf. Bertram T. Lee and H. C. Heaton, *The discovery of the Amazon according to the account of Friar Gaspar de Carvajal* (New York, American Geographical Society, 1934), *passim*.

6. James A. Robertson (tr.), *Antonio Pigafetta, Magellan's voyage around the world* (Cleveland, 1906), vol. 2, pp. 168-170.

7. It is well to recall, perhaps, that the first part of the immensely popular Italian epic of Ludovico Ariosto, *Orlando furioso*, appeared in 1516. Books XIX and XX of this narrative poem describe an encounter with Amazons.

8. Olschki, *op. cit.*, p. 382.

9. Henry Thomas, *Spanish and Portuguese romances of chivalry* (Cambridge, 1920), p. 67.

10. *Ibid.*

11. Ricardo Rojas, *Historia de la literatura argentina* (Buenos Aires, ed. 2, 1924-25; 8 vols.), vol. 3, pp. 26, 103.

12. Benedetto Croce, *La Spagna nella vita italiana durante la Rinascenza* (Bari, 1917), pp. 197-198. "L'Amadis e gli altri libri di cavalleria,

tutti pieni com'erano di amori e di svenevolezze, formavano la lettura prediletta dei soldati. . . ."

13. Diego Clemencín (ed.), *El ingenioso hidalgo don Quijote de la Mancha* . . . (Madrid, 1833), vol. 4, p. 277.

14. A. P. Maudslay (tr.), *Bernal Díaz del Castillo. The true history of the conquest of New Spain* (London, The Hakluyt Society, 1908-1916), vol. 2, p. 37.

15. Part I, chap. 32.

16. H. R. Wagner (ed.), *The discovery of New Spain in 1518 by Juan de Grijalva* (Pasadena, Cortes Society, 1942), pp. 22, 207.

17. "Instrucción que dió el capitán Diego Velázquez en la isla Fernandina en 23 de octubre de 1518 al capitán Hernando Cortés, etc." *Colección de documentos inéditos para la historia de España* (Madrid, 1842-1895; 112 vols.), vol. 1, p. 403.

18. A. P. Maudslay, *op. cit.*, vol. 1, p. 131.

19. Francisco Fernández del Castillo, *Tres conquistadores y pobladores de la Nueva España: Cristóbal Martín Millán de Gamboa, Andrés de Tapia, Jerónimo López* (Mexico City, Publicaciones del Archivo general de la nación, vol. 12, 1927), p. 252.

20. F. A. MacNutt (tr.), *Hernando Cortés. The Five letters* (New York, 1908), vol. 2, p. 177.

21. "Instrucciones dadas por Hernando Cortés a Francisco Cortés su lugarteniente en la villa de Colima. Año de 1524," in Pacheco y Cárdenas, *Colección de documentos inéditos de descubrimientos, conquistas . . . en América* (Madrid, 1864-1884; 42 vols.), vol. 26, p. 153.

22. H. H. Bancroft, *History of Mexico* (San Francisco, 1883), vol. 2, p. 61.

23. "The relation of Nunno di Gusman written to Charles the fifth Emperour" in Samuel Purchas, *Hakluytus Posthumus or Purchase His Pilgrimes* (Glasgow, 1906), vol. 18, pp. 59-60.

24. "Tercera relación de la jornada de Nuño de Guzmán" in Joaquín García Icazbalceta, *Documentos para la historia de México* (Mexico City, 1858-1866; 2 vols.), vol. 2, p. 451.

25. Putnam and Priestley, *op. cit.*, p. 349. Alvaro del Portillo y Díez de Sollano, in his *Descubrimientos y exploraciones en la costa de California* (Madrid, 1947), devotes his third chapter to a discussion of the origin of the name California, and believes that it was given in derision by Cortes' enemies. While he may be correct, some of this scholar's arguments are unsound and can be easily refuted.

CHAPTER V

1. Cf. Enrique de Gandía, *Historia crítica de los mitos de la conquista americana* (Buenos Aires, Madrid, 1929), *passim.*

2. *Anales de la Biblioteca Nacional* (Buenos Aires), vol. 8, p. 124, cited in Ricardo Rojas, *Historia de la literatura argentina* (Buenos Aires, ed. 2, 1924-1925; 8 vols.), vol. 1, p. 280.

3. Arthur Helps, *The life of Las Casas, apostle of the Indies* (London, 1868), pp. 94-99.

4. Antonio Rodríguez Villa, *El Emperador Carlos V y su corte, según las cartas de D. Martín de Salinas, embajador del Infante D. Fernando* (1522-1539) (Madrid, 1903), p. 529.

5. Juan de San Martín y Alonso de Lebrija, *Relación del descubrimiento y conquista del nuevo reino de Granada, años 1536 a 1539* (Madrid, Sociedad de bibliófilos españoles, 1916), pp. 64-65.

6. *Ibid.*, p. 67.

7. Cf. Bertram T. Lee and H. C. Heaton, *The discovery of the Amazon according to the account of Friar Gaspar de Carvajal* (New York, American Geographical Society, 1934).

8. *Ibid.*, p. 214.

9. *Ibid.*, p. 221.

10. "Relación de Hernando de Ribera," in *Comentarios de Álvar Núñez Cabeza de Vaca* (Buenos Aires, Espasa Calpe Argentina, Colección Austral, 304, 1942).

11. Usually listed in Spanish accounts as Ulrich Schmidel.

12. "Voyage of Ulrich Schmidt to the rivers La Plata and Paraguai, from the German original of 1567," in *The conquest of the River Plate* (London, Hakluyt Society, No. 81, 1891), p. 45.

13. Agustín de Zárate, *Historia del descubrimiento y conquista del Perú*, book 3, chap. 11, in *Biblioteca de autores españoles* (Madrid, 1862), vol. 26, *Historiadores primitivos de Indias*, p. 485.

14. Sir Walter Raleigh, *Discovery of Guiana*, in *Hakluyt Voyages* (London, 1927), vol. 7, pp. 295-296.

CHAPTER VI

1. Bernardino de Mendoza, *Comentarios de lo sucedido en la guerra de los payses baxos desde el año 1567 hasta 1577* (Madrid, 1592).

2. Cf. Rudolfo Schevill, "La novela histórica, las crónicas de Indias y los libros de caballerías," *Revista de las Indias* [Colombia], época 2ª, Nos. 59-60 (1943), pp. 173-196.

3. Álvar Núñez Cabeza de Vaca, *Naufragios y comentarios* (Buenos Aires, Mexico City, Colección austral, No. 304, 1942). There are many other editions.

4. This tale is recounted in El Inca Garcilaso de la Vega, *Comentarios reales* (many editions), Book I, chap. 8. Cf. also Lesley B. Simpson, "The Spanish Crusoe. An account by Maese Joan of eight years spent as a castaway on the Serrana keys in the Caribbean sea, 1528-

1536," *Hispanic American Historical Review*, vol. 9 (1929), pp. 368-376.

5. Cf. Adolfo Bonilla y San Martín, *Luis Vives y la filosofía del Renacimiento* (Madrid, 1929; 2 vols.).

6. Juan Luis Vives, *Instrucción de la mujer cristiana* (Buenos Aires, Mexico City, Colección austral, No. 138, 1940), p. 36.

7. Quoted in Henry Thomas, *Spanish and Portuguese romances of chivalry* (Cambridge, 1920), p. 165.

8. *Ibid.*, p. 170.

9. Quoted in Francisco Rodríguez Marín, *Don Quijote de la Mancha* (Madrid, 1916-1917; 6 vols.), vol. 1, p. 209.

10. George Ticknor, *History of Spanish literature* (New York, 1854; 3 vols.), vol. 1, p. 541.

11. Quoted in Thomas, *op. cit.*, p. 171.

12. *Ibid.*, p. 161.

CHAPTER VII

1. Henry Thomas, *Spanish and Portuguese romances of chivalry* (Cambridge, 1920), p. 169. The *Peregrino y Ginebra*, which also was placed on the *Index*, was, apparently, another exception.

2. Quoted in Marcelino Menéndez y Pelayo, *Orígenes de la novela* (Madrid, 1925; 4 vols.), vol. 1, p. cclxix.

3. Francisco A. de Icaza, *El "Quijote" durante tres siglos* (Madrid, 1918), pp. 112-114.

4. Miguel Luis Amunátegui, *Los precursores de la Independencia de Chile* (Santiago de Chile, 1870), vol. 1, p. 224.

5. José Toribio Medina, *Historia de la literatura colonial* (Santiago de Chile, 1878; 3 vols.), p. 27.

6. Vicente Gaspar Quesada, *La vida intelectual en la América española durante los siglos xvi, xvii, y xviii* (Buenos Aires, 1910), p. 61.

7. José María Vergara y Vergara, *Historia de la literatura en Nueva Granada*, quoted in Quesada, *op. cit.*, p. 75.

8. Carlos González Peña, *Historia de la literatura mexicana* (Mexico City, ed. 2, 1940), p. 81.

9. Fernando Montesinos, *Anales del Perú* (Madrid, 1906; 2 vols.), vol. 1, p. 17.

10. Text reproduced in many works such as: José Toribio Medina, *Biblioteca Hispano-Americana* (Santiago de Chile, 1898-1907; 7 vols.), vol. 6, p. xxvii; Pacheco y Cárdenas, *Colección de documentos inéditos relativos al descubrimiento, conquista y colonización de las posesiones españolas en América y Oceanía* (Madrid, 1864-1884; 42 vols.), vol. 42, pp. 466-467; José Torre Revello, *El libro, la imprenta y el periodismo en América durante la dominación española* (Buenos Aires, 1940),

apéndice, iii. Ms. original indicated as in Archivo General de Indias, Seville, (Indiferente general. *Contratación*, 148-2-2).

11. Pacheco y Cárdenas, *op. cit.*, vol. 23, pp. 457-458.

12. Medina, *Biblioteca Hispano-Americana*, vol. 6, p. xxvi-xxvii. An abbreviated form of this decree is cited in the *Recopilación de leyes de los reinos de las Indias* (Madrid, 1756; 4 vols.), libro I, título xxiv, ley iiii, with date of September 29, 1543. Cf. *Disposiciones complementarias de las Indias* (Madrid, 1930; 3 vols.), vol. 3, sec. xxxvii.

13. Cristóbal Pérez Pastor, *Bibliografía madrileña* (Madrid, 1898-1907; 3 vols.), vol. 1, prólogo xiii.

14. Juan de Torquemada, *Monarquía indiana* (Madrid, 1723; 3 vols.), libro ix, chap. xxx.

15. Toribio Motolinia, *Historia ecclesiástica indiana* (Mexico City, 1870), p. 410.

16. *Ibid.*, p. 209. Cf. also Rómulo Velasco Ceballos, *La alfabetización en la Nueva España* (Mexico City, 1945), *passim*. Also, "Enseñanza del castellano como factor político colonial," *Boletín del archivo general de la nación*, vol. 17, no. 2 (Mexico City, 1946), p. 165-171.

17. "Carta de D. Antonio de Mendoza, virrey de Nueva España al Emperador, dándole cuenta de varios asuntos de su gobierno, México, Dic. 10, 1537," *Documentos inéditos para la historia de México* (Mexico City, 1858-1866; 2 vols.), vol. 2, pp. 148-150.

18. Tomás Zepeda Rincón, *La instrucción pública en la Nueva España en el siglo XVI* (Mexico City, 1933), p. 31.

19. Pacheco y Cárdenas, *op. cit.*, vol. 18, p. 472.

20. *Colección de documentos inéditos para la historia de España* (Madrid, 1842-1895; 112 vols.), vol. 94, p. 232.

21. Antonio E. Serrano Redonnet, "Prohibición de libros en el primer sínodo santiagueño (Tucumán)," *Revista de filología hispánica*, vol. 5, No. 2 (1943), pp. 162-166.

CHAPTER VIII

1. José Torre Revello, *El libro, la imprenta y el periodismo en América durante la dominación española* (Buenos Aires, 1940), *passim*.

2. José Torre Revello, *La fundación y despoblación de Buenos Aires (1536-1541)* (Buenos Aires, 1937), p. 87.

3. Ciriaco Pérez Bustamante, *D. Antonio de Mendoza, primer virrey de la Nueva España, 1535-1550* (Santiago de Compostela, 1928), p. 20, and appendix, Documento No. IV.

4. Cf. George P. Hammond and Agapito Rey, *Narratives of the Coronado Expedition, 1540-1542* (Albuquerque, N. M., 1940), *passim*.

5. Lathrop C. Harper, *Catalogue of Americana*, part. I, no. 163 (April, 1941), pp. 46-47.

6. José Torre Revello, *Crónicas del Buenos Aires colonial* (Buenos Aires, 1943), p. 51.

7. Torre Revello, *El libro, la imprenta y el periodismo*, p. 213.

8. Torre Revello, *Orígenes de la imprenta y su desarrollo en América Española* (Buenos Aires, 1940), pp. 93-98; Hildamar Escalante, "Juan Pablos, primer impresor de América," *Revista nacional de cultura* (Venezuela), No. 37 (1943), pp. 76-84; Joaquín Hazañas y La Rua, *La imprenta en Sevilla* (Seville, 1892), *passim;* Wagner, Henry R., "The House of Cromberger," *To Doctor R* (Philadelphia, 1946), pp. 227-239.

9. José Gestoso y Pérez, *Noticias inéditas de impresores sevillanos* (Seville, 1924), pp. 36 ff.

10. *Ibid.*, p. 103.

11. Ibid., pp. 86-99.

12. *Recopilación de leyes de Indias* (Madrid, 1756: 4 vols.), libro I, título XXIV, ley V.

13. Irving A. Leonard, *Romances of chivalry in the Spanish Indies* (Berkeley, 1933), p. 13; Torre Revello, *El libro, la imprenta y el periodismo*, p. 215.

14. These scattered documents are in the Archive of the Indies, Seville, *Contratación*, legajo 1079.

15. Archivo Nacional del Perú, *Protocolos de Sebastián Vásquez, 1551-1554,* fol. 1227v-1228.

CHAPTER IX

1. Rudolph Schevill, "An impression of the condition of Spanish American libraries," *Modern Language Notes*, vol. 20 (May, 1905), p. 143.

2. Marcelino Menéndez y Pelayo, *Orígenes de la novela* (Madrid, 1925; 4 vols.), vol. 1, p. cclxiv.

3. Part I, chap. XVI.

4. Menéndez y Pelayo, *op. cit.*, vol. 1, p. cxli.

5. *Ibid.*, p. cxl. It has been modernly reprinted in Adolfo Bonilla de San Martín, *Libros de caballerías* (Madrid, 1907-1918; 2 vols.), vol. 2, pp. 477-615.

6. Menéndez y Pelayo, *op. cit.*, vol. 1, p. cxxxiv.

7. *Ibid.*, pp. lix-lx.

8. *Ibid.*, p. cccxxx.

9. "Libros de diversas facultades de la testamentaría de Felipe II," *Documentos inéditos para la historia de España*, (Madrid, 1842-1895; 112 vols.), vol. 68, pp. 486, 488.

10. Part I, chap. VI.

CHAPTER X

1. The description of the organization and operation of the House of Trade at Seville offered in this chapter is largely derived from the modern account of C. H. Haring, *El comercio y la navegación entre España y las Indias en época de los Habsburgos* (Paris, Brujas, 1939), and the older and fundamental authority José de Veitía Linaje, *Norte de Contratación de las Indias Occidentales* (Sevilla, 1672).

2. Haring, *op. cit.*, p. 9.

3. Archivo General de Indias, *Contratación*, legajo 1086, "Registro de la nao 'Santa Catalina,'" fol. 91. The text of this document is reproduced in its entirety in Irving A. Leonard, *Romances of chivalry in the Spanish Indies* (Berkeley, 1933), Appendix, Document IV.

4. *Ibid.*, Appendix, VI.

5. See Guillermo Céspedes del Castillo, *La avería en el comercio de Indias* (Sevilla, 1945), *passim*.

6. Haring, *op. cit.*, pp. 326-330.

CHAPTER XI

1. F. de Castro y Bravo, *Las naos españolas* (Madrid, 1927), p. 94.

2. José Torre Revello, "Merchandise shipped by the Spaniards to America (1534-1586)," *Hispanic American Historical Review*, vol. 23 (1943), pp. 773-781.

3. For a fuller account of the Spanish fleets see C. H. Haring, *Trade and navigation between Spain and the Indies in the time of the Hapsburgs* (Harvard University Press, 1918). The Spanish version of this work is here cited: C. H. Haring, *El comercio y la navegación entre España y las Indias en época de los Habsburgos* (Paris, Brujas, 1939), Parte II, *passim*.

4. Paul S. Taylor, "Spanish seamen in the New World," *Hispanic American Historical Review*, vol. V (1922), *passim*.

5. See Earl J. Hamilton, "Wages and subsistence on Spanish treasure ships (1503-1660)," *Journal of Political Economy*, vol. 37 (August, 1929), *passim*.

6. Haring, *op. cit.*, pp. 116-118; José Torre Revello, *Crónicas del Buenos Aires colonial* (Buenos Aires, 1943), chap. 2.

7. Haring, *op. cit.*, p. 247.

8. Torre Revello, *Crónicas del Buenos Aires colonial*, pp. 57-60.

9. The complete diary has recently been printed in R. P. Fray Tomás de la Torre, *Desde Salamanca, España, hasta Ciudad real, Chiapas. Diario de viaje, 1544-1545*. Prólogo y notas por Franz Blom, 1944-45 (Mexico City, 1945). Much of the text is incorporated in Francisco Ximénez, *Historia de la provincia de San Vicente de Chiapa y Guatemala* (Guatemala City, 1929). The part of the diary relating to the ocean

crossing is reproduced in E. Rodríguez Demorizi, *Relaciones históricas de Santo Domingo* (Ciudad Trujillo, R. D.), pp. 93-122.

10. "Cartas de Eugenio de Salazar," in *Biblioteca de autores españoles* (Madrid, 1926), vol. 62, p. 291.

11. These examples are selected and translated from Francisco Fernández del Castillo, *Libros y libreros en el siglo XVI* (Mexico City, 1914), pp. 360-446.

CHAPTER XII

1. *Recopilación de leyes de los reinos de las Indias* (Madrid, 1756; 4 vols.), libro I, título XXIV, ley VII.

2. George Haven Putnam, *Censorship of the Church of Rome* (New York, 1906-1907; 2 vols.), p. 182.

3. Henry Charles Lea, *The Inquisition in the Spanish dependencies* (New York, 1908), pp. 202, 326.

4. See text of edict in Francisco Fernández del Castillo, *Libros y libreros en el siglo XVI* (Mexico City, 1914), pp. 459-463.

5. *Ibid.*, pp. 463-464.

6. Joseph de Veitia Linaje, *Norte de la contratación de las Indias* (Seville, 1672), libro II, cáp. 18, p. 208.

7. Federico de Castro y Bravo, *Las naos españolas* (Madrid, 1927), p. 72.

8. *Ibid.*

9. See Fernández del Castillo, *op. cit.*, pp. 466-467.

10. *Ibid.*, p. 351.

11. *Ibid.*, p. 366.

12. *Ibid.*, 424.

13. *Recopilación de leyes de los reinos de las Indias*, libro I, título XXIV, ley VI.

14. Fernández del Castillo, *op. cit.*, pp. 326-327, 357.

15. *Ibid.*, pp. 351-358.

16. *Ibid.*, p. 358.

17. *Ibid.*, p. 359.

18. *Ibid.*, p. 467.

19. *Ibid.*, pp. 422-423.

20. *Ibid.*, pp. 510-511.

21. José Toribio Medina, *Historia del Tribunal del Santo Oficio de la Inquisición en México* (Santiago de Chile, 1905), p. 417.

22. *Ibid.*, p. 416.

23. Ricardo Rojas, *Historia de la literatura argentina* (Buenos Aires, ed. 2, 1924-25; 8 vols.), vol. 3, pp. 43-44.

24. Fernández del Castillo, *op. cit.*, p. 506.

25. *Ibid.*, p. 363.

26. *Ibid.*, pp. 409, 330, 428.

CHAPTER XIII

1. Pacheco y Cárdenas, *Colección de documentos inéditos relativos al descubrimiento, conquista . . . en América y Oceanía* (Madrid, 1864-1884; 42 vols.), vol. 3, p. 496.

2. *Cartas de Indias* (Madrid, 1877), p. 195.

3. Edmundo O'Gorman, *Reflexiones sobre la distribución urbana colonial de la Ciudad de México* (Mexico City, 1938), p. 39.

4. Angel Rosenblat, "El desarrollo de la población indígena en América," *Tierra Firme* (Madrid, 1935), No. 2, pp. 128-142.

5. Gonzalo Aguirre Beltrán, "The slave trade in Mexico," *Hispanic American Historical Review*, vol. 24 (1944), pp. 412-431.

6. *Cartas de Indias*, pp. 297 ff.

7. Hubert H. Bancroft, *History of Mexico* (San Francisco, 1883-1888; 6 vols.), vol. 2, p. 661.

8. *Cartas de Indias*, p. 331.

9. Alberto M. Carreño (ed.), *Gonzalo Gómez de Cervantes. La vida económica y social de Nueva España al finalizar el siglo XVI* (Mexico City, 1944), p. 188.

10. *Cartas de Indias*, pp. 315 ff.

11. John Tate Lanning, *Academic culture in the Spanish colonies* (New York, 1940), p. 113.

12. Joaquín García Icazbalceta, *Bibliografía mexicana del siglo XVI*, (Mexico City, 1886), p. 168.

13. *Ibid.*, pp. 171, 173.

14. Francisco del Paso y Troncoso, *Epistolario de Nueva España* (Mexico City, 1939-1942; 16 vols.), vol. 12 (1576-1596), p. 13.

15. *Cartas de Indias*, p. 197.

16. Alfonso Méndez Plancarte, *Poetas novohispanos. Primer siglo (1521-1621)* (Mexico City, 1942), p. 13-14.

17. The account of this episode is drawn from Amado Alonso, "Biografía de Fernán González de Eslava," *Revista de filología hispánica*, año II (1940), pp. 213-319, and the correspondence of Archbishop Moya de Contreras and Viceroy Enríquez reproduced in *Cartas de Indias*.

18. *Cartas de Indias*, p. 305.

19. Tomás Zepeda Rincón, *La instrucción pública en la Nueva España en el siglo XVI* (Mexico City, 1933), p. 94.

20. The first of these book lists is analyzed in Irving A. Leonard, "Una venta de libros en México, 1576," *Nueva revista de filología hispánica*, año 2 (1948) No. 2, p. 174-185, to which the document itself is appended.

21. This list is published as an appendix to an analysis of its titles given in Irving A. Leonard, "On the Mexican Book Trade, 1576," *Hispanic Review*, vol. 17 (1949), pp. 18-34.

22. Francis Borgia Steck, "Early Mexican literature," *Hispanic American Essays* (Chapel Hill, N. C., 1942), p. 49.

23. Juan Hurtado y Ángel González Palencia, *Historia de la literatura española* (Madrid, 1925), p. 393.

CHAPTER XIV

1. See Rubén Vargas Ugarte, *Manuscritos peruanos en las bibliotecas del estranjero* (Lima, 1935; 3 vols.), vol. 1, p. 245.

2. See Roberto Levillier, *Don Francisco de Toledo, supremo organizador del Perú. Su vida, su obra, 1515-1582* (Madrid, 1935; 2 vols.); Arthur F. Zimmerman, *Francisco de Toledo, fifth Viceroy of Peru, 1569-1581* (Caldwell, Idaho, 1938).

3. Fernando de Montesinos, *Anales del Perú* (ed. of Víctor M. Maúrtua, Madrid, 1906; 2 vols.), vol. 2, pp. 95-96.

4. Rubén Vargas Ugarte (ed.), *Diario de Lima de Juan Antonio Suardo, 1629-1639* (Lima, 1936) indicates that on July 15, 1634, a play was performed at the viceroy's palace entitled "Prelado de las Indias, Don Toribio Alfonso Mogrovexo, Arzobispo," playwright not mentioned.

5. Philip A. Means, *Fall of the Inca Empire* (New York, 1932), p. 175.

6. At the end of Book II of this *Historia* Acosta wrote, ". . . que los dos libros precedentes se escribieron en latín, estando en el Perú, y así hablan de las cosas de las Indias como de cosas presentes." There is an interesting chapter on Acosta and his writings in Felipe Barreda y Laos, *Vida intelectual del virreinato del Perú* (Buenos Aires, 1937), pp. 99-125.

7. José Toribio Medina, *Escritores americanos celebrados por Cervantes en el Canto de Calíope* (Santiago de Chile, 1926).

8. See Guillermo Lohmann Villena, *El arte dramático en Lima durante el virreinato* (Madrid, 1945), pp. 55-83.

9. José Torre Revello, *Orígenes de la imprenta en España y su desarrollo en la América Española* (Buenos Aires, 1940), pp. 104-117.

10. Genaro García, *Documentos inéditos o muy raros para la historia de México* (Mexico City, 1905-1911; 35 vols.), vol. 15, p. 99.

11. This book list was reproduced and analyzed in Irving A. Leonard, "Best Sellers of the Lima Book Trade, 1583," *Hispanic American Historical Review*, vol. 22 (1942), pp. 5-33.

12. The royal decree of February 5, 1569, granting Monterroso the exclusive right to print and sell his work in the Indies for a period of twenty years, is reproduced in the appendix of José Torre Revello, *El libro, la imprenta y el periodismo en América . . .* (Buenos Aires, 1940), pp. xxi-xxii.

354 REFERENCES

13. See M. de Iriarte, *El doctor Huarte de San Juan y su 'Examen de Ingenios'* (Madrid, 1935), *passim*.

14. Marcelino Menéndez y Pelayo, *Orígenes de la novela* (Madrid, 1925; 4 vols.), vol. 1, p. cclxii.

CHAPTER XV

1. See William Lytle Schurz, *The Manila galleon* (New York, 1939), *passim*.

2. Archivo General de la Nación (Mexico City, *Inquisición* tomo 133); this document is reproduced and analyzed in Irving A. Leonard, "One man's library, Manila, 1583," *Hispanic Review*, vol. 15 (1947), pp. 84-100.

3. Possibly a mistake was made in the date. The newly appointed Commissioner for Manila, Fray Francisco Manrique, received his instructions in Mexico City on March 1, 1583, and must, therefore, have reached the Philippines some months later. Since it was in January, the writer may have inadvertently set down the year just closed, the actual date being 1584.

4. The terminal letter of the name is unlike any other *o* or *a* in the manuscript, but the distinguished Spanish paleographer, Dr. Agustín Millares Carlo, who kindly had a photographic copy of the document made for me, gives the reading "trebiña." This name is thus far unidentified. There was a book merchant in Mexico City about the time of this document by the name of Juan de Treviño. See Francisco Fernández del Castillo, *Libros y libreros en el siglo XVI* (Mexico City, 1914), index.

5. Marcelino Menéndez y Pelayo, *Historia de los heterodoxos españoles* (Madrid, 1911-1932; 7 vols.), vol. 5, p. 425.

6. David P. Barrows, *History of the Philippines* (New York, 1925), chap. vi. James A. Robertson, "Legaspi and Philippine colonization," *American Historical Association Annual Report* (Washington, 1908), vol. 1, pp. 143-156.

7. Pedro Torres y Lanzas, *Catálogo de los documentos relativos a las Islas Filipinas. Precedido de una Historia general de Filipinas por Pablo Pastells, S. J.* (Barcelona, 1925; 2 vols.), vol. 2, pp. ccxxii-ccxxiii.

8. Quoted in *ibid.*, p. clxxxiv-clxxxv.

9. *Loc. cit.*

10. *Op. cit.*, vol. 2, p. ccxxxi.

11. These data are drawn from a long letter of Bishop Salazar, written in Manila in 1583 to Philip II, translated in Emma H. Blair and J. A. Robertson, *The Philippine Islands, 1493-1803* (Cleveland, 1903-1909; 55 vols.), vol. 5, pp. 210-255. See also preface of this volume.

12. Concerning the establishment of the Royal Audiencia of Manila

see Charles H. Cunningham, *The Audiencia in the Spanish Colonies as illustrated by the Audiencia of Manila, 1583-1800* (Berkeley, 1919), chap. II, *passim.*

13. These instructions are translated in full in Blair and Robertson, *op. cit.,* vol. 5, pp. 256-273.

14. *Carta de Diego de Ronquillo a S. M., 8 de Abril, 1584,* quoted in Torres y Lanzas, y Pastells, *op. cit.,* vol. 2., p. ccxxxii.

15. *Carta del Obispo a S. M., 18 de Junio, 1583; Carta de Diego de Ronquillo a S. M., 8 de Abril, 1584,* quoted in *ibid.,* vol. 2, p. ccxxxii; Blair and Robertson, *op. cit.,* vol. 6, p. 74, note 13; Pedro A. Paterno, *Historia de Filipinas* (Manila, 1909), vol. 3, p. 58.

16. The Old City of Manila or Intramuros shared the same fate as the modern city outside its walls and was almost completely destroyed in the fighting between the American and Japanese forces in 1945.

17. Torres y Lanzas, y Pastells, *op. cit.,* vol. 2, p. clxxxix.

18. *Ibid., Documentos* Nos. 2280, 2328, 2915, 2927, 2937, 2964.

19. *Carta del Obispo a S. M., 18 de Junio, 1583,* quoted in *ibid.,* vol. 2, p. ccxxxiii.

20. Blair and Robertson, *op. cit.,* vol. 5, p. 272.

CHAPTER XVI

1. Alberto M. Carreño (ed.), *Gonzalo Gómez de Cervantes. La vida económica y social de Nueva España al finalizar el siglo XVI* (Mexico City, 1944), p. 85. Much of the preliminary material of this chapter is drawn from this interesting document.

2. *Ibid.,* pp. 99-101, 118.

3. Alfonso Méndez Plancarte, *Poetas novohispanos. Primer siglo (1521-1621)* (Mexico City, 1942), p. xxx.

4. *Ibid.,* p. xxxi.

5. This document is reproduced in the *Hispanic Review,* vol. 9 (1941), pp. 1-40, together with an introductory analysis containing reference numbers.

6. *Ibid.,* Nos. 75, 80, 195, 199, 292, 437; cf. No. 540, "Nyculas Rramos, De la bulgata edicion de la Bliblia" (the word is usually so spelled).

7. *Ibid.,* Nos. 64, 72, 117, 305, 432, 71b, 132, 168, 525, 536.

8. There appears to be no trace of conflict between Augustinianism and the Pelagianism of the Jesuits. See A. Harnack, *History of dogma* (Boston, 1905), vol. 7, pp. 73-91.

9. See Nesca A. Robb, *Neo-Platonism of the Italian Renaissance* (London, 1935), *passim;* Eugenio Garín, "Aristotelismo e Platonismo del Rinascimento," *La Rinascita,* vol. 2 (1939), pp. 641-671.

10. Letter to Boccaccio, September 7, 1363; see F. Schevill, *The first century of Italian humanism* (New York, 1928), pp. 22-23.

11. *Cambridge modern history* (Cambridge, 1903), vol. 2, p. 695; and E. Ananigne, *Pico della Mirandola, sincretismo religioso-filosofico* (Bari, 1937), chap. 2.

12. B. A. G. Fuller, *A history of philosophy* (New York, 1938), part 2, p. 19.

13. It should not be forgotten that it was an astrological motive that induced Copernicus to inquire into the mathematical order of the heavens; see F. Thilly, *A History of philosophy* (New York, 1914), p. 235. Milton expressed faith in astrology in *Paradise Lost* and justified his belief in it in his tract on Christian faith. Even Kepler made prognostications in his almanacs. Throughout the seventeenth century cultured opinion was divided and perplexed, although in 1586 Sixtus V had published a constitution forbidding all methods of foretelling the future. See Preserved Smith, *The history of modern culture* (New York, 1934), pp. 426-440.

14. See reference 5, Nos. 52, 121, 299, 310, 315, 534.

15. L. Zanta, *La renaissance du stoicisme au 16e siècle* (Paris, 1914), pp. 167 ff.

16. Four items on this book list testify to the interest in the commentaries of St. Thomas Aquinas. The Thomistic form of scholasticism gained new life in sixteenth-century Spain and Portugal where the Universities of Salamanca and Coimbra "dem aristotlischen Thomismus zu grossen Ansehen und Einfluss verhalfen"; F. Ueberweg, *Grundriss der Philosophie der Neuzeit* (Berlin, 1896), vol. 1, p. 28.

17. Interest in the commentaries of Alexander of Aphrosisias is also shown by an item on the list; see reference 5 and F. Thilly, *op. cit.*, p. 232.

18. See Zabuggin, *op. cit.*, pp. 316-318.

19. Méndez Bejarano, *Historia de la filosofía en España* (Madrid, n.d.), pp. 245-247; M. Menéndez y Pelayo, *La ciencia española* (Madrid, 1915), pp. 249-281.

20. E. W. Brown and others, *The development of the sciences* (New Haven, 1923), p. 222. The interest in zoology is much less pronounced and shows similar leanings. See Avicenna, *De animalibus*, and Nicolas Leonicensus, *De los hierros de Plinio y de otros, y de yerbas, animales, y serpientes*.

21. M. Möbius, *Geschicte der Botanik* (Jena, 1937), p. 33.

22. A. Wolf, *A history of science, technology, and philosophy in the 16th and 17th centuries* (New York, 1935), pp. 396-397.

23. The famous work of Nicolás Monardes, found in many other *registros* of the sixteenth century, is strangely lacking.

24. This author's *Physiognomoniae libri sex* . . . anticipated the theories of Lavater on the human face.

25. H. Haeser, *Lehrbuch der Geschicte der Medicin* (Jena, 1881), vol. 2, p. 112. Cf. *Secreti diversi et miracolosi*, a supposititious work attributed to Gabriello Fallopio.

26. For all these names consult the well-indexed works of Haeser and Wolf.

27. Hasan Ibn Hasan was the greatest of medieval opticians (Wolf, *op. cit.*, p. 244). Campano gave the first European translation of Euclid (from an Arabic text). Sacrobosco was the author of the first work of astronomy published in the West after the fall of the Roman Empire. See C.-F.-M. Marie, *Histoire des sciences mathématiques et physiques* (Paris, 1883), vol. 2, pp. 140, 158. Information on writers in this section will be taken from this work unless otherwise stated.

28. J.-E. Montucla, *Histoire des recherches sur la quadrature du cercle* (Paris, 1831), pp. 204, 297.

29. The presence of the *Dialectica juris civilis otomani* . . . by François Hotman is especially interesting since he was a Calvinist and a leading critic of royal absolutism.

30. See G. Toffanin, *La fine dell' umanesimo* (Torina, 1920), chaps. 8, 9.

31. Miscellaneous items are: P. Mexía, A. de Torquemada, Hernán Núñez, Visorio's poem in six cantos, *Anagrama de la vida humana*, and Boscán's translation of the *Cortegiano*.

32. Also known as *Egloga di Flavia* (by Fillipo Galli?). This edition is apparently unknown.

33. A clerk's notation *"En berso latino"* would appear to be an error for *"en verso italiano."* It is probably a question of *Di M. Antonio Tibaldeo Ferrarese, l'opere d'amore.*

34. J. B. Trend, *Luis Millán and the vihuelistas* (Oxford, 1925), pp. 54, 64.

35. R. Schneider, "Notes sur l'influence artistique de 'Songe de Poliphile'," in *Études italiennes* (1920), vol. 2, pp. 1-16, 65-73.

CHAPTER XVII

1. See Urban Cronan, "Mateo Alemán and Cervantes," *Revue hispanique* (1911) vol. 25, pp. 468-475.

2. Nicholson B. Adams, *The heritage of Spain* (New York, 1943), p. 152.

3. In Part II, Book I, chap. vi of *Guzmán de Alfarache*, Alemán remarks, ". . . habiéndolo intitulado Atalaya de la vida humana dieron en llamarle *Pícaro* y no se conoce ya por otro nombre."

4. Archivo General de Indias, Seville. *Contratación*, 1135, registro de la nao "La Trinidad," fol. 46.

5. Archivo General de la Nación, Mexico City. *Inquisición*, 257, *visita de naos, 1600*, fol. 14.

6. Francisco Fernández del Castillo, *Libros y libreros en el siglo XVI* (Mexico City, 1914), pp. 444-445.

7. See Document VII in Irving A. Leonard, *Romances of chivalry in the Spanish Indies* (Berkeley, 1933). There are abstracts of *registros* of this period in Francisco Rodríguez Marín, *Documentos referentes a Mateo Alemán y a sus deudos más cercanos, 1546-1607* (Madrid, 1933).

8. See *Discursos leídos ante la Real Academia Española por . . . Francisco Rodríaguez Marín y Marcelino Menéndez y Pelayo* (Seville, 1907), pp. 35-36.

9. *Ibid.*, p. 21.

10. *Ibid.*, pp. 36-39.

11. Luis González Obregón, *México viejo y anecdótico* (Paris-Mexico City, 1909), p. 72.

12. See Alice H. Bushee, "The *Sucesos* of Mateo Alemán," *Revue hispanique* (1911) vol. 25, pp. 441 ff.

13. José Toribio Medina, *La imprenta en México (1539-1821)* (Santiago de Chile, 1907-1912), vol. 2, p. 43.

14. Archivo Nacional del Perú, Lima. *Protocolos*, Bartolomé de la Cámara, 1612-1614, fol. 155. This document is reproduced in the *Hispanic Review*, vol. 11 (1941), pp. 218-220.

15. Fernando Montesinos, *Anales del Perú* (Madrid, 1606; 2 vols.), "*Año de 1614.*" A detailed and interesting description of Lima in the early seventeenth century by a contemporary, Father Bernabé Cobo (1582-1657) is included in Raúl Porras Barrenechea, *Pequeña antología de Lima, 1535-1935* (Madrid, 1935), pp. 119-138.

16. Montesinos, *op. cit.*, "*Año de 1613.*"

17. Guillermo Lohmann Villena, *Historia del arte dramático en Lima durante el virreinato. I. Siglos XVI y XVII* (Lima, 1941), p. 87.

18. Sister Mary H. Corcoran, *La Cristiada de fray Diego de Hojeda* (Washington, 1935), introduction.

19. In 1606 two copies of the first and second parts were billed for sale in Cuzco at 20 reales each. See Irving A. Leonard, "On the Cuzco book trade, 1606," *Hispanic Review*, vol. 9 (1941), p. 373.

CHAPTER XVIII

1. Archivo General de Indias, Seville. *Contratación*, 1145a, fol. 259.

2. Francisco Rodríguez Marín, *El "Quijote" y Don Quijote en América* (Madrid, 1911), p. 35.

3. Archivo General de Indias, Seville. *Contratación*, 1145a. Reproduced as Document VIII in Irving A. Leonard, *Romances of chivalry in the Spanish Indies* (Berkeley, 1933), pp. 114-115.

4. Archivo General de la Nación, Mexico City. *Inquisición*, tomo 276, No. 13.

5. *Ibid.*

6. Rodríguez Marín, *op. cit.*, p. 41.

7. Cesáreo Fernández Duro, *La armada española* (Madrid, 1895-1903; 9 vols.), vol. 3, p. 488.

8. Rodríguez Marín, *loc. cit.*

9. Fernández Duro, *loc. cit.*

10. Luis Cabrera de Córdoba, *Relaciones de las cosas sucedidas en la Corte de España, 1599-1614* (Madrid, 1857), p. 264.

11. This document is reproduced in Irving A. Leonard, "Don Quixote and the book trade in Lima, 1606," *Hispanic Review*, vol. 8 (1940), pp. 285-304.

12. The *registro* covering cases 21 to 40 is in the Archivo General de Indias, Seville. *Contratación*, 1145*a*, fol. 36, and cases 41 to 61, *ibid.*, *Contratación*, 1145*b*, fols. 49-53.

13. Rodríguez Marín, *loc. cit.*, p. 41.

14. A description of Puertobelo about the time of this incident is available in the "Descripción corográfico de . . . Puertobelo, 1607," Pacheco y Cárdenas, *Colección de documentos inéditos de descubrimientos, conquistas . . . en América y Oceanía* (Madrid, 1864-1884; 42 vols.), vol. 9, pp. 108-120.

15. "Descripción de Panamá y su provincia sacada de la Relación que por mandado del Consejo hizo y embió aquella Audiencia," *Revista de los archivos nacionales* (Costa Rica), año 2 (1938), Nos. 5, 6, pp. 245-285.

16. Allyn C. Looseley, "The Puerto Bello fairs," *Hispanic American Historical Review* (1933) vol. 13, pp. 314-335.

17. "Descripción de Panamá y su provincia," *loc. cit.*

18. For a discussion of the colonial trails across the Isthmus of Panama, see Roland D. Hussey, "Spanish colonial trails in Panama," *Revista de historia de América* (1939) vol. 6, pp. 47-74.

19. Both passages are quoted in *ibid.*

20. These details concerning Old Panama City and a few relating to Puertobelo were drawn from the "Descripción" cited in note 15 above.

21. Ricardo Palma, *Mis últimas tradiciones peruanas* (Barcelona, 1906).

22. This book list is reproduced and analyzed in Irving A. Leonard, "*Don Quixote* and the Book Trade in Lima, 1606," *Hispanic Review*, vol. 8 (1940), pp. 285-304.

23. Cristóbal Pérez Pastor, *Bibliografía madrileña* (Madrid, 1896-1907; 3 vols.), vol. 2, p. 90.

24. *Loc. cit.*

25. *Ibid.*, p. 51.

CHAPTER XIX

1. Concolorcorvo (Calixto Bustamente Carlos Inga), *El lazarillo de ciegos caminantes desde Buenos Aires hasta Lima* (Biblioteca de cultura, No. 6, Paris, 1938), apéndice, chap. XXV, gives some indications of the route between Lima and Cuzco. With regard to the amount of time required for the journey, the diarist in the *Diario de Lima de Josephe de Mugaburu, 1640-1694* (Lima, 1935; 2 vols.), vol. 2, p. 196, reports that he left Lima with his wife and children on September 12, 1676, and reached Cuzco on November 1, 1676, "after traveling fifty days." Many more details of the route have come to light recently in a contemporary account entitled "Descripción anónima del Perú y de Lima a principios del siglo 17, compuesta por un judío portugués y dirigida a los estados de Holanda," in the *Revista del archivo nacional del Perú,* vol. 17 (1944), entrega 1, pp. 3-44.

2. These are reproduced textually in Irving A. Leonard, "On the Cuzco book trade, 1606," *Hispanic Review,* vol. 9 (1941), pp. 359-375.

3. These data on early seventeenth-century Lima, the route to Cuzco, and on the latter city are drawn from the "Descripción anónima" of note 1.

4. Fernando Montesinos, *Anales del Perú* (Madrid, 1906; 2 vols.), "*Año de* 1606."

5. Preston E. James, *Latin America* (New York, 1942), p. 160.

6. Cieza de León, *Señoría,* chap. 15, quoted in Bailey Diffie, *Latin American civilization: colonial period* (Harrisburg, Pa., 1945), p. 134.

7. It is of interest to note that only one copy of Lope's *comedias* is reported in the 45 cases of books which Sarria had brought down to Lima from Puertobelo.

8. See Roland D. Hussey, "Colonial economic life," in A. C. Wilgus, (ed.), *Colonial Hispanic America* (Washington, 1936), p. 318.

9. Copies of *Remedios contra los pecados* are listed on both the Lima and the Cuzco documents at 8 reales each.

10. See Francisco Rodríguez Marín, *El "Quijote" y Don Quijote en América* (Madrid, 1911), pp. 49 ff.

11. The description of the *Juego de sortija* held in the little town of Pausa in the Peruvian Sierra is drawn from Rodríguez Marín, which reproduces the text of the *relación* in the appendix.

12. Ludwig Pfandl, *Cultura y costumbres del pueblo español de los siglos XVI y XVII. Introducción al estudio del siglo de oro* (Barcelona, 1929), p. 240.

13. In the edition of this novel published at Valencia in 1792, pages 365 to 382 give a detailed description of a *juego de sortija* which was probably closely imitated at Pausa in 1607.

14. The work by Jenaro Alenda y Mira, *Relaciones de solemnidades y fiestas públicas de España* (Madrid, 1903) is a bibliography of some

1,795 *relaciones* and *descripciones* of public festivities from 1402 to 1726, with numerous excerpts from items listed. On pages 100-101 there are full quotations from a *Relación de la sortixa* at Valladolid in 1590, from which some of the data given in the text were drawn. Another detailed account of the same year is the "Relación de la sortija que se hizo en Madrid en 31 de marzo de 1590," reprinted in the series of the *Sociedad de bibliófilos españoles* (Madrid, 1896), vol. 32, pp. 221-232.

15. Rodríguez Marín, *op. cit.*, pp. 110-112.

16. *Ibid.*, p. 118.

CHAPTER XX

1. Dardo Cuneo, "El realismo imaginero," *Cuadernos americanos* (Mexico City), *año* 6 (1947), p. 247.

2. Rudolph Schevill, "An impression of the condition of Spanish American libraries," *Modern language notes*, vol. 22 (May, 1905), p. 143.

3. Of interest in connection with these difficulties of the Creole writer is Agustín G. de Amezúa y Mayo, *Como se hacía un libro en nuestro siglo de oro. Discurso leído por . . . el día 23 de abril de 1946, con la ocasión de la Fiesta del Libro Español* (Madrid, 1946).

4. See Mariano Picón-Salas, *De la conquista a la independencia* (Mexico City, 1944), pp. 96-104.

5. Of interest in this discussion is the prologue of Edmundo O'Gorman to the 1940 edition of José de Acosta, *Historia natural y moral de Indias* (Mexico City), pp. liv ff.

6. See Rudolph Schevill, "La novela histórica, las crónicas de Indias, y los libros de caballerías," *Revista de Indias* (Bogotá), *época* 2ª, Nos. 59-60 (1944), pp. 173-196.

7. Juan Alfonso Carrizo, *Antecedentes hispano-medievales de la poesía tradicional argentina* (Buenos Aires, 1945), p. 79.

8. Rufino J. Cuervo, *Apuntaciones críticas sobre el lenguaje bogotano* (Bogotá, 1939), quoted in Carrizo, *op. cit.*, p. 51.

9. The cultivated Portuguese-Spanish governor of Spanish Louisiana at New Orleans, Don Manuel Gayoso de Lemos, had in his library in 1799 copies of Cervantes' *Galatea*, Gil Polo's *Diana enamorada*, and Suárez de Figueroa's *La constante Amarilis*. See Irving A. Leonard, "A frontier library, 1799," *Hispanic American Historical Review*, vol. 23 (1943), pp. 21-51.

10. Carrizo, *op. cit.*, p. 39.

11. María Cadilla de Martínez, *La poesía popular en Puerto Rico*, p. 76, quoted in Carrizo, *op. cit.*, p. 38.

12. Carrizo, *op. cit.*, p. 864.

INDEX

(This index does not include the documentary references which are assembled on pages 341-361. Except in certain proper names, such as Las Casas and La Marche, the Spanish definite and indefinite articles *(el, la, las, los, un)* are disregarded in alphabetizing subject matter.)

Acapulco, 226
Acoloro, island of Java Major, 38
Acosta, José de, historian, 215, 251; "Pliny of the New World," 216
Acuña, Hernando de, author, 112
Advertentiae theologicae scholasticae, by Vellosillo, 249
Africa, 19; Amazons reported in, 37; fleets skirt its coasts, 127, 143
Agrajes, character of *Amadis of Gaul,* 43
Agricola, Georgius, sixteenth-century geologist, 252
Aguilera, Antonio de, author, 201, 207
Aguilar, Jerónimo de, Cortés's interpreter, 193
Ahumada, Augustín de, brother of Santa Teresa, letter quoted, 23; mentioned, 213
Albertus Magnus, 252
Alcalá de Henares (Spain), 96, 109, 126, 128, 273, 274, 285, 287, 289, 290
Alcalá, Jaime de, author, 204, 255
Alcalá, Pedro de, *Arte y vocabulista arábigo,* 254
Alcántara, San Pedro de, 234
Aldine press, 256
Alemán, Mateo, novelist, career of,

parallels Cervantes', 258; comes to Mexico, 265-266; mentioned, x, 117, 255, 259-264, 267, 268, 326
Alfonso the Catholic, 32
Alfonso VIII, 120
Alfonso X, 221, 252, 298
Alger, Horatio, viii
almiranta, vice admiral's brig, 143, 272
Alonso, Antonio, public scribe, 200
Amadís de Grecia, 18, 33, 107
Amadis of Gaul (Amadís de Gaula), earliest edition of, 16; synopsis of, 16-17; mentioned by Díaz del Castillo, 43: attacked by Vives, 68; attacked by Antonio de Guevara, 69-70; bill to ban presented to Spanish Cortes, 76; decree against shipping (1531), 81; new decree against (1543), 82, 85; copies in Cromberger inventory, 96, 98; read on shipboard, 161, 163; ordered in Lima (1583), 223; mentioned, 15, 18, 20-24, 29-33, 38-42, 71-72, 97, 107, 109, 114-115, 118, 138, 229, 230, 259, 261, 264, 326
Amazon river, 58
Amazons, alleged locations of, 37; episode in *Sergas de Esplandián,* 38-40; reported in Yucatán, 46; quest of by Gerónimo López, 47; Olid's quest of, 48; reported near Colima, 49; Cortés's references to, 49-51; reported by Nuño de Guzmán, 52; rumor concerning in Valladolid, Spain, 55-56; presence in New Granada, 57-58; in Brazil, 58-60; in Paraguay, 60-

363